ENCYCLOPEDIA OF

WOMEN IN AMERICAN HISTORY

ENCYCLOPEDIA OF

WOMEN IN AMERICAN HISTORY

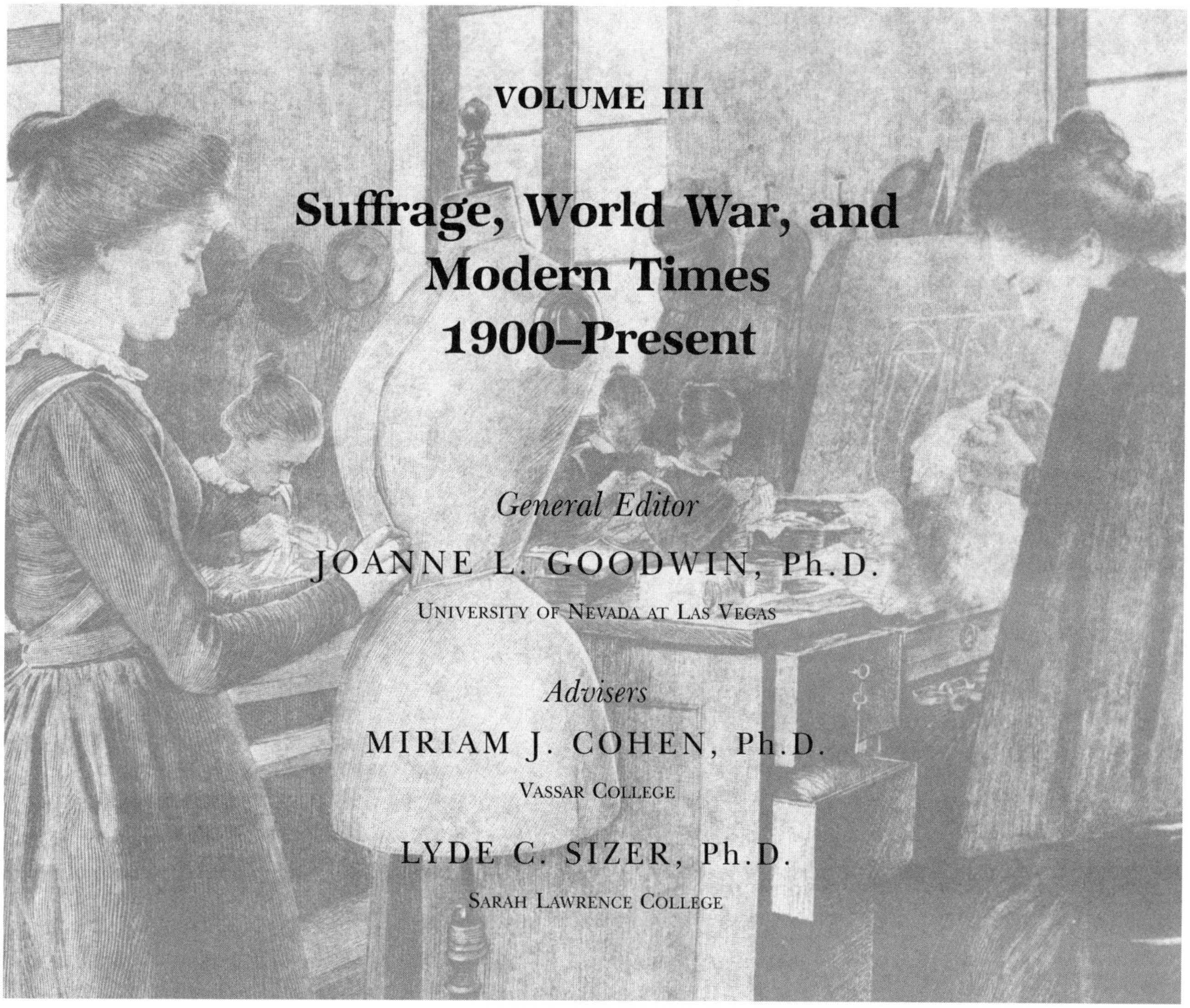

VOLUME III

Suffrage, World War, and Modern Times 1900–Present

General Editor

JOANNE L. GOODWIN, Ph.D.

UNIVERSITY OF NEVADA AT LAS VEGAS

Advisers

MIRIAM J. COHEN, Ph.D.

VASSAR COLLEGE

LYDE C. SIZER, Ph.D.

SARAH LAWRENCE COLLEGE

SHARPE REFERENCE

an imprint of M.E. Sharpe, Inc.

Developed, Designed, and Produced by BOOK BUILDERS LLC

SHARPE REFERENCE

Sharpe Reference is an imprint of M.E.Sharpe INC.

M.E.Sharpe INC.
80 Business Park Drive
Armonk, NY 10504

Library of Congress Cataloging-in-Publication Data

Encyclopedia of women in American history.
p. cm.
Includes bibliographical references.
Contents: v. 1. Colonization, revolution, and the new nation, 1585–1820 / general editor, Joyce Appleby — v. 2. Civil War, western expansion, and industrialization, 1820–1900 / general editor, Eileen K. Cheng — v. 3. Suffrage, world war, and modern times, 1900–present / general editor, Joanne Goodwin.
SET ISBN 0-7656-8038-6 (alk. paper)
1. Women—United States—History—Encyclopedias. I. Appleby, Joyce Oldham. II. Cheng, Eileen K. III. Goodwin, Joanne L.

HQ1410.E53 2001
305.4'0973'03—dc21 2001042025

Printed and bound in the United States of America

The paper used in this publication meets the minimum requirements of American National Standard for Information Sciences--Permanence of Paper for Printed Library Materials, ANSI Z 39.48.1984.

MV (c) 10 9 8 7 6 5 4 3 2 1

Photo Credits

Archive: 163; **Corbis:** iii; **Culver Pictures:** 36, 47, 54, 55, 57, 66, 70, 76, 80, 84, 90, 95, 99, 109, 111, 121, 128, 133, 140, 144, 155, 157, 164, 165, 178, 181, 190, 197, 205, 206, 209, 216, 220; **Robert Foothorap:** 191; Courtesy of **Barry Gossage/Phoenix Mercury:** 213; **Photo Researchers, Inc.:** 35, 41, 45, 110, 123, 126, 145, 153, 169, 172; **Texas State Library and Archive Commission:** 60

CONTENTS

VOLUME III

PART 3: DOCUMENTS

CONSULTANTS AND CONTRIBUTORS

GENERAL EDITORS

Joyce Appleby (Volume 1)
University of California, Los Angeles

Eileen Ka-May Cheng (Volume 2)
Sarah Lawrence College

Joanne L. Goodwin (Volume 3)
University of Nevada, Las Vegas

ADVISERS

Miriam J. Cohen
Vassar College

Lyde Sizer
Sarah Lawrence College

CONTRIBUTORS

Dee E. Andrews
Department of History
California State University

Joyce Appleby
Department of History
University of California, Los Angeles

Ruth Bloch
Department of Women's Studies and History
University of California, Los Angeles

Holly Brewer
Department of History
North Carolina State University

Eileen Ka-May Cheng
Department of History
Sarah Lawrence College

Elsie Crowell
Department of Insurance
State Government of Florida

Rebecca Dresser
Independent Scholar

Sara Dwyer-McNulty
Department of History
Marist College

Elizabeth Faue
Department of History
Wayne State University

Nancy Fernandez
Program of Interdisciplinary General Education
California State Polytechnic University

Bonnie Ford
Department of Women's Studies
Sacramento City College

Edith Gelles
Institute for Research on Women and Gender
Stanford University

Joanne L. Goodwin
Department of History
University of Nevada, Las Vegas

Laura Goodwin
Department of College Resources
Sarah Lawrence College

Christine Grant
Department of Athletics
University of Iowa

Beth Haller
Department of Mass Communication and Communication Studies
Towson University

Rona L. Holub
Department of History
Barnard College

Anna R. Igra
Department of History
Carleton College

Thomas Ingersoll
Department of History
Ohio State University

Gwen Kay
Department of History
State University of New York at Oswego

Jane Lancaster
John Nicholas Brown Center for the Study of American Civilization
Brown University

Peg Lamphier
Department of Social Sciences
Chaffey College

Virginia Leonard-Ewing
Department of History
Western Illinois University

Karen Meyers
Department of Continuing Education
University of Toledo

David Peterson Del Mar
Department of History
Portland State University and Oregon State University

Ann Plane
Department of History
University of California, Santa Barbara

Laura Prieto
Department of History
Simmons College

Jessie B. Ramey
Department of Women's History
Sarah Lawrence College

Mary Reynolds
Department of Women's History
Sarah Lawrence College

Ruth Rubinstein
History of Art Department
Institute of Fashion Technology

Elizabeth Diane Schafer
Independent Scholar

Mary Schweitzer
Department of History
Villanova University

Holly C. Shulman
Program of Studies in Women and Gender
University of Virginia

Camille Pepe Sperrazza
Department of Journalism
Manhattan Community College

Amy Gilman Srebnick
Department of History
Montclair State University

Carole Srole
Department of History
California State University

Brenda Stevenson
Department of History
University of California, Los Angeles

Sarah Swedberg
Department of Social and Behavioral Science
Mesa State College

Sherrie Tucker
Assistant Professor of American Studies
University of Kansas at Lawrence

Doris Weatherford
Department of Women's Studies
University of South Florida

Rosemarie Zagarri
Department of History and Art History
George Mason University

Timeline of Women and American History 1900–Present

1903 Orville and Wilbur Wright make the first successful flight of a self-propelled airplane.

1908 In a landmark case, *Muller v. Oregon,* the U.S. Supreme Court rules that states are constitutionally permitted to limit the work day of women laundry workers to ten hours.

1912 Julia Lathrop is appointed director of the Children's Bureau, becoming the first woman to head a U.S. federal agency.

1914 The Panama Canal is opened, connecting the Atlantic and Pacific oceans.

1916 Jeannette Rankin (R-MT) becomes the first woman elected to the U.S. House of Representatives. Margaret Sanger opens the first birth control clinic in Brooklyn, New York.

1917–18 U.S. fights in World War I.

1920 The Nineteenth Amendment to the U.S. Constitution, guaranteeing women the right to vote, is ratified.

1921 The U.S. Congress establishes a national quota system, which remains in effect until 1965, to limit immigration.

1929–39 The Great Depression. In 1933, President Franklin D. Roosevelt launches the relief and recovery program known as the New Deal. Secretary of Labor Frances Perkins becomes the first woman to serve in a cabinet position.

1941–45 U.S. fights in World War II. The Women's Army Corps (WAC) is made a regular component of the U.S. Army in 1943; the major contribution by women, however, is made on the homefront.

1950–53 The United States fights the Korean War. U.S. Senator Joseph McCarthy attacks alleged communist subversives in the federal government and remains a powerful figure until his allegations are discredited in 1954.

1963 President John F. Kennedy is assassinated. The civil rights movement reaches a climax with antisegregation demonstrations in the South and the historic March on Washington—culminating in the Civil Rights Act of 1964.

1966 The National Organization for Women is founded.

1968 After four years of escalation, U.S. military forces in Vietnam total 500,000; during the course of the war (1964–75), some 1,200 women serve as nurses. At home, massive peace demonstrations begin to turn public opinion against the war. Civil rights leader Martin Luther King, Jr., is assassinated.

1969 The *Apollo 11* space mission successfully lands two men on the moon.

1973 In *Roe v. Wade,* the U.S. Supreme Court rules, with qualification, that state laws prohibiting abortion are unconstitutional.

1974 Under threat of impeachment for his involvement in the Watergate scandal, President Richard Nixon resigns from office.

1981 Sandra Day O'Connor becomes the first woman justice of the Supreme Court.

1982 The proposed Equal Rights Amendment fails to win ratification.

1983 Astronaut Sally Ride becomes the first woman in space.

1984 Democrat Geraldine Ferraro is the first woman nominated by a major political party for vice president of the United States.

1989–91 The Cold War comes to an end, as Soviet-bloc countries throughout Europe install democratic governments and the Soviet Union is dissolved.

1993 First Lady Hillary Rodham Clinton heads a national task force on national health-care reform. Carol Moseley-Braun becomes the first African-American woman to serve in the U.S. Senate.

1999 President Bill Clinton is acquitted on two charges of impeachment stemming from his affair with a young White House intern, Monica Lewinsky.

2000 George W. Bush is declared the winner of one of the closest and most controversial presidential elections in U.S. history.

2001 In the aftermath of attacks on the World Trade Center in New York City and the Pentagon in Washington, the United States declares war on world terrorism.

Part 1

Essays

Industry, Modernity, and Diversity: A Historical Overview of the Twentieth Century

Americans who lived through the twentieth century experienced two world wars, the Korean and Vietnam conflicts, and the greatest economic crisis in our nation's history. Yet even those major events do not begin to describe the transformations in economics, culture, and politics that entirely reshaped women's lives. Women moved from being primarily unpaid workers at home to become consumers and wage-earners. Ideas about a woman's place changed from "a woman's place is in the home" to "a woman's place is where she chooses it to be."

The ways in which women participated as citizens changed as well. In 1900 a woman's rights as a citizen were intertwined with those of her family and represented to the political system by the male family head. By 2000 women not only voted independently, but also held numerous seats in **CONGRESS** and major leadership positions in national movements. These changes for women did not take place in isolation, but affected their families, coworkers, and communities.

This volume introduces the reader to a sample of individual women, events, and organizations that represent a century of change for women in the United States. The overarching changes affected all women, yet we cannot accurately speak of one representative history. The experiences of growing up female varied with the influences of class, ethnicity, religion, race, and region.

Three themes—industry, modernity, and diversity—organize the experiences of women's lives in this introduction. Industry made wage-earners of women and girls. Modernity introduced better **EDUCATION**, birth control, and greater independence in women's lives. Diversity reflects the differences among women as well as the expansion of rights to all Americans. Each theme defines an era in women's history, but they all overlap chronologically.

INDUSTRY

The daily life of a girl or woman in 1900 bore little resemblance to our lifestyles today. Whether in the country or city, few homes had electricity. Telephones were rare and computers did not exist. Consumerism was limited to necessities for most people. Young people amused themselves at dances, concerts, and fairs. In the country these events were less frequent, so entertainment consisted of visiting, reading, or writing letters. The majority of women and girls had only recently begun to buy their clothes "ready made." Canning of home-grown food was a common skill. Industrial production and the reorganization of labor, however, dramatically changed women's lives as workers and consumers.

Women and children worked in agriculture, as waitresses, cooks, and seamstresses, but as the economy became more industrialized additional jobs opened for them in glass factories, textile mills, food processing plants, and garment making industries. In fact, a child's education might end at age 14, the legal age to enter the workforce by the 1910s. In the country, compulsory school attendance was frequently set aside to accommodate planting, harvesting, or other family needs. African-American and Latino children were considered workers first and children second in agricultural economies of the South and West. African-American girls entered the workforce at a young age and worked consistently over their lives. Similarly, Latinas often worked as family groups in agriculture.

Single women composed the largest group of employed female workers. They mixed their wages with those of other family members. As the Western states became more settled, the services of single women in **DOMESTIC SERVICE**, sales, and food service, as well as **NURSING** and teaching, were in great demand and could bring higher wages than in other regions. Most married women worked at home. Their services to the family proved a greater value than the low wages they could earn. If a married woman had young children, she worked intermittently if at all until her children attended school. The exception to that rule applied to women who were the sole or major support of their families. Although the number of women and girl wage earners was increasing, only a small number of occupations were open to them. Jobs were segregated not only by sex, but also by race. Well into the 1960s, domestic service remained largely work performed by women of color.

In 1900, women knew relatively little about their bodies aside from information passed down from family members. Midwives delivered most babies. In rural areas of the country, older daughters learned about childbirth as they helped relatives and neighbors deliver. Information about CONTRACEPTION (see Volume 2) passed in a similar manner from friend to friend and between female relatives. Magazines ran ads for medicines specifically designed for "female troubles." Yet information about managing the number or sequence of births rarely passed between medical practitioners and women. In 1916, when MARGARET SANGER opened her clinic in New York City to distribute birth control information, she was arrested, her materials confiscated and labeled obscene. Regardless of these and other limitations, the birth rate declined considerably by 1920.

Women actively participated in the development of their communities, as volunteers and fund-raisers for churches, schools, clubs, parks and libraries. They led the campaigns to remove garbage from city streets, provide clean water and fresh milk for children, and clean up government. Furthermore, they did so in a context that censured women's public leadership. The term "public woman" referred to a prostitute and was used as a pejorative against assertive women. The parades, strikes, picketing, and public speeches organized by the SUFFRAGE MOVEMENT were considered radical and conduct unsuitable for a woman. At the same time that images of women occupied more public space in advertisements, magazines, and movies, the political activities of women produced debates about women's place and civic engagement. Consequently, women learned to position their public activism within the context of women's duties as mothers and homemakers.

First among all the issues that engaged women during the early twentieth century was the movement to win the right to vote. By 1912 even the nation's most conservative women's groups gave their support to the suffrage campaigns. They convinced their members to support the vote as a tool to accomplish their organizational goals against liquor or CHILD LABOR, or for better working conditions. Furthermore, they appeased members' fears about acting "unwomanly" by linking the vote to their jobs as mothers. MATERNALISM, or the idea that women's public action could be justified on the basis of their fundamental and primary role as mothers, used a traditional argument to open new fields of activity. This strategy worked, and in 1920 the states ratified the NINETEENTH AMENDMENT granting the right to vote to women.

The pre-suffrage image of a woman's voting bloc quickly dissolved amidst the differences that divided women politically. African-American women, especially in the South, continued to be denied their voting rights along with African-American men. Divisions between women who supported equal rights or PROTECTIVE LABOR LEGISLATION defined legislative strategies into the 1960s. Working-class women and women of color often allied with the political objectives of their class, race, ethnicity, or religion over their sex.

MODERNITY

Americans began to describe their lives as a break from the past and a turn toward modern ways of living in the years following **WORLD WAR I**. The new economy led by business and technology promised higher standards of living for all. Despite the disruptions of the Great Depression and World War II, women benefited directly from advances in educational attainment, improved living standards, and the expectation of companionship in marriage. Women gave birth to fewer children, practiced birth control, and explored their sexuality.

The migration to cities continued and offered women greater opportunities not only to work, but also to partake in the consumer culture. Young people made more decisions independent from their families and enjoyed new forms of MUSIC, DANCE, and art. Stores and banks helped women increase their purchasing power with easy credit. Whether the young working woman with new discretionary income or the married **HOMEMAKER** who made the major purchases for the family, women became a vital part of the consumer economy.

Women who moved into cities experienced the advantages of technology and new manufactured goods. Electricity spurred the purchase of "labor-saving" devices in many middle-class homes. Clothes washers, vacuum cleaners, and refrigerators changed the way the homemaker managed her work. The Great Depression sent consumption trends in rapid reverse, and highlighted the economic (if unpaid) value of women's skills in domestic production. Gardening, canning, and sewing saved a great amount of money. With the entrance of the United States into World War II, consumer trends revived and expanded. This time more women worked outside the home because their labor was much needed, and they received higher wages. Women of color who worked in segregated job markets also saw a positive shift. Leaving the domestic service jobs of the South, for example, they moved to cities of the upper Midwest and West to fill wartime production jobs. Segregation did not end, but wages and types of employment improved. Many wartime workers wanted to continue in the higher-paid, higher-skilled jobs when the war ended, but industry jobs were promised to returning servicemen to ease their reintegration into civilian life. Women lost those jobs, but many stayed in the workforce.

Despite the characterization of the 1950s as the age of domesticity and the return to family duties for many married women, the economy continued to need workers. Offices needed typists, stenographers, bookkeepers, and file clerks. Retail stores needed designers, publicists, and salespeople. Factories continued to employ working-class women. Single women predominated in these work settings, but married women entered the workforce in greater numbers. By the 1960s, women workers joined labor unions although they did not hold leadership positions, and many fields were still closed to them.

Civic activism continued as the changes of the prior decades were consolidated into community institutions and everyday life. Women voted, ran for office, sat on juries, and participated in voter registration drives. The **LEAGUE OF WOMEN VOTERS** formed to educate women voters about their government, the campaign process, and candidates' records. The **NATIONAL WOMAN'S PARTY** continued its campaign for sexual equality by introducing the **EQUAL RIGHTS AMENDMENT** in 1923 and repeatedly for decades (see Documents). At the federal level, the women of the New Deal participated in policymaking and government jobs to the greatest extent in history. They headed government bureaus, conducted national research, hired thousands of college graduates, and participated in creating the **SOCIAL SECURITY ACT**. As first lady, **ELEANOR ROOSEVELT** set the standard of public activism. She also brought public attention to the needs of African Americans.

By the 1940s, women of the NAACP worked with their chapters to end lynching, pass desegregation laws, and register African Americans to vote. They made room for civil rights workers in their homes, raised funds, and participated in nonviolent civil disobedience. They integrated schools as children and young adults, mobilized bus boycotts, and offered leadership to a younger generation. Women in Latino communities worked behind the scenes to support churches, social welfare organizations, political groups, and unions. The civil rights movement brought the greatest political changes in the years after World War II. Women and men working together organized local communities to challenge discriminatory practices. In doing so, the women of the civil rights movement enlarged citizenship rights regardless of race. They also helped to create a model of non-violent social activism that the women's movement, Chicanos, and gay and lesbian activists would follow in subsequent decades.

DIVERSITY

During the last three decades of the century, a realignment in global systems of power occurred. Independence movements overthrew imperialist nations at the same time that technology and markets brought once distant countries into the global economy. Evidence of these forces in the United States appeared with civil rights, expanded immigration, and challenges to legal inequality between men and women. The social unrest in the United States resulted not only from the liberation movements of the 1960s, but also from the influence of evangelical religion. The dominant worldview of Protestant, middle-class values that had characterized mainstream culture for much of the century now shared the stage with a multiplicity of perspectives and views. Women participated in all aspects of the century's changes but in a variety of ways.

The changes wrought by technology and social relations near the end of the century emphasized choice over tradition. Divorce and remarriage rates reached new heights during the last quarter of the century. In the terms of the time, "broken families" became "blended families" as the children of first and second marriages merged into one.

The availability of relatively safe contraception methods such as the birth control pill revolutionized sex, giving women the choice to enjoy sex for reasons other than procreation. Twenty years later, technology not only separated sex from reproduction, but separated pregnancy and giving birth from biological parenthood. Artificial insemination, surrogate motherhood, and frozen embryos gave people for whom conception was difficult the opportunity to have children. As new ways of having children became widely known, new forms of families became more widespread. The care of children also underwent change.

By the 1970s, several issues linked to the double shift of working mothers became topics of public discussion. **CHILD CARE**, leave for **PREGNANCY**, flexible time for working mothers, and partner benefits are a few examples. As more married women entered the workforce as part-time or full-time workers, the random and informal methods of child care—relying on relatives or neighbors—broke down. By the 1970s, the need for day-care facilities became a matter of public policy and debate over the American family. Feminists questioned why parents would not share the responsibility of child rearing or at least consider it a matter of choice rather than biology. Some important changes in fathers' involvement did occur. Nevertheless, the number of hours spent attending to family and household duties by mothers declined only slightly by the end of the century. The balance between wage-earning and family continues to preoccupy young women in the early twenty-first century.

The women's movement changed American society in fundamental ways. Women entered the workforce with expectations of fair wages, equity, and workplaces free of harassment. Women expected to live free from violence, and found refuge at shelters for battered women and **RAPE** crisis centers.

Exploring the diverse experiences and perspectives of women's lives gave rise to new ways to understand ourselves. The field of gender studies influenced every academic discipline in the universities and produced **WOMEN'S STUDIES** programs and new degree specializations.

CONCLUSION

Many of the issues of the Second Wave of the women's movement focused on gaining access to areas previously prohibited to women. Women wanted to participate in **ATHLETICS**, attend professional schools, serve in the **MILITARY**, be pop divas, and sit on the Supreme Court. As gains were made, individual women sometimes attributed their success to individual talent and dismissed the importance of the struggle for equal rights. During the 1980s, articulate, well-funded groups formed to oppose choice, access, and diversity.

At the dawn of the twenty-first century, debates about feminism could be found everywhere, despite great changes in the lives of women and girls. We can be sure that the path ahead will be neither predictable nor easy and that women and girls will need new skills to overcome the new obstacles that arise.

Joanne L. Goodwin

See also: Sexual Revolution; "The Civil Rights Movement," p. 21.

FURTHER READING

Evans, Sara. *Born for Liberty, A History of Women in America.* New York: Free Press, 1997.

Hine, Darlene Clark, and Kathleen Thompson. *A Shining Thread of Hope, The History of Black Women in America.* New York: Broadway Books, 1998.

Jameson, Elizabeth, and Susan Armitage. *Writing the Range, Race, Class, and Culture in the Women's West.* Norman: University of Oklahoma Press, 1997.

Ruiz, Vicki. *From Out of the Shadows, Mexican Women in Twentieth-Century America.* New York: Oxford University Press, 1998.

Women in Public Life

From the fight for woman suffrage at the beginning to the rebirth of feminism at its end, the twentieth century has witnessed significant changes in the public lives of American women. Lacking the right to vote in all but a few states in 1900, women found ways to influence American life by creating and participating in civic associations, social service agencies, and public interest groups. Once women gained the vote in 1920, they became active in formal political parties as well. During the **GREAT DEPRESSION** of the 1930s, women organized relief efforts and protested unemployment, and they supported the nation with defense work and **MILITARY SERVICE** during **WORLD WAR II**. Despite these contributions, women continued to face discrimination in the workplace and society. Only when greater numbers of women entered higher education and the paid labor force did their efforts to organize to demand equal rights with men begin to bear fruit. From the 1960s to the present day, women have protested for and won an equal place in public life.

WOMEN'S POLITICS AND WOMAN SUFFRAGE

In the years between 1900 and 1920, lacking many formal political rights, women of different classes, races, and religions organized in voluntary associations to gain the right to vote. Early victories in the West gave women a limited opportunity to engage in party politics, but subsequent state campaigns for the vote left women without much say in forming state and federal policies. In 1900, under the leadership of **CARRIE CHAPMAN CATT** (see Volume 2) the National American Woman Suffrage Association began to change tactics. Taking over from Anna Howard Shaw, Catt coordinated resources for both state and national **SUFFRAGE** campaigns to get the best results for the effort. From 1900 to 1905, and from 1915 on, Catt coordinated national and state efforts in a "winning plan" to keep the suffrage message constantly before the public.

In 1911 Washington state passed a woman suffrage amendment; California followed in 1912. Losses in woman suffrage campaigns in 1915, however, brought a new generation to the fore. Younger leaders such as Harriot Stanton Blatch, the daughter of **ELIZABETH CADY STANTON** (see Volume 2), and **ALICE PAUL** devoted their energies to the cause in such organizations as the College Equal Suffrage League, the Political Equality Association, and, most importantly, the Congressional Union. Crucial to the success of the movement was a shift in suffrage tactics toward public protest, education, and publicity. Suffrage parades and motorcades, whistle-stop campaigns, door-to-door canvassing, and public relations work brought new support to the suffrage cause. The Congressional Union's campaign to picket the White House in 1917, while controversial, aroused public sympathy. The shared experience of disenfranchisement underwrote much of the suffrage appeal as elite, middle-class, and working-class women participated for the first time in broad-based cross-class organizing. Little effort, however, was directed across the racial divide. Despite some interracial cooperation, white woman suffragists in Southern states insisted on racially segregated organizations, and some campaigned exclusively for the right to vote in state primaries for white women only.

Electoral politics and suffrage battles were only a small part of women's public life. The Progressive era was high tide for a distinctive women's political culture. Devoted to "civic housekeeping," a movement to address the problems of poverty and government indifference, women from settlement houses, social agencies, and organizations such as the **NATIONAL CONSUMERS LEAGUE** and the **NATIONAL CONGRESS OF MOTHERS** sought to pressure cities to improve services, safety, and sanitation. The power of organized women established the first day-care centers, created the **MOTHERS' PENSIONS**, fueled the movement for a juvenile justice system, and attempted to clean up government corruption. Such activism led to the creation of many state and federal agencies, including the United States **CHILDREN'S BUREAU**. Voluntary associations existed across class and race lines to support welfare, civil rights, and educational efforts among African Americans in such groups as the **NATIONAL ASSOCIATION OF COLORED WOMEN** and the labor work of the **NATIONAL WOMEN'S TRADE UNION LEAGUE**.

By 1910, most women's organizations were committed to working for suffrage. It was by then clear that women's organizations had reached the limit of what they could do outside formal electoral and institutional channels. Women could educate and lobby, but without the vote, they could not make elected officials fully responsive to their demands. As a result, women's organizations formed for such diverse purposes as **TEMPERANCE** (see Volume 2), labor, civil rights, good government, and child welfare devoted resources to suffrage work. Despite their different and sometimes opposing goals, women achieved unity in the late suffrage campaigns and secured congressional passage of women's right to vote in 1919. The strong state-level organization of the National American Woman Suffrage Association brought about ratification of the **NINETEENTH AMENDMENT** in August 1920.

In the suffrage struggle, the great promise of women gaining the right to vote was that they could form a block to lobby for legislation in social welfare, education, and peace. After suffrage, however, women voted much as men did, and their voting reflected sharp political and social differences. Initial victories in the passage of the **MATERNITY AND INFANCY PROTECTION ACT** (1921), minimum wage legislation, and the **CABLE ACT**, which secured independent citizenship for married women, were thus followed by divisions among women over the **EQUAL RIGHTS AMENDMENT** and the fear of losing legal protections.

Despite their earlier unity, women had, in fact, different visions of what needed to be done. The majority of women did not join either a women's party or nonpartisan organizations like the **LEAGUE OF WOMEN VOTERS**. Most voted in ways that reflected loyalties to a racial or ethnic group, occupation or union, religion, region, or political belief. It was not that women lacked feminist consciousness but rather that, in the decades after suffrage, women were more interested in pursuing partisan interests. The new generation of women activists held more positive views about government than did their elders and sought to expand social programs. By the 1920s, women also had emerged as activists in the Democratic and Republican parties.

WOMEN'S PUBLIC LIVES UNDER THE NEW DEAL

During the **GREAT DEPRESSION** of the 1930s, much of the nation experienced social and political upheaval. Responding to this crisis were many voluntary associations, which women often staffed or led. These acts of private charity and coordination of public resources did much to alleviate suffering. With unemployment as high as 25 percent nationwide and 60 percent in some cities, however, private agencies and local governments found their resources inadequate. As both citizens and public activists, women protested to stop evictions and cuts in relief. They went on strike against unfair employers, and they mobilized in support of political candidates and parties who promised to address the unemployment crisis.

First lady **ELEANOR ROOSEVELT** came to represent the activism of women in political life. She was, however, only the most visible symbol of women's progress in electoral politics. By 1933, women had served in public office—including two governors, one senator, fourteen representatives, and hundreds—if not thousands—of state and local legislators and government officials, yet it was the women in the **NEW DEAL** administration of Franklin Delano Roosevelt who signaled the ascendancy of women to positions of power. **MARY DEWSON**, who headed the Women's Division of the Democratic National Committee; Labor Secretary **FRANCES PERKINS**, the first woman to serve in a presidential cabinet; and Ellen Sullivan Woodward, an administrator assigned to relief agencies, strongly influenced social policy. They proved to be instrumental in drafting such important legislation as the **SOCIAL SECURITY ACT** (1935) and the **FAIR LABOR STANDARDS ACT** (1938).

During **WORLD WAR II**, women were engaged in supporting the war effort in a range of roles. Although the government redirected domestic resources from domestic social programs into national defense, women social workers and administrators were important for the war effort. Such individuals as **MARY MCLEOD BETHUNE** helped to train and mobilize young workers into defense jobs. Similarly, women were to be found in the ranks of civil defense committees, helping to organize bond and scrap drives, establishing day-care centers, and working in civilian government. In the WACs (Army), WAVES (Navy), SPARS (Coast Guard), and the Marine Corps, in the Army and Navy nursing corps, and as pilots (WASPS), more than 350,000 women entered **MILITARY SERVICE** during the war. Women's patriotism and labor led workers to exceed production quotas and dedicate part of their earnings to Liberty Bonds and relief efforts.

WOMEN AND SOCIAL MOVEMENTS IN THE POSTWAR UNITED STATES

After World War II, women seemed to retreat from public life. Expected to return to the home and take up the traditional role of wife and mother, many women, however, shifted their attention to paid employment, volunteer work, and public activism. Women's work for peace and racial justice and their founding of organizations for women's political and sexual rights (including the Women's Strike for Peace, the **DAUGHTERS OF BILITIS**, and the **NATIONAL COUNCIL OF NEGRO WOMEN**) meant that neither feminism nor women's activism disappeared from public view.

Escalating labor force participation, the new wave of women entering college, and the changing political climate opened new opportunities for women's public activism. In the 1950s and 1960s, African-American and white women focused on facing down the racial and sexual discrimination that had long haunted American society. First through the civil rights movement and second through the **WOMEN'S LIBERATION MOVEMENT**, women came to terms with the ways in which they were constrained from full participation in public life.

The emergence of a strong civil rights movement in the South coincided with other efforts to shift the racial and sexual grounds of American democracy. In the mid-1950s, the National Association for the Advancement of Colored People and other civil rights organizations brought suit to challenge racial discrimination in public education, transport, and housing. From the 1950s to the early 1960s, public protests such as the Montgomery bus boycott, student sit-downs in cafeterias, the freedom rides to desegregate public transportation, and voting registration campaigns sought to overturn segregation laws. Women such as **ROSA PARKS** and **FANNIE LOU HAMER** were central to these efforts. In the 1960s and 1970s, consciousness of discrimination also fueled activism among Chicanas, Native Americans, and Asian Americans.

Paralleling these moves for racial equality was the effort of women to dismantle barriers to sex equality under the law. In 1963, the **PRESIDENT'S COMMISSION ON THE STATUS OF WOMEN** published a report which documented pervasive discrimination against women in education and employment. Woman activists including **BETTY FRIEDAN**, labor advocate **ESTHER PETERSON**, and civil rights lawyer **PAULI MURRAY** founded the **NATIONAL ORGANIZATION FOR WOMEN** in 1964. Hundreds of bills for women's rights were considered and passed between 1960 and 1966, including the **EQUAL PAY ACT** of 1963 and the Civil Rights Act of 1964, which gave women equal employment rights under **TITLE VII**.

It was, however, the social movements of the 1960s that shifted the struggle for women's equality from courtroom and Congress to widespread public activism. In the civil rights and antiwar movements, women organized protests, conducted voter registration campaigns, and spoke and wrote for the cause. At the same time, they often were assigned to stuff envelopes, mimeograph newsletters and flyers, and make coffee. The gap between the words of social movements calling for human equality and the reality of men's and women's unequal power, even in democratic movements, came home to women as the ground shifted from civil rights to broader student struggles. By 1967, women had begun talking to each other and organizing caucuses to demand equal representation on committees and a more visible public role. Soon, however, activist women broke from the radical student organizations to form their own groups. In what came to be called women's liberation, college-age women joined older women in creating a social movement that encompassed both public and private concerns, where the personal became political.

Through their efforts, the legal and political rights of women were expanded in the areas of sexual and **REPRODUCTIVE RIGHTS**, economic justice and financial independence, **EDUCATION** and the professions, and personal life. **MARRIAGE** and divorce, child care and **CHILD CUSTODY**, **HEALTH** care, sexual assault, and domestic abuse were issues made more visible by the women's movement. In the economic arena, an ever-growing number of women in the paid labor force faced wage and employment discrimination and occupational segregation, conditions which underwrote women's dependence and inequality. The work of women, both in the political arena and in their voluntary efforts to establish women's clinics, domestic shelters, and workplace and union coalitions to fight discrimination, not only made women visible participants in public life but fundamentally changed the landscape of American politics.

SUMMARY: WOMEN AND PUBLIC LIFE

In the last three decades of the twentieth century, women have made enormous progress. In ever-increasing numbers, they have attended college and graduate school, taken on non-traditional professions, sought and served in political office, refined the character of American politics through innovative campaigns, and shifted electoral and legislative agendas in government.

Not all the changes women made, however, were progressive in character. With greater activism on issues of reproduction and sexual freedom came the reaction of those who opposed women's right to choice over their bodies and the exercise of sexual preference. Conservative women as well as liberal and radical women came to redefine what feminism and women's interests were, some choosing to pursue individual freedom, others preferring to use women's role as maternal protector in support of peace, in protest of the nuclear arms race and the death penalty, or against abortion.

The power of women's electoral and voluntary politics has changed the political landscape. While women's inequality persists, and women lack full and equal representation in many walks of life, they have altered the future through their visible public activism. The enormous changes in women's public life in the twentieth century has shifted the ground of women's struggle from winning the vote to making women's vote and participation count.

Elizabeth Faue

See also: "Violence Against Women," p. 19; "The Civil Rights Movement," p. 21.

FURTHER READING

Chafe, William. *The American Woman: Her Changing Social, Economic and Political Roles, 1920–1970.* New York: Oxford University Press, 1972.

Crawford, Vicki L., Jacqueline Anne Rouse, and Barbara Woods, eds. *Women in the Civil Rights Movement: Trailblazers and Torchbearers.* Brooklyn, NY: Carlson, 1990.

Evans, Sara M. *Born for Liberty: A History of Women in America.* New York: Free Press, 1989.

Gustafson, Melanie, Kristie Miller, and Elisabeth Israels Perry, eds. *We Have Come to Stay: American Women and Political Parties, 1880–1960.* Albuquerque: University of New Mexico Press, 1999.

Rosen, Ruth. *The World Split Open: How the Modern Women's Movement Changed America.* New York: Viking, 2000.

Women and the Labor Force

During the twentieth century, enormous changes took place in women's work lives. They shifted from unpaid, often invisible work to paid labor. Business cycles, wars, and economic structural reorganization set constraints and opened opportunities. However, sociopolitical movements forged new language and policies that changed American understandings of women's work.

The shift from unpaid to paid work was well under way by the opening of the twentieth century. In 1900, over one-third of single women worked for wages. The figures for urban women not in school reached nearly four-fifths. By 1930, nearly all single women either attended school or worked for pay, rather than performing unpaid work at home.

Paid labor slowly contributed to greater autonomy for single women or girls. In 1900, most immigrant and second-generation daughters lived at home and turned their entire paychecks over to their parents. They spent their leisure with their families. By 1930, more young women kept a portion of their pay for themselves, whether sneaking it from their pay envelopes or negotiating a percentage with their parents. They wanted to spend money on clothes and to socialize with their friends at amusement parks and music halls. **WORLD WAR II** expanded opportunities for travel and migration west for new defense jobs. In the 1960s, more women began to live on their own, delaying **MARRIAGE** or avoiding it entirely. However, in the 1980s and 1990s, employed immigrant women still contended with parental expectations that they remain at home until marriage.

Married women's move into paid work accelerated throughout the century, especially in the years after World War II. Before the war, most married women worked at home, rearing children and keeping house. African-American wives and mothers, who worked for wages in larger numbers, were the exception. Some married women kept boarders, did laundry, or took **OUTWORK** (see Volume 2) that enabled them to care for their children while earning money.

The number of married women working outside the home increased with each decade after World War II. Married women worked before childbirth, part-time when their children were at school, and after their children were grown. In the 1970s, a major shift occurred when married women with young children began working full-time.

During the 1930s, the **GREAT DEPRESSION** created massive unemployment. Americans scapegoated married women workers as well as ethnic and racial minorities, despite the dire circumstances pushing them to seek work. Laws outlawed married women's employment. More than 1,600 women lost their jobs. College graduates were discouraged from seeking employment, "career women" were criticized, and women in general were blamed for intensifying the unemployment crisis.

Conversely **WORLD WAR I** and **WORLD WAR II** created a demand for more workers. During both wars, women temporarily found employment in "men's jobs," especially in wartime production. In World War II, even married women were encouraged to work in defense plants, although the companies maintained gender job distinctions. The employment of married women created a demand for child care, but the belief that married women really belonged at home limited the number of federal day-care centers.

In the 1950s, assumptions about women being temporary workers continued, despite the booming postwar economy's demand for more workers. When the numbers of single women fell short, employers hired married women to fill the jobs. Part-time employment rose. Nonetheless, popular attitudes maligned employed married women, who still saw themselves as primarily **HOMEMAKERS** contributing extras to the family, rather than its main support.

These same assumptions influenced employers' decisions, as the United States shifted from an agricultural and manufacturing economy to a service and global economy over the twentieth

Percentage of Men and Women in the Labor Force, 1890–2000

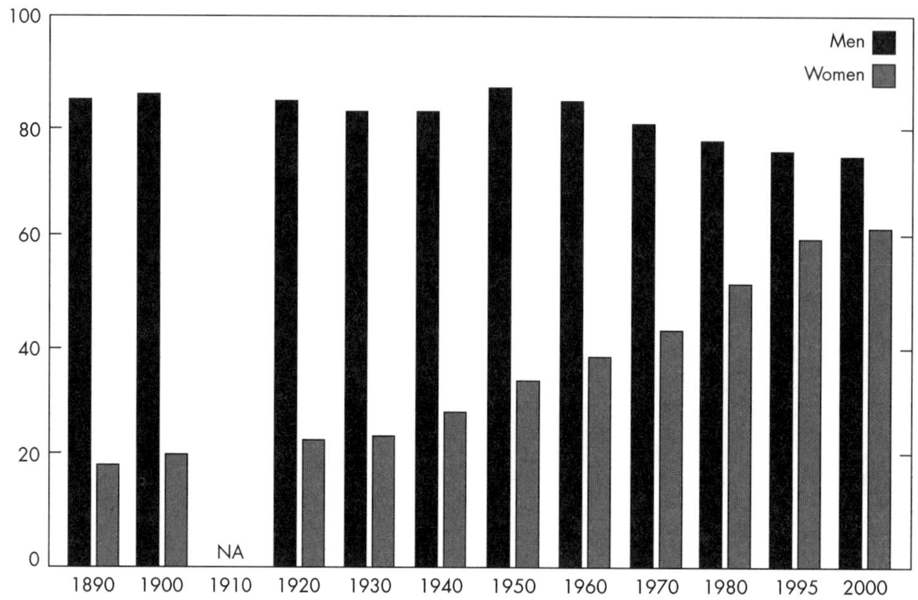

Sources: 1890–1930: Historical Statistics of the United States, Colonial Times to 1970, Part 1, U.S. Department of Commerce, Bureau of the Census (Washington, D.C., 1975), pp. 131–32. 1980–2000: Statistical Abstract of the United States, 1989, U.S. Department of Commerce, Bureau of the Census (Wahington, D.C., 1989), p. 376.

century. The shift was dramatic. In 1900, nearly three-quarters of employed women worked in agriculture, **DOMESTIC SERVICE**, and factories or shops, often in exploitative sweatshops. By 2000, the areas of employment changed. The proportion of women in agriculture and domestic service dropped to under 3 percent each, as women moved into clerical, service, professional and managerial jobs. However, the timing of the change varied by ethnic or racial group. Many Japanese Americans did not leave domestic service until after World War II; most urban **AFRICAN AMERICANS** remained domestics until replaced by **HISPANIC AMERICANS** with the surge of immigration after 1965.

Sweatshops, which had declined in the 1930s, reappeared in the apparel industry in the 1980s. As American businesses opened low-wage factories in other countries, U.S. wages and working conditions deteriorated. In the 1990s evidence surfaced of immigrant women brought to the United States for slave labor as domestic, sex, garment, and field workers.

When employers reorganized the workplace, adopted new technology, or opened new types of establishments, the gender-typed jobs might switch. For example, male shopkeepers selling ready-made clothing replaced women dressmaking and millinery proprietors at the turn of the century. Women supplanted men in **CLERICAL WORK** (see Volume 2), banks, restaurants, and real estate.

However, cultural assumptions influenced employers' choices. Airlines and restaurauteurs assumed that attractive young women would please their predominately male customers. Employers expected to pay low wages to youthful and inexperienced female office and retail workers. These gendered cultural assumptions about who worked and why influenced how contemporaries interpreted business cycles and wars, and how business choices contributed to restructuring the economy.

Throughout the century, sociopolitical movements promoted policies affecting women's employment and provided the language for debates on women's work. Progressives of the early 1900s, for example, debated whether women should have rights equal to men's or be treated differently, and whether women were better served by unions or government laws. Within this context, they considered whether work victimized or "emancipated" women.

Dismayed by the hardships of immigrant and native-born women working in sweatshops and factories, reformers portrayed them as victims of oppressive employers and their own families. To improve their work conditions, reformers promoted **PROTECTIVE LABOR LEGISLATION**, such as minimum wage and maximum hour laws specifically for women. In 1908 the U.S. Supreme Court ruled in ***MULLER V. OREGON*** that states could protect women by limiting their hours of work. In contrast to this image of helplessness, some suffragists hailed new middle-class jobs, like **SOCIAL WORK**, as opportunities for women to become independent or "emancipated."

These two portrayals of working women hardened in the 1920s after the **NINETEENTH AMENDMENT** passed. The **NATIONAL WOMAN'S PARTY** called for an **EQUAL RIGHTS AMENDMENT** (ERA) to extend equal treatment. Most reformers, however, opposed the ERA because it would have eliminated protective labor legislation for women.

The drive for unionization of unskilled and semiskilled factory workers in the 1930s reinforced the reformers' image of working-class women as victims. The union movement's efforts to restore self-esteem and power to failed male breadwinners confined women to the roles of symbolic victims or "Union Maids" who battled bosses in female auxiliaries. The limited role for women nearly erased their contribution to the union movement from historical memory, despite women's major role in earlier labor struggles. Even the federal government's pro-union Works Progress Administration (WPA) theater productions portrayed women as junior partners who inspired their men to take action. This same image of women continued in the celebrated 1954 film ***SALT OF THE EARTH***, which chronicled a real strike by male Mexican-American miners in New Mexico whose overburdened wives pressured their husbands to include household issues as strike demands.

Working women's views about their own work were more complex than those of reformers, unions, or suffragists. They did not share the sense of a division between working-class women as victims (or at best as militant helpers) and middle-class women as "emancipated." Middle-class women had their own struggles at work. Those in men's occupations, like doctors and **LAWYERS**, needed to prove their competence in fields where professionalism was defined as masculine. Those in middle-class "women's" fields, like teaching, social work, library work, and NURSING also agonized about status. Nurses struggled to prove their professional efficiency and still maintain the caring attitude expected of women. Social workers worried about their low wages, low-status clients, "hard-boiled" image, and the need to remain feminine. Some social workers even downplayed the professional traits of ambition and specialized knowledge, and some organized trade unions, rather than the more typical professional association.

At times, working-class women shared the reformers' view of them as victims. Domestics felt victimized when employers did not treat them humanely. Saleswomen resented management efforts to impose dress codes. Nevertheless, working-class women rejected reformers' characterization of their work as degrading and took pride in their skills and resourcefulness. They developed a work culture that gave them influence over their work. For example, waitresses developed informal practices that they taught to new coworkers, such as taking turns calling in sick when bosses overstaffed them. Chicana cannery workers in California shared coping techniques, such as using cold cream to protect their skin from the irritating peach fuzz. Saleswomen scheduled long appointments with special customers, exploiting their relationships with customers to thwart management control. This work culture often gave rise to unions or strike activity.

Although working women held their own self-images, the language and policies of Progressive reformers, suffragists, and the labor movement shaped government policies and national discussions about working women for decades, until the civil rights movement and the Black Power movement inspired Second Wave feminism in the 1970s to develop new ways to think about women workers as well as new policies.

New feminist organizations such as the NATIONAL ORGANIZATION FOR WOMEN (NOW) shared the civil rights movement's emphasis on equality and integration. NOW called for an "equal partnership of the sexes" and went to court to insure an enforcement of the Civil Rights Act of 1964, which prohibited discrimination by sex and race. At first, feminists echoed the older policy goal of "equal pay for equal work," but they soon began to question the formula's effectiveness at equalizing salaries, because men and women occupied different jobs in a "sex segregated" labor market. Feminists then called for a reevaluation of salaries based on "comparative worth," the use of objective criteria like education, skill, and responsibility.

The policy of affirmative action sought to promote equity and integration by the employment of underrepresented groups. Although it benefited women, affirmative action's challenge to men's work cultures contributed to a backlash in the 1990s.

Women also sought to promote equal treatment by establishing rules for defining appropriate behavior at work, particularly by banning SEXUAL HARASSMENT. Such abuse was not new in the workplace. Between 1910 and 1940, African-American mothers in the South sent their daughters to Northern cities to avoid the sexual advances of men in homes where they worked as domestics. Factory workers had long complained about the advances of foremen who had the power to hire and fire. Women in CLERICAL WORK resented the jokes about the "pretty typewriter" girl. Until the 1970s, women accepted sexual harassment as a part of life, even though individuals sometimes retaliated against persecutors. As sexual harassment became recognized as a form of workplace discrimination, some women turned to the EQUAL EMPLOYMENT OPPORTUNITY COMMISSION (EEOC) for redress. The discussion of sexual harassment in the workplace gained national attention in 1991 when Anita Hill, an attorney for the EEOC, accused Clarence Thomas, the head of the agency and President George Bush's nominee for the Supreme Court, of sexual harassment.

The Black Power movement's veneration of African-American culture inspired feminists to celebrate feminine styles of work. Feminists contrasted the nurturing style of nursing and MIDWIFERY with doctors whom they accused of sexism, arrogance, and invasive high-tech birthing procedures.

Conservatives contributed to the shaping of American understanding of working women in the 1980s and 1990s. The economic wing of the New Right believed that the unregulated market could eliminate uncompetitive companies and spread wealth. When small businesses made a resurgence and women's numbers grew dramatically, ENTREPRENEURS such as Debbi Fields of the Mrs. Fields Cookies chain were touted as proof of opportunity for enterprising business women. This new emphasis on business reinforced feminist approval of women who moved into male jobs, giving rise to media attention to the few women in executive positions.

Nonetheless, the long-standing critique of "career women" tempered the glorification of entrepreneurs. Popular culture criticized women wearing "power suits" as symbols of corporate power, wealth, and unnatural womanhood. As early as 1976 Faye Dunaway, in the film *Network*, played a corporate executive with no soul. By the 1990s, such criticism became even more common: The hero in the 1996 film *Jerry Maguire* replaced his driven, high-powered girlfriend with a nurturing, subordinate, working woman. Paid work was fine as long as women maintained perceived feminine qualities. At the same time, feminists complained that a **GLASS CEILING** curbed women's rise up the corporate ladder.

The transformation from unpaid to paid work as well as business cycles, wars, and economic restructuring shaped women's experiences in the workforce. However, until the 1970s, assumptions about single women as temporary workers framed the understanding of those experiences. The contemporary social-political movements shaped the language and government policies that fashioned varied understandings of women's work. Early in the century, the Progressives and labor movement divided women workers into victims or "emancipated" women, although working women themselves held more complex views about their work experiences. Beginning in the 1970s, the civil rights and Black Power movements shaped feminist goals of equality and pride in distinctly feminine skills, while conservatism promoted an ambiguous appreciation of entrepreneurship.

Carole Srole

See also: American Federation of Labor (AFL/CIO); Asian Americans; Business and Industry; Equal Pay Acts of 1963 and 1972; Native Americans; Triangle Shirtwaist Factory Fire; Unions, Labor.

FURTHER READING

Clark-Lewis, Elizabeth. *Living In, Living Out: African American Domestics in Washington, D.C., 1910–1940.* Washington, DC: Smithsonian Institute Press, 1994.

Gluck, Sherna Berger. *Rosie the Riveter Revisited: Women, the War, and Social Change.* Boston: Twayne, 1987.

Honey, Maureen. *Creating Rosie the Riveter: Class, Gender, and Propaganda during World War II.* Amherst: University of Massachusetts Press, 1984.

Kessler-Harris, Alice. *Out-to-Work: A History of Wage-Earning Women in the United States.* Oxford: Oxford University Press, 1982.

Peiss, Kathy. *Cheap Amusements: Working Women and Leisure in Turn-of-the-Century New York.* Philadelphia: Temple University Press, 1986.

Women and the Consumer Society

All people in the modern United States depend on consumer goods to meet their needs. Shopping and buying, however, are generally identified as female activities. Bumper stickers declaring "Born to Shop" remind us that consumption is one of women's most visible contemporary roles. The story of women as consumers begins long before the twentieth century and involves more than simply buying things. Through different uses of their purchasing power, women navigated changing social conditions and found resources to express themselves as workers, citizens, and individuals.

MAKING A CONSUMER SOCIETY

Historians disagree about the origins of a consumer society in the United States. Some scholars focus on the nineteenth century and the **INDUSTRIAL REVOLUTION** (see Volume 2). They argue that mass production led to changes that created a consumer society. Others emphasize the relationship of changes in consumer taste and behavior to economic change. Much recent scholarship explores what historian of technology Ruth Schwartz Cowan has called "the consumption junction": the intersection where producers and consumers struggle over economic, social, and personal interests.

Many historians now believe that the story of the consumer society began during the eighteenth century with the desires of a growing urban population for a greater range of fashionable goods. By the nineteenth century, the new consumer orientation of households combined with emerging ideals about female domesticity to identify women with consumption.

Historians write about a "consumer revolution" but change occurred both gradually and unevenly. The consumer society spread first to urban areas and the affluent and later to rural areas and the poor. New production methods also coexisted with traditional manufacturing practices. Mamie Garvin's experiences illustrate this complex transformation. In 1913 Garvin, an African American, traveled from her home in Charleston, South Carolina, to Boston to earn money for her trousseau. She worked by day in a garment factory, sewing **PIECEWORK** (see Volume 2) with Polish and Italian immigrant women. By night, Garvin and two friends copied styles from ladies' magazines to custom-make fashions for Boston's African-American, middle-class women. If the consumer society created a revolution, it was a long and complicated one.

WOMEN AND WORK

Women's unpaid domestic work as well as their wage labor took new forms in the consumer society. Rising standards of living pressured women to put more time and energy into household consumption while consumer capitalism opened up new types of paid jobs for women.

Mass production of goods made factory work processes more specialized and mechanized, and separated laborers from the final product. Mass consumption, however, had very different effects on housework.

The job of **HOMEMAKER** remained highly unspecialized, personalized, and time-consuming. Fashionable ready-made clothing offered more choices, yet took more time for shopping and washing. The automobile created a new workplace for suburban homemakers: the driver's seat. Advertisers' warnings of the social stigma of "ring around the collar" or "halitosis" manipulated female responsibility for house-hold consumption into social pressure and guilt. Poor women suffered additional indignities when they could not afford the clothing and household furnishings that meant respectability to middle-class employers, teachers, and social workers.

Women's consumer responsibilities in the home also led to new education and employment opportunities. **HOME ECONOMICS** classes in high schools and colleges created more teaching jobs for women instructors. In business, companies anxious to appeal to "Mrs. Consumer" hired college-educated home economists for positions in product development, testing, and demonstration. From her test kitchen at Corning Glass Works, Lucy Maltby wrote recipes as well as shaped the company's market research, technological innovation, and public relations from 1929 to 1965.

Women's **DOMESTIC ARTS** (see Volume 2) also found a new place in the consumer society. Maria Martinez, a Pueblo Indian, learned pottery making from the women in her family. Basing her work on traditional designs rediscovered by archeologists, Martinez became an internationally known artist by the 1920s. Buyers valued the "traditional" and "authentic" qualities of the pottery, and its popularity created new appreciation for Native American culture. At the same time, her buyers' taste for "Indian" pottery limited Martinez's artistic choices. Following the Pueblo "traditions" expected by her clients meant that Martinez could not experiment with new technologies or designs. Consumer society both supported and constrained opportunities for women skilled in domestic arts.

In the twentieth century personal ambitions, economic need, education, and skills encouraged increasing numbers of women to enter the paid workforce. Consumer culture provided resources for working women to express their rights and expand their impact in the workplace.

Young immigrant women who worked in urban factories at the turn of the century used consumer culture to assert their rights as workers and as women. Clara Lemlich, a Jewish immigrant from the Ukraine who became a labor organizer and leader, demanded not only higher wages and shorter hours but also cloakrooms for women workers. Lemlich wanted the owners to recognize the right of factory operatives to be both laborers and ladies. Many working-class women, including Appalachian textile workers, Irish-American telephone operators, native-born stenographers, and Mexican-American cannery workers, bought fashionable things as a way to define their individual identities.

The consumer society created a new arena for consumption, the department store, which became a new workplace for women. Sales clerks balanced the advantages of a glamorous work setting filled with stylish merchandise against the disadvantages of low wages, little opportunity for advancement, and male supervisors' patronizing control. Saleswomen who became buyers forged a female specialty within the male world of management, earning attractive wages and providing role models for female coworkers. In the urban department store, women workers negotiated with middle-class women buyers and male managers to earn income, respect, and recognition.

Consumer society linked women with new roles and opportunities in public life, offering them complicated routes toward economic and personal autonomy.

WOMEN AS CITIZENS

Before and after gaining the vote, women expressed their citizenship through consumer activities. Women used the language and relations of consumption to defend their political interests, demand rights, and shape the practice of American politics.

At the turn of the twentieth century, consumer culture provided the reunited **SUFFRAGE MOVEMENT** with new arguments and tactics to promote women's rights. Some suffrage leaders justified women's capacity for voting on the basis of the skills required for shopping: Women voters would use skills developed through comparison shopping to evaluate different candidates' merits, and apply household thriftiness to scrutinize corporate and government spending. Suffragist organizers also borrowed advertisers' methods. "Votes for Women" appeared on giant billboards and the sides of streetcars; in busy city centers suffragists paraded wearing sandwich boards and selling suffrage newspapers. Portraying women voters as citizen consumers, the suffragists contributed campaign strategies to American politics as they popularized women's rights.

Women reformers also found resources in the consumer society to promote their political agendas. Under the leadership of **FLORENCE KELLEY**, the **NATIONAL CONSUMERS LEAGUE** (NCL) mobilized middle-class woman consumers to oppose exploitative labor practices and protect woman workers. Kelley encouraged woman shoppers to buy goods carrying the NCL White Label, signifying that the manufacturer had met stringent factory, labor, and sanitation standards. The NCL translated female moral responsibility for the welfare of woman workers into a political voice for **PROTECTIVE LABOR LEGISLATION**.

Women's role as purchasers for their families provided a powerful tool for working-class women to fight for their rights. Immigrant Jewish homemakers in early-twentieth-century New York organized boycotts and rent strikes to force merchants and landlords to reduce prices. In the 1930s African-American women in Detroit formed the Housewives League. Members pledged to patronize merchants and professionals in their local community, thus spending their dollars to help black businesses and families survive the hard times. The League's strategy of combining consumer advocacy with boycotts and picketing later became a model for the Montgomery, Alabama, bus boycott and other civil rights activism in the 1950s. In the 1970s, Mexican-American and Chicana women urged middle-class housewives to boycott grapes in support of farm workers' rights. Middle-class women gained new political awareness from their exposure to the civil rights agenda of the United Farm Workers. At the same time Chicana organizers and workers became more conscious of gender inequality and experienced empowerment as women.

Through consumer activism women developed political consciousness and brought about change.

WOMANHOOD

In the consumer society, advertising created new forms of communication to both educate and persuade buyers. Advertisers used images of womanhood to influence consumer attitudes and behavior. At the same time, women found new ways to use consumption to present images of themselves and their hopes. These varied and often competing representations of womanhood reveal the very public and the very personal meanings that consumer society offered women in the modern United States.

By the 1920s advertising trade journals estimated that women were responsible for 85 percent of consumer spending. Popular notions about womanhood powerfully shaped advertisers' messages. In addition, advertisers' preoccupation with women encouraged women to become preoccupied with themselves.

Most advertisements depicted consumers as not only female but also white and middle-class. Women of color encountered few, and often negative, depictions of their roles in consumer society. Aunt Jemima, a housemaid pictured on pancake mix boxes, portrayed African-American women as simple, uneducated, and subservient. Asian, Latina, and other women of color rarely appeared in mainstream advertising until the 1970s.

Despite advertising's limited and often damaging portrayal of female consumers, women found a range of ways to express themselves and their desires through consumption. After passing through Ellis Island in New York Harbor or Angel Island outside San Francisco, a young immigrant woman's first purchase was often ready-made American clothing to symbolize her newly constructed American self. Immigrant mothers, by purchasing foreign-language publications and traditional foods from neighborhood markets, also used consumption to express American ethnic identity. Women of color dressing attractively in current fashions and ethnic styles created public self-images that declared their right to self-definition and provided an alternative to racist stereotypes.

The "consumption junction" where women interacted with changing economic and social institutions presented them with a complex blend of promises and challenges. The study of consumer society helps explain the varied and often contradictory roles of women in the twentieth century.

Nancy Page Fernandez

FURTHER READING

Glickman, Lawrence. *Consumer Society in American History: A Reader.* Ithaca: Cornell University Press, 1999.

Scanlon, Jennifer, ed. *The Gender and Consumer Culture Reader*. New York: New York University Press, 2000.

A Woman's Body

The battlefield for many of women's struggles during the twentieth century was woman's body. Women made tremendous gains in sexuality, **HEALTH** care, and **REPRODUCTIVE RIGHTS** during the twentieth century, but by the end of the century, conservative backlash threatened to erode earlier gains in access to safe, legal **ABORTION**. Though attempts to challenge the dominant conceptions of appearance were made, many feminists believed that by the end of the century the ideal appearance had changed for the worse.

APPEARANCE

Both nineteenth- and twentieth-century feminists struck out against unhealthy **FASHION** standards. In the nineteenth century feminists counseled against corsets and long voluminous skirts. They succeeded in modifying clothing by the 1890s when **GIBSON GIRLS** (see Volume 2), young, healthy, athletic women, loosened their corsets and trimmed their skirts.

In the early twentieth century, clothing followed those simpler lines. In the 1920s short skirts and bound breasts were a major break from the past, displaying a new woman who was more boyish and who might do masculine things like pilot airplanes. Subdued by the **GREAT DEPRESSION** of the 1930s, women turned back to simpler dresses with longer skirts. In the 1940s, they wore slacks and shoulder-padded jackets reflecting the masculine roles women were taking in war industries and the armed services.

With the back-to-the-home movement of the 1950s, fashion turned to a revised interpretation of the nineteenth-century hourglass figure. Women cinched their waists and lifted their breasts with various undergarments—corset-like "merry widows," waist cinchers, girdles, and bras.

In a dramatic turnaround, the youth movement of the 1960s and the feminist movement of the 1970s advocated comfortable, natural clothing without restraint—characterized most forcefully by the protest at the **Miss America Pageant** in 1968 where restrictive garments were thrown into a trash can. Counterculture women abandoned bras and makeup. For the career-minded, pantsuits reflected women's goals of career success.

The post-feminist 1980s and 1990s were notable for a more unattainable and, many believe, unhealthy obsession with slenderness. The body itself became an artistic canvas. Rather than merely using clothing to adorn their bodies, some women decorated them with piercing and tattoos. In trying to achieve the perfect body, many women, at the end of the twentieth century, were turning to fitness programs and rigid discipline over diet—sometimes crossing the line to eating disorders. Because of the complex way in which images are updated for novelty and replicated incessantly in our media-obsessed culture, the goal of healthy realistic ideals for women's appearance was perhaps the most difficult objective to achieve.

SEXUALITY

By the turn of the twentieth century, a **sexual revolution** for women was in progress. Working-class women who lived in cities began to frequent new spaces for leisure—dance halls, movie houses, and amusement parks. Dating in public began to replace visiting at women's homes as a rite of courtship. By the 1920s, middle-class women entered this public space as well. While the dating system took away some of women's power to control sexuality, it also gave them more freedom of sexual expression. Some historians point out that the date implied a bargain. Men paid for dinner and amusement and expected sexual favors in return. With greater privacy and more opportunity, many working-class women were initiated into premarital sexual intercourse.

By the 1920s, middle-class women were adopting these mores. Of the women who became adults in the 1920s, about 50 percent had sexual intercourse before marriage. This proportion remained stable until the 1960s. During these decades, most women reserved premarital intercourse for men whom they planned to marry. During **World War II**, many men and women gave lip service to this moral standard, but became engaged numerous times. In the postwar 1950s, there was an attempt to return to simpler times with steady dating, early **marriage**, and premarital intercourse in committed relationships.

During the 1960s, a different kind of sexual revolution took place. Women no longer restricted their sexual activity to men they could trust, experimenting with partners more freely. By the 1980s, 80 percent of women had experienced sexual intercourse before marriage and marriage was coming at a later age. Acceptance of cohabitation without marriage became commonplace. The AIDS epidemic that began at this time changed contraceptive use, but did not necessarily turn back the sexual revolution. Condom use increased while use of oral contraceptives decreased. At the same time, the percentage of adolescent women who experienced sexual intercourse and multiple partners remained static. A return to the sexual mores of the 1950s did not occur.

During the 1980s and 1990s significant gains were made by **lesbian** women who declared their sexuality and worked for rights that they were denied. By the end of the century, lesbians were expressing their commitment to one another openly. In addition, they were gaining rights of **child custody** and adoption, as well as recognition of their partners by employers, health plans, and hospitals.

WOMEN'S HEALTH MOVEMENT

During the colonial and early national periods, women—as wives, mothers, healers, and midwives—dispensed most health care. With the professionalization of medical care in the nineteenth century, male doctors were able to get laws on the books that prevented the practice of **medicine** by persons untrained at medical colleges (see Volume 2). At first, women were not accepted into medical schools, and only after protracted struggles were they admitted in very small numbers.

By the turn of the twentieth century, though midwives were still delivering many of the babies in the country, medicine, and, most particularly, reproductive practices, were becoming the domains of male doctors. Childbirth had become unnatural, with lengthy periods of hospitalization and separation of mother and baby.

In the late 1960s when the nascent women's movement gave women the encouragement to question their treatment, they found much that was not to their liking. They asserted that they were not allowed to make informed choices about their medical care, and that medical research was most often carried out on men, with no concern about how women would react to treatments being tested. Women also found many male doctors to be condescending and arrogant.

The women's health movement came into its own—publishing self-help manuals like ***Our Bodies, Ourselves*** in 1969 (see Documents) and agitating for changes in the health-care system. Many women learned about their bodies through self-help clinics where they viewed themselves with the aid of speculums and mirrors and learned to diagnose and treat themselves. Women activists testified before Congress and government agencies and filed lawsuits connected to such issues as the safety of contraception, the availability of abortion, and the cessation of sterilization abuse. It helped that women were flocking to medical schools. By 1999, 22 percent of physicians in the United States were women.

REPRODUCTIVE RIGHTS

Of all the changes regarding women's bodies that occurred in the twentieth century, none was more important than the control of reproduction. Without control over whether or not to have children and when to have them, other gains for women would be limited.

Knowledge of birth control was severely hampered by the 1873 **Comstock Law** (see Volume 2) that banned "obscene" materials from the mail, including birth control information. In addition, most states had laws restricting the dissemination of birth control. **Margaret Sanger** was arrested in 1916 for flouting these laws.

Though the Comstock Law's ban on birth control was overturned in 1936, women still had limited options until 1960. In that year, the Food and Drug Administration approved the birth control pill. It was the first reliable contraceptive under the control of women that separated the use of birth control from sexual activity. Within five years, the pill was the most popular form of birth control in the United States.

Though women were flocking to the pill, there were disturbing rumors of possible dangerous side effects—blood-clotting disorders that could sometimes lead to death. Senator Gaylord Nelson (D-Wis.) held hearings on the safety of the pill in 1970. These all-male hearings about a matter that was of primary concern for women galvanized the women's health movement. Feminists did not want to throw out the pill; they wanted women to be able to choose whether to use it, with all the information about the side effects available to them. After a lengthy fight, eventually the Food and Drug Administration required inserts to be packaged with the pill so that women could exercise informed consent. This was a formidable victory for all prescription users, as it became standard procedure for all medications.

This success led feminist health activists to move on to other reproductive rights issues—particularly the legalization of **abortion**. This conflict would prove to be the most difficult battle in the war over women's bodies.

From the second half of the nineteenth century to the mid-1960s, abortion was prohibited in all states. Still experts estimated that hundreds of thousands of abortions took place each year in the late 1940s and early 1950s. During the 1960s, many state abortion laws were repealed and therapeutic abortions were legalized. Usually a woman had to convince a board of doctors that she needed an abortion to safeguard her physical or mental health. In 1973 the Supreme Court made one of the most important decisions in United States history. ***Roe v. Wade*** legalized abortion in the first trimester of pregnancy. Soon after *Roe v. Wade*, abortion became widely available; however, a backlash against the Supreme Court ruling led to a raging battle in the 1980s and 1990s between pro-choice and pro-life groups.

At the turn of the twenty-first century, women were being held to a higher standard of physical perfection than ever before. At the same time, their right to sexual freedom, though opposed by religious groups and clouded by the specter of sexually transmitted diseases, seemed stronger than ever. The women's health movement had made great strides, but its achievements had not reached many poor women. Birth control was safer and more reliable than ever before, but the opportunity for safe legal abortion was diminished. While significant gains were made in the twentieth century regarding a woman's body, none came without considerable struggle.

Bonnie L. Ford

See also: Hyde Amendment; Midwifery; National Abortion and Reproductive Rights Action League; National Right to Life Coalition; Planned Parenthood.

FURTHER READING

Bordo, Susan. *Unbearable Weight: Feminism, Western Culture, and the Body*. Berkeley: University of California Press, 1993.

D'Emilio, John, and Estelle Freedman. *Intimate Matters: A History of Sexuality in America*. New York: Harper & Row, 1988.
Mintz, Steven, and Susan Kellogg. *Domestic Revolutions: A Social History of American Family Life*. New York: The Free Press, 1988.
Seid, Roberta P. "Too 'Close to the Bone': The Historical Context for Women's Obsession with Slenderness." In Fallon, Patricia, et al., eds., *Feminist Perspectives on Eating Disorders*. New York: The Guilford Press, 1991.
Solinger, Ricky, ed. *Abortion Wars: A Half Century of Struggle*. Berkeley: University of California Press, 1998.

Violence Against Women

Violence against women has a complex history that has barely been explored. Even a widely accepted definition has been difficult to agree upon. Violence against women could include **RAPE**, incest, **PORNOGRAPHY**, and various forms of emotional or psychological abuse. This essay will focus on wife beating, the form of violence toward women that has attracted the most attention from American courts and scholars.

Violence against wives has been both accepted and commonplace throughout most of American history. The Massachusetts Bay and Plymouth colonies passed laws against spousal violence in the seventeenth century, but courts were reluctant to separate couples and were critical of wives who acted independently. Indeed, husbands then and later routinely and successfully defended violence as a means of subduing and "correcting" wives who disobeyed them.

Violence against wives apparently declined during the nineteenth century, for several reasons. Growing numbers of middle-class couples believed that relations between spouses ought to be characterized by mutual respect, not masculine dominance and feminine submission. Violence in general, including homicide rates, fell as people became more settled and as society placed more emphasis on self-restraint.

Other forms of violence against women remained commonplace by the turn of the twentieth century, however. Violence toward prostitutes was both widespread and accepted. The concept of marital rape did not exist, for women were expected to submit to intercourse when their husbands required it.

By 1900 these social changes had affected the nation's legal climate. Wives could secure a divorce on the grounds of physical cruelty alone in a growing number of states. The post–Civil War **WOMEN'S RIGHTS MOVEMENT** (see Volume 2) had sometimes focused on wife beating.

Many men continued to hit their wives in the early twentieth century, particularly in rural areas. City women had more options. Police officers, though wary of intervening in family disputes, might arrest a violent husband. Most urban couples did not enjoy a great deal of privacy around 1900. Many lived in boardinghouses, apartments, or in small houses in crowded residential areas. S. C. Hilton of Portland, Oregon, recalled an evening when he and a friend were sitting on his front porch and noticed "quite a gathering" down the street. A neighboring couple was in the middle of an argument. The wife loudly refused to "go back in the house again with you for you to beat me." The husband "seemed to get ashamed" and slunk back home. Hilton invited the wife and her child to stay with him and his wife for a few days. She did—and soon filed for divorce.

This sort of willingness to assist abused wives declined during the twentieth century. One study found that neighbors and friends had constituted 46 percent of people who had intervened against violent husbands in the mid-nineteenth century and just 14 percent in the mid-1950s. Homes had become larger and more isolated. Couples were less likely to live with boarders, servants, and extended family. Attitudes also shifted. In the 1970s a woman who had just been beaten by her husband fled barefoot from her home. She appeared at a neighbor's door, desperate for help, only to be met with rejection: "We don't want to get involved," the woman said.

Violence apparently rose during the twentieth century. **MARRIAGE** became more and more emotionally intense, creating opportunities for both increased intimacy and increased disappointment and conflict as husbands and wives expected more of each other. Husbands were also becoming more violent because society as a whole was emphasizing self-realization at the expense of self-restraint. Twentieth-century advertisers urged people to indulge themselves. Banks invited clients to borrow rather than to save. These shifting norms affected how people acted when they were angry. By the 1920s enraged husbands were more likely to act upon rather than to curb their emotions.

These husbands, moreover, were married to women who were less and less likely to defer to them. Twentieth-century wives enjoyed easier access to divorce and employment than ever before. The growth of government programs for impoverished mothers meant that leaving one's husband did not necessarily lead to losing one's children. All of this meant that wives could afford to expect more from their husbands than just economic support. These wives, like their husbands, increasingly asserted a right to pursue their own happiness.

"Wife beating," as historian Linda Gordon observes, "arose not just from subordination but also from contesting it." This is not to say that assertive wives were responsible for the violence they suffered. Rather, women's growing determination to reject male dominance enhanced both their chances for respect and autonomy and their chances of being hit. Marginal women—poor women and women of color—were especially apt to resist men's attempts to dominate them. A study of women imprisoned for homicide in 1926 found that 124 out of 161 were African-American, and many of these women had killed their husbands or boyfriends. Native American and working-class women were more likely than white, middle-class women to fight abusive spouses.

There were, therefore, many reasons why husbands might have become more violent during the twentieth century. But did violence against wives actually increase? This is a very difficult question to answer, for the vast majority of violent acts that occurred within the family went unrecorded. Testimony presented in divorce suits offers telling clues, however. Twentieth-century wives became more and more likely to describe husbands who utilized violence quickly and without restraint, who hit them rather than calling them names, for example. More so than nineteenth-century divorce seekers, these women spoke of husbands who regularly beat them from head to toe, who broke their bones, or burned them with cigarettes.

Husbands' violence was becoming more extreme in part because its causes were becoming more diffuse, more varied. Violent husbands of the early nineteenth century had usually hit their wives for very specific reasons: an action or attitude on the wife's part that the husband considered unacceptable. But by the 1920s more and more husbands were hitting their wives for reasons that had little or nothing to do with the women's actions or attitudes. One mother recalled that her son-in-law "would come home from the mill cross and cranky, and throw things around." If her daughter "would try to talk to him he would slap her."

Violence against wives became both more commonplace and more recognized during the last half of the twentieth century. Marital expectations reached unprecedented heights, even as husbands and wives alike asserted unprecedented rights to pursue their own happiness. A recovering wife abuser in the 1990s recalled that he had expected his wife to "love me and fix me and be my everything." Violence often flourished in this intense environment.

Other forms of violence against women also rose in the 1960s and 1970s. Reports of rape skyrocketed, as did the availability of violent pornography.

But a profound shift in public awareness regarding violence against women appeared in the 1970s. Feminists, churches, community groups, and social workers across the nation began organizing dozens and then hundreds of hotlines and shelters for battered women. The battered women's movement was part of a growing sensitivity to exploitation in general and to the oppression of women in particular.

The battered women's movement has been extraordinarily successful. In the early 1970s battered wives had virtually no one to turn to other than family and friends. Abused women across the country can now seek refuge in shelters where they and their children can at least begin to sort out their options in a safe and supportive environment. Police officers—who once treated wife beating as a private matter—have become much more likely to arrest husbands, and these husbands are often directed to mandatory counseling. The movement has also brought an unprecedented amount of public attention to wife beating. The press ignored violence against wives during the 1960s. In 1977 the *New York Times* published 44 articles on the subject. Popular culture discovered wife beating and featured it in a number of films. Feminists also identified and publicized related problems, including dating violence, emotional or psychological abuse, and marital rape.

Violence against wives appeared to be declining at the close of the twentieth century. Spousal killings constituted a bit more than 12 percent of homicides in 1974. In 1994, they made up just 5 percent of such deaths. Reported acts of wife beating began to decline in the mid-1990s. But such statistics are difficult to interpret. The falling rate of spousal homicides, for example, may simply indicate that people are marrying later or not at all. Even with increased public funding, violence against wives and the other forms of abuse that accompany it will be difficult to eradicate. The average man still enjoys substantial physical, economic, and social advantages over the average woman. Most marriages are therefore characterized by inequality, and inequality can easily become a breeding ground for cruelty and violence—especially when inequalities are unrecognized.

History shows that the causes and even the extent of wife beating have changed over time. But it also indicates that violence against wives is a deeply rooted part of our national history.

David Peterson del Mar

See also: Divorce; Feminism, Radical; New Woman, the; Welfare.

FURTHER READING

Gordon, Linda. *Heroes of their Own Lives: The Politics and History of Family Violence, Boston, 1880–1960.* New York: Viking, 1988.

Peterson del Mar, David. *What Trouble I Have Seen: A History of Violence against Wives.* Cambridge: Harvard University Press, 1996.

Pleck, Elizabeth. *Domestic Tyranny: The Making of American Social Policy against Family Violence from Colonial Times to the Present.* New York: Oxford University Press, 1987.

The Civil Rights Movement

HISTORICAL BACKGROUND

The images of the civil rights movement are vividly etched in the minds of Americans who witnessed the violence of white Americans upon black American citizens. The televised coverage of police dogs attacking peaceful protestors, tearing their clothing and their flesh; the rush of water from fire hoses knocking them to the ground; and the stinging clouds of tear gas blinding American citizens shocked people across the nation. Racial justice and civil rights could no longer be considered a regional issue.

The United States emerged from World War II a global superpower, having defended democracy abroad. By the 1950s, capitalism became a global image of the American system, particularly when compared to communism. How could the super democracy explain the scenes of civil rights conflicts taking place in U.S. cities? These violent undemocratic practices embarrassed the nation's leaders and shocked the international community even as America staked its claim to moral leadership of the free world. The legal, cultural, and ideological system of race differences had its roots in **SLAVERY** (see Volume 2).

The **CIVIL WAR** and **RECONSTRUCTION** (see Volume 2) brought significant gains, particularly with the three constitutional amendments passed during these years. The Thirteenth Amendment (1865) abolished slavery. The Fourteenth Amendment (1868) granted citizenship to African Americans and guaranteed them equal protection under the law. The Fifteenth Amendment (1870) gave all male citizens the right to vote. Women, regardless of color, could not vote.

When African Americans tried to claim their constitutional rights, however, they encountered bitter resistance, often by institutions of their own government. For a brief period during Reconstruction black men could vote and hold political office in the Southern states. That window closed shut when Northern occupation of Southern states ended in the 1870s. White supremacists quickly turned back the laws within the states and denied not only voting rights, but access to education, employment, and freedom of movement.

The segregationist era of Jim Crow dominated the South but patterns of race-based discrimination existed throughout the United States.

The civil rights movement had earlier precursors in the twentieth century, but the term generally refers to the groups and actions that took deliberate steps to gain equal constitutional protection for Americans regardless of race in the years since 1940. Movement activists struggled for equal education, employment, housing, public accommodations and voting rights. Most civil rights groups used nonviolent methods, including sit-ins, boycotts, and marches. They endured despite murders, lynchings, beatings, bombings, and arrests. Finally, with the passage of the Civil Rights Act of 1964 and the Voting Rights Act of 1965, discriminatory practices against African Americans, other minorities, and women began to erode in earnest.

WOMEN'S CONTRIBUTION TO THE CIVIL RIGHTS MOVEMENT

The women of the twentieth century have a long record of activism. However, the names of only a few are familiar to us. Most histories of the civil rights movement emphasize the leadership of male clergy or black male radicals. Women's involvement in civil rights began to be told in the 1980s by journalist Paula Giddings, activist Angela Davis, and historians such as Darlene Clark Hine and Anne Standley. Yet the actions of legions of women in this campaign continue to be collapsed into a few names. This essay introduces a few less familiar activists and the issues they promoted.

Education

Slaves in the nineteenth century had not been permitted an education; in fact, it was a crime to teach a slave to read. In addition, racial segregation and poverty created poorly staffed and underfunded schools for African Americans. Large numbers of African Americans did not know how to read and write, a fact that contributed to limited economic options. Nevertheless, education became a personal and community responsibility. Clubs and organizations raised funds to support schools locally as well as in other states. Teaching became one of the few avenues for professional jobs, and literacy campaigns became an essential first step for many in the civil rights movement. In 1954, in *Brown v. Board of Education,* the United States Supreme Court ruled unanimously that the "separate but equal" doctrine justifying racial segregation of students in public schools was unconstitutional. Despite this landmark ruling, Southern whites mobilized to fight school integration.

Septima Poinsetta Clark (1898–1987) graduated from high school at 18. She had no teaching experience, yet she served as the principal of a two-teacher school with 132 students in South Carolina. Conditions at the school were deplorable, and attendance sporadic since many students had to work in the fields. These injustices moved Clark to become active in the National Association for the Advancement of Colored People (NAACP), an organization fighting racial inequality. In 1956, when the South Carolina legislature decreed that no state employee could belong to the NAACP, Clark was one of 11 African-American teachers fired. She had taught 40 years.

Clark continued to work in education, but in a different setting. As director of workshops at the Highlander Folk School in Tennessee, she taught African Americans to read and write and prepared them to pass the voter registration test. One of Highlander's better-known students, **Rosa Parks**, applied its principles when she refused to give up her seat on a bus and was arrested, sparking the Montgomery bus boycott.

Public Accommodations

One of the most visible institutions of Southern segregation laws was the separation of blacks and whites in restaurants, hotels, and other public facilities, and on public transportation. The African-American women of Montgomery, Alabama, who often worked as maids in the homes of white families, used public transportation in large numbers. Despite the fact that the bus company relied on their business, drivers treated them rudely, failed to stop at regular bus stops, and on occasion threw them off the bus. After long hours of menial labor, Montgomery's black workers had to stand in the back of the bus, leaving the front seats reserved for whites. Representatives of the black community, men and women, met with politicians and bus company representatives for years without successful resolution.

Much has been written about the Montgomery bus boycott, yet the public rarely associates it with Jo Ann Robinson. Through her leadership of the Women's Political Council (WPC), a black middle-class professional organization, and as a board member of the Montgomery Improvement Association, Robinson was instrumental in organizing and implementing the boycott. As a result, she was one of 17 professors fired from Alabama State University afterward. The boycott succeeded with the full support of the black community, including the cooks and maids who walked long miles to work and back to maintain the boycott. Although it is Rosa Parks and Rev. Martin Luther King, Jr., whose names rose to prominence from this boycott, its success depended upon the planning and efforts of Jo Ann Robinson and the WPC. Similar boycotts were conducted in Tallahassee, Birmingham, and Baton Rouge. In 1956 the United States Supreme Court ruled unconstitutional the Alabama state and local laws that segregated transportation.

Economic Empowerment

The wages of African Americans were much lower than those of whites who performed essentially the same jobs in less grueling conditions. Without equal opportunity in education, housing, health care or the political arena, most African Americans found it difficult to move up from low-paying, menial labor.

Gloria Richardson led the Cambridge Movement, a drive for economic and political equality in a small Maryland town where black unemployment hovered at 50 percent. It was the first such movement outside the Deep South and the only one led by a woman. Richardson, an African American who studied at Howard University, had learned early on that neither her education nor her well-to-do family could protect her from segregation. She focused on the economic status of African Americans in Cambridge. With the help of the Student Nonviolent Coordinating Committee (SNCC) and other flagship organizations of the civil rights movement, Richardson brought the attention of local, state, and federal officials to conditions in Cambridge. On July 23, 1963, in the office of U.S. Attorney General Robert F. Kennedy, the "Treaty of Cambridge" was signed, integrating public schools and hospitals, employment, public accommodations, and housing. It also established a human rights commission.

Voting Rights and Political Empowerment

Although the Fifteenth and Nineteenth Amendments extended voting rights to all men and women, African Americans still faced huge obstacles to voting. They were forced to take literacy tests designed for failure; a typical "test" question was to count the bubbles on a bar of soap. African Americans were required to pay poll taxes that most could not afford, and many were beaten or fired for trying to exercise their constitutional rights.

No one showed a more indomitable spirit in rising above these obstacles than **FANNIE LOU HAMER**, the youngest of 20 children of a Mississippi sharecropper. Due to family illness and poverty, she left school to go to work at 12 years of age. Hamer worked weighing cotton, a job she lost, at the age of 40, for trying to vote. She was the victim of severe beatings, numerous arrests, and constant threats; she, her husband, and her daughter all lost their jobs as Hamer became known to the world for her activism.

In 1964, Hamer helped found the Mississippi Freedom Democratic Party (MFDP), an alternative to the all-white Mississippi Democratic Party, which had broken with the national Democrats over civil rights: it excluded the state's 400,000 African Americans. Hamer led the MFDP to the 1964 Democratic National Convention, where her appearance drew the nation's attention to the sad state of human rights in Mississippi. The work of Hamer and the MFDP bore fruit in 1968 and 1972, when the Democratic conventions included blacks, women, and other groups previously denied representation.

Shirley Chisholm, the nation's first African-American congresswoman, walked the trail blazed by Hamer. In 1972, she ran for president of the United States and received 151 delegate votes at the Democratic convention.

These are just a few of the women who devoted themselves to the struggle for civil rights. Across the country, women of all ages and ethnicities were active in the movement. Casey Hayden, Penny Patch, Dorothy Miller, and Mary King were SNCC volunteers whose bravery and early commitment paved the way for other whites to join the movement. Jewish women, according to historian Debra Schultz, joined the civil rights movement in disproportionate numbers; half the Freedom Riders and attorneys going south were Jewish. They had helped to establish the NAACP, and they contributed generously to civil rights organizations.

Institutions and Organizations

Several organizations were established during the civil rights movement to fight segregation and Jim Crow laws. SNCC included numerous women leaders, including Doris Smith, a highly visible and effective volunteer recruiter who died at the age of 26 in 1966. One of the first women to hold a leadership position in the Southern Christian Leadership Conference (SCLC), **Ella Baker** was an inspirational organizer and motivator who gained a reputation for excellence at building bridges between groups, sharing ownership of projects, and minimizing the role of a single leader.

Among the institutions working to create a foundation from which to mobilize citizens to action advance the status of black America, no organization did more than the black church. Segregated society contributed to the dominant role of black churches, one of the few cohesive institutions to emerge from slavery. The churches with their predominantly female membership anchored their community. The church was the place for meetings, strategy sessions, worship, and a sense of sanctuary from the white world. It was also one of the few places large enough to accommodate great numbers of people. Black women mobilized their congregations to seek support for the civil rights movement.

CONCLUSION

The focus of the civil rights movement was discrimination based on race, not sex, but the social upheaval it created made a path for black women of courage and leadership to gain valuable political experience. It also taught ordinary citizens how injustice works and how to fight it—lessons many women applied to the struggle against sexism that followed.

Today, many of their accomplishments are being challenged by reverse discrimination lawsuits and the abolition of affirmative action. Recent court rulings denying special consideration on the basis of race for college admissions and employment have raised concerns that opportunities for women and minorities will be curtailed.

Many African Americans have mobilized to resist these actions. On March 7, 2000, some 11,000 people marched in Florida against a program to end affirmative action. It was the largest civil rights march in state history. During the aftermath of the bitterly contested presidential election of 2000, Florida A&M University students staged a silent sit-in at the state capital. In both efforts, women of all ages and colors played key roles.

Elsie Bradwell Crowell

See also: African Americans.

FURTHER READING

Cowan, Toma and Maguire, Jack. *Timelines of African American History—500 years Of Black Achievement.* New York: Perigee Books, 1994.

Crawford, Vicki L., et al., eds. *Women in the Civil Rights Movement Trailblazers & Torchbearers, 1941–1965.* Bloomington: Indiana University Press, 1990.

Giddings, Paula. *When and Where I Enter: The Impact of the Black Women on Race and Sex in America.* New York: Bantam Books, 1984.

Morris, Alton D. *The Origins of the Civil Rights Movement: Black Communities Organizing for Change.* New York: Free Press, 1984.

Olson, Lynne. *Freedom's Daughters: The Unsung Heroines of the Civil Rights Movement from 1830 to 1970.* New York: Scribner's, 2001.

Shultz, Debra. *Going South—Jewish Women in the Civil Rights Movement.* New York: New York University Press, 2001.

Walker, Melissa. *Down from the Mountaintop: Black Women's Novels in the Wake of the Civil Rights Movement, 1966–1989.* New Haven: Yale University Press, 1991.

The Changing American Family

By the early 1900s the United States had evolved from a primarily agricultural economy to an industrial giant. Railroad magnates connected the country with thousands of miles of track, and developers built cities up and out to accommodate the burgeoning population. Just as labor and landscape adjusted to this transformation, so did women and their families.

In working-class families all able-bodied members contributed to the household economy. Fathers filled positions in factories, mines, and farms while wives cared for their children and kept the home. Depending on their ethnicity, many married women took jobs outside of the home as well. Jewish women, for instance, often worked in factories. Italian, Polish, and Irish women, however, were less likely to work outside of the home after marriage. They supplemented the family income by taking in boarders or doing piecework in their homes. For poor **African-American** women, racial discrimination all but eliminated their chances of finding factory work. They were forced to take **DOMESTIC SERVICE** jobs to make ends meet.

In middle-class families the father was the sole provider. He might be a skilled professional in the field of medicine, business, or labor while his wife was a **HOMEMAKER**. These families could separate themselves from the busy urban environment by purchasing homes in residential communities at the edge or outside of the cities. Wives carried on the nineteenth-century Victorian ethos of devotion to the domestic sphere. For the most part these women did their own household chores, those at the upper end of the middle class assisted by servants.

The wealthiest families in the United States, by far the minority, might own more than one home, each equipped with hired help. Husbands might or might not have to work, while wives were responsible for directing the household employees. These women had plenty of time for leisure activities.

Although life experiences varied greatly among young women of different social and economic classes at the turn of the twentieth century the gap narrowed significantly by the 1920s. **CHILD LABOR** restrictions, decreasing unemployment, and the availability of high school **EDUCATION** temporarily kept the children of poor families out of work and in school. After graduation young women, regardless of economic class, usually delayed marriage and entered the workforce or went off to college.

While young women of the previous generation had worked at home or in single-sex environments, after 1900 women often worked in offices or department stores alongside men. At the end of the day, female workers went out to social clubs and dance halls. Freed from her parents' watchful eyes the **NEW WOMAN** smoked, drank, and participated in sexual experimentation.

The growing independence of women contributed to the emergence of a new familial ideal, the companionate family. Women and men, less restricted by parental control and the arduous chores formerly demanded in **MARRIAGE**, chose partners based on sexual interest and intellectual and emotional compatibility. Modern conveniences supposedly freed up wives so that they could focus on familial relationships. The availability of birth control enabled women to spend more time nurturing fewer children.

Although new attitudes had seemingly relieved wives of loveless marriages, backbreaking labor, and burdensome numbers of children, the new model of the family was equally challenging. Rather than relying on female friends for companionship, wives were expected to find it in their spouses. New appliances may have made work easier, but standards of cleanliness became more rigid. Women may have had fewer children, but the expectations of "good parenting" became more difficult to live up to.

Just as women and men were more likely to enter marriage based on individual satisfaction with their partner, they were more likely to abandon marriage if they became dissatisfied. In the nineteenth century restrictions on divorce, social pressure, and moral obligation kept unhappy couples together. By the 1920s one out of every seven marriages ended in divorce.

Changing attitudes toward marriage and family life in the 1920s signaled a social crisis to some observers, but those concerns were quickly overshadowed by the **GREAT DEPRESSION** in 1929. People lost jobs and property overnight, and families were forced to pool their resources to survive. By 1932 the unemployment rate in the United States approached 25 percent. Those of marriageable age often delayed weddings. Those who did marry often limited their family size. Although the average number of children born to a family had been steadily declining, for the first time Americans experienced negative population growth. Divorce rates slowed. A couple was more likely to endure an unhappy marriage before paying for a divorce or losing a potential wage earner. During the Depression, many people believed women should not work if their husbands were employable. Some blamed high rates of unemployment, low wages, and the general malaise that seemed to infect men on married women who worked. Both the government and independent businesses fired married women during the Depression to create jobs for men. Yet more married women took jobs than ever before.

WORLD WAR II finally brought an end to the Depression. The government called men to military service and women to the factories. Women's employment grew from 28 percent to 37 percent during the war. Three-quarters of those newly employed were married. They trained and worked as welders, burners, and riveters, among other jobs.

When the war ended so too did women's newly won achievements in the labor force. Employers laid off women first to make room for returning veterans. Those who had to work out of economic necessity returned to stereotypically women's jobs such as clerical work. African-American women retained some war benefits. More jobs were open to them than before the war, but like other women they lost the higher wages brought about in the crisis.

After more than a decade of family dislocation due to depression and war Americans were eager to embrace family life. Women and men married early and had large families. The generation born during and after the war came to be known as the "baby boomers." Eager to take advantage of the postwar housing development, middle-class parents moved their growing families away from the city. These suburban pioneers left behind the familial support networks that had sustained their parents' generation, and had to rely on their neighborhood and organizational connections rather than blood ties. It was up to mothers to make and sustain these vital lifelines.

Critics of postwar **SUBURBANIZATION** argue that the houses resembled boxes and that both the buildings and the gadgets inside them promoted consumerism and subsequently debt. The neighborhood support system that seemed like a reasonable substitute for extended family demanded political conformity. And finally, mothers, whose domestic roles were so central to family life, often felt unfulfilled. Cleaning, child care, and cooking left little time to attend to their own interests. **BETTY FRIEDAN'S** famous critique, *The Feminine Mystique* (see Documents), described women suffering from "the problem that has no name." Middle-class women found themselves with everything society told them they should want: a husband, children, and a house, but none of these seemed to make them happy.

Some women turned to alcohol to solve their problems while others took prescription drugs such as Valium. Some found more constructive answers to their needs. Women took jobs outside of the home once their children went off to school, or blended their domestic devotion with social and political activism to form or join movements that would ultimately benefit children and families, such as the La Leche League, Women Strike for Peace, or the civil rights movement.

The 1950s created a culture of self-awareness. Young baby boomers had less economic responsibility, more education, leisure, and time spent with their peers than any previous generation. When they arrived at adulthood in the 1960s and 1970s many carried with them a sense of entitlement and a willingness to challenge the status quo. Both women and men challenged the style of marriage they had inherited from their parents' generation.

Feminists encouraged women to pursue education and gain economic self-sufficiency. The birth control pill, developed in 1960, also encouraged women's independence, offering married women a reliable method of limiting **PREGNANCY** and unmarried women a chance to experience sexual fulfillment outside of marriage. Although birth control had been available for centuries, the pill's simplicity made it uniquely liberating.

Just as women questioned their dependence on men, men questioned their duty toward women. New attitudes toward rights and responsibilities kept unwilling expectant couples from marrying. The number of children born out of wedlock more than tripled. Divorce rates climbed along with the number of single-parent families. Once divorced, women more often than not became the primary caretakers.

The 1980s produced varied reactions to changes that occurred in the previous two decades. Women blending marriage, children, and career became the norm. Just as women took on additional responsibilities they expected more from their marriage partners regarding child care and housework.

Despite the controversies over the modern family, it continues to thrive. Foreign adoption and new reproductive technology have enabled single women, homosexuals, and infertile couples to have children. Women, as they gain higher levels of education and move into better-paying jobs, are less likely to find themselves in a situation of economic dependency on men, and are therefore financially better equipped to handle divorce. And the federal government, while it lags behind other industrialized countries in the area of paid maternity leave and subsidized child care, nevertheless enacted the **FAMILY AND MEDICAL LEAVE ACT** into law in 1993, recognizing that family is a priority for everyone.

Sara Dwyer-McNulty

FURTHER READING

Coontz, Stephanie. *The Way We Never Were: American Families and the Nostalgia Trap.* New York: Basic Books, 1992.

May, Elaine Tyler. *Homeward Bound: American Families and the Cold War Era*. New York: Basic Books, 1988.

Mintz, Steven and Susan Kellogg. *Domestic Revolutions: A Social History of American Family Life*. New York: Free Press, 1988.

Women and the Media

As mass media developed in the twentieth century, so did women's roles within them. In the early 1900s, women held influential positions at women's **MAGAZINES** and on women's sections of newspapers. Many magazines had woman editors; for example, *Vogue* has only had woman editors since its 1892 beginning. In 1900, 2,193 of 30,098 **JOURNALISTS** in the United States were female, according to the Census. By 1910, the number of women in writing or editing jobs doubled. This early precedent allowed women to gain a foothold in most mass media.

Savvy publishers and editors understood that as half the population, women had purchasing power that their advertisers desired. Thus, their role as consumers produced an expansion of woman-focused media throughout the century. Women had a hand in all the major media: newspapers, magazines, photography, radio, television, film, cartooning, public relations, advertising, and the Internet.

Women who wrote for the print media in the early twentieth century followed flamboyant role models. A tradition of "stunt reporting" began in the late nineteenth century with women such as the renowned **NELLIE BLY** (see Volume 2), who made the country aware that women could be reporters. It would prove impossible for the women journalists who followed to match Bly's amazing feats. But some did learn to infuse as much drama as possible into their stories. They were known as the "sob sisters." In covering such sensational stories as the 1906 trial of coal heir Harry Thaw, who was accused of murdering his wife's lover, they influenced American culture in a number of ways, including the development of soap operas and advice columns, as publishers sought to attract more woman readers.

Women had become an integral part of the world of newspapers, as consumers. Stores directed their advertising toward them, and newspapers created sections specifically for them. These sections initially focused on homemaking. But by the late twentieth century, most newspapers retooled "women's pages" as lifestyle sections for a broader audience.

In 1865, the country had 700 magazines; by 1890 that number had grown to 4,400, and in 1999 the *National Directory of Magazines* listed 20,000 titles. A number of women led the magazines from the beginning. Gertrude Battles Lane edited *Woman's Home Companion. The Ladies Home Journal,* the first U.S. magazine to reach 1 million subscribers (in 1903), was started by Cyrus H.K. Curtis, but his wife, Louisa May Knapp, who had been the editor of his newspaper's women's section, was its first editor. These magazines continually reinvented themselves to focus on issues of interest to women: By the late 1980s, 65 percent of American women were still reading one of the "seven sisters," *Ladies Home Journal, Better Homes & Gardens, Good Housekeeping, McCall's, Family Circle, Redbook,* or *Woman's Day.*

The subject content of women's periodicals historically extended beyond home and family. Women began a number of publications, some focused exclusively on gaining the right to vote for women, while others featured a wide array of timely subjects. For example, **MARGARET SANGER** edited *The Woman Rebel,* which she used to lobby for **REPRODUCTIVE RIGHTS** for women in 1917 (see Documents). These publications appealed to the audience of reformers during the Progressive era of the early 1900s.

Another journalistic innovation of the era was muckraking, which produced about 2,000 investigative articles in the first 15 years of the twentieth century. One of these muckrakers, **IDA TARBELL**, is now revered as the "patron saint" of investigative journalism. She dug into documents and interviewed experts, instead of relying on gossip as many muckrakers did. Her 18-part exposé of the Standard Oil Company and its head, John D. Rockefeller, published in

McClure's magazine in 1902, led to government investigations of the company and a landmark antimonopoly Supreme Court decision.

Journalist **IDA B. WELLS BARNETT** (see Volume 2) used her pen to raise awareness of racial violence. As a part owner of the Memphis *Free Speech,* Barnett exposed the prevalence and horrors of **LYNCHING** (see Volume 2), and she later took over the editorship of the *Conservator,* the first black newspaper in Chicago.

Feminist and racial issues in women-directed media surged again in the 1960s and 1970s. **GLORIA STEINEM,** the editor of ***MS.* MAGAZINE**, founded in 1972, appealed to educated, middle-class women who made up the majority of the women's rights movement. *Ms.* covered many issues at the heart of the movement: maternity leave, spouse abuse, equal pay, date rape, and sexual harassment. *Essence,* founded in 1970, linked the issues of the civil rights movement with the lives of young, urban black women. *Essence* gained a circulation of 890,000 by 1990, making it one of the fastest-growing women's publications of its time.

Women had the vote after 1920, but they still had less access to media jobs than men. First lady **ELEANOR ROOSEVELT** helped that situation by holding 348 weekly press conferences during her time in the White House, and insisting that only woman journalists could attend. Except for one time during World War II, Roosevelt stuck by her rule. This policy encouraged media outlets to hire women to cover her.

Roosevelt understood the challenges faced by women working in the media because she was a writer herself. Before becoming first lady, she edited a baby magazine with her daughter, and she wrote a syndicated column, "My Day," for daily newspapers from 1936 until 1962. Her column's underlying message was one of independence and equality for women (see Documents).

Roosevelt's interest in social issues ensured that her press conferences produced substantive stories for journalists, that would appear in the news sections, rather than the society or homemaking pages. Similarly, her all-women press conferences allowed for women's issues to have a platform. For example, in 1933 she chastised the government for laying off married women from the federal workforce as a money-saving effort. During the war, Roosevelt used the conferences to support servicewomen. Many of the women at her press conferences went on to illustrious careers in journalism after Roosevelt left the White House. With the advent of World War II, women also began to have more access to the newer media of the time: broadcasting.

Women had a tough time in early news broadcasting because their higher-pitched voices were not believed to be authoritative. However, women had been involved in broadcasting from the beginning as radio actresses. In the tradition of women's pages, networks wanted women on the radio to focus on homemaking. Ruth Crane's radio show, "Mrs. Page's Home Economy," ran on WJR in Detroit from 1929 to 1944. Some women had to give up more serious media work just for a chance to get on air. Mary Margaret McBride, formerly a journalist for magazines and newspapers, became a radio announcer in 1934. Producers told McBride to mimic a grandmotherly voice for her show, but halfway through she burst into her real voice as she told listeners that she had no children or husband and would rather her show focus on people and places, rather than homemaking. Listeners supported her and her radio interview show lasted until 1960.

WORLD WAR II opened many opportunities for women in broadcasting. In 1946, women made up 28 percent of the broadcasting workforce in jobs ranging from sales to the control room. These gains proved temporary, however, as returning service men forced women out.

Women slowly gained more on-air time, but it took until the late 1970s and early 1980s for women to appear frequently. **BARBARA WALTERS** became the highest-paid news personality in 1976 with a five-year, $5 million contract, when she left NBC's "Today" show to co-anchor the evening news on ABC. By the end of the twentieth century, women could be seen and heard all over radio and TV. In fact, women made up 40 percent of the television workforce in 2001. However, they have not broken the **GLASS CEILING** to executive jobs. Only 13 percent of the top executives at the major media and telecommunications companies were women in 2001.

Just as women wrote for all aspects of media, they also created much of the visual fabric of the media in the twentieth century through photography, cartooning, film, and video. In photography, Jessie Tarbox Beals was reportedly the first female press photographer; she began her career at the *Buffalo Inquirer and Courier* in 1902. Dorothea Lange and Margaret Bourke-White, two of the most renowned **PHOTOGRAPHERS** of the century, documented major events ranging from bread lines during the **GREAT DEPRESSION** to India's Mahatma Gandi.

Women's visual sensibilities also found an outlet through cartooning. Louise Quarles illustrated puns in 1901 and is believed to be the first woman cartoonist. Cute images filled the early cartooning of women, with cartoonists like Rose O'Neill drawing a comic strip featuring the cupid-like Kewpies in 1909. (Later, they became the well-known dolls.) However, one cartoon transformed women's image in comics. Begun in 1940 by Dalia "Dale" Messick, "Brenda Starr" featured a red-headed news reporter, a strong career woman character admired by both men and women.

Women were prominent film makers in the early days of the cinema, before 1920, when many actresses had their own production companies and directed films, too. However, the burgeoning Hollywood structure made it difficult for women to be directors. Between 1939 and 1979, women directed only 14 of the 7,332 Hollywood feature films produced. By 1990, women directed 4 to 5 percent of feature films annually.

Women worked in the business side of media for all of the twentieth century in areas such as publishing, advertising, production, and public relations. The *New York Herald-Tribune* appointed Helen Reid vice president of its merged newspaper in 1924. Dorothy Schiff became publisher of the *New York Post* in 1939. Eleanor "Cissy" Patterson bought two newspapers in Washington, D.C., combined them into the *Washington Times-Herald,* and ran it beginning in 1939. Her niece, Alicia Patterson, began publishing *Newsday* on Long Island in 1940 based on an accurate hunch that Americans would move to the suburbs. One of the most well-known woman publishers, **KATHARINE GRAHAM,** oversaw *The Washington Post* during the paper's coverage of the Watergate scandal.

Women have found success in the world of advertising as well. Since advertising agencies began in the 1920s, woman copywriters have developed slogans for top products.

Although difficult to break into in the early years, public relations is now dominated by women. By 1993, 60 percent of PR specialists were female compared to 25 percent in 1968.

As opportunities exploded for women in all types of media in the late twentieth century, they claimed an equal share of many jobs. Many college women are attracted to media professions. In 1999, women made up about 63 percent of mass communication graduates. Of these, 26 percent sought public relations jobs, 24 percent advertising agency jobs, and 19 percent TV jobs.

Throughout the century, women gained power as both media consumers and media workers. From TV programming to ad copy to magazine startups, media companies realized they must address the interests and needs of women if they were to succeed. This trend gave women the ability to guide the media as well, through their increased roles as publishers, producers, editors, writers, and creators. After a century, women are truly integral in defining all aspects of U.S. mass media.

Beth Haller

FURTHER READING

Abramson, Phyllis Leslie. *Sob Sister Journalism.* New York: Greenwood Press, 1990.

Beasley, Maurine and Sheila Gibbons. *Taking Their Place: A Documentary History of Women and Journalism.* Washington, DC: American University Press, 1993.

Robbins, Trina. *A Century of Women Cartoonists.* Northhampton, MA: Kitchen Sink Press, 1993.

Rosenbloom, Naomi. *A History of Women Photographers.* New York: Abbeville Press, 2000.

Sanders, Marlene, and Marcia Rock. *Waiting for Prime Time: The Women of Television News.* New York: Harper & Row, 1990.

Streitmatter, Rodger. *Raising Her Voice: African-American Women Journalists Who Changed History.* Lexington: University Press of Kentucky, 1994.

Feminism

In the early twentieth century, Americans began using the term *feminism* to describe the women's movement. Feminists sought to transform gender relations in every part of life—cultural, economic, political, and personal. They challenged nineteenth-century values of womanly submission and self-sacrifice, and stressed freedom and aspirations. As one early twentieth-century feminist declared, "We intend simply to be ourselves, not just our little female selves, but our whole big human selves."

Every other Saturday, a group of these new feminists met in Greenwich Village, New York, beginning in 1912. Calling their club "Heterodoxy," they discussed a wide range of topics related to women's emancipation. Club member **Charlotte Perkins Gilman** (see Volume 2), devised strategies for reducing the time women devoted to taking care of their families, such as living in apartment buildings equipped with communal kitchens and day-care centers. Other club members included birth control advocate Mary Ware Dennett, Grace Nail Johnson of the National Association for the Advancement of Colored People, and Henrietta Rodman, a high school vocational counselor. Rodman founded the Feminist Alliance to fight for the right of married women to hold jobs even after bearing children.

In the early 1900s, women became active in civic life on an unprecedented scale. In settlement houses, women's clubs, and labor unions, they organized not only for suffrage but also to clean up cities, improve working conditions, and reduce infant mortality. Among them were African-American feminists, who faced barriers to opportunity across the nation. Inspired by journalist **Ida B. Wells Barnett** (see Volume 2), the **National Association of Colored Women** (NACW) joined her crusade against the **lynching** (see Volume 2) of **African Americans**. At the same time, they defended African-American women against sexually demeaning treatment and stereotypes. Activists such as Nannie Burroughs wove feminism into their social reform work. Burroughs, a member of the NACW, fought for women's rights in the black **Baptist** church (see Volume 2) and devoted much of her energy to enabling African-American women to be economically self-sufficient.

Virtually all feminists supported women's right to vote, with various strategies. The National American Woman Suffrage Association (NAWSA), facing well-financed opposition, courted well-to-do women. Other activists took suffrage into the streets. Groups like the College Equal Suffrage Association canvassed door-to-door and held outdoor meetings. Harriot Stanton Blatch brought factory workers and professional women together in 1907 to found the Equality League of Self-Supporting Women, which staged the first in a series of large suffrage parades in 1910.

The militant British suffragettes provided a model for Alice Paul, who headed the NAWSA's Congressional Committee. Paul and her companions picketed the White House, staged a counter-inaugural parade in 1913, and captured headlines by going on hunger strikes when they were arrested and sent to prison in 1917. In contrast, NAWSA politely lobbied congressmen of both parties and demonstrated patriotism by supporting the war effort. After **World War I** ended, the combination of strategies culminated in victory for the **suffrage movement** with the ratification of the **Nineteenth Amendment**.

Historians puzzle over what happened in the 1920s. The early-twentieth-century wave of feminism seemed to wane just as women gained an important political tool in the vote. Some historians point to internal conflicts in the women's movement, particularly between supporters of the **Equal Rights Amendment** (ERA) and those who advocated **protective labor legislation** for women workers. In 1923 Alice Paul, as the leader of the **National Woman's Party** (NWP), began the campaign to pass the Equal Rights Amendment (see Documents). Many feminists opposed the ERA because they believed it would nullify laws that set maximum hours and minimum wages for many women workers. **Florence Kelley** hoped that labor laws for women would eventually extend to male workers as well. Until that happened, she believed women workers were particularly vulnerable to exploitation and needed protection, not the ERA. Other conflicts divided feminists along racial lines. During the suffrage movement, African-American feminists had experienced the racism of white suffrage organizations. After 1920, they sought white allies in the struggle against their disfranchisement. In a typically disappointing encounter, **Mary Church Terrell** (see Volume 2) asked for the NWP's support in defending African-American women's voting rights. Alice Paul refused.

External pressures as well as internal conflicts served to mute feminism after 1920. In the aftermath of World War I, the Red Scare threw suspicion on anyone organizing for justice and equality. The outspoken anarchist feminist **Emma Goldman** was deported in 1919, and many others feared that they would be jailed or fired for associating with radical women like her. The burgeoning consumer culture co-opted feminist themes, enticing women with the promise of a good life achieved without the necessity of political activism. A pro-business government found an ally in the Supreme Court, which struck down minimum wages for women in 1923. Feminists faced obstacles in the political arena. Armed with their new political importance as voters, women participated actively in party politics, but they did not vote as a bloc. In 1921 feminists in the federal **CHILDREN'S BUREAU** won passage of the Sheppard-Towner **MATERNITY AND INFANCY PROTECTION ACT,** but its funding was eliminated in 1929. The wartime **WOMEN'S BUREAU** became a permanent part of the Department of Labor in 1920, but its staff lacked the support of a powerful grass roots women's movement. Although women were joining a variety of interest groups, they no longer composed a visible feminist movement.

Many women participated as workers and mothers in the wave of labor and consumer organizing during the **GREAT DEPRESSION**. However, few claimed to be feminists in a climate that renewed the emphasis on feminine self-sacrifice. In the federal government, some tried to combat discrimination in **NEW DEAL** assistance programs. **MARY MCLEOD BETHUNE**, founder of the **NATIONAL COUNCIL OF NEGRO WOMEN,** served as director of the Negro Division of the National Youth Administration. First lady **ELEANOR ROOSEVELT** brought members of her women's reform network into the government. They included **FRANCES PERKINS** and **MARY DEWSON**, both of whom opposed the ERA. The **FAIR LABOR STANDARDS ACT** of 1938 extended labor legislation to men as well as women, but special rules for women workers continued. The ERA did not become a widely shared feminist goal until the 1960s.

The "Second Wave" of feminism seemed to burst on the scene in the 1960s. However, it had been percolating since **WORLD WAR II** when women workers found new opportunities in war production jobs. They developed a heightened consciousness of their own abilities and took pride in their new skills. After the war, most "Rosie the Riveters" lost their "men's jobs" and returned to work in the service and clerical sectors, but millions of working-class women joined unions to improve conditions in "women's jobs." They demanded paid maternity leave, minimum wages, and **CHILD CARE**. By 1955 they had won equal pay statutes in sixteen states plus Alaska, and in 1963 the federal **EQUAL PAY ACT** mandated equal pay for equal work.

In 1952 labor journalist **BETTY FRIEDAN** published *The UE Fights for Women Workers,* an account of one union's role in improving the lot of working-class women. Eleven years later, Friedan soared to fame with the publication of *The Feminine Mystique,* which described the discontent of many **HOMEMAKERS** (see Documents). Across the country, women who felt trapped in suburban domesticity recognized themselves in the book. Friedan recommended that such women pursue careers outside the home, but her book did not say how they could attain careers beyond the low-paid world of "women's work." Friedan saw an opportunity to broaden women's access to jobs when Congress passed the Civil Rights Act in 1964. **TITLE VII** of the act made sex discrimination in employment illegal and set up the **EQUAL EMPLOYMENT OPPORTUNITY COMMISSION** (EEOC) to hear workers' complaints. The EEOC failed to take sex discrimination seriously and even upheld the practice of sex-segregated job listings in newspapers. Friedan and a group of other frustrated feminists founded the **NATIONAL ORGANIZATION FOR WOMEN** (NOW) in 1966. NOW became the leading organization in the "women's rights" branch of Second Wave feminism.

While labor union activists and professional women tackled inequality in the workplace, other women were developing a feminist perspective through their work in a variety of social movements. The civil rights movement heightened women's expectations for equality. In the early 1960s, young women joined the Student Nonviolent Coordinating Committee (SNCC), where they worked in freedom schools and voter registration drives. In 1965 two white members of SNCC, Mary King and Casey Hayden, wrote "A Kind of Memo" that listed examples of sexist practices in the organization. Empowered by the civil rights movement's vision of equality, SNCC volunteers carried their analysis of sexism into other social movements as well.

In the late 1960s and early 1970s, feminism emerged in the antiwar and social justice movements of the New Left. The black nationalist movement provided for African-American women what the New Left provided for many white women—an experience of sexism that came up against expectations raised by the civil rights movement. Kathleen Cleaver observed, for example, that in the Black Panther Party if she brought up an idea it would be rejected, but if a man raised the same suggestion it would be implemented. In 1973, the **National Black Feminist Organization** (NBFO) was founded, in its statement of purpose criticizing the way women had been treated in the Black Power movement. In the Chicano nationalist movement, Francisca Flores responded to sexism by stating, "The issue of equality, freedom and self-determination of the Chicana—like the right of self-determination, equality, and liberation of the Mexican community—is not negotiable." **Chicana**, **Asian-American**, and African-American feminists confronted sexism in their communities as well as racism among white feminists. Women of color insisted that feminism address the ways sexism intersects with racism and economic oppression.

Women who became feminists in the social movements of the 1960s forged the **women's liberation** wing of the Second Wave. Liberation meant more than equal rights with men. Like the feminists of Heterodoxy at the beginning of the century, women's liberationists sought to transform society. The key political tool of Second Wave feminism was "consciousness raising," which took place when a small group of women gathered to discuss an aspect of their lives, such as relationships with partners, housework, body image, or discrimination at work. Consciousness raising went public in speak-outs about women's issues. In 1969 12 women in New York City spoke to an audience of 300 about their illegal abortions. Journalist **Gloria Steinem**, recognizing her own experience in the stories she heard, became a feminist. In 1972 she launched ***Ms.* magazine** as a consciousness-raising tool for women around the country.

Feminist institutions and organizations blossomed in the Second Wave. Shelters for battered women and **rape** crisis hot lines met urgent needs, while women's **music** festivals and coffee houses nurtured feminist culture. The National Welfare Rights Organization (NWRO) fought for rights and respect for poor mothers. The Boston Women's Health Collective published the first edition of ***Our Bodies, Ourselves*** in 1970 to spread the findings of feminist **health** groups (see Documents). After the Supreme Court overturned antiabortion laws in 1973, the **National Abortion Rights Action League** defended the reproductive right women had won in ***Roe v. Wade***. **Women's Studies** programs at colleges and universities transformed academic disciplines.

Historians are only beginning to assess feminism at the end of the twentieth century. Some see the decline of feminism in the 1920s being repeated. Bitter divisions over whether to give women the right to sue producers of **pornograhy** generated lasting animosities among feminists. Political gains seemed to be dissipating. After passing Congress in 1972, the ERA fell short of ratification in the states. In 1989 the Supreme Court hemmed in abortion rights. The commercial media and advertisers were again selling a form of "lifestyle" feminism to women. More optimistic historians point to the lasting effects of both the first and second waves of feminism. Feminism ushered in many changes, from greater employment and educational opportunities to women's sports and gender-neutral language. The fruits of suffrage could be seen in the gender gap that emerged in 1980 and in the increasing numbers of women who attained political office. In 1993 Rebecca Walker and a group of young feminists declared themselves the "Third Wave" and dedicated themselves to "Continuing the Women's Movement."

Anna R. Igra

See also: Feminism, Radical; "A Woman's Body," p. 16; "The Civil Rights Movement," p. 21.

FURTHER READING

Anzaldua, Gloria, and Cherie Moraga, eds. *This Bridge Called My Back: Writings by Radical Women of Color.* Watertown, MA: Persephone Press, 1981.

Cott, Nancy F. *The Grounding of Modern Feminism.* New Haven: Yale University Press, 1987.

Crow, Barbara A., ed. *Radical Feminism: A Documentary Reader.* New York: New York University Press, 2000.

Garcia, Alma M. *Chicana Feminist Thought: The Basic Historical Writings.* New York: Routledge, 1997.

Heywood, Leslie, and Jennifer Drake, eds. *Third Wave Agenda: Being Feminist, Doing Feminism.* Minneapolis: University of Minnesota, 1997.

Rosen, Ruth. *The World Split Open: How the Modern Women's Movement Changed America.* New York: Viking, 2000.

Rupp, Leila J., and Vera Taylor. *Survival in the Doldrums: The American Women's Rights Movement, 1945–1960s.* New York: Oxford University Press, 1987.

Part 2

Articles

A

ABBOTT, EDITH (1876–1957)

A pioneer in American **SOCIAL WORK**, education, and reform. Edith Abbott was born in Grand Island, Nebraska, to parents who were passionate about social and political issues. Her father was the first lieutenant governor of Nebraska and her mother a pacifist who championed woman suffrage and abolishing slavery in the United States. Both Edith and her younger sister, **GRACE ABBOTT**, became involved in the social problems of the day.

At a time when few women attended college, Edith Abbott graduated from the University of Nebraska in 1901 and went on to earn a doctoral degree in economics from the University of Chicago in 1905. Under a Carnegie fellowship, Abbott went to England, where she continued her studies at University College, London, and the London School of Economics and Political Science. After teaching for a year at Wellesley College in Massachusetts, Abbott was offered a position as assistant director of the research department at the Chicago School of Civics and Philanthropy, a new education venture. It was a somewhat risky career move, but Abbott relished the challenge and moved to Chicago, where she lived at **HULL HOUSE** (see Volume 2), one of the first social settlements in North America, with her sister and a host of remarkable women of the time, among them Hull House founder **JANE ADDAMS** (see Volume 2).

During the early 1900s, social workers received their education and training in the field, basically as apprentices to caseworkers in social agencies. Abbott, on the other hand, firmly believed that social work should be taught at the university and graduate-school level, and was instrumental in transferring the School of Civics and Philanthropy to the University of Chicago, where it was renamed the School of Social Service Administration. It was the first university-based graduate school of social work, and Abbott served as its dean from 1924 until 1942. She also helped establish the Cook County Bureau of Public Welfare, assisted in drafting the Social Security Act of 1935, served as president of the National Conference of Social Work, and was a founder and editor of *Social Service Review,* which examines and evaluates social welfare policy and practice.

ABBOTT, GRACE (1878–1939)

Director of the U.S. Children's Bureau under four presidents. Abbott played an instrumental role in getting **AID TO DEPENDENT CHILDREN** included in the Social Security Act of 1935.

Born in 1878 in Grand Island, Nebraska, Abbott and her sister, **EDITH ABBOTT**, grew up listening to their father argue law cases and learning from their mother about the rights of all Americans. Grace graduated from Grand Island College, and taught high school. She began intermittent summer graduate classes at the University of Chicago in 1904, moved to Chicago in 1907, and completed her M.A. degree in political science in 1909. In the middle of her studies, she moved into the city's most famous social settlement, **HULL HOUSE** (see Volume 2) to participate in the community of intellectuals and reformers.

Her career in social work built on Hull House relationships throughout her life. Soon after arriving at the settlement house, Abbott was recruited to direct the Immigrants' Protective League, founded in 1908 to provide legal and social services to newcomers. She met Julia Lathrop at Hull House who, a few years later, became the first director of the U.S. **CHILDREN'S BUREAU.** Lathrop invited Abbott to join her in Washington, D.C., to head up the Children's Bureau child labor division in 1917. Her primary responsibility was to oversee the first federal child labor law. The law passed in 1916 but was declared unconstitutional in 1918, and Abbott had to dismantle the apparatus she had set up. After completing a few more duties for the bureau, Abbott returned to Chicago in 1919. Two years later, she returned to the Children's Bureau as director and served until 1934. During her tenure, the Children's Bureau worked on stricter regulation of child labor, supported the development of **MOTHERS' PENSIONS** laws in the states, and administered the first **MATERNITY AND INFANCY PROTECTION ACT** passed by Congress in 1921.

After Abbott retired from the Children's Bureau in 1934, she returned to Chicago to teach social welfare at the School of Social Service Administration at the University of Chicago and become managing editor of the *Social Service Review*. Her sister and Sophonisba Breckinridge founded the school and the journal. Within a short time, Abbott was involved again in welfare policy, this time working to draft a provision for aid to dependent children in the Social Security Act. She died in Chicago in 1939, but her ideas on social welfare continued to influence generations of students through her books. They included *The Child and the State*, a compendium of American legal and policy directives toward children; and *From Relief to Social Security*, a history documenting welfare policies through the Depression.

FURTHER READING

Costin, Lela B. *Two Sisters for Social Justice: A Biography of Grace and Edith Abbott*. Urbana: University of Illinois Press, 1983.
James, Edward T., ed. *Notable American Women: A Biographical Dictionary*. Vol 1. Cambridge, MA: Harvard University Press, 1971.

ABORTION

The termination of a pregnancy. Ancient medical texts describe both oral and surgical methods to induce abortion. While the instruments have changed, the methods remain largely the same.

Beginning in the 1820s, a growing number of states began to outlaw the procedure. Still, abortions remained widely available and relatively safe through the early 1900s. Then, in the 1930s, as abortion moved from women's homes and doctors' offices into hospitals, it came under increasing scrutiny from obstetricians and law enforcement. By 1940, anti-abortion laws were being enforced and physicians providing abortion prosecuted. As abortion was pushed underground, it became increasingly dangerous. By 1965, it had become a crime in every state, and it was during this period that health risks from abortion became widespread. In response to the growing dangers to women's health that resulted from "back alley" abortions, an organized movement to decriminalize the procedure took hold, led by physicians and women's rights advocates.

In 1973, the U.S. Supreme Court in ***Roe v. Wade*** established a limited right to abortion based on a constitutional right to privacy, with the result that most state laws banning abortion were thereafter considered unconstitutional. Since then, efforts have been made to reverse *Roe v. Wade*. Led largely by evangelical Christians and the Roman Catholic Church, the right-to-life movement has been somewhat successful in limiting abortion rights, in part by returning some authority to states and by intimidating doctors.

ABZUG, BELLA SAVITSKY

(1920–1998)

A lawyer, feminist, and outspoken member of the United States House of Representatives from 1970 to 1974. Born Bella Savitsky on July 24, 1920, she graduated in 1942 with a bachelor of arts degree from Hunter College in New York.

Bella Abzug, lawyer and feminist, was an avid supporter of the ERA.

Two years later, she married Maurice Abzug, a stockbroker. The couple would have two daughters. In 1945, she earned her law degree from Columbia University.

Abzug practiced labor law in New York City for 23 years. She then won a seat in the House of Representatives in 1970, where she served two terms. During her tenure in the House, she chaired the Committee on Public Works and Transportation and the Subcommittee on Government Information and Individual Rights. She also served as assistant Democratic Whip, a key position within the party leadership. Throughout her career, Abzug was active in the women's rights movement, an avid supporter of the **Equal Rights Amendment** (ERA), and an outspoken member of the **National Organization for Women** (NOW).

Soon after her election to the House, she drew public attention with her wide-brimmed hats and flamboyant style. Abzug challenged the maledominated Congress and admonished her colleagues as elite white males who were out of touch with mainstream America. She vocally advocated the immediate withdrawal of American troops from **Vietnam** as the war raged on. She was equally outspoken on such issues as women's and minority rights and federal aid to cities. Despite her popular appeal, some of her political allies criticized her style as too confrontational, noting that she was unwilling to compromise to pass key legislation.

Among Abzug's successes in Congress were the passage of the "Government in the Sunshine Act," which increased the public's access to government records. She cofounded the **National Women's Political Caucus** in 1971 and authored several bills designed to improve the status of women and prevent sex discrimination.

Abzug gave up her seat in Congress to run unsuccessfully for the United States Senate. She later ran unsuccessfully for mayor of New York City and then again for the House. In 1978 President Jimmy Carter appointed Abzug cochair of the National Advisory Committee for Women, but dismissed her a year later after the committee criticized the president for cutting funds for women's programs.

After Abzug returned to private practice, she remained in the public spotlight as a news commentator, lecturer, and author. Abzug followed her successful 1972 book *Bella! Ms. Abzug Goes to Washington* with *The Gender Gap: Bella Abzug's Guide to Political Power for American Women* in 1984.

Abzug served on a number of international bodies and was an organizer of the 1991 Women's Congress for a Healthy Planet. In 1995 she played a key role at the UN's Fourth World Conference on Women.

Abzug's health declined in the late 1990s. She died on March 31, 1998, from complications after heart surgery.

ACTORS

Women have starred on the American stage and screen throughout the twentieth and twenty-first centuries and have taken increasing control of the financial and production aspects of the business.

Stage actor Maude Adams (1872–1953) was most famous for her portrayal of Peter Pan in the play written expressly for her by James Barrie in 1905. Academy Award–winner Helen Hayes (1900–1993), often called the "first lady of the American theater," is best known for portraying women possessed of an inner core of steel. In 1964 Hayes founded the Helen Hayes Repertory Company to promote the reading of Shakespeare's plays in American universities.

Bette Davis's career as an actress spanned nearly six decades and included two Academy Awards for best actress.

Women's roles in silent film represented stereotypes: divas and innocents, vamps and flappers. With a complexion described as "a rose blushing through old ivory," Anna May Wong (1905–1961) was featured alongside a number of Hollywood's leading men during the era of silent film. Within the pantheon of the stars of silent films that included Theda Bara (1890–1955), **Clara Bow** (1905–1965), Lillian Gish (1893–1993), and Gloria Swanson (1899–1983), Mary Pickford (1893–1979) reigned as "America's Sweetheart" until her retirement in 1933. She was also a cofounder of United Artists and winner of an Academy Award for her role in the 1929 film *Coquette*.

The 1940s was a golden age in Hollywood. Legends such as the comic actress Carole Lombard (1908–1942), the red-haired beauty Rita Hayworth (1918–1987), and the dynamic Barbara Stanwyck (1907–1990) set the standards of glamour and talent to which later generations of women would match their own achievements. It was reputed that actress and dancer **Betty Grable** (1916–1973) insured her famous legs for a million dollars. Whether or not this was so, her shapely limbs made her the favorite pinup girl of men serving in the United States armed forces during **World War II**. Bette Davis (1908–1989) was known as much for her short temper and difficult behavior as she was for the complex characters she portrayed. African-American Dorothy Dandridge (1923–1965) appeared in a number of "race films," or pictures made for the African-American audience. She became a star in the title role of *Carmen Jones* but her talents were not encouraged and valued in the 1950s and 1960s.

Marilyn Monroe (1926–1962) remains an enigmatic figure and an icon of female beauty and sexuality to this day. A star of romantic comedies in the 1950s, her acting gifts allowed her to transcend otherwise two-dimensional roles. **Katharine Hepburn** (b. 1907) won a record four Academy Awards for best actress and received 13 nominations in all, the first in 1933 and the last in 1981. Of similar name, but no relationship, was the Belgian-born Audrey Hepburn (1929–1993), whose petite frame and large, expressive eyes made her one of the most appealing presences in films of the second half of the twentieth century.

Throughout the twentieth century, leading roles often called for young, beautiful women. From the 1970s on, however, actors such as Jessica Tandy (1909–1994), Joanne Woodward (b. 1930), Anne Bancroft (b. 1931), Ellen Burstyn (b. 1932), Cicely Tyson (b. 1933), Shirley MacLaine (b. 1934), Jane Fonda (b. 1937), Faye Dunaway (b. 1941), Sally Field (b.1946), Diane Keaton (b. 1946), Susan Sarandon (b. 1946), Meryl Streep (b. 1949), Michelle Pfeiffer (b. 1958), Julia Roberts (b. 1967), and Gwyneth Paltrow

TRAILBLAZERS

Bette Davis once described herself as having "eyes like a bullfrog, a neck like an ostrich, and limp hair." Nonetheless, her intense personality and unforgettable stare made her a legend of American film. She won Oscars for her portrayal of an actress fallen on hard times in *Dangerous* (1935) and for her work in *Jezebel* (1938).

Born Ruth Elizabeth Davis on April 5, 1908, in Lowell, Massachusetts, she renamed herself "Bette" after the heroine of Balzac's novel, *Cousin Bette*. Davis studied acting in New York City, where her dance teacher was the choreographer **Martha Graham**. After working in live theater and failing her first screen test for the Metro-Goldwyn-Mayer studio (MGM), she was hired by Universal Pictures.

Davis was most popular for the menacing or sharp-tongued characters she played in films like *The Letter* (1940), *The Little Foxes* (1941), and the classic *All About Eve* (1950). In later years she often played eccentric older women. In *What Ever Happened to Baby Jane?* (1962), Davis, as the title character, terrorized her sister, played by fellow veteran actor Joan Crawford (1904–1977).

Davis began appearing on television in the 1950s, and from the 1970s made a number of made-for-television films. Her last appearance came in the 1987 theatrical release *The Whales of August*, in which she was paired with another film legend, Lillian Gish (1893–1993).

Bette Davis succumbed to cancer in Neuilly-sur-Seine, France, on October 6, 1989, just after she was honored at a film festival in Spain.

(b. 1972) turned in award-winning performances as aging, eccentric, or unglamorous characters.

Television has provided a range of opportunities for actors, including work in series programs as well as films produced for the small screen. Mary Tyler Moore (b. 1936) became known to television audiences in the 1960s and went on to headline her own series, *The Mary Tyler Moore Show*. Candice Bergen (b. 1946) also made her mark in both fields.

In 1987, Marlee Matlin (b. 1966) became the first deaf actor to win an Academy Award (for *Children of a Lesser God*) and continues to be a regular presence in films and television.

ADAMS, EVA B. (1908–1991)

Director of the U.S. Mint (1961–1969). A native of Nevada, Eva Adams's career as a public servant took one of the few paths open to women of her time. She worked as an administrative assistant for three senators from the state of Nevada.

Adams was born in Wonder, Nevada, in 1908 where her father worked for mining and banking magnate George Wingfield. She loved school and took advantage of opportunities to expand her knowledge. She graduated from high school at the age of 14, earned her bachelor's degree in 1928 from the University of Nevada, and by the age of 19, moved to southern Nevada to teach at Las Vegas High School. Several years later, she continued her education at Columbia University in New York City and earned a master's degree in English in 1936. That same year, she returned to Reno to teach in the English Department at the University of Nevada.

Her career took a different turn in 1940 when she accepted an invitation from Senator Patrick McCarran (D-NV) to join his staff in Washington, D.C. She worked as McCarran's assistant until his death in 1954. McCarran's powerful role in the Senate and his Cold War positions on national security and foreign affairs placed Adams at the center of national politics. That experience served her well after McCarran's death when she became administrative assistant to his successors, Nevada Senators Ernest Brown (appointed in 1954) and Alan Bible (elected in 1954). While working in Washington, D.C., she earned a law degree from American University's Washington College of Law (1950) and a masters degree in law from George Washington University (1952). Adams was admitted to the bars of Nevada and the District of Columbia.

In 1961, President John F. Kennedy appointed her Director of the U.S. Mint. President Lyndon B. Johnson reappointed her in 1964. She was the first woman to receive this position which she held until 1969, when she retired and returned to Reno. She continued to serve as a consultant for public service organizations and held positions on federal commissions. One notable example of that service was the Health, Education, and Welfare Secretary's Advisory Committee on the Rights and Responsibilities of Women in 1975. Adams died in Reno in 1991.

ADKINS v. CHILDREN'S HOSPITAL

A 1923 U.S. Supreme Court case. The case was important in the history of efforts to pass laws guaranteeing minimum wages to workers.

In the early years of the twentieth century, many state legislatures passed laws to improve conditions for workers. Some of these laws regulated the number of hours employees could be required to work; others established a minimum wage. Progressives saw these statutes as important victories in the fight for social reform, but many business owners opposed them. In their view, these laws interfered with private property rights and with the right of workers to contract freely to provide their labor to employers.

Adkins v. Children's Hospital arose from the federal Minimum Wage Act of 1918, which established a minimum wage board in the District of Columbia to set minimum wages for women and minors and ensure that employers paid these wages. The Children's Hospital in the District of Columbia employed several women at wages lower than the standard, and when the minimum wage board took action against the hospital, the women lost their jobs. The Children's Hospital brought suit to prevent Adkins and other board members from enforcing the wage orders. The women said they were satisfied with their pay and working conditions, so the hospital sued on their behalf to stop enforcement of the law and allow the women to take whatever jobs they wanted. At issue was whether the women had been denied due process under the Fifth Amendment of the U.S. Constitution, which guarantees that "due process of law" has to be followed before someone can be denied "life, liberty, or property."

In its five-to-three decision, the Supreme Court ruled against the minimum wage board, saying that "the right to contract about one's affairs is part of the liberty of the individual protected by the Fifth Amendment." The Court went on to say that "the statute in question is simply a price-fixing law forbidding two parties to contract in respect to the price for which one shall render service to the other." The Court concluded, "To uphold individual freedom is not to strike down the common good, but to further it by the prevention of arbitrary restraint upon the liberty of its members."

The effect of *Adkins v. Children's Hospital*, combined with the Great Depression of the 1930s, was to put an end to efforts to establish minimum wages in the United States. However, popular pressure continued to build for minimum wage laws, and in 1937 the Court overturned its ruling in *Adkins* by upholding a minimum wage law for women in *West Coast Hotel v. Parrish*. By 1939 twenty-five states had enacted minimum wage laws, and in 1941 the Court upheld federal minimum wage standards for both men and women.

TRAILBLAZERS

Among the many contributions of Margaret Mead (1901–1978) to the field of anthropology, those for which she is best known stem from her early work in American Samoa and New Guinea. After studying adolescent girls in Samoa and young children in New Guinea, Mead concluded that while adolescence was a biological process, there were significant differences in how this process was handled by different cultures. Among her great discoveries is the idea that "human nature is malleable," that people behave as they do largely because they were trained to do so, not because it is part of "human nature" to do so. Mead extended her insights into gender roles and demonstrated that many of the ideas prevalent in Western society about gender and gender roles were cultural rather than biological in origin. In particular, her work among three different cultures in New Guinea, the Arapesh, the Mundugumor, and the Tchambuli, showed women in gender roles quite different from those they typically adopted in Western culture. Among the Tchambuli, for example, women were dominant and men submissive.

Mead received a degree in psychology from Barnard College, then did a Ph.D. in anthropology at Columbia, studying under Franz Boas and RUTH BENEDICT. In 1925 she traveled to American Samoa to study adolescent girls. The results of her research were published as *Coming of Age in Samoa* (1928), a work that was an immediate best-seller, partly because of its open and frank treatment of adolescent sexuality. Her second work, *Growing Up in New Guinea* (1931), pointed out that Western cultures had much to learn from so-called "primitive" cultures about how children were reared and educated.

Mead taught at a number of colleges and universities, but her primary affiliation was with the American Museum of Natural History in New York. She wrote more than 20 books and coauthored another 20. She received numerous honors during her life and was elected president of many professional organizations, including the American Anthropological Association and the American Association for the Advancement of Science. Mead died of cancer in 1975.

ADOLESCENCE

It is only in the twentieth century that adolescence has been seen as a separate and distinct period of development. In earlier centuries, young people married and went to work at younger ages, and most people slipped from childhood to adulthood fairly easily; girls married in their teens, and boys embarked on their careers. In the early decades of the twentieth century, psychologist G. Stanley Hall published *Adolescence,* a work that revolutionized the perception of teenagers and how they should be treated. One of his most important insights was that adolescence should be prolonged. He also saw adolescence as a period of "storm and stress" as young people struggled with their emerging sexuality. In the 1920s anthropologist Margaret Mead countered many of Hall's insights, pointing out that emerging sexuality among Samoan adolescents was not fraught with difficulty and demonstrating that gender assumptions were cultural rather than biological in origin.

In keeping with Hall's ideas about prolonging adolescence, Progressive-era reformers campaigned against **CHILD LABOR** and for compulsory **EDUCATION** laws. Reformers also worked to raise the age at which people could marry. Through most of the 1920s Mary Richmond worked to end what she called "child marriage." In many states at the time, girls could legally marry at the age of 12.

The twentieth-century view of adolescence has been particularly hard on girls. As Joan Jacobs Brumberg notes in her ground-breaking work, *The Body Project,* "The process of sexual maturation is more difficult for girls today than it was a century ago because of a set of historical changes that have resulted in a peculiar mismatch between girls' biology and today's culture." Girls tend to reach sexual maturity much younger than they did a century ago. But the process of psychological maturation has not accelerated and society simply does not offer the same protection to girls as they received in the nineteenth century when young women were carefully watched and chaperoned.

Moreover, television and print advertising places tremendous pressure on adolescent girls to reach a standard of physical attractiveness that was unheard of a hundred years ago. In contrast to modern teenage girls' obsession with appearance, Brumberg notes that most nineteenth-century homes did not even have mirrors. Twentieth-century adolescent girls receive mixed messages constantly. On the one hand, they are forbidden by law to marry, while on the other hand they are constantly reminded of their sexuality and taught to use their sexuality to attract men. Although many girls develop into healthy, well-adjusted adults, some react to all the pressure by a series of rebellious acts; others develop eating disorders; others emerge from adolescence with little self-confidence or self-esteem.

FURTHER READING

Brumberg, Joan Jacobs. *The Body Project: An Intimate History of American Girls.* New York: Vintage, 1998.

Pipher, Mary. *Reviving Ophelia: Saving the Selves of Adolescent Girls.* New York: Ballantine, 1995.

AFRICAN AMERICANS

At the outset of the twentieth century, African Americans were overwhelmingly poor, rural, and Southern. A century later the vast majority lived in cities across the nation, and about half were relatively well educated and prosperous. African-American women were at the heart of this transformation.

Many women participated in the migration of blacks out of the rural South to Southern and then Northern cities, a migration that began late in the nineteenth century. Married or not, urban African-American women often earned money as domestic servants, laundresses, peddlers, or seamstresses.

WORLD WAR I stimulated northward migration. African-American women soon dominated domestic service in Northern cities, although most insisted on living in their own homes, where they could care for their children, rather than with their employers. **WORLD WAR II** offered opportunities for African-American women in defense plants at wages that were many times higher than they had earned during the Depression. Growing numbers of female African-American entrepreneurs appeared beginning in the 1920s, fueling the emergence of a substantial black middle class. Thousands of seamstresses and hairdressers set up shops, often in their homes. Growing numbers of college-educated African-American women worked as teachers and nurses.

Whether they earned money or not, African-American women were strong wives, mothers, and community members. They raised their children to be hardworking and autonomous and took leading roles in community groups, from churches to antilynching campaigns. **MARY MCLEOD BETHUNE** and members of the **NATIONAL ASSOCIATION OF COLORED WOMEN** were among the leaders of such movements.

The role of African-American women grew still larger during the second half of the twentieth century. In refusing to give up her seat on a bus to a white person, **ROSA PARKS** helped to ignite the civil rights movement in 1955, and, though male leaders enjoyed the most publicity, women organizers such as **ELLA BAKER**, **FANNIE LOU HAMER**, and JoAnn Robinson played critical roles.

African-American women were also assuming greater familial and economic roles. They headed just 18 percent of black families in 1950, but that number had increased to 40 percent by 1980. The percentage was much higher among those living in poverty, where single mothers struggled, with the help of family and neighbors, to keep their children fed and safe. Middle-class African-American women were also becoming more powerful. By the later years of the century they outnumbered their male counterparts in colleges and many professions.

FURTHER READING

Giddings, Paula. *When and Where I Enter: The Impact of Black Women on Race and Sex in America*. New York: Morrow, 1984.

Jones, Jacqueline. *Labor of Love, Labor of Sorrow: Black Women, Work, and the Family from Slavery to the Present.* New York: Basic Books, 1985.

AID TO DEPENDENT CHILDREN

The first federal program to support mothers with young children who were desperately poor and without adult male support. The policy became a part (Title IV) of the **SOCIAL SECURITY ACT** (1935), a comprehensive program designed during the 1930s to provide a safety net against economic disaster for Americans. The idea behind Aid to Dependent Children (ADC) was to keep poor families together, to provide a subsidy for the poor mother, and to prevent children from leaving school to enter the workforce. It built on earlier state-level experiments called mothers' aid or **MOTHERS' PENSIONS**. By the 1960s, ADC became the largest poverty program paid for by federal and state tax revenues. In 1996, President Bill Clinton ended the safety net program and replaced it with Temporary Assistance for Needy Families (TANF).

The widespread economic disruption of the Great Depression during the 1930s created the context for aid to dependent children. Americans elected Franklin D. Roosevelt as president in 1932 on his promise to provide economic security for all Americans. The plan that passed Congress, the 1935 Social Security

WOMEN'S FIRSTS

The first African-American woman elected to the U.S. House of Representatives was early childhood expert Shirley Chisholm (b. 1926), who took her seat in 1969 and served for 15 years. In 1972 she achieved national recognition by becoming the first African-American woman to run for president.

Born Shirley St. Hill to West Indian immigrant laborers, Chisholm had the opportunity at 14 to meet **ELEANOR ROOSEVELT**. In an interview in later life she named Roosevelt as one of three great influences in her life (the others were her grandmother and **HARRIET TUBMAN**—see Volume 2) and recalled Roosevelt's words to her: "You are black and you are a young woman, but don't you let anybody stand in your way. Because you've got it!"

In Congress she made a name as a critic of the war in Vietnam and an advocate of the interests of the urban poor. She retired from politics in 1982, seeking a more private life. She once remarked: "Of my two 'handicaps' being female put more obstacles in my path than being black."

Her two books are *Unbought and Unbossed* (1970), a memoir, and *The Good Fight* (1973), an account of her presidential bid.

Shirley Chisholm

Act, took social responsibility for the elderly, the very young, the unemployed, the sick, and the disabled and subsidized their income through a plan of social insurance. Some features of the act were new, but the provisions for dependent children had been used in many states for two decades.

The U.S. **CHILDREN'S BUREAU**, created in 1912 to research all aspects of children's lives, wrote the provision and lobbied for its inclusion in the Social Security Act. The bureau knew the state-level mothers' pension laws better than anyone, and they believed that any social insurance plan must provide a measure for families without fathers. In part, this reflected contemporary moral values, but it also recognized economic realities. At the time, most women worked in a small sector of jobs that paid meager wages. Consequently, employment programs, while successful for male heads of families, would leave hundreds of thousands of mother-only families in poverty. In addition, some supporters argued, a mother's first job was in the home raising her children. That work proved of far greater value to society than the wages she could earn or the costs of ADC.

The "proper" role for mothers as care-givers or wage-earners remained at the heart of debates over ADC, with the balance shifting increasingly toward self-support. States, seeking to reduce welfare expenses, enforced work rules mandating wage work by mothers. In 1962, 33 states had work rules and the federal government began focusing on jobs and training. The trend coincided with an increase in the number of working mothers throughout the United States as well as an increase in unmarried mothers and African-American women who received ADC. The program, already unpopular in many states, began to symbolize all that was wrong with federal programs.

The issue of welfare reform became a campaign theme during the 1992 presidential campaign. Clinton, having won that election, carried out his campaign promise to "end welfare as we know it" in 1996, when he signed legislation ending AFDC. A program with far greater limits called Temporary Assistance for Needy Families replaced it.

ALBRIGHT, MADELEINE K.

(b. 1937)

U.S. government official and diplomat; the first woman to serve as secretary of state. Broadly experienced in international diplomacy and U.S. foreign policy, respected by her peers as a consummate professional, and with a reputation for directness, Madeleine Albright was a natural choice for President Bill Clinton to name as secretary of state at the start of his second term in 1997.

The start of her tenure as a high-profile cabinet official was dominated by a personal revelation. Soon after taking office, Albright—the daughter of a Czech diplomat who had taken the family to America after the Communist takeover in 1948—learned that her parents, who raised her as a Roman Catholic, had been born Jewish; a number of her relatives had been killed in the Holocaust.

Born Madeleine Korbel in Prague, Czechoslovakia, she came to the United States at age 11 with a grant of political asylum. After earning her B.A. from Wellesley and M.A. and Ph.D. from Columbia, she worked on national security affairs in the departments of defense, state, and treasury during the early 1960s. She later held positions in the Export-Import Bank, the National Security Council under President Jimmy Carter, and the faculty at Georgetown University's School of Foreign Service. During Clinton's first term (1993-97), Albright served as chief U.S. representative to the United Nations.

As secretary of state, she took an active role in enforcing trade sanctions on Iraq after the Persian Gulf War, seeking resolutions to the crisis in Kosovo and the Yugoslav War, and adding new members to NATO. Albright is the author of several books and numerous articles. She has three daughters from her marriage to journalist Joseph Albright, which ended in divorced.

AMERICAN ASSOCIATION OF UNIVERSITY WOMEN

The oldest national organization dedicated to expanding opportunities for women's **EDUCATION**.

The Association of Collegiate Alumnae, formed in 1882, merged with regional organizations to form the American Association of University Women (AAUW) in 1921. At that time, only a small percentage of women attended colleges and universities, and many schools legally denied women admission. Within a few years, the AAUW established not only a scholarship program but also a research branch. In 1938, the organization published its first study of sex discrimination on campuses; similar studies would be repeated over the years. The organization has been a consistent advocate of both sex equity and **CIVIL RIGHTS**. It supported the passage of the Civil Rights Act, **TITLE IX** (prohibiting sex discrimination in athletics), and the Family and Medical Leave Act.

Today, the AAUW has 150,000 members with more than 1,500 branches across the United States. It is also a member of the International Federation of University Women making the network global.

AMERICAN CIVIL LIBERTIES UNION

National nonprofit organization dedicated to preserving and protecting constitutional rights through litigation and legal defense, legislative lobbying, and public education. The American Civil Liberties Union (ACLU) was founded in 1920 by a group of civil libertarians that included **JANE ADDAMS** (see Volume 2), **HELEN KELLER**, Norman Thomas, Felix Frankfurter, and Roger Baldwin, who served as director until 1950. Its predecessor organization, the National Civil Liberties Bureau, was founded in 1917 to protect the right to free speech of citizens who spoke out against U.S. participation in **WORLD WAR I**. Other women instrumental in the formation of the organization included the labor organizer and Communist party leader Elizabeth Gurley Flynn and the social reformer Crystal Eastman.

Headquartered in New York and with chapters in every state, the ACLU has been active since its formation in defending free speech, civil rights, due process of law, separation of church and state, the right to privacy, and other constitutional freedoms; it has opposed segregation, capital punishment, and government censorship. ACLU leaders and attorneys have supported a number of controversial groups and causes, including the First Amendment rights of the American Nazi Party in the late 1970s. Conservative groups and politicians have criticized the organization for what they perceive to be liberal excesses.

The ACLU has been active in opposing gender discrimination and defending abortion rights. In 1971, **RUTH BADER GINSBURG**, then a law professor at Rutgers University and later appointed to the U.S. Supreme Court, founded the ACLU Women's Rights Project to promote legal reform for women and their political and economic rights. In 1992, the ACLU's abortion rights team broke away to form the Center for Reproductive Law and Policy (for organizational efficiency rather than policy differences). The ACLU was also active during the 1990s in establishing standards and definitions of **SEXUAL HARASSMENT** and in making it easier for women to file complaints.

AMERICAN FEDERATION OF LABOR AND CONGRESS OF INDUSTRIAL ORGANIZATIONS

Federation of labor **UNIONS** in the United States, Canada, Mexico, and Panama. Headquartered in Washington, D.C., the organization was formed in 1955 by a merger of the American Federation of Labor (AFL) and the Congress of Industrial Organizations (CIO). As of 2001, the AFL-CIO included 64 unions, representing 13 million working women and men. The unions are self-governing but cooperate within the federation; they are represented at the biennial AFL-CIO convention, the federation's supreme governing body. The chief functions of the AFL-CIO are to lobby government and employers on behalf of organized labor; give legal assistance; provide research and information services; and resolve disputes between members.

The AFL was organized in 1886 as a decentralized federation that emphasized the organization of skilled workers into craft unions (as opposed to industrial unions made up of workers with diverse skills). In 1935 it set up the Committee for Industrial Organization to organize workers in mass-production industries. That body established its own federation in 1938 and changed its name to the Congress of Industrial Organization. Its dramatic rise in membership and prestige, as well as a mutual desire to confront anti-labor policies in the federal government, finally led to the merger.

Many unions with traditionally heavy female membership are, or have been, affiliated with the AFL-CIO. Among these are the Amalgamated Clothing and Textile Workers Union, the **AMERICAN FEDERATION OF TEACHERS**, and the International Ladies Garment Workers Union. The Working Women's Department of the AFL-CIO works with civil rights, community, and religious organizations to promote equal pay, flexible hours, child-care benefits, and other issues important to female members. In 1995, **Linda Chavez-Thompson** became the highest-ranking woman in the labor movement when she was elected to the new position of AFL-CIO executive vice-president.

AMERICAN FEDERATION OF TEACHERS

Labor organization for teachers, school counselors, custodians, and school bus drivers. Founded in 1912 and formally joined with the American Federation of Labor in 1915, the American Federation of Teachers (AFT) was based on the educational philosophy of John Dewey, who believed that the worker and employer should work together to serve each other's interests. **Margaret Haley**, who had established the Chicago Teacher's Federation in 1897—the first teacher's union to join forces with organized labor—helped found the AFT. However, she left the organization in 1916 because of philosophical differences with the union president, Charles Stillman.

At the turn of the twentieth century, teachers hoped that by forming a union they were more likely to be accepted as professionals and have a larger voice in educational policy and curriculum. They might have joined the **National Education Association** (NEA), which was founded in 1857, but many believed that the NEA did not give them enough professional support. Because NEA membership was comprised mainly of school administrators and college professors, it was they whom the NEA primarily served.

Female teachers felt a particular need to organize. Between 1900 and 1920, 80 percent of the nation's teachers were female. However, they were only paid half as much as their male counterparts. With no labor support, teachers could be fired for little or no reason. In addition, a woman who married usually lost her job. During **World War II**, teacher shortages forced school administrations to allow married women to teach.

With help from unions, teaching has allowed women access to the professional world and the political arena. Classroom teachers were among the first groups to advocate equal pay for men and women. Teacher unions have influenced educational bureaucracies, have given teachers a voice in structuring school curriculums, and have professionalized education. Today the AFT, an AFL-CIO affiliate, works to support educators across the United States: It fights for higher salaries, pensions, and tenure for educators; it negotiates contracts; and it influences state and local educational policies.

ANDERSON, LAURIE (b. 1947)

Multimedia performance artist, writer, and musician. Born June 5, 1947, in Chicago, Anderson moved to New York to study art at Barnard College in 1968 and received an M.F.A. in sculpture from Columbia in 1972.

One of her first public performances was in 1968 on a New York City street, where she played a duet with a tape recorder inside her violin, while wearing ice skates frozen in two blocks of ice. The performance ended when the ice melted. Anderson has been at the forefront of avant-garde art ever since, frequently performing with musical instruments of her own creation, including a harmonizer that filters her natural voice into a low male-sounding voice, which she dubs "the voice of authority" and uses whenever assuming the persona of a lecturer. Long fascinated with technology, Anderson describes herself as a "techno ice-queen observer."

Anderson's art, in any of its multiple forms—sculpture, spoken word, writing, music—examines the points of view afforded Anderson as an urbanite, a woman, a feminist, and an artist. She uses multidisciplinary presentation to increase the impact of her work, integrating images through photographs, film, or fine art with text, music, or performance.

In 1984, Anderson presented her debut single, "O Superman," a spoken-word piece, to mainstream airwaves. It reached number one in Britain. She tours extensively with her multimedia shows and concerts, which have included *United States, Empty Places,* and *Nerve Bible*, the last of which was published in book form.

ANDERSON, MARY (1872–1964)

Labor organizer, first **Women's Bureau** chief. Born in Sweden in 1872, Mary Anderson emigrated with her sister to the United States in

1882 and found work washing dishes in a Michigan boarding house for lumberjacks. She then worked for several years in Chicago garment and shoe factories before becoming an organizer for the National Boot and Shoe Workers' Union; she eventually became the local branch president. In 1903, she joined the Chicago branch of the Women's Trade Union League (WTUL) after experiencing difficulties working with all-male executive boards. By 1910, she was the WTUL representative for the Garment Workers' Union. In that position, she organized, lectured, and investigated strikes. In 1914, Anderson began researching women's war work for the federal government. Her research and union leadership gained the attention of political figures. She became chief of the U.S. Department of Labor's Women's Bureau in 1919. She helped lead a fight to defeat the **EQUAL RIGHTS AMENDMENT**, which she believed would be detrimental to women's lives. She published vital evidence backing a series of laws reforming working conditions and pay. She retired in 1944 and spent the rest of her life lecturing about women and labor issues.

Maya Angelou has worked as a writer, actress, and director.

ANGELOU, MAYA (b. 1928)

Writer, and actress, and director. Born Marguerite Johnson, Maya Angelou had a difficult childhood. At the age of eight, she was raped by her mother's boyfriend and suffered several episodes of muteness as a result. Her early childhood is covered in her autobiography, *I Know Why the Caged Bird Sings* (1970). Angelou's other autobiographies, including *Gather Together in My Name* (1974) and *The Heart of a Woman* (1981), focus on economic, racial, and sexual oppression, as do her novels, poetry, and screenplays.

Marguerite Johnson became "Maya Angelou" while working as a dancer in San Francisco in the 1940s. Angelou worked several seedy jobs, including one as a prostitute. She relocated to New York City in the 1950s, where she was encouraged by the Harlem Writer's Guild to develop her writing talent. In the meantime, she acted in several stage productions, including *Porgy and Bess*.

Angelou moved to Cairo, Egypt, in the early 1960s. While there she worked to improve conditions for Third World women and was the associate editor of the *Arab Observer*. On returning to the United States, she became the first African-American woman to have one of her stories made into a film (*Georgia, Georgia*, 1972). In addition, she received two Tony nominations for her acting in *Roots* and was the first female African-American director in Hollywood.

Angelou has been a professor of American Studies at Wake Forest University since 1981. In 1993, she was the inaugural poet for President Bill Clinton, where she read her poem "On the Pulse of the Morning."

ANOREXIA NERVOSA

An eating disorder. Anorexia is most often found in **ADOLESCENT** girls and young women and is characterized by an exaggerated preoccupation with body size. A young woman afflicted with anorexia believes that she is fat even when her body weight falls well below what is healthy for her height and bone structure. Anorexia may lead to severely reduced calorie intake, compulsive exercise, and bulimia—binge eating followed by vomiting to purge what has been consumed. Young women who lose significant amounts of weight stop menstruating and may experience reduced heart rate, low blood pressure, and depression. Among women afflicted with anorexia, 10 percent will die, most from heart problems.

Biological, social, and psychological factors have been identified as causes of anorexia. Not much is known about the biological factors, but there is some evidence that anorexia may occur as a result of mood swings and depression. Social factors include the pressure on women to be thin. Psychologically, young middle-class women who are achievement oriented and who hope for a traditional lifestyle, including marriage, tend to develop anorexia. Psychologists speculate that the competing desires to be successful at school and work and yet feminine and attractive to men may create confusion and a sense of being overwhelmed. Anorexic young women are often perfectionists, and their families may have very high expectations for them.

Treatment for anorexia is difficult, and many victims must be hospitalized. A combination of psychotherapy, antidepressant medication, and education about nutrition can help many recover.

ANTI-MISCEGENATION LAWS

State laws that prohibited marriage between people of different races. The term "miscegenation" dates only to 1864, but anti-miscegenation laws in America were in force for more than 300 years.

Maryland enacted the first anti-miscegenation law in 1661; by the nineteenth century similar laws were in place in most states. Interracial relationships were regarded as both a breach of morality and a threat to the economic structure of slavery.

Anti-miscegenation laws soon included other races. In 1880, California barred licenses for marriages between a white person and a "Negro, mulatto, or Mongolian," in a reaction to the influx of mostly Chinese immigrants. In 1909 it added people of Japanese heritage to this list.

Laws did not prevent either interracial marriage or the birth of children of mixed race, and following **WORLD WAR II**, many of the statutes were challenged. In 1948, the California Supreme Court ruled that such laws were based on racial distinctions that were "by their very nature, odious to a free people." Civil rights gains in the 1950s and 1960s drew attention to the anti-miscegenation laws, although a Gallup poll conducted in 1958 on the subject of interracial marriage showed that 94 percent of the white people questioned opposed such marriages. In 1967, 16 states still had anti-miscegenation laws on their books when, in ***LOVING V. VIRGINIA***, the U.S. Supreme Court struck down a 1924 Virginia law forbidding interracial marriages as unconstitutional and a denial of Fourteenth Amendment rights.

ARDEN, ELIZABETH

(1878–1966)

Beautician and cosmetics entrepreneur. Elizabeth Arden was born Florence Nightingale Graham in Ontario, Canada. She attended nursing school in Toronto, but upon becoming a nurse discovered a path that she considered more interesting—cosmetics. Arden believed that creams and salves used for medical purposes could also serve as beauty creams and lotions.

Unable to find the perfect beauty cream on her own, Arden moved to New York City in 1908 and formed a partnership with a chemist. At that time, the concept of beauty cream was unheard of. Cosmetics were used mainly by stage performers. Undiscouraged, Arden worked in a beauty parlor until she could afford to open her own salon in 1910.

Arden's Fifth Avenue salon, which offered superior products and services, was popular with New York's elite. Soon her products were being sold in exclusive department stores around the world. In addition, Arden was the first to use beauty advisors and made "makeovers" commonplace in stores that sold her products.

Among Arden's innovations in cosmetics were foundations made to match skin tone, coordination of colors for face and nails, and anti-aging creams. By 1920, there were over 100 Elizabeth Arden products on the market. Overall, Arden made cosmetics a socially acceptable—and perhaps even essential—part of everyday fashion. After establishing herself in the cosmetic industry, from the 1930s until her death in 1966 Arden ran the Maine Chance Stables in Kentucky where the 1947 Kentucky Derby winner was bred.

ARTISTS

Creators of visual images whether painting, prints, sculpture, environmental, or performance.

In 1971, art historian Linda Nochlin published an article entitled, "Why Have There Been No Great Women Artists?" Nochlin's question raised two related issues: Women had created art for centuries, but they were excluded from the history of art and the institutions of cultural power. Whether they were denied admission to schools and academies to study, patrons to finance their work, or acceptance into galleries to exhibit their work, women had to leap great barriers to turn their art into a profession.

During the twentieth century some of these barriers fell. The academy system that had controlled access to professional training in the visual arts during the nineteenth century fell apart by the end of **World War I**. New artists experimenting with new styles replaced the academic traditions and created modern art schools. Women participated in every movement from surrealism to abstract expressionism and performance art. They worked in every medium, such as **photography** at the beginning of the century and electronic media at its close.

Berenice Abbott and Imogene Cunningham became noted photographers of urban and natural landscapes, respectively. Margaret Bourke-White and Dorothea Lange used the photographic image to document the United States during the Depression and **World War II**. Diane Arbus, Mary Ellen Mark, and Annie Liebowitz use documentary portraiture as social commentary.

The woman artists with the greatest international reputations during the second half of the century, Georgia O'Keeffe and **Louise Nevelson**, used aspects of minimalism and abstraction in their painting and sculp-

TRAILBLAZERS

Georgia O'Keeffe (1887–1986) was a painter whose abstractions of natural forms—clouds, flowers, desert landscapes—became her signature work. Born in Sun Prairie, Wisconsin, she began her art studies as a child and by age 16 had five years of private lessons. She spent one year (1905) studying at the Art Institute of Chicago and another (1907) with the Art Students' League in New York City. Unsettled about the direction of her artwork, O'Keeffe spent the next several years teaching art and taking classes.

Beginning in 1916, the photographer and gallery owner Alfred Stieglitz displayed her drawings in his gallery. He also preserved some of the best images of O'Keeffe in photographs of the artist. In 1918, she returned to New York City, and she and Stieglitz married in 1924. That year, O'Keeffe began to paint her enormous abstractions of flowers.

Looking for new visual stimulation, O'Keeffe traveled west by train in 1929 to Taos, New Mexico. She stayed with Mabel Dodge Luhan. The colors of the land, the Native American and Spanish cultures of the Southwest, and the distance from all she knew captivated her. After that summer, she returned to New York and Stieglitz but returned each subsequent summer to further explore northern New Mexico.

O'Keeffe's work became less popular during the postwar years when abstract expressionism was in vogue. She had only a few solo shows. However, by the 1970s a new generation of admirers renewed interest in her work and she held two major exhibitions. She stopped painting in the early 1970s as her eyesight failed. O'Keeffe died at the age of 98 in 1986 in Santa Fe, New Mexico. An art museum dedicated specifically to her life and work was built in her honor a few years later.

Georgia O'Keefe is best known for her large, visually stimulating canvases.

tures, respectively. Although neither appreciated being called a *woman* artist, they both broke barriers for the next generation.

After World War II, New York replaced Western Europe as the center of the art world and created the context for a new school of painting called abstract expressionism. For decades, only male practitioners of abstract expressionism gained attention, and yet prominent women such as Lee Krasner, Elaine de Kooning, and Helen Frankenthaler worked alongside Jackson Pollock, William de Kooning, and others.

The **WOMEN'S LIBERATION MOVEMENT** of the 1960s and 1970s brought new energy into the art world, challenging the subjects and institutions yet again. Some women began to examine the way in which gender shaped their lives and incorporated their observations into their artwork. Issues that had previously been taboo—rape, incest, menstruation, childbirth, and sexuality—became the subject matter of visual and performance artists. Judy Chicago's paintings and *The Dinner Party* installation brought into full public view women's bodies, experiences, and histories. Women's lives became a subject of the visual arts as women's bodies and mythical attributions had been a century earlier. Ana Mendieta's performance work, Betye Saar's and Faith Ringgold's sculptural pieces, and Jenny Holzer's electronic message installations captured the social changes underway with their unconventional art works.

It took longer to gain access to the art world's exhibitions, critics, collectors, and historians. Yet, the change occurred because of the persistence, dedication, and political mobilization of women to end their exclusion and marginalization. As with other forms of creative expression—**DANCE**, acting, **MUSIC**, and **LITERATURE**—women make their own choices to work as visual artists today, rather than having those choices made for them.

ASH, MARY KAY

(b. 1915)

Business executive and entrepreneur. Mary Kay Wagner was born in Hot Wells, Texas, in 1915 and grew up during the Depression. After her father, Edward Wagner, contracted tuberculosis, she ran the household and cared for him while her mother, Lulu, worked as a restaurant manager to support the family. During the 1930s, after graduating from high school, Wagner married Ben Rogers and had three children. She sold books door to door to earn additional income for her family and was divorced from her husband in 1938 after he returned home from serving in the armed forces. She joined the Stanley Home Products company, selling housewares and cleaning products, and eventually became a manager in the organization. In 1952, she became national training director at the World Gift Company and helped expand the company's business. However, she encountered a **GLASS CEILING** and could not be promoted to a top position because those jobs were only open to men, so she left.

In 1963, she used $5,000 of her own money to found Mary Kay Cosmetics in Dallas, Texas, hiring women to sell beauty products door to door and rewarding outstanding salespeople with pink Cadillacs, diamonds, and other incentives to motivate them to sell. By the 1990s, the company employed over four hundred thousand salespeople in 25 countries across the globe. It is the largest company selling cosmetics through direct sales.

Ash has been married three times and has a daughter and two sons.

ASIAN AMERICANS

At the beginning of the twentieth century, few Asian women had managed to overcome the legal barriers necessary to emigrate to the United States. Having arrived only recently from many different countries, most had not yet forged identities as Asians and Americans.

The earliest Asian immigrants to come to the United States were the Chinese. By the beginning of the twentieth century, a small number of Chinese women were employed in domestic service, but many others were still trying to escape past legacies of slavery and oppression. While the 61-year ban on Chinese immigrants finally ended in 1943, the National Origins Act of 1924 banned the entry of Koreans, Japanese, and Asian Indians, and the 1934 Tydings-McDuffie act restricted the number of Filipino immigrants to 50 a year. With the exception of the 1908 Gentlemen's Agreement, which allowed Japanese women to enter the country as family members of Japanese men, resulting in near equal proportions of men and women Japanese immigrants, legislation existed that restricted the immigration of Asians and had the particular effect of barring women.

It was not until 1965 that all Asian immigration laws were lifted and quotas finally increased to reunite families. Today, Asian women emigrate from a multitude of Asian countries, such as Laos, Cambodia, and Indonesia, representing numerous cultural and national backgrounds and religions.

While some women arrived independently, in large part, women emigrated with family members. Many women followed men, both husbands and would-be husbands. Some Japanese and Korean women came as picture brides, a form of arranged marriage. Many Asians emigrated first to Hawaii or California.

While legal barriers have been lifted against their entry, Asian-American women continue to face prejudice. A 1990 study showed that Asian immigrant women without proficiency in English were more likely to be impoverished than other immigrant groups. Additionally, negative portrayals of Asian women in the media perpetuate negative stereotypes of Asian women as submissive and subservient or, in the equally unfavorable alternative, as ruthless "dragon lady" caricatures.

In reality, Asian women are struggling to advance themselves in all areas and are now becoming visible as journalists, Cabinet members, mayors, and activists. And Asian-American women possess a growing consciousness of their dual identities, which is slowly being introduced to mainstream white culture by writers such as Chinese-American **Amy Tan**.

ATHLETICS

By the dawn of the twentieth century, upper-class women were participating recreationally in the socially acceptable sports of archery, bowling, tennis, and golf, while others played croquet or enjoyed the freedom of bicycling. At the collegiate level, women's competitive experiences were available at some institutions, but the quantity and quality of these opportunities varied greatly from campus to campus. The most popular college sports were basketball, tennis, field hockey, swimming, softball, and archery.

In this era, tennis star Suzanne Lenglen won Wimbledon (1919) and Gertrude Ederle swam the English Channel, shattering the men's record by over two hours.

The Growth of Sporting Opportunities for Women

By the late 1920s, industries and municipal recreation departments and agencies were running recreational and competitive basketball, bowling, and baseball/softball leagues for women, with top teams participating in national championships. Women in the middle and upper classes, however, continued to focus their abilities on individual sports, such as golf, tennis, fencing, figure skating, and swimming, rather than on teams. In the first quarter of the twentieth century, national championships were established for these women.

In 1920, the United States entered a full women's swimming team and two figure skaters in the Olympic Games in Antwerp, Belgium; in 1928, a women's track-and-field team was sent to the Amsterdam Olympic Games.

The most outstanding female athlete of the 1932 Olympics, and perhaps the finest female athlete of the twentieth century, was **Mildred "Babe" Didrikson Zaharias**, who won two gold medals and one silver in track-and-field events. A great all-around athlete, Babe went on to become one of America's best golfers ever.

Ironically, as women's sporting opportunities in society at large were expanding, the opportunities for women in intercollegiate sports were diminishing and soon would almost disappear, supplanted by several less competitive approaches, such as intramurals. Not until the 1960s would intercollegiate opportunities for women reappear.

African-American women were able to participate in athletics primarily through traditionally African-American colleges. Tuskegee Institute dominated the Amateur Athletic Union (AAU) national track-and-field competition from 1937 to 1948 and Tennessee State University dominated AAU and Olympic competition from 1947 into the 1960s. Sprinter Wilma Rudolph was one of Tennessee State's stars.

Major league baseball suffered from a lack of manpower during **World War II**, leading to the creation of a women's baseball league in 1943. By 1948, it consisted of ten teams and attracted almost a million fans, but as the soldiers came back from World War II, the women's league struggled to compete for spectators. It finally dissolved in 1954. Industrial leagues also folded in the 1950s when society returned to more traditional views of

WOMEN'S FIRSTS

In 1960 at the Olympic Games in Rome, Wilma Rudolph became the first American woman to win three gold medals. What made her accomplishment so amazing was the fact that, after contracting polio at age four, she was told that she would never walk again.

Born in 1940 in Tennessee, Wilma was the twentieth of 22 children. Her poverty-stricken family additionally suffered from the injustices of a segregated society. Throughout her childhood, she was afflicted with measles, mumps, chicken pox, double pneumonia, scarlet fever, and then polio, which left her with a crippled left leg. Several members of her family provided daily physical therapy exercises which, in time, allowed Wilma to walk with the support of a metal leg brace. Eventually, by age 12, she walked normally, thanks to her great determination.

Fours years later, she ran in the four-by-four relay at the 1956 Melbourne Olympic Games and won a bronze medal. The following year, she enrolled at Tennessee State University, whose track and field athletes had dominated AAU and Olympic teams for years.

In the 1960 games, she won gold medals in the 100 meters and 200 meters (Olympic record); a third gold was won for anchoring the 400-meter relay (world record). Dubbed the "World's Fastest Woman," she was feted throughout Europe before returning to the United States.

In her hometown of Clarksville, Tennessee, the first racially integrated event ever held in the town was a welcoming home parade and banquet in her honor. That year she was named United Press Athlete of the Year and Associated Press Woman Athlete of the Year. In 1962, she won the Babe Zaharias Award as the most outstanding athlete in the world.

After retiring from track at age 22, Rudolph worked as a coach and inspirational speaker. In 1967, she was selected to work in Operation Champ to train ghetto children in track then later worked with Chicago's Youth Foundation. In 1981, she founded the Wilma Rudolph Foundation to train young underprivileged athletes.

Rudolph died of a malignant brain tumor in 1994 at age 54.

women's roles in society, emphasizing femininity, domesticity, and motherhood.

The Impetus for Significant Changes in Opportunities for Women

The 1960s saw a radical requestioning of women's roles in society. Following the 1960 Report of the Commission on the Status of Women, the 1963 Equal Pay Act, and the 1964 Civil Rights Act, the modern women's rights movement began. The **NATIONAL ORGANIZATION FOR WOMEN (NOW)** was formed in 1966, and women started entering fields formerly closed to them.

Concomitant with this push toward equality for women on many fronts was the growing interest in high-level competitive opportunities in collegiate sports. This resulted in the development of the Commission on Intercollegiate Athletics for Women (CIAW) in 1966. In 1971, the CIAW evolved into the Association for Intercollegiate Athletics for Women (AIAW), which set out to create an educationally sound and student-oriented model for athletics, offering state, regional, and national championship opportunities for women.

In 1972, the passage of **TITLE IX** gave sportswomen the biggest boost toward equality in the twentieth century, prohibiting discrimination based on sex in educational institutions receiving federal funding. With this law, the world of educational sport was to be forever changed.

In 1973, former Wimbledon tennis champion Bobby Riggs, then in his fifties, belittled women tennis players as inferior and challenged **BILLIE JEAN KING**, the top female tennis player, to a match. Promoted as the "Battle of the Sexes," the event attracted a worldwide television audience of fifty million. Many considered the match a contest to determine if a woman could defeat a man in sport and prove herself to be as skilled, as popular, and as entertaining. King won in straight sets, and another giant step toward equality for women was taken. For all her many contributions, especially for her fight for equal pay for female tennis players and also for the establishment of the Women's Sports Foundation in 1974, King is regarded by many as the most influential female athlete of the twentieth century. The Foundation, comprised of national, international, and Olympic female champions, has become the strongest collective voice for women in sport.

The Setbacks

Throughout the 1970s, the growth of opportunities for girls and women in sport was phenomenal because institutions not in compliance with Title IX risked the loss of federal funds. Opposing Title IX, however, was the National Collegiate Athletic Association (NCAA). Unsuccessful in its attempt to exempt football and men's basketball, the NCAA then maneuvered to achieve the next best result—to take control over all women's sports. Using its dominant power and its great financial resources, the NCAA competed with the AIAW by offering championships for women. By June 1982, the AIAW had been put out of business. Women were subsumed into the male model of sport, losing several national championship opportunities, athletic scholarships, and hundreds of leadership positions.

Another huge setback for athletic equality was the U.S. Supreme Court ruling in *Grove City College v. Bell* (1984), in which the justices held that only athletic programs that directly received federal funding were required to comply with Title IX. Almost no athletic departments in the country receive direct federal funding. Title IX was resurrected with the 1988 Civil Rights Restoration Act, but it was not enforced until 1993, when President Clinton took office.

Conclusion

Despite enforcement of Title IX in the 1990s, women in educational institutions still do not receive comparable opportunities, support, treatment, or coverage in sport at any level. These collegiate results demonstrate that many educational institutions continue to discriminate in violation of a federal law mandating equal opportunity for all.

Despite the discriminatory treatment, American sportswomen continue to excel. Jackie Joyner-Kersee was the first woman to win the heptathlon in consecutive Olympic Games in 1992. In 1996, U.S. women won Olympic gold medals in soccer, basketball, softball, synchronized swimming, and gymnastics. The women's ice hockey team won its first gold medal at the Winter Olympics in Nagano, Japan, in 1998, and in that same year the U.S. soccer team won the World Cup before a worldwide television audience. The growth of women's sports in the 1970s, in the 1990s, and since has been phenomenal.

Christine Grant

FURTHER READING

Gerber, E., J. Felshin, P. Berlin, and W. Wyrick. *The American Woman in Sport.* Reading, MA: Addison-Wesley, 1974.

AVERY, BYLLYE (b. 1937)

Women's health care activist and founder of the National Black Women's Health Project (NBWHP). Born in Deland, Florida, Avery received her MA in special education in 1969 from the University of Florida. After the 1973 Supreme Court decision ***Roe v. Wade***, Avery became involved in women's reproductive health issues. That same year, Avery, a young widow with two small children, became pregnant and made the difficult choice to have an abortion. She subsequently left her job as a special-education teacher to help open a clinic in Gainesville, Florida; five years later, in 1979, she helped found the Birthing Center there. Eventually she focused on the health of African-American women and families, and in 1981 became the founding director of the National Black Women's Health Project, headquartered in Atlanta, Georgia. Avery later broadened her efforts to include education and national health policy. One of her projects was the film *On Becoming a Woman: Mothers and Daughters Talking to Each Other* (1987), a documentary depicting two generations of African-American women engaged in discussions about menstruation, sex, love, and communication.

The recipient of a MacArthur Foundation fellowship in 1989, Avery has also been a visiting fellow at the Harvard University School of Public Health; a consultant on women's health care in Latin America, Africa, and the Caribbean; and an advisor on health issues to the Kellogg Foundation for its International Leadership Program.

AVIATION AND SPACE

The operation of airplanes and spacecraft. The first woman to obtain a pilot's license was barnstormer Harriet Quimby in 1911, from the Aero Club of America. Quimby had been working as a writer and was inspired to become a pilot after attending the Belmont Park Aviation Meet. She became the first woman to fly over Mexico City and, on April 16, 1912, gained further notoriety for flying across the English Channel. Her achievements paved the way for **Amelia Earhart**, perhaps the most famous female American aviator.

In 1928 Earhart became the first female passenger to fly across the Atlantic Ocean. After this successful venture, she decided to make the transatlantic flight as a pilot in 1932. Flying solo, she broke the existing time record for crossing this ocean, completing the flight in 13 hours and 30 minutes.

Earhart was a strong advocate of commercial air travel. In 1927 she worked as a sales representative for a commercial airport. Later, she cofounded Boston and Maine Airways, one of the first commercial airlines. With fellow pilot Ruth Nichols, she also helped form the **NINETY-NINES**, an association of women fliers. Earhart was the first president of the Ninety-Nines, so named for the number of members in the group.

Other female pioneers in aviation include Clara Trenchmann, who worked for the Curtis Flying Service; Olive Anne Beech, owner of Beech Aircraft; and Jacqueline Cochran, the woman responsible for supervising hundreds of women pilots in the Women's Air Service during **WORLD WAR II**.

Planes were not the only crafts in which women flew. In 1924 Jeanette Piccard became the first woman to pilot a hydrogen balloon, taking a 175-foot zeppelin (a craft designed by German military officer Ferdinand Graf von Zeppelin that was used in **WORLD WAR I** air raids) to an altitude of 57,559 feet.

Many women took to the skies in 1935 when they became the first "air hostesses," serving food and beverages to airline passengers. To work in this capacity, women had to meet certain age and weight restrictions, and were often subjected to sexual harassment by passengers and pilots. Antidiscrimination laws later eliminated these restrictions, and the job title changed to "flight attendant" when equal employment laws allowed men to gain entry into the field.

The first American woman astronaut was **SALLY RIDE**, who in 1983 spent six days orbiting the earth as part of the space shuttle *Challenger*'s crew. Ride later directed the Space Institute of the University of California. Mae Jemison became the first African-American woman astronaut in 1992 when she spent eight days in space on the *Endeavour*.

B

BAEZ, JOAN (b. 1941)

Musician and social activist. With a three-octave vocal range and a strong sociopolitical focus in her traditional folk songs, it is no surprise that Joan Baez has been labeled "Queen of the Folk Singers." Baez was born in Staten Island, New York, on January 9, 1941. Her father, Albert Baez, a physicist, undoubtedly influenced her pacifism when he turned down a job making high-tech war weapons.

Because she was half Mexican, half Anglo, Baez faced racial issues at school. Believing that music was the key to being accepted by other students, she took up the ukulele and the guitar. Her first performance was at a high school talent show when she was 14 years old. She quickly became known as a girl with a voice.

Baez studied drama at Boston University but she did not graduate. She gained a strong following due to her regular musical gigs at coffeehouses, and in 1959 she made her musical debut at the Newport Folk Festival. The Vanguard label immediately signed her and released a recording of her festival performance. A year later, she released her first studio album *Joan Baez*.

Throughout the 1960s, Baez used her musical career to promote civil rights and to protest the **VIETNAM WAR**. She organized and performed in a musical tour of black Southern colleges because African Americans were not allowed access to concerts at all-white colleges. In 1965, Baez founded the Institute for the Study of Non-Violence (now called the Resource Center for Non-Violence) in Palo Alto, California. In 1967, she was arrested for protesting the Vietnam draft. Baez's tour of Vietnam inspired her 1973 album *Where Are You Now, My Son?*

Baez also cofounded Amnesty West Coast (a division of Amnesty International, a worldwide human rights organization). In addition, she founded Humanities International, an organization that focuses on human rights, disarmament, and nonviolence. She was the opening act at the Live Aid concert for Ethiopian relief in 1985 and costarred with musical acts Sting, U2, and Peter Gabriel in Amnesty International's 1986 "Conspiracy of Hope" tour.

Baez continues her work in music and politics today. Her autobiography, *And a Voice to Sing With,* was released in 1987.

FURTHER READING

Garza, Hedda. *Joan Baez.* New York: Chelsea House, 1991.

BAKER, ELLA (1903–1986)

Ella Baker is one of the least-known leaders of the civil rights movement. She wanted it that way.

She was born in Norfolk, Virginia, to Georgianna Ross Baker, a powerful and compassionate woman who profoundly shaped Ella's life. She went to college at Shaw University, where the president became so vexed by her insistence that male and female students ought to be able to socialize with each other that he tried—unsuccessfully—to expel her.

Unlike many African-American women who graduated from college, Baker did not pursue a teaching position. Instead she went to Harlem, in 1927 the center of African-American art and thought. She was soon deeply involved in several reforms. She helped to convince the New York City Public Library to hire African Americans and then got a job there. She married T. J. Roberts in 1941, but kept her maiden name (which was then very unusual) and her independence.

Baker moved onto the national scene in 1941 when she became a field secretary for the National Association for the Advancement of Colored People (NAACP). This position showcased her talents for grassroots organizing, and she quickly increased the civil rights organization's membership. She resigned five years later, frustrated by the leadership's unresponsiveness to its rank and file. She worked and volunteered for a number of organizations over the next decade and often spoke on issues of race and justice.

The bus boycott in Montgomery, Alabama, brought Baker back to the South. She helped found the Southern Christian Leadership Conference (SCLC) in 1957, but resigned a few years later, frustrated that Martin Luther King and other young ministers seemed more comfortable with "a leadership-centered group" than a "group-centered leadership."

She was much more optimistic about the young idealists of the Student Non-Violent Coordinating Committee (SNCC), an organization that she helped found in 1960. Like Baker, they believed strongly in organizing and educating ordinary Southerners to achieve political and social change. Indeed, SNCC soon began registering Southern black voters. Hundreds of these activists learned the trade from "Miss Baker."

Baker spoke on and worked for a broad array of increasingly radical causes after returning to New York City in the 1960s. She helped establish the Mississippi Freedom Democratic Party (MFDP) in 1964, and gave the keynote address at its founding convention. At her memorial service in 1983, civil rights leader Bob Moses asked that people who considered themselves her children come forward. Hundreds of people of all ages moved to the front of the church.

FURTHER READING

Grant, Joanne. *Ella Baker: Freedom Bound.* New York: John Wiley & Sons, 1998.

BAKER, JOSEPHINE (1906–1975)

Music hall dancer, nightclub entertainer, blues singer, and film actress. Born on June 3, 1906, in the slums of St. Louis, Missouri, Freda Josephine Carson spent her life pursuing her love of the stage and became well-known in the United States and Europe as a versatile intertainer. The daughter of washerwoman Carrie McDonald and vaudeville drummer Eddie Carson, she worked as a maid and babysitter for wealthy white families while pursuing her interests in musical theater and cabaret. She began appearing in comical skits with the Jones Family Band and the Dixie Skippers at age 13 and attracted attention in 1923 as a member of the chorus in a touring production of the all-black musical *Shuffle Along.* She was married and divorced four times; her second marriage, in 1921, was to Willie Baker, whose last name she chose to keep.

After appearing in several New York theater and nightclub productions, Baker accepted a

Josephine Baker was well known in the United States and Europe as a versatile entertainer.

dancing role in a Paris stage show called *La Revue Nègre* in 1924. Her feathered skirt, sensual dance routines, and exotic beauty make her an overnight senasations. Moving to the famous Folies Bergères music hall, she received star billing—and the adoration of audiences—for her no-holds-barred dance routines and banana skirts. Performing her notorious *Danse Sauvage* (Savage Dance), she became known by such nicknames as the Black Venus, Black Pearl, and Creole Goddess. Her immensely popular stage performances in the 1920s and 1930s personified American "hot jazz" for European audiences. She starred in two movies in the early 1930s, *Zou-Zou* (1934) and *Princesse Tam-Tam* (1935), and earned international acclaim as a blues singer.

Thriving professionally and finding refuge from American racism, Baker became a French citizen in 1937. During **World War II**, she performed for the troops and served undercover in the French Resistance. She was later awarded the Medal of the Resistance with Rosette and named a Chevalier of the Legion of Honor, two of France's most prestigious honors, for her efforts. Beginning in the 1950s, Baker adopted and raised dozens of children of various nationalities—whom she referred to as her "Rainbow Tribe"—at her château in southwestern France. She also remained a frequent performer and international celebrity, making triumphant apearances on Broadway in 1964 and 1973, and in Paris just before her death on April 12, 1975.

BARBIE

A doll first manufactured by Mattel, Inc., in 1959. Barbie has become the best-selling fashion doll in the world, with annual sales of more than $1.5 billion.

Barbie was the brainchild of Ruth Handler, who noticed that her daughter liked to play with paper dolls that represented adult women. Handler modeled Barbie on the Lilli doll, a large-breasted, provocatively dressed German doll. The first Barbies—named after Handler's daughter—sold for three dollars. In the doll's first year of production, a record 351,000 were sold.

Barbie is best known for her figure. The $11\frac{3}{4}$-inch doll's measurements, transferred to human size, would result in a woman with a 39-inch bustline, an 18-inch waist, and 33-inch hips. Many women have objected that Barbie sets an unrealistic standard of appearance for young girls. It has also been criticized for embodying traditional attitudes toward women and women's work—the doll was originally marketed as a teenage fashion model, and her first outfits included a wedding dress. When the first talking Barbie was introduced in the late 1960s, feminists were outraged that one of her utterances was, "Math class is tough."

Over the years Mattel has responded to some of the criticism by introducing a variety of new editions that show the doll as an astronaut, physician, and computer programmer. The line has also added Barbie dolls that are African American, Asian American, and members of other ethnic groups.

BEARD, MARY RITTER

(1876–1958)

A women's rights leader, labor organizer, and historian. Ritter was born in Indianapolis, Indiana. While studying at DePauw University, she met and married Charles Beard. In 1900, they moved to England so Charles could continue his studies at Oxford University. There, the couple became active participants in the British woman suffrage movement.

Returning to the United States in 1904, the Beards entered New York's Columbia University for graduate training, but Mary found social activism far more invigorating and directed her energies to labor reform and women's rights. In 1907, she began working with the Women's Trade Union League, an organization committed to helping working-class women. The group boasted an impressive list of members, including **JANE ADDAMS** (see Volume 2), **FLORENCE KELLEY**, and Sophonisba Breckinridge. From 1910 to 1912, Beard also edited a suffrage journal *The Woman Voter* and played a critical role in organizing New York City textile workers into unions.

After women in the United States won the right to vote with the **NINETEENTH AMENDMENT**, Beard broke with suffragists who favored an **EQUAL RIGHTS AMENDMENT**. She opposed such an amendment because she feared it might destroy governmental legislation put in place specifically to aid women.

Along with organizing labor and championing women's rights, Beard became the most prominent female historian in the United States, and her books remain extremely influential. In 1927, she and her husband published the first of a four-volume series on U.S. history *The Rise of American Civilization*, and in the 1930s and the 1940s, she wrote several books on how women have influenced U.S. and world history. These studies include *Understanding Women, America Through Women's Eyes* and *Laughing Their Way: Women's Humor in America*. In 1946, Beard published her most important work in women's history, *Women as Force in History*. In this ground-breaking study, she attacked other historians for neglecting women. To combat these scholars, she positioned women at the center of history and argued that they had made important contributions to all parts of society.

Beard's scholarly accomplishments still influence historians today. In fact, many late–twentieth-century feminist historians acknowledge her scholarship. Gerda Lerner, one of the most accomplished of these female historians, vividly recalled her first encounter with *Women as Force in History*: "I was able to connect with her central idea, that women have always been active and at the center of history. I was struck by a sudden illumination, by the simplicity and truth of her insight."

BENEDICT, RUTH FULTON

(1887–1948)

Anthropologist who helped popularize the concept of cultural relativism. Born Ruth Fulton in New York City on June 5, 1887, Fulton's childhood was marred by the death of her father and periodic bouts of depression. After moving with her mother to St. Joseph, Missouri, and then Buffalo, New York, she attended Vassar College. A gifted student, Fulton graduated Phi Beta Kappa in 1909. She then toured Europe for a year and worked briefly as a social worker before marrying a biochemistry professor, Stanley Benedict, in 1914.

Seeking intellectual stimulation, Benedict began taking classes at the New School for Social Research. Working with **ELSIE CLEWS PARSONS** there introduced her to the study of anthropology and inspired her in 1921 to begin graduate work at Columbia University under the tutelage of famed cultural anthropologist Franz Boas. After earning her doctorate in 1923, she became a lecturer at Columbia and served as Boas's administrative assistant.

From 1922 to 1939 Benedict conducted research among the Serrano, Zuñi, and Cochiti Indians that became the basis for books including *Tales of the Cochiti Indians* (1931), *Zuñi Mythology*

Ruth Benedict introduced anthropological concepts to a mass audience.

(1935), and *Patterns of Culture* (1934). A bestseller, *Patterns of Culture* introduced anthropological conceptions to a mass audience and popularized "cultural relativism," the notion that cultures cannot be ranked hierarchically.

Although her research was influential, Benedict experienced sexual discrimination throughout her career. Columbia University assumed that her husband earned a sufficient income as a biochemist, and consequently refused to pay her for her work as a lecturer. Only after Benedict and her husband separated in 1931 (by which time she was an assistant professor) did the university begin paying her a salary. Thereafter, despite her landmark research, Columbia continued to deny her promotion to full professor.

During **World War II** Benedict worked in the Office of War Information (OWI). The research she conducted there served as the basis for an examination of Japanese culture, *The Chrysanthemum and the Sword* (1946). Following the war, Benedict returned to Columbia, where she headed the Research in Contemporary Cultures project and finally won promotion to full professor in July 1948. Benedict never taught in that capacity, however, as she died of a coronary thrombosis only two months later, on September 17, 1948.

BERRY, MARY FRANCIS

(b. 1938)

Educator, author, and civil rights leader. Mary Francis Berry was born on February 17, 1938, in Nashville, Tennessee. After attending local public schools, she graduated from Howard University and then received a doctorate as well as a law degree from the University of Michigan.

Dr. Berry served as provost of the Division of Behavioral and Social Sciences at the University of Maryland, then was appointed Chancellor of the University of Colorado. From 1977 to 1980, Dr. Berry was assistant secretary for education in the administration of President Jimmy Carter, and in 1980 President Carter appointed her as a member of the U.S. Commission on Civil Rights. President Ronald Reagan dismissed Dr. Berry after she expressed criticism of his positions on civil rights. She took legal action against the president and was returned to the commission.

In 1993, President Bill Clinton appointed her chairperson of the commission, and she was reappointed to that position in 1999. She is also a professor of law and history at the University of Pennsylvania and is the author of seven books, including *The Pig Farmer's Daughter and Other Tales of American Justice: Episodes of Racism and Sexism in the Courts from 1865 to the Present* and *Long Memory: The Black Experience in America*.

BETHUNE, MARY McLEOD

(1875–1955)

Educator and social activist. Patsy McLeod was reportedly surprised that Mary, her fifteenth child, was a girl, for she had asked God "to send us a child who would show us the way out." Mary McLeod had many barriers to overcome. She was born black, poor, and female in South Carolina, yet she would become one of the most respected and prominent African-American leaders—man or woman—of the twentieth century.

McLeod's parents wrung enough money from their farm to send their precocious daughter to a nearby mission school. She later won a scholarship to Scotia Seminary in North Carolina and spent a year at Dwight L. Moody's religious institute in Chicago, then she became an educator. In 1898 she married Albertus Bethune, with whom she had one child before he left her.

> ***"If we accept and acquiesce in the face of discrimination, we accept the responsibility ourselves and allow those responsible to salve their conscience by believing that they have our acceptance and concurrence. We should, therefore, protest openly everything. . .that smacks of discrimination or slander."***
>
> —Mary McLeod Bethune, "Certain Unalienable Rights" (1944)

Bethune's star was by this time rising. She founded Daytona Educational and Industrial School for Negro Girls, which would eventually merge with another institution and become Bethune-Cookman College. In 1917 she became president of the Florida Federation of Colored Women's Clubs. In 1924 she was named president of the **National Association of Colored Women**, which gave her a national platform. In

Mary McLeod Bethune was one of the nation's most respected and prominent African-American leaders.

1935, she founded the **National Council of Negro Women**.

She became a Democrat in 1936, when Franklin D. Roosevelt invited her into his administration, where she headed the National Youth Administration's Division of Negro Affairs, a position that made her the highest-salaried African American in government. She organized the National Conference on the Problems of the Negro in 1937, played a crucial role in mobilizing African Americans during World War II, and spoke and wrote frequently and eloquently on a wide range of economic and political issues that affected African Americans.

McLeod Bethune was more pragmatic than radical. She emphasized conciliation and cooperation. An ardent patriot, she believed strongly in the democratic promise of the United States. She counseled African Americans to pull themselves up by their own bootstraps and reportedly liked to remark, "I have faith in God and in Mary Bethune." But she also resolutely and repeatedly opposed white supremacy, from lynching to segregation.

A tireless and gracious leader, McLeod Bethune was extremely popular. The poet Langston Hughes remarked that chickens became nervous upon her approach, sensing that "some necks would be wrung in her honor to make a heaping platter of southern fried chicken." Her very presence, along with her many accomplishments, made African Americans feel proud and strong.

FURTHER READING

McCluskey, Audrey Thomas, and Elaine M. Smith, eds. *Mary McLeod Bethune: Building a Better World: Essays and Selected Documents*. Bloomington: Indiana University Press, 1999.

BLACK, CATHLEEN (b. 1944)

A Chicago native, Cathleen Black began her career selling advertising for magazines such as *Holiday, Travel & Leisure,* and *New York*. She helped launch ***Ms.* Magazine** and later became associate publisher. She became the first woman to publish a weekly consumer magazine when she was named publisher of *New York* magazine in 1979. In 1983, she moved to *USA Today,* helping to raise its circulation to 1.8 million readers. Eight years later, Black became the president and CEO of the Newspaper Association of America, the newspaper industry's largest trade group, where she served for five years before joining Hearst.

In 1995, she was hired to run Hearst Magazines, the largest publisher of monthly magazines in the world. Its 16 publications include *Cosmopolitan, Esquire,* and *Good Housekeeping*. Her focus has been on promoting growth in licensing and new media in the international market.

Black is a graduate of Trinity College, Washington, D.C. She serves on the board of the Hearst Corporation, IBM, and the Coca-Cola Company. She is married with two children.

BONNIN, GERTRUDE SIMMONS (ZITKALA-SHA) (1876–1938)

Writer, musician, and Native American activist. Gertrude Simmons was born in 1876 to a white father and Sioux mother on the Pine Ridge reservation in South Dakota. She left home at the age of eight to attend a Quaker school in Indiana for **Native Americans**, but at her mother's behest, she returned home to finish her schooling.

In 1895, Simmons entered another Quaker institution in Indiana, Earlham College, where she won an oratory contest. After graduation, she taught at the Carlisle Indian School in Pennsylvania but was disheartened by the conditions of Native American students there and left after two years. In 1900, she published articles under her pen name, Zitkala-Sha (Red Bird), criticizing

Carlisle for degrading Native Americans and their cultures through forced conversions to Christianity.

Simmons excelled at the violin and entered the Boston Conservatory of Music. In 1900, she toured Paris as a soloist. She would eventually coauthor an opera in 1913 entitled "Sun Dance" with William Hanson. She was also active as a writer, contributing to *Harpers* and *The Atlantic*.

Simmons married Captain Raymond Bonnin, a mixed-blood Nakota who worked for the Bureau of Indian Affairs, in 1902. She gave birth to a son, Ohiya, and for 14 years, they lived on the Ute reservation in Utah, where she worked as a clerk and teacher.

The Bonnins moved to Washington, D.C., to lobby on behalf of Native Americans. Gertrude was elected secretary of the Society of American Indians in 1916 and edited *American Indian Magazine*. She assisted with the passage of Indian Citizenship Bill in 1924 through a grassroots campaign in which she urged Native Americans to support the bill and accept the responsibilities of suffrage. In the same year, she coauthored a history of the exploitation of Oklahoma Native Americans by the U.S. government. An advocate of pan–Native American power, she sought to build unity among tribes and, in 1926, formed the National Council of American Indians, over which she presided until her death in 1938.

BRICE, FANNY (1891–1951)

Singer and comedian whose career took her from the stage to radio and film. Born Fannie Borach on New York City's Lower East Side, Brice's earliest success came at age 13 when she won first prize singing "When You Know You're Not Forgotten by the Girl Who Can't Forget" in a contest. In an effort to break into show business, she worked as a pianist, singer, and assistant projectionist in a movie house. She was fired from the chorus line of the show *Talk of the Town* when it was quickly discovered that she could not dance.

Brice joined the famous Ziegfeld Follies musical variety show in 1910. A plain woman with a remarkable voice, Brice used her comedic skills to create a unique stage personality. Immensely popular for her amusing routines, she became a star in 1921 for her rendition of "My Man," a song that became her trademark. She was also known for the songs "Second-Hand Rose," "I Should Worry," and "Rose of Washington Square."

Brice made her first film, *My Man,* in 1928; she also appeared in *Be Yourself!* (1930), *The Great Ziegfeld* (1936), and *Everybody Sing* (1938). Brice introduced "Baby Snooks," a character she created on the stage, to radio audiences in 1936, and played the role almost continuously until her death.

In 1964, **BARBRA STREISAND** starred as Fanny Brice in the Broadway musical *Funny Girl*. She went on to reprise the role in the 1968 film and in the 1975 sequel *Funny Lady*.

BROOKS, GWENDOLYN

(1917–2000)

Poet. Gwendolyn Brooks is known as "Chicago's poet," as she lived there most of her life. She was born to David and Zeziah (Williams) Brooks on June 17, 1917, in Topeka, Kansas. The family moved to Chicago soon after her birth. Brooks attended three separate high schools, including Hyde Park High School, an all-white school; Wendell Phillips High School, an African-American school; and finally, Englewood High School, which was integrated. She graduated from Wilson Junior College in 1936.

Gwendolyn Brooks is known for her poetry about the urban experience. Her style ranges from traditional ballads and sonnets to blues rhythm and free verse. Her experimental poetry expresses the problems of everyday life in inner-city neighborhoods. Her first poem, "Eventide" (1930), was published in *American Childhood Magazine* when she was 13 years old. By 1934, she was writing a weekly poetry column called "Shadows and Light" in *The Chicago Defender*, an African-American newspaper.

After winning the 1943 Midwestern Writer's Conference Poetry Award, Brooks published her first book of poetry, *A Street in Bronzeville* (1945). She drew the subjects of the poems in this collection from her experiences in urban Chicago. Her second collection of poems, *Annie Allen*, won the Pulitzer Prize in 1950, making her the first African-American woman to win this prestigious award.

From 1963 until her death, Brooks taught creative writing at various colleges throughout the United States. In 1994, she was named the National Endowment for the Humanities' Jefferson Lecturer, the highest award for humanities given by the U.S. government. In addition, she was Illinois Poet Laureate, a position she held from the time of Carl Sandburg's death in 1968 until her own death from cancer in 2000.

BROWN, HELEN GURLEY

(b. 1922)

Writer, editor. Helen Gurley was born into a poor rural Arkansas family on February 18, 1922. She graduated from Texas State College for Women in 1941 and then took a job as an advertising copywriter. Because of her talent, she progressed quickly in the field, and by 1958, she had won two Frances Holmes Advertising Copywriter awards.

Helen Gurley married David Brown, a movie producer, in 1959. Together, they created the idea for a new type of women's magazine, one that would go beyond the typical women's magazines of the era that focused on cooking and sewing. They planned to focus on issues confronted by the modern "working girl." Lacking the resources to realize this dream, Brown instead devoted her talents to writing a book, *Sex and the Single Girl*. Released in 1962, it became a best-seller, and Brown left her job in advertising.

The Hearst Corporation took notice of Brown's ideas, and in 1965, named her editor-in-chief of its floundering *Cosmopolitan* magazine. The magazine was redesigned to appeal to the 18-to-35-year-old single career woman and included articles about women at work, consumerism, and dating. Under Brown's editorship, *Cosmopolitan*'s circulation rapidly increased to 3 million copies per year, outselling its competitors. Although her editorship ended in 1996, Helen Gurley Brown remains editor-in-chief of *Cosmopolitan* international editions.

See also: Entrepreneurs.

BROWN, RITA MAE (b. 1944)

Writer, women's rights activist. Rita Mae Brown was born in Hanover, Pennsylvania, on November 28, 1944. She was later adopted by Ralph and Julia (Buckingham) Brown, who moved her to Florida. Brown attended Fort Lauderdale High School, where she excelled in both academics and athletics.

Brown entered the University of Florida on a scholarship, which was revoked in 1964 because of her involvement in the **CIVIL RIGHTS** movement and the fact that she was a lesbian. The dean of the college called her "a neurotic, a lesbian, and demented." Unable to pay tuition, Brown hitchhiked to New York City and acquired a scholarship to New York University. There she studied English and the classics, and founded the Student Homophile League. After receiving her B.A. in 1968, she attended the Manhattan School of Visual Arts and became certified in cinematography. She earned her Ph.D. in political science from Federal City College in Washington, D.C., in 1976.

As a women's rights activist, Brown cofounded the first women's center in New York City and was an early officer of the **NATIONAL ORGANIZATION FOR WOMEN** (NOW). However, she was forced to resign from NOW because of her outspokenness on lesbian issues. In response, she cofounded several feminist/lesbian organizations including the Radicallesbians, the Redstockings, and the Furies, the last of which was a female separatist commune. In the 1970s, Brown also worked with the National Gay Task Force and the **NATIONAL WOMEN'S POLITICAL CAUCUS**.

As a writer, Brown has created novels, essays, and screenplays. Like her best-selling novel ***RUBYFRUIT JUNGLE*** (1973), her writing focuses on contemporary feminism, lesbianism, and the Southern identity. Her other works include *A Plain Brown Rapper* (1976), a collection of political essays; *The Slumber Party Massacre* (1982), a film; and the NBC television miniseries *The Long Hot Summer* (1985). Brown makes her home in Charlottesville, Virginia, and lists her cat, Sneaky Pie Brown, as coauthor of some of her works.

BROWNMILLER, SUSAN

(b. 1935)

Journalist, author, and feminist. Susan Brownmiller was born in Brooklyn, New York, on February 15, 1935. She attended Cornell University from 1952 to 1954 and became a writer for several magazines, including *Coronet* and *Newsweek*. She left journalism to join the Student Non-Violent Coordinating Committee (SNCC), which was registering African Americans to vote in the South during the 1960s.

In the the late 1960s, she returned to journalism, working for the *New York Times*, *Vogue*, and *The Nation*, among other publications. She also became active in the feminist movement. In 1975, she published *Against Our Will: Men, Women, and Rape*, an examination of the history of rape that explains how women have been exploited by men over time. In 1999, Brownmiller published *In Our Times: Memoir of a Revolution*, an account of her experiences in the feminist movement. She is a lecturer on sexual assault as well as the women's movement.

BUSH, BARBARA PIERCE

(b. 1925)

First lady (1989–1993), wife of the forty-first U.S. president and mother of the forty-third president. Barbara Pierce was born on June 8, 1925, in New York City, the daughter of a publishing executive. She grew up in Rye, New York, and graduated from Ashley Hall, a boarding school in Charleston, South Carolina. After attending Smith College for one year, she married George Herbert Walker Bush in 1945. They would have six children; one daughter died of leukemia in 1953.

Bush accompanied her husband to his military postings and during his college education and oil industry employment. She supported his political aspirations and moved with him to Washington, D.C., in 1967, after he was elected to Congress. She relocated upon his assignment to various other political posts, including diplomatic liaison to China in 1974.

As the wife of a prominent political leader, Barbara Bush became an active supporter of community service and promoter of volunteerism. She initiated a national literacy program during her husband's eight years (1981–1989) as vice president under Ronald Reagan. After her husband became president in 1989, she established the Barbara Bush Foundation for Family Literacy. In 1992, she became the first wife of a presidential candidate to make a major speech at a party convention.

Her nurturing, empathetic image, and loyalty to her family resulted in her being among the nation's most popular first ladies. Her son George Walker Bush was elected president in 2000, and Bush became the only former first lady to witness her son's inauguration.

BUSH, LAURA LANE WELCH (b. 1946)

First lady, wife of the forty-third U.S. president. Laura Lane Welch was born on November 4, 1946, in Midland, Texas, the daughter of a homebuilder. In 1968, she earned a bachelor's degree in education from Southern Methodist University. In 1973, she completed a master's degree in library science at the University of Texas at Austin. She worked as a teacher and school librarian prior to marrying George W. Bush, an oil executive, in 1977. They have twin daughters.

Laura Bush first campaigned for her husband in his unsuccessful bid for a seat in Congress in 1978. In 1987 the family moved to Washington, D.C., where she helped her husband work on his father's victorious presidential campaign. After the 1988 election, the Bushes relocated to Dallas, where George became the managing partner of a major-league baseball team.

With Laura supporting his return to politics, George W. Bush defeated incumbent Texas Governor Ann Richards in 1994 and was reelected in 1998. As the governor's wife, she was instrumental in promoting the humanities in education and organizing the Texas Book Festival. She was also an active supporter of breast cancer research. In 1998, Laura Bush launched a statewide early-childhood development initiative, emphasizing family literacy and preschool reading programs.

During the 2000 presidential campaign, Bush advised her husband on his speeches and choice of running mate. She campaigned vigorously for the votes of women and arranged for her hus-

Laura Bush is an avid supporter of teaching humanities in education.

band's highly successful appearance on the television talk show, "Oprah."

As first lady, Bush has continued her advocacy of **EDUCATION** and literacy, and introduced Texas themes to entertainment and social events at the White House. She has stated in televised interviews that she does not favor the overturning of ***ROE v. WADE.***

BUSINESS AND INDUSTRY

Women have always worked, but the biggest change in the twentieth century was in the percentage of white mothers in the labor force; black mothers and many immigrant women had long worked the double shift of work and family. A second major change was the emergence of female professionals, the first generation of women graduates.

Women in Industry

In 1900 wages were low and conditions harsh for all workers, male and female. About 5 million women worked, many of them in Southern mills which paid as little as a dollar a day. Others worked in sweatshops and laundries. Industrial accidents were common: 146 women died in 1911 in the **TRIANGLE SHIRTWAIST COMPANY FIRE** in New York City. Labor union membership was low, partly because women were denied apprenticeships and the **AMERICAN FEDERATION OF LABOR** did not recruit unskilled or semiskilled workers. Efforts by the National Women's Trade Union League helped little in this regard. Although women were active in some strikes, notably the Lawrence "Bread and Roses" strike of 1912, efforts at pay parity were unsuccessful, and reformers tried another approach, namely **PROTECTIVE LABOR LEGISLATION**: a Supreme Court decision in 1908, ***MULLER V. OREGON,*** limited women's working hours and regulated conditions.

During the **WORLD WAR I** labor shortage, women moved into men's jobs and received equal pay. These gains were short-lived, however, and most munitions workers either returned home, took low-paying unskilled factory jobs, or moved into the service sector. Most black women were still confined to housework. During the **GREAT DEPRESSION** some married women were dismissed, but many others became the family breadwinner if their husbands were unable to find work. Between 1940 and 1945, during **WORLD WAR II** the number of employed women rose from 14 million (26 percent of the total workforce) to 19 million (36 percent). Almost one quarter were married, compared with 15 percent in 1940. Women took over "male" jobs, and "Rosie the Riveter" working in the shipyard became a popular icon.

Although many were laid off in 1945, by 1951 the number of women in the workforce was higher than it was at the end of the war though almost 75 percent of them were in unskilled or semiskilled traditionally "female" jobs in textiles and jewelry assembly work.

WOMEN'S FIRSTS

Born to wealthy parents in Oakland and raised to be a "lady" Lillian Moller Gilbreth (1878–1972) became world famous as the "First Lady of Engineering." Part of the scientific management movement, she has been described as the "human face" of Taylorism, a system of time and motion study.

In 1900 she was the first woman to speak at graduation at Berkeley, started on a doctorate, but abandoned it to marry Frank Bunker Gilbreth. She bore 13 children over the next 17 years. Meanwhile, she found time to write two doctoral dissertations on the application of psychology to management problems and partnered with her husband in studying work and training industrial workers.

Gilbreth combined career and family to an extraordinary degree. After her husband's sudden death in 1924, she put her 11 surviving children through college. She continued to work until she was 90. She headed her own consultancy firm, Gilbreth Inc., and applied motion study to numerous places where women worked—kitchens, fast-food outlets, and department stores and offices as well as factories. During World War II she helped keep "Rosie the Riveter" fit to work by organizing calisthenics classes. She served five presidents on commissions dealing with civil defense, war production, aging, and rehabilitation of the physically handicapped. She was the first female professor of management at Purdue University, and received 23 honorary degrees and numerous gold medals from engineering societies worldwide.

Women in Business

Until the 1960s the term *businesswoman* usually denoted a clerical worker, a telephone operator, or a department store saleswoman. Such "pink-collar" jobs became reserved for women and were relatively low paying. Only in the last decades of the twentieth century did women achieve some kind of parity of access to corporate and managerial jobs, though the **"GLASS CEILING"** and the "mommy track" prevent a proportionate number from reaching the top.

Though most businesses were run by men, a few women became very successful. They included African Americans, such as Maggie Lena Walker, a banker, and Madame C. J. Walker (no relation), who manufactured hair products for African-American women. They also included Jewish immigrants and their daughters, such as Estee Lauder, the cosmetics tycoon, and Lena Himmelstein Bryant, who headed Lane Bryant, a producer of women's clothing. As three of these four examples suggest, women found it easier to compete in "feminized" areas of the economy. Similarly some jobs in commerce and industry became the province of women, notably personnel work, public relations, advertising, and department store buying. By century's end women ran a majority of small businesses, and a few women led their own large firms. They include **OPRAH WINFREY** in entertainment, **MURIEL SIEBERT** in finance, and **KATHARINE GRAHAM** in publishing.

The **WOMEN'S BUREAU**, created in 1920, gathered statistics and agitated for protective legislation; although **NEW DEAL** agencies did little specifically for women, postwar administrations supported the principle of equal pay. **TITLE VII** of the 1964 Civil Rights Act prohibited discrimination based on sex. President Lyndon B. Johnson then created the **EQUAL EMPLOYMENT OPPORTUNITY COMMISSION** (EEOC). Its lack of success in promoting equality for women contributed to the formation of the **NATIONAL ORGANIZATION FOR WOMEN** (NOW) in 1966.

The ratio of women's to men's earnings remains low in almost all sectors of the economy. This reflects women's continuing domestic responsibilities, their choice to work part time (which often means loss of benefits), and gender discrimination.

See also: Arden, Elizabeth; Ash, Mary Kay; Division of Labor, Sexual; Earhart, Amelia; Entrepreneurs; Equal Credit Opportunity Act, 1974; Equal Pay Act of 1963 and 1972; National Federation of Business and Professional Women's Clubs; Perkins, Frances; Petersen, Esther; President's Commission on the Status of Women.

Jane Lancaster

C

CABLE ACT

Passed by Congress in 1922, it entitled women to their own rights of citizenship, independent of the citizenship of their husbands. Also known as the Married Women's Act, the Cable Act repealed a 1907 law that stated that women acquired their husband's nationality on marriage. Under the 1907 law, a woman born in the United States forfeited her citizenship if she married a non–United States citizen. With the Cable Act, women could not lose their citizenship on marriage. Furthermore, the act loosened the naturalization process for immigrant women. If a husband obtained citizenship, his wife simply had to petition for citizenship. She did not have to follow the entire naturalization process.

The Cable Act was the fruit of lobbying efforts by the **LEAGUE OF WOMEN VOTERS**. Dedicated to the legal protection of women and children, league leaders, such as Maud Wood Park, advocated and obtained a number of significant pieces of legislation in the 1920s, including the **MATERNITY AND INFANCY PROTECTION ACT** of 1921 and the Cable Act. Together, these laws protected married women and authorized federal aid for mothers and children.

CADET NURSES CORPS

A program established in 1943 by Congress to encourage young women between the ages of 17 and 35 to enter nursing schools. At the time, more than 20 percent of the country's nurses were in the armed forces. Consequently, there was a tremendous shortage of nurses for the civilian population. To ease this shortage, Congress passed the Bolton Act, which provided federal funds for tuition, books, monthly stipends, and uniforms for women who enrolled in undergraduate nursing schools. In addition to providing more nurses, the program changed the face of nursing education by requiring nursing schools to upgrade their curricula and facilities to meet federal standards. The Cadet Nurses Corps was administered by the U.S. Public Health Service and ended in 1949.

CALDERONE, MARY STEICHEN (1904–1998)

Physician, writer, and crusader for sex education. Mary Steichen was born on July 1, 1904, in New York City. Her father was the great photographer Edward Steichen and her uncle was the poet Carl Sandburg. Steichen graduated from Vassar College in 1925 and became a stage actress. She eventually decided to pursue a career in medicine and received her medical degree from the University of Rochester in 1939.

As a physician, Calderone served as medical director of Planned Parenthood–World Population from 1953 to 1964. In 1954 she cofounded the Sexuality Information and Education Council of the United States (SIECUS) and served as its executive director from 1964 to 1982. The organization distributed materials on contraception and sex education. Calderone strongly believed that young people should understand their own sexuality, and that with adequate sex education in school they might avoid many unwanted pregnancies.

Calderone published the *Manual of Family Planning and Contraceptive Practice* in 1970 and *Talking with Your Child About Sex: Answers for Children from Birth to Puberty* in 1983. She died on October 24, 1998.

CALDICOTT, HELEN BROINOWSKI (b. 1938)

Physician and antinuclear activist. Helen Mary Broinowski was born in Melbourne, Australia. In 1956, she was among the first women to be accepted to the Medical School at the University of Adelaide, where she specialized in pediatrics. After graduation, she married William Caldicott, a doctor.

In 1966, the Caldicotts moved to Massachusetts so Helen Caldicott could work at Harvard Medical Center, treating children with cystic fibrosis. In 1975, she returned to Australia and founded the Cystic Fibrosis Clinic in Adelaide.

During the 1970s, Caldicott led the opposition to the testing of nuclear weapons in the atmosphere. She returned to the United States in the late 1970s and helped organize Physicians for Social Responsibility, which later became International Physicians for the Prevention of Nuclear War. For its work alerting the world to the dangers of nuclear weapons, the organization was awarded the Nobel Peace Prize in 1985.

Caldicott has written several books, including *Nuclear Madness* (1979) and *If You Love This Planet: A Plan to Heal the Earth* (1992). During the 1990s, Dr. Caldicott returned to the United States and continues to lecture.

CALIFORNIA FEDERAL SAVINGS AND LOAN v. GUERRA

A 1987 U.S. Supreme Court case that helped to end discrimination against pregnant women in the workplace. Mark Guerra was the director of the California Department of Fair Employment and Housing. In 1982 a receptionist at the California Federal Savings and Loan Association (Cal Fed) took a disability leave because she was pregnant. When she later notified Cal Fed that she was able to return to work, she was told that her job had been filled and no similar jobs were available. She filed a complaint with the state's Department of Fair Employment and Housing, charging that Cal Fed had violated the California Fair Employment and Housing Act. This act requires employers to provide leave and reinstatement to employees on maternity leave.

Before action was taken on the complaint, Cal Fed went to federal district court, arguing that the California law was inconsistent with **TITLE**

VII of the U.S. Civil Rights Act of 1964, which prohibits discrimination based on sex, and with the Pregnancy Discrimination Act, which says that sex discrimination includes discrimination based on pregnancy. Cal Fed argued that if discrimination based on pregnancy was against federal law, then any law (such as the California law) that required Cal Fed to treat pregnant women as a separate, distinct class of persons contradicted federal law. The district court agreed with Cal Fed, but the court of appeals reversed the district court. In 1987 the U.S. Supreme Court affirmed that reversal, saying that the two laws were not inconsistent. In its decision, the Court restated one of the goals of Title VII: "to achieve equality of employment opportunities and remove barriers that have operated in the past to favor an identifiable group of . . . employees over other employees." The *Cal Fed* case made it clear to employers that they could not discriminate against pregnant women.

CALLAS, MARIA (1923–1977)

Opera singer. Cecilia Sophia Anna Maria Kalogeropoulos was born in New York City to a Greek immigrant family on December 2, 1923. She returned to Greece with her mother in 1937 and soon afterward began her operatic training at the Elvira de Hidalgo in Athens, appearing in the operetta *Bocaccio* in 1940. Two years later she appeared in Giacomo Puccini's opera *Tosca* at the Athens opera.

During the 1940s she sang in the Venice opera, performing works by Richard Wagner. On April 21, 1949, she married Giovanni Battista Meneghini in Verona, Italy. In 1950, she sang the leading role in Giuseppe Verdi's opera *Aida* at Milan's famous La Scala opera house. During the 1950s, Callas performed in the United States, singing the lead roles in operas such as *Madame Butterfly* and *Norma*.

In 1959, Maria separated from her husband and began a nine-year relationship with Aristotle Onassis, the Greek shipping magnate. Meanwhile, she continued her singing career, performing at La Scala and the Paris opera during the 1960s. In 1970, a reported suicide attempt halted her career; however, she may have only taken an overdose of sleeping pills by mistake. She began a comeback in 1973, singing in Germany, the United States, and Japan. Callas died on September 16, 1977. She is considered one of the great opera sopranos of the twentieth century.

CAMP FIRE GIRLS

National, nonsectarian community and service organization for girls. In 1910, in Thetford, Vermont, William Chauncy Langdon organized a group he called the Camp Fire Girls as an alternative to the Boy Scouts. At the same time, Charlotte and Luther Halsey Gulick expanded the vacation they ran each year for their four daughters at Lake Sebago, Maine, into a summer camp. The camp was called "WoHeLo," a word Charlotte Gulick created out of the first two letters of each of the principles she wanted the camp to embody: work, health, and love.

The Gulicks and Langdon met in a group with other educators and decided to form the Camp Fire Girls, which was officially incorporated in 1912 in Washington, D.C., with Luther Gulick serving as the first president. They chose the name Camp Fire Girls because a camp fire symbolized the foundation of the first community and the centrality of domestic life. The group emphasizes family, youth leadership, community, youth–adult partnership, and inclusiveness through a program of youth education and outdoor activity.

In 1954, the Camp Fire Girls issued a statement of its commitment to diversity and inclusiveness, and in 1975, the organization expanded to include boys. Today, the Camp Fire Boys and Girls serve approximately 650,000 youth each year, nearly half of which are boys. The Camp Fire Girls and Boys do not discriminate on the basis of gender, race, religion, or sexual orientation. The organization is headquartered in Kansas City, Missouri.

CANNON, ANNIE JUMP (1863–1941)

Preeminent woman astronomer, known for her work on the classification of stellar spectra. Annie Jump Cannon was born on December 11, 1863, in Dover, Delaware, the daughter of a politician. Her mother encouraged her to stargaze by converting the family attic into an observatory. Cannon studied astronomical research methods at Wellesley College, graduating in 1884.

A decade later, after devoting herself to the piano and photography, Cannon returned to

Wellesley as a researcher in the physics laboratory. Studying astronomy at Radcliffe College with Edward C. Pickering, director of the Harvard Observatory, Cannon was hired in 1896 to assist in the study of stellar spectra.

Based on studies of photographic spectra obtained by Pickering, Cannon developed the Harvard classification, which was based on spectral colors, temperature, and brightness determined by the radiation and wavelengths emitted by the stars. Cannon demonstrated that the spectra of stars could be classified into a continuous sequence of categories. Her system defined ten categories identified by letters instead of numerals. The International Solar Union accepted Cannon's classification system for standard use by observatories, and leading astronomers from around the world visited her to learn the methodology.

An important aspect of Cannon's work was the classification of some 350,000 stars in both the northern and southern hemispheres. Catalogued in *The Henry Draper Catalogue* (1924) and the two-volume *Henry Draper Extension* (1925–49), her classifications provided accurate, consistent information that helped elevate astronomy from amateur to professional status. She also discovered 300 variable stars, five novas, and a double star.

In 1931, Cannon became the first woman to receive the National Academy of Science's prestigious Draper Medal. In 1933, she established the Annie Jump Cannon Prize of the American Astronomical Society to support research by women astronomers. And in 1938, she was named the William Cranch Bond Astronomer at Harvard, with the rank of professor. Cannon died on April 13, 1941, in Cambridge, Massachusetts.

See also: Science and Technology.

CARPENTER, CANDICE (b. 1952)

A cofounder of iVillage.com. iVillage.com is a website that publishes articles on subjects of interest to women 18 and over, provides opportunities for women to communicate with one another through the Internet, and provides access to experts via online resources. With the site's launch in 1995, Carpenter became a media innovator for women's interests and education in technology, and a leader in Internet business ventures. Prior to iVillage.com, Carpenter was president of Q2, an arm of the QVC, Inc., shopping channel. She was also an executive with Time Warner and won an Emmy Award for the 1995 NBC documentary series *Lost Civilizations*.

Carpenter grew up in Florida, received a bachelor's degree in human biology at Stanford University and an MBA at Harvard Business School. While at Stanford, she became an instructor at the National Outdoor Leadership School in Landor, Wyoming. Carpenter is a single mother with two daughters.

CARSON, RACHEL (1907–1964)

A marine biologist, writer, and environmentalist. Carson's most famous and influential work is *Silent Spring* (1962). This provocative study of the dangers of certain chemical insecticides is generally acknowledged to have stimulated the modern environmental movement. The book aroused worldwide concern for nature, demonstrating that DDT and other chemicals that were being widely used to enhance agricultural productivity were poisoning America's lakes, rivers, and oceans and ultimately affecting water supplies for humans.

Carson grew up in the small town of Springdale, Pennsylvania. She graduated from the Pennsylvania College for Women (now Chatham College), studied at Woods Hole Marine Biological Laboratory, and received a master's degree in zoology from The Johns Hopkins University. Carson began her career as a professor of zoology at the University of Maryland from 1931 to 1936. She was hired by the U.S. Bureau of Fisheries to write radio scripts and also wrote feature articles on natural history for the *Baltimore Sun*. Carson eventually became editor-in-chief of all publications for the U.S. Fish and Wildlife Service and published several books on the sea—*Under the Sea Wind* (1941), *The Sea Around Us* (1951), for which she was awarded the 1952 National Book Award in nonfiction, and *The Edge of the Sea* (1955).

Shy by nature, Carson devoted much of her writing to teaching people about the wonders of nature. When she realized that aerial spraying of DDT had killed birds in a neighbor's sanctuary, Carson thoroughly researched the impact of chemicals on the environment and became alarmed at the results. She was publicly criticized and attacked by the chemical industry, agricultural scientists, and some government officials for her "alarmist" writings. She died before seeing DDT banned from use in the United States, but because of Carson, "environment" and "ecology" became household words.

CARTER, ROSALYNN SMITH (b. 1927)

First lady of the United States (1977–1981) and wife of James Earl "Jimmy" Carter, Jr., the nation's thirty-ninth president. Rosalynn Smith was born in Plains, Georgia, on August 18, 1927, the oldest of four children. Her father died when she was 13, and she helped her mother, who had become a dressmaker, to support the family. In 1944, Rosalynn enrolled in Southwestern College in Americus, Georgia, where she met Jimmy Carter in 1945. The couple was married in 1946.

Since Jimmy Carter was a naval officer, the couple were stationed in different parts of the world. After the death of his father, Carter left the navy in 1953 to run the family agricultural business. Rosalynn handled the finances.

Rosalynn Carter helped her husband win a seat in the Georgia Senate in 1962 and campaigned with him when he successfully ran for governor of Georgia in 1970. She also delivered speeches on the campaign trail in 1976, when Carter ran for president. As first lady, Rosalynn Carter strengthened the nation's commitment to the performing arts and programs to help the mentally ill and the elderly.

The Carters returned to Plains in 1981, where Rosalynn Carter wrote her autobiography, *First Lady from Plains*, published in 1984. She has also written *Helping Yourself Help Others* (1995). Rosalynn Carter is vice chairperson of The Carter Center in Atlanta, Georgia, which promotes world peace.

CATHER, WILLA (1873–1947)

An accomplished muckraking journalist and feminist author. Born on December 7, 1873, in Virginia, Cather moved with her family to Red Cloud, Nebraska, in 1884. Later in life, her experiences in Virginia and on the frontier of Nebraska would provide settings for most of her novels. As a young woman, Cather found that she could express herself best through writing. Not only did she become an important magazine writer and editor, but she also won a Pulitzer Prize.

While a student at the University of Nebraska, Cather wrote and edited the *Hesperian*, the university's literary magazine. As part of the increasing number of women attending colleges and universities in the late 1800s, she used her education to become a social critic of both industrialization and the destruction of the U.S. frontier.

After graduating in 1895, Cather moved to Pittsburgh, Pennsylvania, to become the editor of a magazine for women, *Home Monthly*. In 1901 she began teaching high school English, and in 1903 her first book, *The Troll Garden,* was published. In 1906, Cather began writing for *McClure's*, a New York monthly magazine dedicated to exposing social inequalities, dangerous working conditions, and mistreatment of workers. Cather's writing abilities and her knack for recognizing a good story helped her rise to the position of managing editor with *McClure's*.

Willa Cather, journalist and author, wrote novels about pioneering and independent women.

Although Cather enjoyed working for *McClure's*, she disliked urban living. "I like trees," she told one reporter, "because they seem more resigned to the way they have to live than other things do." In 1912, she left *McClure's* and New York City to become a full-time novelist. Over the next ten years, she published several highly acclaimed books, including *O Pioneers!* (1913), *My Antonia* (1918), the Pulitzer-Prize winning *One of Ours* (1922), and *A Lost Lady* (1923). In these novels, Cather created pioneering and independent women who strove to tame the prairies. By placing women as central figures in the West, she showed how women were critical in agriculture and westward expansion. In an era when many people viewed women as weak and passive, Cather's strong-willed and persistent heroines controlled their homes and, through perseverance, mastered the land.

Cather's final novels, *Death Comes for the Archbishop* (1927), *Shadows on the Rock* (1931), and *Sapphira and the Slave Girl* (1940), described the pioneering spirit of French and English travelers to North America. Cather's writing earned her honorary doctoral degrees from some of the most prestigious institutions in the United States, including the University of Michigan, the University of California, Columbia, Princeton, and Yale. In the 1940s, poor health hindered her writing, and on April 24, 1947, she died of a cerebral hemorrhage in New York City. One obituary simply and eloquently summed up Cather's life in a way that she likely would have appreciated: "She was an artist in telling a story simply."

CHAVEZ-THOMPSON, LINDA (b. 1944)

Labor union activist. Chavez-Thompson was born to parents who worked as sharecroppers in Lubbock, Texas. One of eight children, she toiled along with her siblings in the cotton fields, dropping out of school in the ninth grade to help her parents support the family. At 19, she married her first husband and cleaned houses for a living.

Chavez-Thompson joined the Laborers' International Union in 1967 and served as secretary and as a union representative for the Hispanic-American members. In 1971, she became a representative of the American Federation of State, County, and Municipal Employees (AFSCME) and later rose to the position of vice president, directing the union's activities in seven western states considered unfriendly to labor. In 1995, Chavez-Thompson became the executive vice president of the AFL-CIO, the highest-ranking woman in the labor movement. She was appointed by President Bill Clinton to serve on the President's Initiative on Race, and in 1998 was elected vice chair of the Democratic National Committee. In her leadership position, Chavez-Thompson worked to forge closer ties between the labor movement and women and minorities.

Chavez lived in San Antonio, Texas, prior to moving to Washington, D.C., in 1998. She is a widow and has two children.

CHICANA

A term that refers to Mexican-American women living in the United States. (A Mexican-American male would be called a "Chicano.") Originally an informal expression in both English and Spanish, it became a term of ethnic pride in the context of literary and political movements of the 1960s and 1970s. Because of its strong political associations, Mexican Americans do not uniformly accept the term "Chicana".

Chicana is therefore not synonymous with Latina (short for *latinoamericana*, meaning person from Latin America) or with Hispanic (from the Latin word for "Spain," meaning a Spanish-speaking person).

In 1972 the National Association for Chicana and Chicano Studies (NACCS) was founded to encourage academic research and advance political awareness and engagement in the Mexican-American community. Prominent Chicanas include political journalist, television commentator, and former member of the U.S. Commission on Civil Rights Linda Chavez; **Dolores Fernandez Huerta**, cofounder of the United Farm Workers; and artist, scholar, and curator Amalia Mesa-Bains.

CHILD CARE

Working mothers and the need for child care have been closely associated in the United States. Although both grew much more common during the twentieth century, the nation has remained ambivalent over both.

The nation's first day-care centers appeared in the mid-nineteenth century in Eastern cities. They were founded by wealthy women concerned over the plight of poor children, whose mothers often worked outside the home.

Child Care for Impoverished Mothers

Day nurseries grew rapidly around the turn of the twentieth century, as immigrants from Southern and Eastern Europe flocked to large cities. The founders of these institutions hoped to take the children of poor, working mothers off the street so that they could learn, as one philanthropist put it, the "habits of truthfulness, honesty, and cleanliness." Indeed, staff members of day nurseries inspected their charges daily, and many also bathed them and changed their clothes. They investigated each family that applied and were especially concerned that mothers worked only out of dire economic necessity. As these practices suggest, the well-to-do women in charge of these institutions generally distrusted the mothers whose children they cared for. They also, as historian Sonya Michel points out, tended to see child care as a "temporary expedient" to be discarded once families attained a state of "normalcy," with mothers at home rather than at work. African-American club women also started day nurseries, but were more accustomed to and less critical of employed mothers than were their white counterparts.

Although the day nurseries were free, most impoverished mothers both detected and resented the staff's criticism of their parenting. Working mothers usually relied on family, neighbors, and daughters over the age of six to care for their young children.

Progressive reformers of the early twentieth century proposed a different solution for working mothers: **MOTHERS' PENSIONS**. Though the program was poorly funded and administered, the federal government began paying mothers whose husbands had died or deserted them so that these women could stay home to raise their children.

Growing numbers of well-to-do mothers, on the other hand, were concluding that their preschool children required exposure to child experts. They paid to send their sons and daughters to nursery schools, where psychologists and other professionals both molded children and advised mothers.

Nurseries expanded during the **GREAT DEPRESSION** and **WORLD WAR II**, but largely from necessity. Increasing numbers of mothers worked during the 1930s as many husbands lost their jobs. The federal government began involving itself with child care by funding Emergency Nursery Schools, which employed out-of-work teachers. These institutions were intended to be educational, but economic need was the primary criterion for admission. An acute shortage of wartime workers prompted the federal government to advocate that women workers place their children in nurseries during World War II, and many women—able to make a good wage for the first and last time in their lives—heeded the call. Although day-care facilities expanded dramatically, most working mothers had to scramble. Finding adequate child care was especially difficult for women who left home to take jobs in distant cities. Some African-American mothers tried to solve the problem by leaving their children with relatives in the South.

The Struggle for Universal Child Care

Many working mothers returned to their homes after World War II, but many did not. Such mothers were the first to advocate for what historian Elizabeth Rose terms "a *right* to day care." Increasing numbers of wives and mothers were working to increase their families' standard of living. Some public child-care centers in large cities responded to this pressure by staying open, but the great majority were closed by the early 1950s. In an era in which both the birthrate and the cult of motherhood was increasing, working mothers and public day care enjoyed little public support.

Child care was transformed in the last four decades of the twentieth century as women flooded into the workplace. In 1950 about 12 percent of mothers with children under age six worked for wages. By the late 1980s more than half did. This led to an explosion of all sorts of day care: large centers run by nonprofits or private businesses, small operations located in homes, and worksite centers operated by large employers. Only care by family members declined.

Still, the federal government balked at providing universal day care. In 1965 it began Head Start, an ambitious program that functioned as a preschool for children at risk of doing poorly in elementary school. The federal government also allowed parents to deduct child-care expenses from their incomes but was hesitant about instituting a comprehensive program.

Feminists in particular urged universal child care as a way of promoting women's economic and social rights. But they were opposed by many members of the religious right, who encouraged mothers of young children to remain in the home.

Conservatives were eager to put some children in day care: the sons and daughters of welfare mothers. Welfare reform in the 1990s forced growing numbers of mothers into the workplace and their children into child care. Elizabeth Jones, an African-American single mother of three children in the District of Columbia, had been on welfare for nine years when she began working outside the home. By the end of the twentieth century she was successful but logging so many hours to keep her family's finances afloat that during most days she saw her children only in passing and found it "hard not to think sometimes about a life where I could have real time" with them.

As the twenty-first century began, the nation's day-care system was a massive and diverse patchwork of programs. The quality of care varied greatly. Well-to-do parents hired nannies or sent their children to facilities staffed by well-trained professionals and characterized by low teacher-to-student ratios. But most families had to rely upon overcrowded centers or homes staffed by poorly trained providers. Meanwhile the proportion of children who spend their days in child care continues to grow.

David Peterson del Mar

FURTHER READING

Michel, Sonya. *Children's Interests/Mothers' Rights: The Shaping of America's Child Care Policy*. New Haven: Yale University Press, 1999.

Rose, Elizabeth. *A Mother's Job: The History of Day Care, 1890–1960*. New York: Oxford University Press, 1999.

WOMEN'S FIRSTS

Arthur Wright, a Baptist minister, reacted to segregation by building a park for African-American children behind his church in Bennettsville, South Carolina. His youngest daughter Marian (b. 1939) took note and would become one of the nation's leading advocates for children.

Marian Wright was an excellent student. She was valedictorian of her class at Spellman College and then got her law degree at Yale University in 1963, later becoming the first black woman to pass the Mississippi bar. Long involved in the civil rights movement, she soon put her law degree to work in the South, serving as an attorney for the National Association for the Advancement of Colored People (NAACP). In 1968 she moved to Washington, D.C., to work on Martin Luther King's Poor People's March, and married Peter Edelman, with whom she had three children.

As the civil rights movement declined, Wright Edelman turned her energies to poor children. She advocated for Head Start and founded and headed the Children's Defense Fund, which became the nation's leading lobbying group for impoverished children.

Wright Edelman believes passionately that government can and ought to play a role in improving the lives of poor families. Sharply critical of federal budget priorities and bloated defense budgets, she has been a tireless advocate for expanded child care, prenatal care, and a wide variety of other anti-poverty programs.

Among Wright Edelman's many honors is the Albert Schweitzer Humanitarian Prize and the Presidential Medal of Freedom, which she received in 2000. She has written five books and remains a powerful and articulate advocate for people too young to speak for themselves.

CHILD CUSTODY

Until the middle of the nineteenth century, fathers were almost always granted custody when couples divorced. But by 1920, the situation had reversed, and women were usually granted custody of children in divorce situations. Many factors influenced this gradual change. Family life had undergone profound changes as a result of the INDUSTRIAL REVOLUTION (see Volume 2). Whereas fathers once worked either at home or close to home, they increasingly worked long days in factories far from home, leaving mothers in charge of the domestic sphere. Judges began to grant custody to women, especially when the children were young.

Beginning in 1920, the right to vote gave women an enhanced legal status, which, in turn, led to legislation that favored women in custody cases. Freudian psychology, which stressed the importance of the mother's role, had a significant impact on social philosophy beginning in the 1940s, further strengthening mothers' claims to their children in custody cases.

The trend began to change again in the 1960s, as divorce rates began to climb. Fathers began to claim that the automatic preference accorded to mothers constituted sex discrimination; women began to enter the workforce in greater numbers; and feminists asserted that parenting should be shared by fathers and mothers alike. Laws favoring women in custody cases were replaced by gender-neutral laws. The Uniform Marriage and Divorce Act of 1970 established a new standard for custody decisions. Custody decisions were no longer made based on who was the primary caregiver but on the basis of the "best interests" of the child. Also in the 1970s fathers began to campaign for joint custody. In 1979, California, Kansas, and Oregon enacted laws that made joint custody an option in divorce cases. By 1991 more than 40 states had laws that not only allowed but actually preferred joint custody. In practice, most divorced parents who have joint custody actually have joint legal custody but physical custody arrangements in which the children actually live more than half the time with one parent, usually the mother.

Some feminists have begun to question the current preference for joint custody. Women, who usually earn less than men, are often disadvantaged by such arrangements, since **CHILD SUPPORT** may be limited or not granted at all. It can be confusing for children to move back and forth between two "homes," especially as they grow older. Sometimes joint custody arrangements that are imposed on parents by courts, actually increase conflict between parents, which can be damaging to children.

CHILD LABOR

Work for children that harms or exploits them. Until the beginning of the twentieth century, child labor was common and expected. Children helped their parents with farming and household chores and were apprenticed to trades at very young ages. With the advent of the **INDUSTRIAL REVOLUTION**, children were sent to work in textile mills and factories.

Although social reformers began to question the wisdom of child labor in the mid-nineteenth century, it was not until the beginning of the twentieth century that concerted efforts were made to eliminate the practice. In 1904, the National Child Labor Committee (NCLC) formed in an effort to end child labor. This group hired Lewis Hine to photograph "breaker boys" working in mines, "newsies" peddling papers on city streets, and tiny children working in cotton fields in the South. Through publicizing these pictures, writing pamphlets, and lobbying, the NCLC influenced many state legislatures to pass laws restricting child labor.

Federal child labor legislation was enacted in 1916 and 1918 but were quickly declared unconstitutional by the Supreme Court, because judges felt that regulation of child labor should be done at the state level.

The first successful federal legislation prohibiting child labor was the Fair Labor Standards Act of 1938 which prohibited children under the age of 16 from working in manufacturing and mining.

While this law substantially eliminated child labor in the United States, problems still exist. The children of migrant farm workers work long hours and are directly exposed to dangerous pesticides. And the children of recent immigrants still labor in the garment industry, working at home in an effort to circumvent the law.

In the early 1900s, child labor was still prevalent in the United States.

CHILD SUPPORT

In earlier centuries, the issue of child support centered on illegitimate children. Communities pressured men to marry women who were pregnant, precisely so the children would not become burdens on the community. By the beginning of the twentieth century, most states attempted to deal with the financial problem of illegitimate children by criminalizing desertion and nonsupport. Even with strict laws, however, few fathers were successfully prosecuted for nonsupport, and most illegitimate children of poor mothers eventually became wards of the state. When **Aid to Dependent Children** was adopted as part of the Social Security Act in 1935, Congress initially regarded the program as assistance to children whose fathers had died and the law allowed states to determine eligibility requirements. Many states withheld aid based on the so-called moral character of the mother, which left many illegitimate children without aid. Some states also withheld aid if there was a man living in the house, on the assumption that a mother's current boyfriend was obligated to support her children whether he was the father or not. In 1968, however, the Supreme Court invalidated such state-imposed barriers to aid, stating that "immorality and illegitimacy should be dealt with through rehabilitative measures rather than measures that punish dependent children." The court also held that states could not use the income of a man in the household who was not the father of the children to deny aid to the children. As barriers to aid were relaxed, lawmakers began to strengthen legislation to ensure that absent fathers paid child support.

A similar process occurred with respect to court-ordered child support following a divorce. Early in the twentieth century, when women began to be awarded **child custody**, few men were were obliged to pay child support. Many courts reasoned that a father who was "deprived" of the "services" of his children was not obliged to support those children. As divorce became more common, courts began to order child support in cases where they once might have ordered alimony. By 1986, however, it had become clear that children in America were increasingly living in poverty, that these poor children were likely to be living in single-parent families, usually headed by a woman, and that the failure of noncustodial parents, often fathers, to pay child support was part of the problem. It was also clear that courts were not ordering noncustodial parents to pay enough in support. By the late 1990s, courts were increasingly using a model to determine support payments that tried to maintain something like a predivorce standard of living for children. Organizations such as Association for Children for Enforcement of Support (ACES) have helped custodial parents, often mothers, collect back child support. Federal laws now help to track and punish parents who do not pay court-ordered support. As part of the 1996 welfare reform law, a Directory of New Hires was established to help match delinquent parents with wage records. The Deadbeat Parents Punishment Act of 1998 made it a felony to cross state or county lines to evade child support. Willfully failing to pay child support for more than two years was also made a felony.

Also beginning in the 1990s, men's groups mounted campaigns to change how child support is awarded, claiming that men are disadvantaged by the current system. Men's groups advocate "shared parenting" as preferable for children, but it is also increasingly used as a way of avoiding the obligation to pay child support. Men's groups also claim that failure to pay child support is most often a result of inability to pay—either because the awards are unreasonable or because the noncustodial parent is unemployed or poorly paid.

See also: Child Custody.

CHILDREN'S BUREAU

A federal agency designed to collect and publish research on public policy issues concerning children and families. Established in 1912, the Children's Bureau is the oldest federal agency serving children. Today part of the Department of Health and Human Services, its mission is to help states strengthen families and protect children by providing grants to prevent child abuse and neglect and by funding foster care and adoption programs.

The bureau hired women to conduct surveys and analyze data for its research projects. Benefiting from an entire generation of women who graduated from college as well as graduate programs—a first in U.S. **education**—the bureau has the distinction of being the first federal

TRAILBLAZERS

Julia Clifford Lathrop (1858-1932), the first head of the Children's Bureau (and the first woman appointed by a president to head a federal bureau) grew up in Rockford, Illinois, the eldest of five children. After graduating from Vassar College in 1880, she worked as a secretary in her father's law office, but at 32, in 1890, she joined JANE ADDAMS (see Volume 2) at the newly founded HULL HOUSE (see Volume 2), where she lived and worked for 20 years. In 1893 she was appointed to the Illinois Board of Charities and undertook a detailed study of county farms and almshouses throughout the state. This experience led her to campaign vigorously against the grouping together in state institutions of the young and the old, the physically and the mentally ill, and to work to improve the caliber of staff in such institutions. In 1903 she helped to organize the Chicago Institute of Social Science (later the School of Social Service Administration of the University of Chicago). Lathrop also helped create the world's first juvenile court system, in Cook County, Illinois, and helped to found the Immigrants' Protective League.

After President Taft appointed her to the Children's Bureau in 1912, Lathrop worked tirelessly with her staff of 15 to investigate the incidence and causes of infant mortality and to ensure that all births were registered through birth certificates. Reappointed by President Wilson, she commissioned studies on CHILD LABOR, juvenile delinquency, and MOTHER'S PENSIONS, and worked in support of the Sheppard-Towner MATERNITY AND INFANCY PROTECTION ACT.

Lathrop resigned from the Children's Bureau in 1921 because of ill health. She died in Rockford, Illinois, on April 15, 1932.

agency headed and staffed by professional women. The first director, Julia Lathrop, and her successor, GRACE ABBOTT, had earned advanced degrees and had gained experience in social research during their stay at HULL HOUSE (see Volume 2) in Chicago.

Three major initiatives in the early years of the bureau's existence demonstrate the applications of social research to policy. The first supported efforts to reduce infant and maternal mortality; the second focused on child labor; and the third—the nationwide campaign to register births—became a standard public health responsibility.

The results of bureau research were published as pamphlets to educate women in new scientific knowledge about hygiene and nutrition. These pamphlets were influential in the passage of the Sheppard-Towner Act of 1921, which provided for state programs to disseminate information about nutrition and hygiene, to train midwives, and to provide visiting nurse services to pregnant women and new mothers. The bureau's 1914 pamphlet "Infant Care" became the best-selling government publication ever. From 1912 to 1930, rates of infant death were reduced by half, in large part due to the efforts of the bureau.

The bureau also enforced the Keating-Owen Act (1916), which limited CHILD LABOR. This involvement angered some poor women, who felt that their families' survival depended on the financial contribution of children.

During the Depression of the 1930s, the bureau played a crucial role in the push to include AID TO DEPENDENT CHILDREN (ADC) within the Social Security Act. The bureau had provided parties interested in the MOTHERS' PENSIONS programs with volumes of research when it was a local and state program. This information was applied to NEW DEAL initiatives for impoverished children. The Children's Bureau also helped to secure funding to help states provide maternity services to the wives of military men and to provide grants to universities to help them establish public health programs.

CISNEROS, SANDRA (b. 1954)

Chicana novelist and poet whose writing reflects her identity as a woman and an Hispanic. Cisneros was the only daughter in a family of seven children. She was born in Chicago, but her parents shuttled the family between the north and Mexico City. Cisneros often felt isolated, and found companionship in books; she began to write poetry while still in high school and earned her M.A. from the Writers Workshop at the University of Iowa. Before moving to San Antonio, Texas, Cisneros worked in Chicago, teaching high-school dropouts and absorbing to the voices of young Latinas in the barrio.

Cisneros's first book, *The House on Mango Street,* received critical acclaim, winning the Before Columbus American Book Award in 1985. It is the story of a young female writer struggling with life in a large city and her Hispanic community. In 1987 published a collection of poems, *My Wicked Wicked Ways*. Cisneros received two fellowships from the National Endowment for the Arts, for fiction (1982) and poetry (1987). Her collection of short stories, *Woman Hollering Creek* (1991) won the PEN Center West award for best fiction that year. Other awards followed, including a MacArthur Foundation Fellowship in 1995. Cisneros is a member of the writers' group PEN and the women's peace group, *Mujeres por la paz*.

CLINTON, HILLARY RODHAM (b. 1947)

Lawyer, first lady (1993–2001), wife of President Bill Clinton, U.S. senator. Hillary Rodham Clinton has a long list of achievements in the areas of politics, law, and social activism. Hillary Rodham was born in Chicago, Illinois, on October 26, 1947, and had a middle-class, suburban upbringing in Park Ridge, Illinois. In high school, she excelled in academics, music, dance, sports, debate, and student government. Upon her graduation she was voted "most likely to succeed" in her class. As a teenager she campaigned for 1964 presidential candidate Barry Goldwater; like her parents, she was a staunch Republican.

Rodham continued her education at Wellesley College, where she was head of the college's Young Republicans. However, her political views changed in the late 1960s. After living through the assassinations of leaders like President John F. Kennedy and Martin Luther King, Jr., as well as the violence of the 1968 Democratic National Convention, Rodham was inspired to take on social causes. She organized antiwar protests and began a campaign to enroll more black students at Wellesley. She also began her work for children's rights and is still involved in the Children's Defense Fund, a group that lobbies for children's rights. After earning her degree in political science, Rodham moved on to Yale Law School in 1969. There she did extensive research on the legal rights of children, especially in regards to education and health care. She graduated in 1973.

After law school, Rodham served on the 1974 Impeachment Inquiry Staff of the Judiciary Committee during the Nixon hearings. In 1975, she married Bill Clinton, also a graduate of Yale Law School, and moved to Arkansas, where both taught at the University of Arkansas. She founded the Arkansas Advocates for Children, was chairperson of the Arkansas Educational Standards Committee, and introduced a home instruction program for preschoolers. After her husband was elected governor of Arkansas in 1978, she continued her work at Rose Law Firm, but also served as chairperson of the Arkansas Rural Health Advisory Committee.

When Bill Clinton was elected president of the United States in 1993, he appointed Rodham Clinton the head of the Task Force on National Health Care Reform—which ultimately failed in its effort to revamp the nation's health-care system. She has been twice named among the most influential lawyers in the United States by the *National Law Journal*. In 2000, she was elected U.S. senator for the state of New York.

FURTHER READING

Clinton, Hillary Rodham. *The Unique Voice of Hillary Rodham Clinton: A Portrait in Her Own Words*. New York: Avon Books, 1997.

Milton, Joyce. *The First Partner, Hillary Rodham Clinton*. New York: Morrow, 1999.

CONGRESS, WOMEN IN

In 1916, four years before the **Nineteenth Amendment** to the Constitution gave women nationwide the right to vote, Jeannette Rankin, a Republican from Montana, became the first woman elected to the U.S. House of Representatives. Rankin achieved her unique status because Montana had granted women suffrage when it achieved statehood in 1889. Rankin was reelected in 1940.

The first woman to serve in the Senate, Georgia Democrat Rebecca L. Felton, served for a single day. Appointed in 1922 to fill a vacancy, she resigned to make way for the man who had been elected to fill the opening. In the 80th Congress (1947–1949), there were seven women members of the House and one woman in the Senate, **Margaret Chase Smith** of Maine. More than 75 years after Rankin's first election victory, the 102nd Congress (1991–1993) included only two women senators and 28 representatives.

The 1992 election saw a record-breaking number of women elected, leading to the 103rd Congress boasting six women senators and 47 women members of the House of Representatives. Several factors accounted for this increase. A large number of incumbent members of Congress retired, thus providing opportunities for newcomers, and the 1990 reapportionment created new seats in the South and West. At the same time, the public's general dissatisfaction with government allowed women to portray themselves as outsiders. Perhaps most significant was the reaction to the televised confirmation hearings of Supreme Court nominee Clarence Thomas. The public, seeing the all-male Senate Judiciary panel brusquely question Anita Hill, a law professor who accused Thomas of sexual misconduct, highlighted the low number of women in Congress. Still, after the 1992 election, women continued to hold only about 10 percent of the congressional seats, despite making up more than 50 percent of the population. By the 107th Congress (2001–2003), however, there were 61 women in the House and 13 women in the Senate.

Many women began their congressional careers through the "widow's mandate." Through this practice, widows of congressmen were appointed to fill their late husband's seats, often until a special election could be called. This custom often allowed state leaders more time to choose a successor. Sometimes the widow was chosen to run for the office by party leaders so that a sympathy vote would help her eventually win the seat. Several outstanding women came into office through this tradition. Margaret Chase Smith of Maine filled her husband's House seat in 1940 and went on to serve four terms in the Senate. Others include Representative Edith Nourse Rogers of Massachusetts, Senator Hattie Caraway of Arkansas, and Representative Corrine "Lindy" Boggs of Louisiana.

As women have become more politically active, the role of the widow's mandate has faded. In 1978, Nancy Landon Kassebaum of Kansas became the first woman elected to the Senate without coming in through the mandate; in 1992, only one of the women elected to Congress—Cardis Collins of Illinois—had been appointed to fill her late husband's seat. Also in 1992, California became the first state to send two women senators to Washington (Barbara Boxer and **DIANNE FEINSTEIN**), and **CAROL MOSELEY BRAUN** of Illinois became the first **AFRICAN-AMERICAN** woman elected to the Senate.

FURTHER READING

Thomas, Sue. *How Women Legislate*. New York: Oxford University Press, 1994.

White, Florence M. *First Woman in Congress, Jeanette Rankin*. New York: J. Messner, 1980.

CONSENT LAWS, AGE OF

Laws that determine the age at which any person may consent voluntarily to sexual activity. Sexual intercourse with a person under this age is known as statutory rape. Although age-of-consent laws now protect both male and female juveniles, they were originally established for the protection of women.

The notion of "consent," like so many American legal ideas, is derived from English common law, which set the age of consent at ten years of age. At the beginning of the twentieth century, attitudes toward sexual activity began to change. Ten-year-old girls were no longer regarded as mature enough to make such decisions. California was one of the first states to change the age of consent, raising it to 15 in 1889, 16 in 1897, and to 18 in 1913. A number of other states followed, including Arizona, Colorado, Florida, South Dakota, and Wyoming. Tennessee took the most extreme position, making it a felony to have sex with any woman under the age of 21.

At present there is no agreement at the national level as to the age at which a person can reasonably be expected to make an adult decision about sexual activity. Age-of-consent laws vary considerably from state to state and are subject to revision. These laws do not have any direct relationship, moreover, to laws governing a person's right to marry without his or her parents' consent.

COOLIDGE, GRACE GOODHUE (1879–1957)

First lady of the United States (1923–1929) and wife of Calvin Coolidge, the nation's thirtieth president. Grace Anna Goodhue was born in Burlington, Vermont, on January 3, 1879. She attended the University of Vermont, graduating in 1902, and taught at the Clarke School for the Deaf in Northampton, Massachusetts.

While teaching at the Clarke School, she met Calvin Coolidge in 1904, and the couple were married on October 4, 1905. They had two sons. Her husband pursued a political career, becoming mayor of Northampton in 1910 and governor of Massachusetts in 1919. In 1920, he was elected vice president of the United States on the Republican ticket with Warren Harding.

When Harding died suddenly in 1923, Coolidge became president. Grace Coolidge was a popular hostess for her husband in Washington and served as a volunteer for the Red Cross and other charities. After Coolidge left the White House in 1929, the couple retired to Northampton. In 1931 Grace Coolidge was honored as one of America's 12 greatest living women by the National Institute of Social Sciences because of her "fine personal influence exerted as First Lady of the Land."

After her husband's death in 1933, Grace Coolidge continued her charity work, serving as a trustee of the Clarke School. She died on July 8, 1957.

COONEY, JOAN GANZ

(b. 1929)

Television executive. Nearly any American born in the last three decades of the twentieth century can identify "Bert and Ernie," "Big Bird," and "Oscar the Grouch" as part of their memories of *Sesame Street*. But when Sylvan and Pauline Ganz looked at their newborn child, Joan, on November 30, 1929, they could not have anticipated that she would grow up to revolutionize educational mass media. After all, television had not even been invented yet.

Ganz became interested in social and political issues as a teenager. Deeply influenced by one of her teachers, she came to believe that "if the right thinking people don't get into mass communications, the other will." Therefore, after earning a bachelor's degree in education from the University of Arizona in 1951, she became a newspaper reporter, and later a publicity writer for the National Broadcasting Company (NBC).

Between 1962 and 1967, Cooney wrote and produced several documentaries for public television. It was during that time that she began to study the use of public television in preschool education. Her research revealed three important statistics. In 1966, 96 percent of American families owned television sets. In homes with children, the television was on up to 60 hours per week. And educational research suggested that children needed to begin formal learning earlier than the typical age of five or six years old. Cooney concluded that television was a viable form of educational media for preschoolers. Her report, "The Potential Uses of Television in Preschool Education" (1966), was the first step toward the creation of the new broadcasting company, Children's Television Workshop. On November 10, 1969, the company aired the first episode of *Sesame Street*.

The creators of *Sesame Street* had the following goals for children who watched the series: recognition of letters and numbers, beginning reasoning skills, and increased self-awareness. The show relied on color, humor, fast action, and catchy music to hold the attention of its young viewers. The show received immediate rave reviews. Today, *Sesame Street* has an estimated 235 million viewers in 85 countries.

Joan Ganz Cooney has won several awards, including the Daytime Emmy of Lifetime Achievement (1989), the Presidential Medal of Freedom (1995), and the Nancy Dickerson Whitehead Medallion of Excellence in the Field of Mass Communication (1998). She is the president of the Children's Television Workshop, a position she has held since 1970.

D

DANCE

A series of movements, performed in patterns, and set to music. Dance may be performed alone, with another person, or as part of a group. It is an art form that celebrates the emotional, mental, and physical self.

Dance is part of every society's culture and at times has tested society's tolerance. The Turkey Trot was considered risqué in the 1910s. When the Twist was introduced in the 1960s, it was considered indecent because of the suggestive movement of the dancer's hips. Yet, unlike many other dances, people did not dance close to each other when they danced the Twist. Eventually, this innovative dance created a new, informal style. One no longer needed a partner to hold onto, and because there were no formal steps, anyone could get on the floor and simply move to the rhythm.

During the early part of the twentieth century, the Charleston was the rage. Its roots date back to **World War I**, when African Americans left Southern states to work in Northern factories. Their high-stepping dance style was featured in African-American musicals such as "Runnin' Wild." The dance peaked during the 1920s, a decade that also introduced the Shimmy, the Toddle, and the Black Bottom, all reflecting the rhythms of Dixieland jazz.

Musical productions were at their peak from the late 1920s through the 1930s, and showgirls often wore elaborate costumes as they danced in groups, creating flowers, fans, or other patterns by positioning themselves on stage. Some became parts of huge, revolving Ferris wheels or abstract designs, while others managed to position themselves to spell words. One popular group of these showgirls was the Ziegfeld Follies.

Often hundreds of showgirls were used to make a single motion picture. Warner Brothers used 500 women for the movie *The Show of Shows*. According to the December 1929 issue of *Photoplay*, the ideal movie chorus girl dancer possessed "a $32\frac{1}{2}$ inch bust, 23 inch waist, 34 inch hips, $12\frac{1}{2}$ inch calf, [and] $7\frac{1}{2}$ inch ankle." **Betty Grable** and Lucille Ball were two women who started their careers as dancers and went on to Hollywood fame.

Katherine Dunham created an original dance technique in the 1930s by combining ballet with African and Caribbean dance movements. Noted for its creative interpretations of black dance in the West Indies and United States, her pioneering technique soon became part of mainstream modern dance.

Ginger Rogers (1911–1995) became an international star of ballroom dancing through her films with Fred Astaire, setting standards of style with her graceful movement.

By the 1940s, Esther Williams was dancing in water to elaborate production numbers. Couples were moving to the Jitterbug and the Lindy Hop. The 1950s brought rock and roll. Dancing to this strong beat required no physical contact, something that appealed to adolescents. Broadway was alive with musicals such as *West Side Story*, famous for its lavish dance numbers. By the 1960s, some women were working as go-go girls, dancing solo inside cages, wearing miniskirts, and displaying a frenzy and assertiveness that reflected the anxieties and excitement of the time.

In the 1970s, the movie *Saturday Night Fever* helped create the disco dance craze, bringing young people to discotheques where dancing either stylishly with a partner or by oneself was in vogue.

On August 1, 1981, MTV (short for "Music Television") was born. An entire television channel was now devoted to bringing a variety of music, dance styles, and fashion into people's living rooms every day. In particular, MTV was instrumental in bringing the dance form called hip hop to mainstream America. This African-American style of dance, said to have been born on city streets, featured dance movements that stressed head, hand, and feet action as well as spinning on floors and even rolling over. Dancers moved to the steady rhythms of hip hop (or "rap") songs that often addressed the turmoil of city life.

Maria Tallchief (b. 1924) is an Osage Indian whose work with choreographer George Balanchine brought her international acclaim and helped make ballet a beloved American dance form.

DAUGHTERS OF BILITIS

Founded in the mid-1950s in San Francisco and named after a poem, this was the first organized group of **LESBIANS** in the United States. It began as a social organization to give middle-class lesbians a place to meet and soon became the center of a growing political movement.

Joining this organization required a great deal of courage. In the 1950s, women suspected of being lesbians were routinely fired from their jobs, especially if they were public employees. The Daughters of Bilitis worked hard to keep their membership lists secret, but they were only partially successful. The FBI and the CIA infiltrated their meetings, and at the organization's first national convention, in 1960, attendees were greeted by San Francisco law officers who asked if they supported cross dressing. This sort of harassment kept the organization's membership small.

The Daughters of Bilitis began with the modest political goal of winning acceptance from mainstream society. Members were urged to avoid "butch haircuts and mannish manner[s]" that might alienate heterosexuals.

The Daughters of Bilitis became bolder in the 1960s. They helped organize the Council on Religion and the Homosexual, which drew support from some liberal Protestant clergymen. The organization's magazine, *The Ladder*, began exhorting its members to resist oppression, in the manner of other persecuted minorities.

In the 1970s more radical organizations formed and took over the work of advocating for lesbian rights. By 2000 the Boston Daughters of Bilitis claimed to constitute the only surviving chapter of what had once been a national organization. Nevertheless, the Daughters of Bilitis had accomplished a great deal under extremely hostile conditions.

DAVIS, ANGELA (b. 1944)

Educator, author, advocate of Black Power. Born in Birmingham, Alabama, Angela Yvonne Davis was the daughter of two teachers. In 1959, she was sent to New York City by her parents to attend an integrated high school instead of the segregated schools of Birmingham. From there she enrolled at Brandeis University in Massachusetts, graduating in 1963.

In 1968, Davis joined the Black Panther Party (a group that advocated Black Power) and the Communist Party. She believed that these organizations would enable African Americans to liberate themselves from the white majority in the United States. From 1969 to 1970, she taught philosophy at the University of California, but she was fired because of her communist beliefs.

In 1970, Davis was accused of supplying weapons to prisoners trying to escape from a courtroom. Four people were killed, including a judge. Davis went into hiding, but she was finally arrested after being placed on the FBI's Ten Most Wanted list. She spent 16 months in jail but was found not guilty of all charges after a well-publicized trial. In 1980 and again in 1984, she ran for the office of vice president of the United States as a communist.

Meanwhile, Davis continued her career in education, at San Francisco State University from 1979 to 1991 and since then at the University of California.

DAY, DORIS (b. 1924)

Actress and singer. Doris Mary Ann von Kappelhoff was born on April 3, 1924, in Cincinnati, Ohio. As a child, she had hoped to become a ballet dancer, but a serious automobile accident ended her plans.

By the 1940s, Day was singing with the Bob Crosby and Les Brown big bands. After she appeared on the *Saturday Night Hit Parade* with Frank Sinatra, he suggested that Day audition for movie roles. In 1948, she appeared in her first film, *Romance in the High Seas*.

Building an image as a blonde, sweet "good-girl," with a pleasant personality, Day became a star during the 1950s, appearing in such films as *Calamity Jane* (1953), Alfred Hitchcock's *The Man Who Knew Too Much* (1956), and the musical *The Pajama Game* (1957). During the 1960s she appeared in a series of films with Cary Grant and Rock Hudson. Her last film was *With Six You Get Eggroll* (1968).

During the late 1960s, Day starred in a television show that remained on the air until 1973. Day has been married four times. Since the 1980s, she has run the Doris Day Animal Foundation in Carmel, California, an advocacy group for effective pet care.

DAY, DOROTHY (1897–1980)

Journalist, religious leader, pacifist. Dorothy Day was born on November 8, 1897, in Brooklyn,

New York. When she was a child, her family moved to Chicago, where her father, John Day, worked for a newspaper. Dorothy entered the University of Illinois in 1914 but left after two years to become a reporter on a socialist newspaper in New York. As a young woman, she had learned how the poor lived by traveling to their neighborhoods, and she wanted to help them. Socialism seemed to be the best answer.

Day lived with Forster Batterham from 1924 until 1928, and the couple had one child, Tamar Theresa, born on March 3, 1927. Although she had been raised an Episcopal, Day began attending the Roman Catholic Church while working as a New York journalist during this period, and eventually converted. In 1932, in the depths of the **Great Depression**, Day reported from Washington, D.C., on a hunger march staged by thousands of unemployed workers. She was greatly moved by the march and the plight of the poor.

On December 9, 1932, Day met Peter Maurin, a former Catholic clergyman, and the two founded a newspaper called *The Catholic Worker*. It was first published on May 1, 1933, and called on Christians to help the homeless and the unemployed. Day's articles led to a series of Catholic Worker houses opening across America to help the poor.

Over the next few decades *The Catholic Worker* took a strong position in support of pacifism and against war. Day and her editors found themselves in jail repeatedly for their antiwar statements. In 1963 and again two years later, Day traveled to Rome as part of an effort to promote world peace. Day is considered one of the great pacifists and religious leaders of the twentieth century. She died on November 29, 1980. She has become a candidate for sainthood in the Catholic Church.

DELORIA, ELLA CARA

(1889–1971)

Author, teacher, linguist, and anthropologist. Ella Cara Deloria was born on a Yankton Sioux reservation near Lake Andes, South Dakota. A Native American, her Dakota name, Yankton Dakota, means Beautiful Day. She attended a mission school on the reservation, then enrolled in the University of Chicago in 1910. The following year, she transferred to Oberlin College in Ohio, and finally to Teacher's College at Columbia University in New York City, where she worked with the anthropologists Franz Boas and Ruth Benedict and from which she received a bachelor's degree in 1915.

Deloria pursued a career in education, teaching at the All Saints Episcopal High School in Sioux Falls, North Dakota from 1915 to 1919 and at the Haskell Indian School in Lawrence, Kansas, from 1923 to 1927. That year, at Boas's request, she returned to Columbia to teach American Indian dialects. Her early life among the Dakotas motivated her to conduct fieldwork among the tribe to record information about their language and culture. These studies led to several books, including 1932's *Dakota Texts*, which presented stories from Dakota culture. In 1941, she coauthored *Dakota Grammar*, and in 1944 published *Speaking of Indians*.

Following publications of her anthropological works, she became director of St. Elizabeth's mission school in South Dakota, in 1955. In 1984, 13 years after her death, Deloria's novel *Waterlily* was published. It describes life among the Dakota.

DEL RIO, DOLORES

(1905–1983)

Mexican screen actress who became internationally famous, Del Rio was a source of national pride for many Mexican immigrants in the United States.

Lolita Dolores Asúnsolo López Negrete was born on August 3, 1905. The only child of wealthy Mexican parents, she grew up on her family's Durango estate and attended European schools. In 1920, when she was 15 years old, her parents arranged her marriage to Jaime Martinez del Rio.

Del Rio was considered to be a very beautiful woman, which brought her both opportunities and challenges. In 1925 Hollywood director Edwin Carewe, after meeting her at a party, offered her a contract to act in his films. Del Rio starred in five major motion pictures between 1926 and 1929. Fluent in English, she made a successful transition from silent to talking movies.

From 1930 to 1942, Del Rio struggled to develop her career. She wanted to play modern and sophisticated women characters similar to her own background. Instead the Hollywood studios promoted her as Spanish rather than Mexican, and offered her stereotypical parts as exotic *femmes fatales* or wealthy European beauties. Because of these experiences, Del Rio sympathized with the problems of Mexican immigrants in the United States and helped raise money for Mexican-American civil rights organizations.

In 1942 Del Rio, frustrated with the roles available to her in Hollywood, returned to Mexico. She soon became that country's leading movie star. Del Rio earned four Ariels and one Quixote (Mexican and Spanish "Oscars," respectively). In her Spanish-language films, Del Rio expressed her talents and Mexican immigrants in the United States found positive images of Mexican women and national identity. She died April 11, 1983. Del Rio's career is commemorated in a Hollywood, California, mural created in 1990 by Alfredo de Batuc.

DE VARONA, DONNA E.
(b. 1947)

Olympic swimmer and sportscaster. Donna de Varona was born on April 26, 1947, in San Diego, California. In 1960, at the age of 13, she was selected to become a member of the U.S. Olympic team competing at the summer games in Rome, Italy. Although she did not win any medals that year, de Varona did become the youngest person ever to compete for the United States.

Over the next few years, de Varona won a number of national championships, including the 100-meter backstroke in 1962, the 200-meter individual medley in 1963 and 1964, and the 200-yard butterfly in 1964. That same year, at the Olympics in Amsterdam, Netherlands, de Varona won two gold medals, in the 400-meter individual medley and in the freestyle relay event. She retired in 1964, after winning a total of 37 national championships.

In 1965, de Varona became a network sportscaster, the first woman to hold this position. De Varona later worked at ABC Sports for 26 years but lost her job in 2000. She sued the network for age and sex discrimination.

DEWSON, MARY WILLIAMS (MOLLY) (1874–1962)

Economist, social reformer. Molly Dewson was born to Edward and Elizabeth (Weld) Dewson on February 18, 1874, in Quincy, Massachusetts. She attended Wellesley College and graduated in 1897.

Dewson began her career as a social reformer in 1912, when she joined a full-time campaign to establish a minimum wage law for women workers in the United States. Between 1912 and 1917, Dewson and her life partner, Polly Porter, ran a dairy farm in Massachusetts and both became highly active in the women's **SUFFRAGE MOVEMENT**.

After spending 15 months working for the Red Cross Bureau of Refugees in France during **WORLD WAR I**, Dewson became a research secretary for the **NATIONAL CONSUMER'S LEAGUE**. Again she wrote in support of a minimum wage for women and promoted changes in labor organization that would benefit women on a national level.

While fighting for social reform in New York, Dewson met **ELEANOR ROOSEVELT** in 1928. By 1932, Dewson was organizing women to campaign for presidential candidate Franklin D. Roosevelt. After his election, she ran the Women's Division of the Democratic National Committee, where she promoted the equal representation of women in political parties. She used her friendship with the Roosevelts to lobby for the appointments of women to high-level positions in the **NEW DEAL** administration. Dewson also used her skills as an economic advisor to influence the creation of the **SOCIAL SECURITY ACT** and served on the Social Security Board until 1938.

After retiring in 1940, Dewson lived with Porter in Maine and New York. She died on October 22, 1962.

DIVISION OF LABOR, SEXUAL

The way work is divided between the genders; the difference in job opportunities available to men and women. At the turn of the twentieth century, the majority of women still worked as caretakers and **HOMEMAKERS**, tending to their homes and raising children while their husbands went off to work. Some of the wealthier women hired nannies and maids—many of them young immigrant women—to perform these duties for them. Of the relatively few educated women who were not married, many worked as schoolteachers.

In cities, uneducated unmarried women typically worked in factories, in **DOMESTIC SERVICE**, or as **CLERICAL WORKERS**. Even though woman factory workers were paid meager wages and often labored under terrible conditions, some people believed that women should not work at all, because hiring them meant taking jobs away from men who needed to support families. In 1903 working women joined forces with upper-class women to form the Women's Trade Union League (WTUL) to persuade companies to hire more women, increase their pay, and improve working conditions. Throughout the early decades of the twentieth century, women were active in the formation of **UNIONS** and the spread of the labor movement, but improvements were slow in coming.

1911 Katherine Gibbs created the first school for women who wanted to become secretaries and office clerks, and this became an expanding opportunity for women through the course of the century. In the office as in the home, however, low-wage female workers played a supporting role to that of men, who were the bosses. The situation remained largely unchanged until the women's movement of the 1960s and 1970s.

In the male-dominated professional fields, opportunities for women also remained scarce for much of the twentieth century. The ranks of doctors, lawyers, professors, and scientists had included notable women since the mid-1800s, but openings in professional education—and the recognition of peers—were largely reserved for men until the late 1900s. It was commonly held that this division of labor best served the traditional male responsibility for family income.

WORLD WAR II marked an important transition in the sexual division of labor. Six million women entered the industrial workforce, contributing directly to the manufacture of war materiel and domestic goods. Nevertheless, men retained most of the supervisory positions and, when the war was over, women were forced to forfeit their jobs to returning veterans.

The women's movement of the 1960s and 1970s both reflected and engendered a change in social values and gender stereotypes, by which women now were entitled to—and sought—the same employment opportunities as men. Legislative and judicial action dismantled barriers based on gender and required equal employment opportunity in new ways. In 1991, for example, Congress passed the Non-Traditional Employment for Women Act, requiring male-dominated industries to train women for such jobs as truck driving, construction work, and carpentry. In the white-collar world, the **GLASS CEILING** that blocked women from advancement slowly gave way. At the end of the century, however, top-level executive positions still remained heavily male and women were paid less, on average, than men with similar positions. In the year 2000, more than 60 percent of American women were in the labor force, compared to 38 percent in 1960. Women accounted for more than 47 percent of all employed workers, up from 33 percent four decades earlier

Many women took factory jobs during World War II, but supervisory positions were still largely reserved for men.

DIVORCE LAWS

A divorce is a court judgment that ends a marriage. Divorce laws have changed dramatically in the past 200 years. During the early history of the United States, a man virtually owned his wife and children as he did his material possessions.

Until the middle of the nineteenth century in the United States, grounds for divorce were limited to adultery and cruelty. Divorces could only be granted by legislative action. New laws substituted judicial for legislative divorce and broadened the grounds of divorce to include desertion. In the 1970s, feminists advocated for "no-fault" divorce and new laws were passed. These laws no longer required proof of marital misconduct by one spouse or the other. By the 1990s, every state and the District of Columbia had enacted "no-fault" divorce laws.

Ever since the liberalization of the laws in the mid-nineteenth century, divorces have been easier to obtain, and more of them have been granted to women. Nevada has the most relaxed divorce laws, requiring that the plaintiff only live in the state for six weeks before filing for divorce. Divorce was relatively rare in the United States (although there were surges after each world war) until the mid-1960s.

By the 1990s, the rising divorce rate led many states, including Iowa, Idaho, Georgia, and Pennsylvania, to reexamine their legislation and consider restoring the assignment of fault. Other states, such as Minnesota and Michigan, have introduced bills mandating premarital counseling. Bills in Colorado, Washington, West Virginia, and Minnesota allow couples to enter a voluntary agreement to make their marriages harder to dissolve. By 2000, Louisiana, Arizona, and Arkansas had enacted covenant marriage laws, which allowed couples to enter into a stronger marital contract than a standard state contract. Some states, including Iowa, require divorcing parents to take classes to help them understand the emotional impact of divorce on their children.

See also: Child Custody.

DOLE, ELIZABETH HANFORD (b. 1936)

A lawyer and government official who served in five U.S. presidential administrations and ran for the Republican nomination for president in 2000. Mary Elizabeth Hanford was born on July 29, 1936, in Salisbury, North Carolina, the daughter of a flower wholesaler. In 1958, she graduated from Duke University, where she was student government president. She earned a master's degree in 1960 and a law degree in 1965 from Harvard University.

Hanford began her government service as a Democrat, working on a presidential consumer affairs commission (1968–1971) and, as an Independent in the administration of President Richard Nixon, in the White House Office of Consumer Affairs (1971–1973). In 1975, during a six-year appointment to the Federal Trade Commission (1973–1979), she married Senator Robert J. Dole and registered as a Republican.

President Ronald Reagan named Dole secretary of transportation in 1983, making her the first woman to hold that job. During her tenure, she won legislation that required automobile manufacturers to add a third brake-light and air bags as basic equipment and stressed road safety and airport security. In 1989, President George H. W. Bush appointed her secretary of labor, a role in which she was credited with peacefully resolving an Appalachian coal strike.

In 1991, after Bush left office, Dole accepted the position of president of the American Red Cross. She took a leave of absence in 1996 to devote her energies to her husband's unsuccessful campaign for the Republic presidential nomination. Dole then returned to the Red Cross, resigning in August 1999 to seek the 2000 Republican nomination in her own right. Short of funds, she withdrew from the race two months later. She was suggested as a potential running mate for George W. Bush but not selected.

DOMESTIC SERVICE

Paid employment for work done within the home by nonfamily members. Domestic service may include cooks, washerwomen, maids, housekeepers, and nannies. Domestic service employed more women than any other nonagriculture occupation in the early twentieth century.

By the end of the nineteenth century, the tradition of apprenticing young girls in the homes of neighbors to learn domestic skills had given way to paid employment for specific ethnic groups. Many families in the Northeast preferred to hire single Irish women, either immigrants or the daughters of immigrants. They lived in and were on call throughout the day. In the mid-Atlantic and Southern states, African-American girls and women were exclusively hired for domestic work. In the mining camps of the West, Asian men worked as cooks, laundry men, and house servants, until young women of Asian, Native American, and Mexican descent filled the ranks of domestic workers. In fact, the education for Native American and African-American girls included domestic service training because of the job segregation at the time.

New job opportunities during the 1940s made domestic service unappealing and the supply of workers dried up. Teenagers filled some of the gap, taking on babysitting, house cleaning, and even ironing jobs as more women entered the workplace. Domestic service also became commercialized, and businesses replaced individual workers with commercial laundries, home-cleaning services, window washing companies, and day-care centers. By the 1980s, equal employment laws changed the job landscape. The need for domestic workers continued, but a formal employment structure of agencies supplying workers replaced the informal structure of hiring "help."

DREW, NANCY

A fictional teenage detective and the lead character in the Nancy Drew Mystery Stories. Nancy Drew was "born" in 1930 with the publication of *The Secret of the Old Clock*, published by Grosset & Dunlap. The character was the brainchild of Edward Stratemeyer, owner of Stratemeyer Syndicate and creator of other popular series and characters for young readers such as the Bobbsey Twins, Tom Swift, and the Hardy Boys. He hired a young journalist to write the stories based on plotlines he gave her.

Independent, smart, and daring, Nancy Drew challenged the stereotype of females as the weaker, meeker sex and provided young girls with a new role model. And Nancy Drew has grown with the times. Her image was updated in 1986 to appeal to adolescent readers in a new series called Nancy Drew Files. In the 1990s, Nancy Drew went off to college. Millions of copies of her books are read each year by young and teenage girls.

DUNCAN, ISADORA

(1878–1927)

Dancer. Angela Duncan was born on May 27, 1878, in San Francisco, California. Raised in poverty, she began dancing as a child, developing a free-form style of dance that was not then popular with American audiences, so at 21 Duncan traveled to England, where she began appearing at private gatherings. It was during this period that Duncan changed her name to Isadora.

Duncan went to Russia in 1905, where she danced in sheer garments, sometimes barefoot. Meanwhile she had begun a series of love affairs, first with the stage designer Gordon Craig and later with Paris Singer, the sewing machine heir. She had one child by each man. In 1913, both children were tragically killed in an automobile accident.

Duncan tried to overcome her grief by touring South America, Germany, and France. In 1920 she opened a ballet school in Moscow where she taught her students the free forms of ballet that she had made famous. Two years later she married the Russian poet Sergey Aleksandrovich Yesenin, who was much younger than Duncan. They toured the United States, then returned to the Soviet Union, where Yesenin committed suicide in 1925.

Duncan herself was killed in a freak accident on the French Riviera in 1927 when her scarf became tangled in the wheel of the convertible in which she was riding, strangling her. Her innovative forms of dance were the forerunner of modern ballet.

DUNIWAY, ABIGAIL SCOTT

(1834–1915)

Advocate of women's rights. Born in a log cabin in a recently settled part of Illinois in 1834, Abigail Scott crossed the Oregon Trail as a child, married in Oregon, and labored many hard years on an isolated homestead. She eventually became the most prominent and determined advocate of women's rights in the Pacific Northwest.

Duniway forcefully entered public life in 1870, at age 36, founding Oregon's first suffrage association and laying the groundwork for *New Northwest*, a newspaper devoted to women's rights, which debuted on May 5, 1871. She was soon criss-crossing the region—"by stage, rail, steamer, buggy, buckboard and afoot"—to speak, sell subscriptions, gather material, and exhort all manner of Pacific Northwest women to better themselves and their communities. At the close of 1886 she paused to recount the previous year's work: 181 lectures and 3,000 miles, all in the face of "more than the usual quota of persecution, hypocrisy, malice, gossip and hate."

Duniway advocated a wide range of reforms. She argued that men should not monopolize well-paying professional positions and that wives ought to have more control over their earnings. But the SUFFRAGE MOVEMENT remained her central concern. In 1912, more than four decades after Duniway had begun her work, Oregon's voters at last gave women the vote. Two years later, shortly before her death, she at last cast a ballot.

DYK, RUTH BELCHER

(1901–2000)

Women's rights advocate. Ruth Belcher was born in Portland, Maine, on March 25, 1901. Her mother, Annie Belcher, had been a student at Tufts Medical School in the late nineteenth century and inspired Ruth Belcher to follow a professional career. Her father, Arthur Belcher, was a lawyer. She graduated from Wellesley College in Massachusetts during the 1920s and did graduate work at Simmons College in Boston, as well as at the University of Wisconsin. Ruth Belcher and her mother campaigned for the passage of the **Nineteenth Amendment** to the Constitution, which gave women the right to vote.

Dyk eventually became a psychiatric social worker, specializing in the treatment of delinquents in upstate New York. In 1950, she published *Anxiety in Pregnancy and Childbirth*, followed by *Left Handed* in 1980. Meanwhile, she worked closely with her husband, anthropologist Walter Dyk, studying the Navajo Indians. She died on November 18, 2000.

E

EAGLE FORUM

A conservative Christian women's organization founded by **Phyllis Schlafly** in 1972. Schlafly founded the Eagle Forum upon unofficially breaking from the National Federation of Republican Women (NFRW) after being passed up for the presidency of the organization by a more liberal candidate. She felt that the NFRW was becoming too liberal and sought to promote more conservative values.

The Eagle Forum promotes traditional Christian family values. Its 80,000 members, both men and women, believe that women should not be held financially responsible for their families and that men ought to be the heads of their households. Eagle Forum opposes "radical feminism" and the **Equal Rights Amendment** on the premise that such an amendment would send women into combat in war and has the potential to legalize homosexual marriages. The organization is also against **abortion**.

In **education**, the Eagle Forum opposes contemporary methods such as "Outcome Based Education," which abandons traditional methods such as teacher-centered classrooms, student testing, and memorization of factual knowledge. The organization demands a rise in public education standards. Also, it calls for the freedom of students to practice Christian religious values in school. The Eagle Forum condemns the use of learning materials that promote "alternative lifestyles, profanity, and immorality." It also opposes materials that are "anti-biblical" or promote New Age religious practices.

The Eagle Forum promotes capitalism. It believes in military isolationism, although it supports the buildup of a strong ballistic missile defense. Its members oppose a strong central government and believe legislative power should be left in the hands of the states.

EARHART, AMELIA

(1897–1937)

Aviator. Amelia Earhart was born on June 24, 1897, in Atchison, Kansas, to Edwin and Amy (Otis) Earhart. Her maternal grandparents were wealthy and paid for Amelia and her sister Muriel to attend private schools. When she was ten years old, Earhart saw her first airplane at the Iowa State Fair. However, it was not until she was in her twenties that she got the urge to fly one. In 1921, Earhart met Neta Snook, the first woman graduate of the Curtis School of Aviation. Snook became her teacher, and Earhart worked odd jobs to pay for flying lessons. In 1922, Earhart purchased her first plane, a yellow Kinner Canary.

Earhart's name is associated with many "firsts" in aviation. She was the first woman to fly a plane at altitudes over 14,000 feet. In 1932, she was the first woman to fly solo across the Atlantic Ocean; that same year, she broke the women's transcontinental speed record. She helped found the

Amelia Earhart was a woman of many "firsts" in aviation.

Ninety Nines, Inc., a women's flying organization, and was the first female vice president of the National Aeronautics Association.

The big mystery surrounding Amelia Earhart is her final flight in 1937. Earhart and her navigator, Fred Noonan, were attempting to circumnavigate the world. The plane was scheduled for a refueling stop on Howland Island in the Pacific Ocean. However, after their last radio transmission on July 2, 1937, Earhart, Noonan, and the plane were never heard from again. Neither the plane nor the passengers were ever found, despite a search over 250,000 square miles at the cost of $4 million. Most believe that Earhart's plane simply ran out of gas during the dangerously long stretch from New Guinea to Howland Island, although more colorful theories involve Earhart being captured by the Japanese. Whatever the circumstances surrounding her death may have been, Earhart and her navigator took them to the grave.

EDUCATION

Education has played a key role in the advancement of women in the twentieth century. Throughout the 1900s increasing numbers of girls and women attended high school and college, and by the end of the century female graduates outnumbered male graduates. In 1997–1998, women earned 57 percent of master's degrees and 42 percent of doctorates. By 2000, the majority of students were female at all three levels—primary, secondary, and higher.

One of the most important laws expanding educational opportunity for women was the **Civil Rights Act of 1964,** which outlawed discrimination on the basis of race, color, religion, national origin, or sex in public accommodations, employment **(Title VII),** and public education **(Title IX).** Amended in 1972, Title IX countered sex discrimination against students and employees in educational institutions. Since 1988, Congress has made it clear that Title IX covers all areas within institutions including financial aid, admissions (except for private undergraduate and single-sex institutions), employment, and extra-curricular activities. Title IX especially opened up **athletics** to women and resulted in a huge increase in the number of women participating in intercollegiate athletics. Courts opened up military academies to women. The development of community colleges by local and state governments encouraged more high school graduates, especially females and minorities, to continue on to college.

Nongovernmental organizations, such as the **American Association of University Women** (AAUW), have promoted education and equality for girls and women. At first concerned with the status of women in higher education, the AAUW has provided financial assistance to individuals charging discrimination and has awarded fellowships. Recently it has focused on equity issues of girls in elementary and secondary schools. In the early 1970s, the AAUW worked with the **League of Women Voters** and the **National Organization for Women** to support Title IX and the **Equal Rights Amendment**.

Women have traditionally entered sex-segregated occupations such as **Nursing** and **Teaching**. At the end of the twentieth century, over two-thirds of elementary school teachers were women, and as many women as men entered secondary school teaching. Teaching as a profession continued to suffer from low status and pay. On the college level, women instructors were few until the women's movement of the 1960s. Governmental affirmative action programs also helped women gain access to research and teaching. However, men still dominate full-time, tenured, and full professor positions and earn higher salaries.

Fewer women than men enter administration. This has been attributed to discrimination, family obligations, and lack of experience. Principals are more likely to be male. About 30 percent of college administrators are female, mostly at lower echelons and salaries. Administrators often have higher salaries and status than teachers and professors. Approximately 20 percent of college presidents are women; few of them are at major research universities.

The **WOMEN'S LIBERATION MOVEMENT** that followed the civil rights drive of the 1960s led to demands for changes in curricula at all levels. Women's history courses began in 1969. There are currently more than 30,000 **WOMEN'S STUDIES** courses in the United States. Most scholars viewed coeducation as positive for women, but proponents of single-sex classrooms and colleges point out that in such settings girls and women seem to gain more self-confidence and achieve more.

The increasing education of women and access to the same curricula and schools as men has meant a betterment of women's social and economic positions in America. American women have provided leadership for women around the world. Women have increasingly entered the labor force, and the higher the level of education the more likely women are to work. However, many women, especially non-Hispanic, white females, still do not pursue math, science, technology, computer science, and engineering, which locks them out of higher paying jobs. Gender discrimination and social traditions still undermine advancement and performance.

FURTHER READING

Eisenmann, Linda. *Historical Dictionary of Women's Education in the United States*. Westport, CT: Greenwood, 1998.

Solomon, Barbara M. *In the Company of Educated Women*. New Haven: Yale University Press, 1985.

EISENHOWER, MARY (MAMIE) GENEVA DOUD

(1896–1979)

Wife of Dwight David Eisenhower, the thirty-fourth president of the United States. Mamie Geneva Doud was born in Boone, Iowa, the daughter of a meatpacking plant owner. She married Eisenhower, a young army officer, in 1916. They had two sons.

Eisenhower usually traveled wherever her husband was posted. During **WORLD WAR II**, she lived in Washington, D.C., performing volunteer work for military organizations while her husband commanded Allied troops in Europe. She moved to New York City when her husband was named president of Columbia University in 1949 and to France when he became supreme commander of North Atlantic Treaty Organization (NATO) forces in 1950.

Eisenhower also accompanied her husband on his 1952 presidential whistle-stop campaign across the country. Serving two terms as first lady, from 1953 to 1961, she focused her energies on domestic life within the White House. Emphasizing simplicity and frugality, she directed menu planning, budgeting, and housekeeping, and was considered a gracious hostess. She preferred to avoid involvement in political issues and, at press conferences, refused to answer political questions. Withstanding the crises of her husband's military and political careers, as well as his heart attack, she earned the admiration of the American public. Her banged hairstyle and pink clothing became popular fashions.

After leaving the White House in 1961, Eisenhower settled on a farm with her husband in Gettysburg, Pennsylvania. She died on November 1, 1979, in Washington, D.C.

EISENSTADT v. BAIRD

U.S. Supreme Court case. *Eisenstadt v. Baird*, which the Supreme Court decided in 1971, was one of a series of cases in the 1960s and early 1970s affecting reproductive rights. The case arose when William Baird was arrested and convicted of violating a Massachusetts law forbidding the distribution of contraceptives—in this case, contraceptive foam—to unmarried persons. He named the arresting officer (Thomas S. Eisenstadt) in appealing his conviction.

Like an earlier case, ***GRISWOLD v. CONNECTICUT*** (1965), this case involved birth control. But while *Griswold* focused on the distribution of contraceptive devices and information to married people, *Eisenstadt* arose because of a statute that prohibited distribution of contraceptives to unmarried people. The Supreme Court found this statute was unconstitutional because it violated the Equal Protection Clause of the Fourteenth Amendment to the U.S. Constitution.

In reaching its decision, the Court said that it was unable to find any way to distinguish between the use of birth control by married and unmarried people. The Court rejected the idea that the purpose of the statute was to prevent premarital sexual relations, for that would imply that the legislature wanted to punish unmarried people for having sex by forcing unwanted children on them. In sum, the Court's decision in *Eisenstadt v. Baird* more firmly established a right of privacy and equal protection in matters of contraception and sexual behavior.

EMILY'S LIST

A political action committee (PAC) that raises money for women candidates for political office. In 1985, discouraged by the low numbers of women in elective office and recognizing the role played by money in successful candidacies, political activist Ellen Malcolm founded EMILY's List. "EMILY" is an acronym for the expression "Early Money Is Like Yeast." "Just as yeast makes dough rise," Malcolm says, "early money helps women raise more money and become credible candidates."

Representative Barbara Mikulski of Maryland was the first to receive support in her ultimately successful bid for the Senate in 1986. In 1992, in what was called "The Year of the Woman," EMILY's List helped elect four prochoice women to the Senate and 20 women to the House of Representatives. Since then EMILY's List has supported hundreds of politically liberal, prochoice women in their bids for the U.S. Senate, House of Representatives, and governorships.

EMILY's List invites women (and men) to join, requiring not only a membership fee of $100 but also a pledge to contribute at least $100 to at least two women on a list of approved candidates. Since 1996, EMILY's List has expanded its goals beyond fund-raising to include the training of campaign managers, fund-raisers, and press secretaries for women candidates.

ENDO, MITSUYE (b. 1920)

Japanese American who challenged the constitutional right of the United States to imprison Americans of Japanese heritage during **World War II**. When the Japanese bombed the U.S. military base at Pearl Harbor on December 7, 1941, Mitsuye Endo was a U.S. citizen living in Sacramento, California, and working as a clerk at the Department of Motor Vehicles. In February 1942, President Roosevelt signed an executive order allowing the removal of all "enemy aliens" of Japanese descent from "military areas" and U.S. territory bordering the Pacific Ocean. Shortly thereafter Endo was among thousands of Japanese Americans living on the West Coast sent to internment camps. In July, from the Tule Lake War Relocation Center in Newell, California, Endo filed a petition for a writ of *habeas corpus* on the grounds of illegal imprisonment.

Endo's petition was denied and shortly thereafter she was sent to the Central Utah Relocation Center near Delta, Utah. In 1944 her appeal was heard by the Supreme Court, which ruled in her favor. On December 18, Justice William O. Douglas read the majority opinion, declaring that Endo could not be held any longer in the Relocation Center, and that it was beyond the power of the War Relocation Authority "to detain citizens against whom no charges of disloyalty or subversiveness have been made for a period longer than that necessary to separate the loyal from the disloyal." After this judgment, on January 2, 1945, all Japanese Americans forcibly interned in the camps were allowed to return to their homes.

ENTERTAINMENT

Amusement and the enjoyment of the arts. The emergence of electronic media in the twentieth century brought about a profound change in entertainment patterns. Sound recordings, radio, and television brought entertainment into the home and reduced the need to create one's own music or go out to seek it. **Literature** remains a primary source of enjoyment for many, and **athletics** has acquired a new importance for women. Still there is no doubt Americans depend on television as their primary source of entertainment, and much of society's ideas about women's roles are influenced by this powerful medium.

During the mid–twentieth century, women on television were portrayed as housewives who obeyed their husbands, catered to men's needs, and raised children. They were often depicted wearing attractive dresses, makeup, and jewelry, even when cleaning the house.

While some women were powerful and self-sufficient off camera, they still earned success portraying helpless housewives. One of television's most famous shows, *I Love Lucy*, which first aired in 1951, featured Lucille Ball and Desi Arnaz, a real-life married couple who also played a married couple on the show, which ran until their divorce in 1957. On television, Ball portrayed a ditzy woman who got herself into outrageous situations because of her inability to foresee the consequences of her actions, but in real life Ball was a tough, successful businesswoman who succeeded in a field dominated by men. After her divorce, Ball emerged as president of Desilu Productions, went on to star in *The Lucy Show* for six years, then sold the business for $17 million. Her next sitcom, *Here's Lucy*, ran until 1974. Although Lucy's character was a working woman in these later shows, this was not because her character craved a career—we were to assume she was a widow forced to return to work for financial reasons.

Women were not portrayed as single and successful, pursuing careers by choice, until *The Mary Tyler Moore Show* emerged and dominated the CBS Saturday-night lineup during the 1970s. Paving the way was Diahann Carroll, who broke television's color barrier in 1968 when she became the first black actress to have a show built around her character. Playing a nurse on NBC's *Julia*, she portrayed a single mom who had to work to support her son.

In **MUSIC,** many lyrics from songs of the 1950s and 1960s reflect the concept of women in supporting roles, dependent upon men to feel complete. Songs that come to mind are "Bobby's Girl," "My Boyfriend's Back," and "Goin' to the Chapel." But during and after the women's movement of the 1960s, songs that emphasized women's strength and independence emerged—certainly songs such as "You Don't Own Me," "I Am Woman," "I Will Survive," "Girls Just Wanna Have Fun," and "Express Yourself" reflect these ideals. At the end of the century, there was much controversy about lyrics that condoned violence toward women, portraying them only as objects of sexual pleasure. But while artists like Eminem were singing about women in derogatory ways, the female group Destiny's Child was singing the praises of "Independent Women."

TRAILBLAZERS

The controversial pop singer and movie actress Madonna has been called both the ultimate feminist and the ultimate tramp. Enormously successful since the 1980s, she has been outspoken on behalf of women's rights and unafraid to speak her mind on and off stage. At the same time, she has reinvented her public image as a sex symbol in guises ranging from street waif to glamour girl. A pioneer of the music video, she has derived much of her success from sexually charged performances by scantily clad women—most notably herself.

Madonna staunchly defends her portrayal of women, saying that she's just doing what she wants to do. When a television reporter asked her about her appearance in the music video *Express Yourself*—in which she crawls on the floor wearing chains—she responded, "Isn't that what feminism is all about, you know, equality for men and women? And aren't I in charge of my life, doing the things I want to?" Of the chains, she said, "I have chained myself. There wasn't a man that put that chain on me. . . . I do everything of my own volition. I'm in charge." Among the many feminist thinkers who support Madonna's art and image, the cultural critic Camille Paglia says that the singer combines "a full female sensuality with a masculine political astuteness."

Madonna Louise Ciccone was born on August 16, 1958, in Bay City, Michigan. She worked as a singer, drummer, dancer, and model before rising to stardom in 1985 with her second album, *Like a Virgin*. That record became the first by a female artist to sell more than 10 million copies since Carole King's 1971 album *Tapestry*. In addition to her many hit recordings and music videos, Madonna is known for her roles in such movies as *Desperately Seeking Susan* (1985), *Dick Tracy* (1990), *A League of Their Own* (1992), and *Evita* (1996).

Whether one considers her a pioneer of women's freedom or a supporter of sexism and denigration, one thing about Madonna is certain: She loves the controversy. In her documentary film *Madonna, Truth or Dare* (1991), she says, "I know I'm not the best singer. I know I'm not the best dancer. But I'm not interested in that. I'm interested in pushing people's buttons."

Music Television—MTV—began on August 1, 1981, courtesy of cable television, forever replacing whatever images listeners may have carried in their heads with the specific pictures that flashed across the television while the music blared. Visions such as Madonna wearing pointy brassieres will forever be associated with her songs. MTV not only revolutionized the music industry, it influenced fashion and culture. Cable television grew because many wanted MTV. It provided another medium through which women would be scrutinized.

ENTREPRENEURS

Those who assume the responsibility and the risk for a business with the expectation of making a profit. Entrepreneurs develop new products, find new markets, or invent new means of production. While the American business world has not always welcomed women into the workplace, a number of women have gained respect, influence, and wealth in creating businesses of their own, often developing goods and services tailored to the "women's market" and focused on women's unique concerns. According to the U.S. Department of Commerce there were 5.4 million women-owned businesses in the United States in 1997.

Madame C. J. Walker (1867–1919) was the first African-American businesswoman to become a millionaire. In 1914, **Elizabeth Arden** (1878–1966) founded what would become a multimillion-dollar cosmetics empire. In 1944, Helen Valentine addressed the need for a magazine devoted to young women, founding *Seventeen* magazine and serving as editor-in-chief until 1950. To supplement her new husband's small salary, Lillian Vernon (b. 1927) started a mail-order company under her name in 1951, providing monogrammed accessories for young women. Martha Stewart (b. 1941) built a catering business begun in the late 1970s into an empire of "lifestyle" businesses.

Financial independence was often beyond the reach of many women. Shortly after the end of **World War I**, sisters Lillian and Clara Westropp opened the Women's Savings and Loan Company in Cleveland, Ohio. They employed only women, provided loans to women, and by 1965 the institution had amassed assets of $137 million. In 1932, during the **Great Depression**, Tillie Lewis (1901–1977) made $12,000 selling securities in New York City. In 1934 she brought the Italian tomato industry into the United States and earned a fortune of $100 million. Margaret Fogarty Rudkin (1897–1967) likewise found opportunities in the food industry in those dismal economic times and in 1938 launched her baking company, Pepperidge Farm.

Entrepreneurs looked at the office as well as the kitchen: In 1956, Bette Clair Nesmith Graham (1924–1980) invented Liquid Paper, a correcting fluid that soon became indispensable to offices everywhere.

Perhaps the greatest entrepreneurial phenomenon of the twentieth century, **Oprah Winfrey**, parlayed her success as a talk-show host into Harpo Entertainment Group, a conglomerate including film, television, and video production and magazine publishing.

THE EQUAL CREDIT OPPORTUNITY ACT

A 1974 federal statute stating that individuals cannot be denied credit because of sex, marital status, race, religion, color, or national origin. In part, the Equal Credit Opportunity Act (ECOA) was designed to redress the unfair treatment of women who were denied credit because they were female and/or single and not considered good risks by lending institutions.

ECOA prevents lenders from asking personal questions of a prospective borrower that may have nothing to do with her creditworthiness, including whether the woman intends to eventually have children and may even consider leaving the workplace.

EQUAL EMPLOYMENT OPPORTUNITY COMMISSION

A federal commission that investigates discrimination in employment based on age, disability, race, color, religion, gender, or national origin. The Equal Employment Opportunity Commission (EEOC) was established by **Title VII** of the Civil Rights Act of 1964 and began operation in July 1965. If the commission finds evidence of discrimination, it issues a "notice of right to sue" that enables the charging party to bring an individual action in court.

The commission began as a way of addressing the growing unrest in the nation over racial discrimination and segregation. In the struggle to pass the legislation, Congress reached a compromise that eliminated enforcement authority for the EEOC. Instead, the commission is only able to receive, investigate, and conciliate complaints where it finds reasonable cause to believe that discrimination has occurred. If the EEOC is not able to negotiate an agreement between the two parties, the statute provides only that individuals may bring private lawsuits and where EEOC finds evidence of "patterns or practices" of discrimination, EEOC can refer these matters to the Department of Justice for litigation. In its first year, 8,852 charges were filed. One-third of these charges alleged sex discrimination. To gauge possible discriminatory practices, in 1966, the EEOC began requiring companies to submit reports that showed the representation of men and women in five racial/ethnic groups in nine basic job categories.

Through its guidelines the EEOC has ruled it a violation of equal employment opportunity to classify jobs as male or female, light or heavy, or to maintain separate seniority lists. In addition, the EEOC has made clear that it is illegal to refuse to hire or promote a woman because she is married or has children, unless men are similarly treated. The Supreme Court endorsed this interpretation when it held in *Phillips v. Martin Marietta Corp.* (1971) that employers could not have hiring policies for women with young children that differed from those for men with children of a similar age. In the 1990s, Congress expanded EEOC's authority with the passage of the Americans with Disabilities Act of 1990, the Older Workers Benefit Protection Act of 1990, and the Civil Rights Act of 1991.

EQUAL PAY ACTS OF 1963 AND 1972

Federal laws that prevent discrimination on the basis of sex in the payment of wages. Although legislation had been initially proposed in 1945, it was not until the 1963 act that it became illegal to pay women at a lower rate than men for the same work. Between 1950 and 1960, the number of wives who went to work increased from 21 percent to 30 percent. Greater numbers of working women and their greater involvement in unions encouraged the **Women's Bureau**, headed by **Esther Peterson**, to promote the policy of equal pay.

Women and men did not work in similar jobs in 1960. Several versions of the bill appeared before Congress in 1961 and 1962 that emphasized

WOMEN'S FIRSTS

Sarah Breedlove McWilliams Walker—Madame C. J. Walker—was one of the first women in the United States to become a millionaire through her own efforts and ingenuity. Born in Louisiana on December 23, 1867, Walker parlayed her hair-care treatments for black women into an international cosmetics empire.

This daughter of former slaves began selling her treatments—a regimen of vigorous brushing, shampoo, and a medicinal pomade worked through the hair with a hot comb—in 1905 in St. Louis, Missouri. She moved the following year to Denver, Colorado, where she became "Madame C. J. Walker" after her marriage to Charles J. Walker. In 1908 she opened a second office in Pittsburgh, Pennsylvania, then consolidated her operations in 1910 in Indianapolis, Indiana. By 1919, Walker claimed that more than 20,000 agents sold her products in the United States, Central America, and the Caribbean. She preached "cleanliness and loveliness" as a matter of self-respect and also as a means to improve the attitudes of white people toward African Americans. Walker set high standards of hygiene and social responsibility for her agents, encouraging them also to support black philanthropies. Walker moved to New York in 1916 and built a mansion known as the Villa Lewaro in Irvington-on-Hudson.

Walker's philanthropies were many. She helped save the home of abolitionist Frederick Douglass, supported the National Association for the Advancement of Colored People (NAACP) and several organizations in St. Louis and Indianapolis, and funded scholarships at the Tuskegee Institute.

When she died on May 25, 1919, Madame C. J. Walker was a millionaire and one of the most successful businesspeople of the early twentieth century. In 1997, Walker was honored by the U.S. Postal Service with a commemorative postage stamp.

"comparable work" requiring "comparable skills," rather than "equal work." After several amendments and much compromise, the Equal Pay Act of 1963 was passed.

In 1972 the legislation was expanded to include more of the workforce and more than 171,000 women received more than $84 million in increased wages. Two court cases further established the power of the acts. In *Schultz v. Wheaton Glass Company* (1970), a federal circuit court ruled that jobs needed to be "substantially equal but not identical" to be included under the act. In *Corning Glass Works v. Brennan* (1974), the U.S. Supreme Court ruled that employers cannot pay women lower wages because they had been paid previously under the "going market rate."

This legislation did not challenge discrimination in the types of jobs women took, but it did mark the first time that the federal government defended women's right to equal pay in employment. It prevented employers from reducing the wages of either sex to equalize pay between men and women. The legislation also made it a violation when a different wage was paid to a person who worked in the same job before or after an employee of the opposite sex. Many states and communities have their own fair employment laws and agencies that enforce equal pay protections and other prohibitions against sex discrimination on the job. These laws are similar to and sometimes stronger than federal laws.

TRAILBLAZERS

Alice Paul (1885–1977), a lawyer and social reformer, advocated the use of militant tactics to publicize the need for an Equal Rights Amendment. Paul was involved in both the British and American woman suffrage movements, particularly in Emmeline Pankhurst's suffrage demonstrations in England. Paul was arrested and jailed on six occasions for leading political protests but was never swayed from her dedication to the feminist cause.

Paul headed the Congressional Commission of the National American Woman Suffrage Association (NAWSA) in 1912. In 1913, she founded the Congressional Union for Woman's Suffrage, which merged with the Woman's Party in 1917 to form the NATIONAL WOMAN'S PARTY. As a leader of the National Woman's Party, Paul led the first picket protest ever held in front the White House. In 1923, Paul drafted the Equal Rights Amendment and campaigned for its ratification until her death.

Paul was a member of various women's rights organizations throughout her life. She was chairperson of the Women's Research Foundation (1927–1937) and a member of the Nationality Committee of the International American Committee of Women (1930–1933).

EQUAL RIGHTS AMENDMENT

The proposed Twenty-Seventh Amendment to the U.S. Constitution to outlaw sexual discrimination in the United States. Alice Paul, leader of the **NATIONAL WOMAN'S PARTY** and author of the Equal Rights Amendment (ERA; see Documents), saw her idea first introduced to the U.S. Congress in 1923. The ERA intended to end discrimination on the basis of sex, and specifically to end special treatment for women based on sexual difference.

Opposition to the ERA began immediately after its introduction to Congress. Trade unions and women's groups such as the **LEAGUE OF WOMEN VOTERS** opposed the ERA on the grounds that it might invalidate female-specific **PROTECTIVE LABOR LEGISLATION** that had already

After approval by Congress in 1972, the Equal Rights Amendment was the subject of nationwide ratification marches. By the 1982 deadline, however, the necessary three-fourths of states had not ratified.

been passed, such as minimum wage requirements and maximum hour laws. However, the **Fair Labor Standards Act** (1938), which granted the same protection to men as to women, eased these uncertainties and working-class women became more supportive of the ERA.

But the ERA was never ratified. After years of deliberation, the U.S. Senate defeated the bill for the first time in 1943. Alice Paul reintroduced the ERA at every new session of Congress, albeit to no avail. The ERA finally received house approval in 1971 and Senate approval in 1972. When it went to the states to be ratified by the mandatory three-fourths majority by the 1982 deadline, the ERA fell short by three states.

Credit for the defeat of the ERA has been given to **Phyllis Schlafly**, who founded the **National Committee to Stop ERA**. This committee argued that the biological and psychological differences between men and women are natural, and that the ERA would ruin marriage, family, and the "benefits" of economic dependence of women on men.

Despite its defeat, the ERA continued to be introduced at every new session of Congress. Beginning in 1995, the **National Organization for Women**, which has advocated the ERA since 1966, worked to expand the amendment under the new title "The Constitutional Equality Amendment." The purpose of the proposed law was extended to prohibit discrimination not only against women, but also against race, sexual orientation, marital status, ethnicity, age, and disability.

FURTHER READING

Berry, Mary Frances. *Why ERA Failed: Politics, Women's Rights, and the Amending Process of the Constitution.* Bloomington: Indiana University Press, 1986.

Mansbridge, Jane J. *Why We Lost the ERA.* Chicago: University of Chicago Press, 1986.

F

FAIR LABOR STANDARDS ACT

U.S. federal legislation enacted in 1938 that established minimum wages and maximum hours for many workers in companies involved in interstate commerce. A centerpiece of late **New Deal** economic reform, the Fair Labor Standards Act affirmed federal responsibility for maintaining purchasing power and ensuring a minimal standard of living for employed workers. The law set a minimum wage of $.25 per hour in 1938 (increased gradually over the years) and prohibited the employment of children under age 16 during school hours or under 18 in dangerous working conditions. Amendments to the legislation have extended its protections to more low-income workers and reduced the number of hours that could be worked without mandatory overtime time (from 44 to 40). The law also requires equal pay for equal work without regard to gender.

The mandatory minimum wage has been opposed by some economists, who argue that it limits job opportunities for minorities and young people entering the workforce. For women, the establishment of a minimum wage proved beneficial to the millions who took manufacturing jobs during **World War II**, and the requirement of equal pay for equal work mirrored a tenet of the women's rights movement into the twenty-first century.

See also: Infant and Child Health.

FAMILY AND MEDICAL LEAVE ACT

Federal legislation passed in 1993 that protects the jobs of employees who must leave work temporarily to care for family members. The Family and Medical Leave Act (FMLA) of 1993 is one of several labor laws that attempt to equalize treatment of men and women in the workplace. In the first half of the twentieth century, unions pushed for and succeeded in obtaining protective labor legislation, laws designed to protect workers against exploitation in the workplace. Many of these laws were specifically intended to protect women as well as poor, unskilled, and immigrant workers, but some had unwanted consequences. For example, laws forbidding employers to force women to lift heavy loads were used to keep women from better-paying jobs. The Family and Medical Leave Act, however, applies equally to men and women and provides for both men and women to take time off work to deal with family medical issues, such as the birth of a child or the illness of a family member.

Before the passage of this legislation, employers were more likely to expect women to be caregivers. Many threatened men with job loss if they took time off, in essence forcing women to take charge in most medical situations. Before the passage of this and similar legislation, many women lost their jobs when they took time off to have and care for newborn babies or when ill children or spouses needed their attention.

Unions such as the American Federation of State, County, and Municipal Employees (AFSCME), which is mostly composed of women and men of color, and the Coalition of Labor Union Women (CLUW) were among organizations that worked for the passage of this law.

FMLA provides that eligible employees may take a leave of up to 12 weeks in a 12-month period to take care of a newborn baby, a newly adopted child, or a sick family member, or to recover from illness or surgery, without jeopardizing his or her job or medical benefits. The employee is granted the right to return to his or her original position or an equivalent one at the end of the leave. The law also provides that the employer must maintain health benefits during the employee's absence and also allows the employee to work a part-time schedule if needed so that he or she can be available to manage a family medical situation.

The law applies to all public-sector employers and private-sector employers who have 50 or more workers. Employees must have worked for the employer for at least 12 months (at least 1,250 hours) prior to requesting the leave. They must also provide the employer with as much advance notice as possible and may be required to submit proof from a physician of the need for the leave. Since the passage of this law, many men have been allowed to take time off work when a child is born, a benefit that had generally not previously been available to most families.

FASHION

Fashion design, unlike architecture, landscaping, and other design areas from which women were excluded, was from the onset a field in which women figured prominently. American women had long been making clothing for themselves, their families, and for others, so at the turn of the twentieth century, designing clothing professionally was seen as an appropriate "feminine" career choice for the middle-class woman, one that could provide her with a means of income. Until the second half of the twentieth century, women who were not a part of the white middle class generally did not have access to a professional career in fashion design.

In the nineteenth and early twentieth centuries, Paris was the undisputed center of fashion. Charles Frederick Worth established *haute couture*, the professional art of custom clothing design. Working-class women, unable to afford dressmakers who might copy *couture* styles, wore manufactured clothing. It was American designers who would introduce the concept of democracy with ready-to-wear clothing, extending fashion to the average woman.

American Women Designers

While **World War II** disrupted Paris's *couture* industry, it ushered in the age of the American designer. Dorothy Shaver, the vice president of Lord & Taylor, had set the stage a few years earlier when she began crediting American designers (instead of manufacturers) with clothing creations. In 1941, when contact with Paris was severed, the American designer gained prominence.

American fashion designers can trace their beginnings to dressmakers in the nineteenth century, most of whom were female. Dressmakers worked in relative anonymity, on their own or for dress shops or department stores. Ellen Curtis Demorest, known as Madame Demorest, was one of the first dressmakers to attain national stature. In addition to managing her own store in New York beginning in 1860, she invented the mass-produced paper clothing pattern and published a quarterly fashion magazine.

Hattie Carnegie was to further advance fashion as a business in the United States. Starting out in 1909 by pinning hats in a millinery workroom, in 1915 she and a partner opened a custom dressmaking salon in New York. Carnegie soon bought out her partner to gain sole ownership of the business, which grew into a multimillion-dollar enterprise. Carnegie was known for quality fabrics, fine workmanship, and sophisticated designs.

Two important American designers, Pauline Trigère and Clair McCardell, worked for Hattie Carnegie early in their careers. Twenty-year-old Trigère, married with two children, had come to New York from Paris in 1932. She became an assistant designer at Hattie Carnegie and in 1942 opened her own business. Trigère worked directly from fabric, cutting and draping. Her designs, simple in appearance, are noted for their intricate artistry.

Claire McCardell is regarded by many as the most important twentieth-century American ready-to-wear designer. During the 1940s, McCardell was influential in establishing a unique style referred to as the "American Look." McCardell's designs were intended to be both fashionable and comfortable. McCardell worked with carefree materials such as denim, ticking, gingham, and jersey wool.

California native Bonnie Cashin was a dressmaker's daughter. Cashin is considered one of America's most innovative designers. Rather than looking to Paris for inspiration, she designed functional clothing for women's active lifestyles. Her clothing allowed for a woman's individual expression, she often said. After 1952, Cashin did freelance work for companies interested in manufacturing her designs.

By the 1950s women were increasingly recognized as accomplished designers, yet men too gained ground. The spotlight turned to Parisian male *couturiers*, most notably Christian Dior. Contrary to the more egalitarian attitude reflected in the clothing of the female American designers, Christian Dior's designs were seen as more elitist, ignoring the practical needs of everyday life.

In the early 1960s, London designers captured the fashion world's attention by adapting the youthful nonconformity of street dress into their designs. People were called upon to reject commercial fashion in favor of their own natural look, epitomized by "hippie" styles. American women designers of this decade responded by making clothing that met the needs of the modern woman, as had their predecessors. Anne Klein designed practical and elegantly tailored separate skirts and blouses for the businesswoman, as well as sophisticated sportswear. Liz Claiborne and Donna Karan (Anne Klein's former assistant) continued, each in her own way, in this direction.

Liz Claiborne, Inc., formed in 1976, found success by providing women with moderately priced career clothing. Claiborne's intuitive understanding of her customer and keen management skills made hers the first business started by a woman to become a Fortune 500 company.

In 1985 Donna Karan left her longtime position of chief designer at Anne Klein to launch her own company. Taking a more daring turn than her mentor, Karan found immediate success with her body suits. Karan describes her designs as simple, savvy, sophisticated, and easy to wear.

In the early 1970s, Betsy Johnson saw the fashion garment industry and the country as a whole as uninspired and conservative and she decided to act as a balance to this trend. Johnson's designs use elements of popular culture in innovative ways. She has found a niche with the teenage market.

From the 1980s on, American fashion became more diverse. Asian-American designers Vera Wang, Anna Sui, and Vivienne Tam achieved international recognition. As fashion's scope continues to broaden, women designers from underrepresented groups will find greater acceptance.

While female designers span the creative range from the conservative tailored-style to fashions that are on the cutting edge, there is a commitment to making clothes that are versatile and attractive. Clothing that is sexually objectifying, exaggerated, and overly restrictive is not associated with female designers. Male designers tend to concentrate on the total visual effect, one that intends to dazzle or excite the viewer. Ruth Rubinstein contrasts the overtly sexual and aggressive male approach to design with the sensual, gentler effect created by women designers.

Veronica Manlow

FURTHER READING

Rubinstein, Ruth P. *Dress Codes: Meanings and Messages in American Culture*. Boulder, CO: Westview Press, 1995.

FEINSTEIN, DIANNE GOLDMAN (b. 1933)

Politician. Dianne Emiel Goldman was born in San Francisco, California, on June 22, 1933. She entered Stanford University, graduating in 1955 with a B.S. in political science and history. A year later, she married lawyer Jack Berman. The couple were divorced in 1959. During the 1960s, Diane Goldman was involved with the California prison system, serving as chair of the San Francisco Advisory Committee for Adult Detention. In 1962, she married Bertram Feinstein and began pursuing a political career. In 1969 she was elected to the San Francisco Board of Supervisors, the governing body for the city.

As president of the Board of Supervisors, Feinstein became mayor of San Francisco after the assassination of Mayor George Moscone in 1978. The following year, she was elected mayor in her own right and continued to hold the office until 1988. Meanwhile, her husband had died, and she remarried in 1980. Feinstein and Richard C. Blum have one daughter, Katherine.

In 1992, Feinstein was elected to the U.S. Senate from California, filling the final two years of the unexpired term of Pete Wilson, who had just been elected governor. Feinstein was reelected in 1994 and 2000. As California's senior senator, she serves on the Senate Appropriations Committee and the Senate Judiciary Committee.

FEMINISM, RADICAL

The belief that women constitute an oppressed group and that the oppression of women constitutes the first oppression in society. Radical feminism was articulated as a theory in the second wave of feminism that arose in the 1960s and 1970s. Women are seen as a class, much like a social class, although radical feminists reject the idea that capitalism has created (or that socialism would solve) women's oppression. Instead, they examine patriarchy, a universal system of male dominance created by men to subordinate women. Radical feminists argue that this system is prevalent throughout the world (although it takes on different forms in different places) and believe that the oppression of women crosses boundaries of race, class, geography, and culture.

As a theory, radical feminism rejects reform. Radical feminists do not believe that having women adapt to the existing system is a solution. Instead they demand revolution, a complete change in the structures of society. They argue that in order to undermine patriarchy, women must come together as a group and act rather than theorize. For radical feminists, examining oppression is not enough—action must be taken.

FERRARO, GERALDINE (b. 1935)

The first female vice presidential candidate nominated by a major party, Geraldine Ferraro was born in Newburgh, New York, and educated at Marymount College (B.A., 1956) and Fordham University Law School (J.D., 1960).

Before beginning her political career, Ferraro worked as a teacher in Queens, New York, and with the New York Investigations Bureau. She also worked for the Special Victims Bureau, where her experiences with abused women and children compelled her to move into politics.

In 1978, Ferraro became the first woman to be elected to the U.S. House of Representatives from New York's Ninth Congressional District. She was reelected in 1980 and 1982. In 1982, she cosponsored the Economic Equity Act, which achieved many of the aims of the **Equal Rights Amendment**. After chairing the 1984 Democratic Platform Committee (the first woman to hold this position), Democratic presidential candidate Walter Mondale chose her as his running mate. Ferraro's politics were liberal and profeminist. However, she was criticized for her lack of experience in both military and foreign affairs. On the other hand, she was popular with many women and received $4 million in campaign contributions from women alone. Mondale and Ferraro lost the 1984 presidential election, but Ferraro set a precedent for future female candidates.

In 1992, Ferraro ran in the primary race for the Democratic Senate nomination for New York state, but lost to Robert Abrams. In 1993, she served as the U.S. representative to the U.N. Human Rights Commission. She lives with her husband, John Zaccaro, in New York.

FIORINA, CARA CARLETON S. (b. 1954)

A leader and innovator in telecommunications and technology. Carly Fiorina, as she is known, received a bachelor's degree in medieval history and philosophy from Stanford University in 1976 and a master's degree in business administration from the University of Maryland in 1980. She began her career at telecommunications giant AT&T as an account executive and rose to hold a number of senior positions with that company. In 1996, Fiorina helped manage the spinoff from AT&T of Lucent Technologies, a company specializing in broadband and mobile Internet technology. She spearheaded the initial public offering of Lucent stock and for two years served as president of Lucent's global service provider business, selling equipment to telephone companies. In 1999, Fiorina became chief executive officer and president of Hewlett-Packard, the world's second-biggest manufacturer of computers. By becoming one of only a few women to hold top positions in the technology field, Fiorina helped shatter the **GLASS CEILING** keeping women from leading large companies.

Ella Fitzgerald became known as "The First Lady of Song."

FITZGERALD, ELLA

(1917?–1996)

Jazz singer and lyricist. Ella Fitzgerald was born on April 25th in Newport News, Virginia. Sources disagree on her actual year of birth. It is assumed she lied about her age when she began her career because of child labor laws. Also in question are facts about her father, William Fitzgerald. Some sources claim he died when she was an infant, while others state that he never married her mother, Temperance Williams, and he disappeared soon after Ella's birth. When Fitzgerald was 15, her mother died, and Fitzgerald lived many places, including with her maternal aunt, in an orphanage, and at a girls' school, from which she ran away. She lived on the streets of Harlem and made money tap dancing.

Ella Fitzgerald's career began on a dare. Her friends convinced her to enter a talent contest at the Apollo Theater in Harlem. She was supposed to dance, but changed her mind at the last minute and sang "The Object of My Affection" instead. She won first place. Afterwards, she won various other amateur talent contests before being discovered by bandleader Chick Webb, who hired her as the vocalist for his band. Within a few short years she earned the title "The First Lady of Song."

In addition to singing and popularizing scat, a freeform jazz vocal style, Fitzgerald wrote lyrics. Her first major songwriting success was "A Tisket, A Tasket" (1938). Her songs were recorded by Duke Ellington, Nat King Cole, and **BILLIE HOLIDAY**. In 1943, she was the youngest person ever to be inducted into the American Society of Composers, Authors, and Publishers (ASCAP). Throughout the 1950s and 1960s, Fitzgerald's Songbook Recordings repopularized the songs of Irving Berlin and George Gershwin. She also added film to her list of achievements when she appeared in *Pete Kelley's Blues* (1955) and *St. Louis Blues* (1958). She continued her work as a vocalist into the 1980s, performing 40 weeks a year despite health problems. In 1986 she had open heart surgery, and in 1987 her legs were amputated below the knees due to complications with diabetes.

Fitzgerald retired in 1994, two years before her death on June 15, 1996. In her lifetime, she earned eight honorary doctorates in music and humane letters, although she only had a tenth grade education. She also received various lifetime achievement awards.

FLORENCE CRITTENDON HOMES

A nonprofit organization to assist women in need. When wealthy businessman Charles Crittendon lost his daughter, Florence, to scarlet fever in 1882, he underwent a religious conversion that led him to become a philanthropist. While doing missionary work in New York City's red light district, Crittendon encountered two prostitutes and convinced them to seek comfort in Christianity as he had when his daughter died. Within a year, Crittendon founded the "Florence Night Mission" for women seeking shelter and other assistance. In 1893, the organization changed its name to the "Florence Crittendon Mission" and opened several branches in various parts of the United States.

Florence Crittendon Homes became well known for assisting unwed pregnant women. In the 1950s and 1960s, some parents sent their daughters to Crittendon facilities to hide unwanted pregnancies. When the babies were born, they were usually adopted. Today, Florence Crittendon Homes still assist unwed mothers and function as adoption agencies. In addition, they also offer emotional counseling to teenage girls, parenting classes for young mothers, and substance abuse services for mothers and their unborn babies.

FORD, ELIZABETH (BETTY) BLOOMER (b. 1918)

The wife of Gerald R. Ford, the thirtieth-eighth president of the United States. Elizabeth Ann Bloomer was born on April 8, 1918, in Chicago, Illinois, the daughter of a traveling salesman. She grew up in Grand Rapids, Michigan. After studying **DANCE** at Bennington College, she became a member of the **MARTHA GRAHAM** professional company and a **FASHION** model. Bloomer married William Warren in 1942 but was divorced five years later. She married Ford in 1948, during his first campaign for Congress. They would have four children together.

Betty Ford raised the children and supported her husband during his 26 years in Congress. He became vice president of the United States following the resignation of Spiro Agnew in 1973 and president one year later, when the Watergate scandal forced Richard Nixon to leave the White House. Betty Ford was first lady from 1974 to 1977—and highly visible.

Within months of moving into the White House, Ford underwent breast cancer surgery. Her candid discussion of the disease and mastectomy raised public awareness and led to a sharp increase in the number of women who requested mammograms. As first lady, Ford actively promoted women's rights, calling for more career opportunities for women, supporting legalized abortion, and urging passage of the **EQUAL RIGHTS AMENDMENT**. Her candor regarding consultations with a psychiatrist and her concern for personal **HEALTH** issues led the public to identify with her as with few other first ladies.

During the 1960s, while suffering from a pinched nerve, Ford had become addicted to prescription painkillers and alcohol. In 1976, when her husband lost the presidential election to Jimmy Carter, Ford intensified her alcohol and pill consumption. After a family intervention in 1978, she sought treatment.

As a result of her experiences, Ford dedicated her efforts to combatting chemical dependencies. In 1982 she established the Betty Ford Center, a well-known and highly respected alcohol and addiction treatment facility in Michigan.

FRANKLIN, ARETHA (b. 1942)

Singer. When she was born in Memphis, Tennessee, on March 25, 1942, Aretha Franklin's parents had no idea that she would one day earn the title "Queen of Soul." The daughter of a minister, Franklin had her musical start in her father's parish choir. After her mother abandoned the family, Franklin was cared for and inspired by many of her father's colleagues, including such gospel greats as Mahalia Jackson. With a vocal range spanning five octaves, Franklin landed her first recording contract at the age of 14.

Franklin dropped out of high school in 1958 to have a baby. She moved to New York three years later and by 1961 she had a recording contract with Columbia Records. However, her biggest success occurred in 1967 when she gained platinum sales (1 million records sold) with the single "I Never Loved a Man (The Way I Love You)" on the Atlantic label. Soon afterward, "Respect" became her first international hit. Her career with Atlantic Records pushed her into the spotlight as a crossover artist, as she gained a broad white audience. Between 1967 and 1974, Franklin won the Grammy Award for Best R&B Vocal Performance by a Female an astonishing eight times.

Between 1975 and 1985, Franklin's musical career was subdued. When her father was shot by a burglar in 1979 and went into an irreversible coma, Franklin cared for him. By the time he died five years later, she had spent countless hours and over half a million dollars for his care. During this period she married actor Glynn Turman. Including her previous children (one from a marriage to her former manager, Ted White), the couple raised four sons.

During Franklin's musical hiatus she played a role in the 1980 film *The Blues Brothers*. Then, in 1985, she made a comeback with *Who's Zoomin' Who,* her biggest album since *Lady Soul* in 1968. Two years later, she became the first woman ever inducted into the Rock and Roll Hall of Fame.

Franklin's other achievements include a Lifetime Achievement Grammy (in addition to her other 15 Grammy Awards) and an honorary doctorate from Wayne State University in Detroit, Michigan, where she was raised. In 1986, the state of Michigan proclaimed Aretha Franklin's voice one of the state's "natural resources" as a tribute to America's Queen of Soul.

FRIEDAN, BETTY GOLDSTEIN (b. 1921)

Feminist, social reformer. Friedan was born Betty Naomi Goldstein in Peoria, Illinois, on February 4, 1921. Throughout her childhood, Friedan experienced anti-semitism first hand, which prompted her early interest in social issues. As a high school student, she edited her high school newspaper and a student literary magazine, which she cofounded. In 1942, Friedan received her B.S. in psychology from Smith College, where she also edited the student newspaper and founded a literary magazine. She studied for a master's degree at the University of California at Berkeley, but completed only one year before moving to New York City to write for a workers' newspaper. While covering strikes and labor issues, Friedan noticed discrimination against women and became politically active in the fight for women's rights.

When Friedan and her then–husband, actor Carl Friedan, were expecting their second child in 1949, she was fired from her job at the newspaper because of her pregnancy. She was a stay-at-home mother for several years, over which time she developed her theory on feminism. She argued against the notion that women should choose between a career and a family. Curious about how other women felt, Friedan surveyed Smith College graduates and found that many of them suffered depression as a result of giving up their careers to become homemakers. From her data, Friedan penned an article and submitted it to the *Ladies' Home Journal*. The story was rejected by the male editors.

Undiscouraged, Friedan spent five more years completing her research. The result was a book entitled *The Feminine Mystique* (1963) (see Documents), her name for the suffering women endured due to the social convention that women should remain in the home rather than pursue careers. The book sold three million copies by 1966 and made Friedan the "Mother of the Feminist Movement." The positive public response to *The Feminine Mystique* prompted Friedan to work with others to found the **National Organization for Women** (NOW) in October 1966. As the president of the organization, she wrote a feminist magazine column in *McCall's* and lectured extensively until 1970. That year she left NOW. Betty Friedan was named Humanist of the Year in 1975, and today she continues to write, lecture, and teach.

FURTHER READING

Friedan, Betty. *Life So Far.* New York: Simon & Schuster, 2000.

Horowitz, Daniel. *Betty Friedan and the Making of* The Feminine Mystique: *The American Left, the Cold War, and Modern Feminism.* Amherst: University of Massachusetts Press, 1998.

FRONTIERO v. RICHARDSON

Supreme Court case (1973) involving gender discrimination. The case involved the right of a woman (Sharron Frontiero) in the armed forces to claim her husband as a dependent for the purpose of obtaining a larger housing allowance and covering him under her medical and dental benefits. Under federal law at the time, a serviceman could automatically claim his wife as a dependent, whether or not she was employed, but a servicewoman had to prove that her husband was dependent on her for over half his support.

With just one dissenting vote, the Court ruled that by setting up an arbitrary distinction based on sex, the law violated the due process clause of the Fifth Amendment to the U.S. Constitution. The Court did not strike down all classifications based on sex but said that any classification of who was a dependent and who was not had to serve a legitimate legislative purpose. As in *Reed v. Reed* the Court was showing a growing willingness to strike down state and federal laws that it found discriminatory.

G

GARLAND, JUDY (1922–1969)

Singer and actress. Judy Garland was born Frances Ethel Gumm to Frank Gumm and Ethel Milne, vaudevillian actors. In 1926, her family moved from Grand Rapids, Minnesota, to Hollywood. There they performed a family act with the three daughters as "The Gumm Sisters." When they were incorrectly introduced as "The Garland Sisters" in 1934, the name stuck. At age 13, Garland signed her first contract with MGM studios. She is most remembered for her role as Dorothy in *The Wizard of Oz* (1939). Following this success, Garland worked a rigorous schedule, making two to three films per year in the 1940s. She starred in many popular movies, including *Meet Me in St. Louis* (1944) and *Royal Wedding* (1950) with Fred Astaire.

Overworked, by age 21 Garland had become addicted to barbiturates and amphetamines, prescribed to aid her constant hyperactivity and insomnia. Later addictions to diet pills and alcohol caused many downfalls and comebacks in her career. By 1959, she was a semi-invalid because of liver damage and had attempted suicide. She died of a barbiturate overdose in London on June 22, 1969. Her legacy lives on through her films, her vocal recordings, and her daughters.

GIBSON, ALTHEA (b. 1927)

Professional tennis player and golfer. Althea Gibson was the first African American to compete in the U.S. Nationals and break the color barrier at the Wimbledon Championships in lawn tennis in London. Tennis, like many amateur and professional sports, was segregated before 1950.

Gibson was interested in sports from an early age, first playing basketball, then paddle tennis. She took up tennis after a friend gave her a racquet. During high school, Gibson began playing tennis in the nearly all black American Tennis Association in New York. She won the national black women's tennis championship twice but, because of segregation, was not invited to the U.S. Championships at Forest Hills until 1950, after white tennis champion Alice Marble advanced her cause in *American Lawn Tennis* magazine. Despite the fact that she was not allowed into the clubs where the tournaments were held and hotels often refused her rooms, Gibson persisted in tennis and in the 1960s joined the professional golf tour. Althea Gibson paved the way for other black athletes, such as Arthur Ashe, Venus Williams, and Tiger Woods.

Gibson lives in East Orange, New Jersey, where she is reclusive after suffering a series of strokes.

GINSBURG, RUTH BADER (b. 1933)

U.S. Supreme Court justice. Ruth Joan Bader was born in Brooklyn, New York, on March 15, 1933, to Nathan and Cecelia (Amster) Bader. Cecelia Bader, who supported women's rights, encouraged her daughter to excel in academics. At age 12, Ruth wrote an essay entitled "Landmarks for Constitutional Freedom," which was published in her school newspaper and showed her early interest in justice.

Bader received her bachelor's degree in government from Cornell University in 1954, just before her marriage to Martin Ginsburg. Martin was drafted into the military soon after the wedding. As a military wife, Ruth Ginsburg encountered sexual discrimination for the first time. Upon applying for a GS-5 (government servant, level 5) position, she was demoted to GS-2 when her pregnancy was discovered. The GS-5 position went to another woman who was also pregnant but lied in order to get the job.

After her husband's discharge, Ginsburg attended Harvard Law School. She was one of only nine women at the school. Because men at the law school were taken more seriously than women, Ginsburg was determined to prove her academic worth. Her perseverance earned her the nickname "Ruthless Ruthie." When her husband acquired new employment in New York, Ginsburg transferred to Columbia University Law School in 1958. One year later she graduated as valedictorian of her class.

Within a few years she became the second woman to join the faculty at Rutgers University

Law School. By the late 1960s, the American Civil Liberties Union was referring its sexual discrimination cases to Ginsburg—not because she expressed interest in them, but because she was a woman. However, upon becoming involved in the discrimination lawsuits, Ginsburg became an advocate of the **WOMEN'S LIBERATION MOVEMENT**.

Ginsburg's first important case was ***REED v. REED*** in 1971. As a result of this case, the Supreme Court overturned an Idaho law granting preference to men over women as administrators of estates. Over the course of the 1970s, Ginsburg argued six sexual discrimination cases before the Supreme Court and won five of them.

Her successes prompted President Jimmy Carter to nominate her to the U.S. Court of Appeals for Washington, D.C., in 1980. On August 3, 1993, she was confirmed as the 107th Supreme Court Justice, the second female jurist in U.S. history. Her other achievements include the founding of the **AMERICAN CIVIL LIBERTIES UNION** Women's Rights Project (1972) and several articles in support of abortion rights, gay rights, and affirmative action.

GIRL SCOUTS OF AMERICA

A social and service organization for girls founded in 1915. When an educated woman of diverse interests named Juliette Low met Robert Baden-Powell, the founder of the scouting movement and the Boy Scouts and Girl Guides in England, she wanted to establish a similar group for girls in the United States. With the Girl Scouts of America (GSA), she hoped to follow Baden-Powell's example and establish an organization encouraging the development of morals and citizenship through the study of nature.

She began in her own backyard, holding troop meetings in the stable of her Savannah, Georgia, home. In 1913, she published an adaptation of the English "Girl Guides" handbook entitled *How Girls Can Help Their Country*. The Girl Scouts was incorporated as an organization in 1915. In 1938, the GSA expanded to accommodate different age groups and in the 1960s and 1970s expanded their scope of membership and social awareness.

Predicated on the idea of preparing girls for the responsibilities of womanhood and citizenship in a rapidly changing world, the Girl Scouts offers education on a broad variety of subjects. With an emphasis on outdoor education and mental and physical health, the Girl Scouts provides activity, community, and purpose for girls from all racial, religious, and economic backgrounds. A range of programs, such as the Daisy Scouts for girls aged five to seven, Brownies for girls seven to ten, and Seniors, for high school girls, provides opportunities for positive activity within a community of girls throughout a girl's development.

The Girl Scouts is a worldwide organization that encourages self-sufficiency and cooperation.

GLASS CEILING

Term signifying the invisible, extra-legal barriers preventing the upward mobility of women and minorities, particularly in corporate environments. Journalists Carol Hymowitz and Timothy Schellhardt originally coined the term in 1986 to connote the absence of women in upper-level management and executive jobs in corporate America. Since then, the definition has grown to include the same phenomenon in other industries, as well as the exclusion of minorities from high-level positions.

While the disparity is shrinking, women overall as a group are still only making 75 percent of men's salaries. One reason for this is that women are denied access to the positions that offer higher salaries. This is known as a job segregation effect, in which women are corralled into lower-level staff positions that afford little room for growth. Other names given to this phenomenon that helps to keep the glass ceiling intact are "sticky floor" and "pink ghetto." Positions that offer the possibility of promotion frequently fall outside the gendered division of labor adopted by many companies.

Other contributing factors to the glass ceiling within companies are sex discrimination and racism in hiring and promotion practices, sexual harassment, the exclusion of women and minorities from the communication networks of higher-level management, a "glass wall" that discourages the lateral movement of women and minorities from staff to management-track positions, and unfair standards in performance evaluations and salary decisions.

In 1989, the Department of Labor Glass Ceiling Commission began an investigation of the phenomenon. In 1991, it issued findings that concluded that corporations were not committed to ending gender and race discrimination in the workplace. It identified a low priority placed on equal access, no appraisal systems and record keeping of access monitoring, and informal practices such as "old-boy" networks (all-male cliques) as key problem areas. Also, they found that minorities hit a ceiling even lower than women, which disadvantaged women of color in particular. In 1993, the commission issued directives for companies such as eliminating barriers for women and minorities to management-track positions, cultivating high-potential women and advocating support from high-level management for the directives.

The glass ceiling has only been broken to a significant extent in a few instances. In 1999, **Carly Fiorina** became the first woman CEO of a Fortune 500 Company when she joined Hewlett-Packard. In 1999, women held still only 11.2 percent of executive-level positions in Fortune 500 Companies, and only 7 percent of women served as officers.

GOLDMAN, EMMA

(1869–1940)

Anarchist. Born June 27, 1869 in Kovono, Lithuania, Goldman emigrated to the United States in 1885 to live with her sister in Rochester, New York. As a garment worker, Goldman participated in a strike for the eight-hour workday in 1886, just three days before Chicago's famous Haymarket strikes, in which anarchists were blamed for a bomb that killed seven during a clash between police and workers protesting the eight-hour workday. She rapidly became active in social politics.

In 1887, she gained U.S. citizenship by marrying fellow factory worker Jacob Kersner, whom she divorced a year later. In 1889, Goldman met Alexander Berkman, who became her lover and ideological partner. Together, they fought for many causes. In 1890, she launched a lecture tour, espousing beliefs such as free speech, workers' rights, and anarchism. Her impassioned speeches and bold oration skills on behalf of the anarchist cause earned her the nickname "Queen of the Anarchists."

Goldman's beliefs in anarchism and communism emphasized absolute liberty and freedom from all institutions. For this reason, she did not support the **SUFFRAGE MOVEMENT**. Her anarchism was closely tied to other feminist beliefs, however, and she wrote and lectured extensively on birth control and **LESBIAN** rights, and likened **MARRIAGE** to the degradation of **PROSTITUTION**.

In 1892, Berkman attempted to assassinate Henry Clay Frick, the plant manager of Carnegie Steel in Pennsylvania, to avenge the deaths of nine striking workers killed by plant guards. He was arrested and sentenced to 22 years in prison, and Goldman was implicated in the crime. In 1901 she was linked with President McKinley's assassination by an anarchist.

In New York in 1893, Goldman gave a trademark incendiary speech urging hungry workers to steal bread and was sentenced to prison. The U.S. government viewed her as a highly dangerous agitator and, in 1909, invalidated her ex-husband's citizenship, on which her own was based. Goldman was sentenced to prison once more in 1917 for antidraft agitation. A few months after her 1919 release, she and Berkman were deported. She returned to Russia but was disappointed by corruption within the leadership of the Bolshevik Revolution. The Revolution incited a "Red Scare" throughout Europe, as countries feared Marxist revolt. This made it difficult for Goldman as she traveled through Europe advocating on behalf of her many causes. Eventually, she settled in Canada. Although Goldman died there on May 14, 1940, she was buried in Chicago, next to her Haymarket heroes.

GRABLE, BETTY

(1916–1973)

Film and stage actress. Ruth Elizabeth Grable's mother primed her in dance, song, and saxophone, and she began her career in vaudeville at age five. At the age of 13, Grable and her mother moved from St. Louis, Missouri, to Los Angeles, where Grable signed her first contract with 20th Century Fox. She was soon dismissed, however, because she was underage. She signed with MGM Studios three years later.

Grable was a major sex symbol of the **World War II** era. A common slogan of the 1940s was "As American as apple pie and Betty Grable." Her image, borrowed from her film *Pin-Up Girl* (1944), was painted on World War II fighter planes. She was especially noted for her legs, which were insured for $1 million by her film studio. Grable's many film credits include *The Gay Divorcee* (1934) and *How to Marry a Millionaire* (1953). She spent a great deal of her career starring in musical film and was the highest paid woman in the United States in the mid-1940s. She died in Santa Monica, California, of lung cancer on July 2, 1973.

GRAHAM, KATHARINE MEYER

(1917–2001)

Newspaper publisher. Katharine Meyer was born on June 16, 1917, in New York City. Her father, Eugene Meyer, a wealthy financier, bought the *Washington Post* newspaper in 1933. After graduating from the University of Chicago in 1938, Katharine Meyer became a reporter at the *Post*.

Two years later, she married Philip Graham, who became publisher of the *Post* in 1946. Although Graham was an effective publisher, he and Katharine had an unhappy marriage. He was a heavy drinker who abused his wife and carried on affairs with other women. Graham was also afflicted with manic depression and eventually committed suicide in 1963.

Following his death, Katharine Graham took over running of the *Post*. "I had very little idea of what I was supposed to be doing," she wrote in her autobiography, "so I set out to learn. What I essentially did was to put one foot in front of the other, shut my eyes, and step off the edge."

Under her leadership, the newspaper enlarged its circulation and became one of the most powerful publications in America. Defying the government, Graham published the Pentagon Papers in 1971, revealing secret information about U.S. conduct of the **Vietnam War**. *Post* reporters also investigated the Watergate scandal, which led to the resignation of President Richard Nixon in 1974. Graham served as chair and CEO of the paper from 1973 until 1991. In 1999, she was awarded the Pulitzer Prize for her autobiography, *Personal History*. She died on July 17, 2001, of a brain hemorrhage.

GRAHAM, MARTHA

(1894–1991)

Pioneer of modern dance. Born on May 11, 1894, in Allegheny, Pennsylvania, to a doctor with puritanical views, Martha Graham arrived relatively late to the art of dance. After attending

TRAILBLAZERS

A one-time student of Martha Graham's, Twyla Tharp has been a leader in the modern dance movement. Born July 1, 1941, in Indiana, Tharp's mother encouraged her daughter in the arts at an early age. A serious and driven student, Tharp excelled in school and extracurriculars. She transferred to Barnard College from Pomona College and received a degree in art history but discovered her desire to become a dancer.

Tharp immersed herself in the study of dance, training formally with masters of both classical and modern dance such as Martha Graham, Paul Taylor, and Merce Cunningham. She gave her first concert on April 29, 1965, in a Hunter College performance space. The entire performance lasted seven minutes and was entitled "Tank Dive."

Not long thereafter, Tharp assembled her own group of four women dancers. In 1967, they were commissioned to create and perform at the Bang Festival in Richmond, Virginia. Her style was an energetic, highly physical blend of modern dance and classical ballet. And while the dances were deeply expressive, Tharp maintained a very cool facial demeanor which puzzled some critics. Nonetheless, as she gained exposure, she began to receive favorable reviews. Seen as a daring and avant-garde artist, she was frequently approached to choreograph projects in collaboration with other artists. Among the more notable of these collaborations were *Deuce Coupe* for the Joffrey Ballet; *Push Comes to Shove* for Mikhail Baryshnikov, whose first experience in avant-garde dance with Tharp prompted a newfound love for modern dance; *Hair*, for the film director Milos Forman; and *The Catherine Wheel* with Talking Heads frontman David Byrne.

Tharp continues to direct and choreograph for her own dance company, as well as for film and television.

an arts high school and junior college, she joined the Denishawn Dance Company at age 22.

In 1923, she moved to New York to dance with the Greenwich Village Follies and left in 1925 to teach at the University of Rochester's Eastman School of Dance, where she choreographed her first solos. She approached the Follies for support. The Follies agreed, but on the condition that Graham return to it for another year if she did not achieve success. However, her first performance in 1926 earned promising reviews and a small following, so she established her own company in 1929, which would later produce dancers such as Paul Taylor, Merce Cunningham, and Twyla Tharp. In 1935, Graham established a school of modern dance at Bennington College in Vermont.

Graham created many dances based on famous women and accompanied her work with music by modern composers such as Aaron Copland and sets created by avant-garde sculptor Isamu Noguchi. She viewed dance as a means of expressing her heart, and created and performed with a passion and fierce physicality that would both enchant and unsettle critics. Most of her pieces were too austerely modern and too volatile to endure, but she also choreographed classics such as *Appalachian Spring*, a celebration of a Quaker wedding. This piece remains as a hallmark of a remarkable career at the forefront of modern dance.

Graham danced until age 74 and continued to choreograph until her death on April 1, 1991. She was awarded the Presidential Medal of Freedom in 1976.

GRASSO, ELLA (1919–1981)

The first woman to win a state governorship on her own merits. Ella Grasso rose to national prominence through devotion to her roots in her local community. Her accessibility, her honesty, and her plain-spoken style ensured that she never lost an election. Born in Windsor Locks, Connecticut, Grasso graduated from Mt. Holyoke College in 1940. She became involved in politics in 1943, when she joined the **League of Women Voters.** She served on the Windsor Locks Democratic Town Committee, then was elected to the Connecticut General Assembly in 1952 and again in 1954. Her children were small then, and she relied on her extended family in Windsor Locks for help with child care. She was appointed Connecticut's secretary of state in 1958, and served for three terms. In 1970 and again in 1972, she was elected to the U.S. Congress, where to make herself accessible to her constituents she set up a 24-hour toll-free "Ella-phone." In 1974 she ran successfully for governor of Connecticut. She won a second term in 1978, but had to resign in 1980 because of illness; she died on February 5, 1981.

GREAT DEPRESSION

The worldwide economic disaster of the 1930s. The 1920s were a time of prosperity in the United States. Wages were high, businesses made large profits, retail sales boomed, and many people invested money in the stock market. However, the farming market was shrinking. This collapse in the farming industry, along with the failure of 600 banks in the 1920s and the stock market crash of 1929, contributed to the Great Depression.

By 1930, more than 6 million people in the United States were jobless. By 1933, over 14 million Americans were without work. Because of the sexual segregation of labor, women were more likely to remain employed than men because clerical positions, which were predominantly held by women, were not hit as hard as unskilled labor and the trades. However, working-class women suffered because people could not afford their services (such as domestic service and laundries).

The Great Depression also affected housewives. Homes were overcrowded because poor families shared residences. Those housewives who remained in the home found themselves responsible for more cooking, cleaning, and care taking than before the Depression. Some housewives entered the labor force when their husbands lost their jobs. However, some businesses refused to hire married women.

Franklin D. Roosevelt won the 1932 presidential election on the promise of a **New Deal** for people of the United States. Roosevelt assured voters that he could provide economic relief, recovery, and reform. By the time he became president in 1933, the unemployment rate was an astounding 25 percent—the highest during the twentieth century.

Government aid such as grocery vouchers, used clothing, and coal rations helped families maintain their homes and provide for their chil-

TRAILBLAZERS

Dorothea Lange (1895–1965) depicted the desperation of the Great Depression and influenced other photographic journalists. Her black and white photographs of homeless men, such as *White Angel Breadline* (1932), were so poignant that the federal Resettlement Administration hired her to visually document the hopelessness of the impoverished, thus giving the dilemma mass public attention. Her photographs of migrant workers, captioned with the words of the workers themselves, were so moving that they prompted the state of California to establish migrant camps to help the homeless. Her most famous portrait, *Migrant Mother, Nipomo, California* (1936) now hangs in the Library of Congress.

Dorothea Lange received a Guggenheim Fellowship in 1941 but quit after Pearl Harbor was bombed in December 1941 to photograph the 1942 evacuation of Japanese Americans to detention camps. Her collection of Depression photographs, entitled *An American Exodus: A Record of Human Erosion* (1939) is one of the most emotive and influential records of the people of the United States in the twentieth century.

See also: Photographers.

dren. However, under the New Deal, only heads of families, who were usually men, were eligible for direct cash assistance. In addition, the public works projects designed to relieve unemployment were more available to men than women.

Many women were active in Depression relief efforts. **Eleanor Roosevelt**, wife of President Franklin Roosevelt, had an active role in the New Deal administration. **Frances Perkins**, the secretary of labor, led efforts to pass the **Social Security Act** of 1935, which introduced unemployment insurance, aid to dependent children, and old-age insurance.

GRIFFITHS, MARTHA WRIGHT (b. 1912)

Lawyer, U.S. congresswoman, lieutenant governor of Michigan. Martha Wright was born on January 29, 1912, in Pierce City, Missouri, to Charles Elbridge and Nell (Sullinger) Wright. She was educated at the University of Missouri (A.B., 1934) and the University of Michigan (LL.B., 1940).

Griffiths's was admitted to the Michigan bar in 1941. During the war years, she worked as a contract negotiator for the Army Ordinance in Detroit. In 1946 she opened her own legal office, and two months later her husband, Hicks G. Griffiths, joined her. With a former college classmate they formed the Legal Offices of Griffiths, Williams, and Griffiths.

Griffiths, a Democrat, was elected to the Michigan House of Representatives in 1948. During her two terms, she sponsored liberal causes such as the Unemployment Compensation Act. Because of her abilities, the Capitol Press Corporation named her one of Michigan's ten best legislators in 1951.

In 1953, Griffiths became the first woman appointed recorder and judge of the Detroit Recorder's Court. She was noted for her keen sense of justice and her consistency in acting in the best interest of the community. In 1953 alone, Griffiths presided over 430 criminal investigations, including a teamsters' conspiracy case.

After two grassroots campaigns, in 1954 Griffiths became the first woman from the seventeenth district in Michigan to be elected to the U.S. House of Representatives. During her 20-year tenure in Congress, she introduced bills to increase the pay of government employees, distribute food stamps, and provide low-income housing for the elderly. However, her addition to the 1964 **Civil Rights Act** is considered her most notable accomplishment—it was her idea to include the prohibition of sexual discrimination.

In 1983, the year she was inducted into the National Woman's Hall of Fame, Martha Griffiths was elected the first woman lieutenant governor of Michigan. She held this position until 1991. Griffiths currently lives in Detroit, Michigan, where she practices law with her husband.

GRISWOLD v. CONNECTICUT

U.S. Supreme Court case (1965) that overturned a Connecticut law banning the distribution of birth control devices. Estelle Griswold, a doctor and an executive of the Planned Parenthood League, appealed to the Supreme Court after being convicted for distributing information and medical advice to married couples about the use of contraceptives.

In 1961 the Supreme Court had heard a similar case, *Poe v. Ullman*, which challenged a Connecticut law banning the use of birth control devices. The Court, however, did not overturn the law, primarily because it did not believe Connecticut intended to enforce it. The Court was wrong, and it grappled with the issue once again in *Griswold v. Connecticut*. In its decision the Court held that the Connecticut law violated married persons' right of privacy. The Court's landmark decision effectively ended laws interfering with the right to use or distribute information about birth control. The decision also set the stage for the Court's historic 1973 decision in ***Roe v. Wade***.

Griswold v. Connecticut was an important case in judicial history because the U.S. Constitution does not expressly recognize a "right to privacy"—a right that in effect was created by Justice William O. Douglas in this case. In now-famous language, Douglas wrote that several express guarantees in the Bill of Rights create "penumbras" (or shadows) and "emanations" that strongly imply such a right. Following Douglas, the Supreme Court has been more willing to recognize a right of privacy in personal affairs.

H

HALEY, MARGARET

(1861–1939)

Educator and labor leader. Margaret Angela Haley was born in the Chicago suburb of Joliet and attended both public and Catholic schools. She joined the fledgling Chicago Teachers' Federation (CTF) soon after it was formed in March 1897, taking an active role as an advocate for teachers and battling the Chicago Board of Education for promised wage increases. Haley became district vice president in 1900 then left teaching in 1901 to work full time for the CTF. Among her successes were the enactment of the Illinois State Pension Plan for teachers in 1907 and the 1915–1917 effort to ensure tenure for the state's teachers. Haley also edited and wrote for the CTF *Bulletin* from 1901 to 1908.

Haley's leadership was felt nationally as president of the National Federation of Teachers (NFT). She rallied the NFT membership to exert its influence on the larger National Education Association (NEA), which was at that time dominated by college administrators.

In the early 1900s Haley used her influence to build support for a number of social causes, including woman suffrage and **child labor** laws. Haley also joined the **National Women's Trade Union League**, and in 1916 she helped organize the **American Federation of Teachers**. She continued to write, publishing *Margaret Haley's Bulletin* in 1915–1916 and again from 1925 to 1931.

HAMER, FANNIE LOU

(1918–1977)

Civil rights activist. Fannie Lou Townsend was born in poverty as the youngest of 20 children to sharecroppers in Ruleville, Mississippi. Mississippi at the time was still heavily segregated, and **African Americans** were disenfranchised through a number of formal and informal practices, many of which were constitutionally unsound. Although she dropped out of school at an early age, Townsend attended church regularly. She married Pap Hamer in 1944, and together they worked on a Ruleville plantation. She was 44 before she began civil rights work.

Groups such as the Southern Christian Leadership Conference (SCLC) sought to educate rural African Americans about civil rights. In 1962, Hamer volunteered to register to vote and was denied when she took a citizenship test designed to intimidate African Americans. When the bus home was stopped by police for a bogus violation, she led the riders in song. Hamer's employer fired her, and Pap was fired when Hamer finally registered successfully on her third attempt in 1963. Although she endured death threats and a beating in jail by police because of her civil rights activities, Hamer would not be deterred and began serving as an SCLC field secretary.

In 1964, the Council of Federated Organizations (COFO) formed the Mississippi Freedom Democratic Party (MFDP) to challenge Mississippi's all-white delegation to the Democratic National Committee (DNC) convention. Hamer was elected vice chair and was one of the six representatives to the convention. She spoke before the Credentials Committee. COFO leaders were forced to accept a 2-seat compromise proposal that was in part negotiated by Hubert Humphrey. Hamer, angered by the compromise by both African-American leaders of COFO and by the DNC, held a vigil in protest.

By 1968, Hamer had registered 42 percent of African Americans in her county. She served as an official delegate to the 1968 DNC convention and also promoted community welfare with Head Start programs and established a county farm cooperative. She also helped found the National Women's Political Caucus in 1971, but often felt that the political needs of women of color were overlooked. Hamer died in poverty in Ruleville on March 14, 1977.

HAMILTON, ALICE (1869–1970)

A pioneer in the study of industrial working conditions, ailments, and poisons. Alice Hamilton was born in New York City and raised in Indiana. Her family was well-to-do, and after graduation from the University of Michigan Medical School in 1893, Hamilton became a professor of pathology at Woman's Medical School of Chicago's Northwestern University. She chose medicine because, "as a doctor I could go anywhere I pleased—to far-off lands or to city slums—and be quite of use anywhere." While in Chicago, Hamilton lived at **HULL HOUSE** (see Volume 2). During this time, Hamilton ran a clinic for infants and treated people for diseases associated with their occupations. Increasingly she began to notice that lead poisoning was a significant problem in many industrial workers, and so she turned her attention to investigating toxic substances in factories. In 1911, the U.S. Bureau of Labor appointed her a special investigator, and as a result of her surveys of occupational diseases, Illinois established job-related safety measures. Harvard University selected Hamilton to become its first woman faculty member in 1919.

Because of Hamilton's research and social reform activities, Americans began to benefit from safety standards in the workplace.

HARDING, FLORENCE KLING (1860–1924)

First lady, wife of Warren G. Harding, U.S. president from 1921 to 1923. Born in Marion, Ohio, Florence Kling grew up in luxury; her father was a leading banker in Marion. As a girl, she loved the piano and took part in music classes, but at 19 she gave up a musical career to elope with Henry De Wolfe. A spendthrift and an alcoholic, he abandoned her and their child in 1882.

After the divorce, Florence De Wolfe moved back to Marion and taught piano. There she met Warren Harding, the owner and editor of a local newspaper, the *Daily Star*. After a quick courtship, they wed in 1891. She joined her husband in running the newspaper. She managed the circulation department. "No pennies escaped her," a friend recalled, and the paper prospered. Ohioans recognized that Florence Harding deserved credit for the *Star's* accomplishments. As one remarked "Florence Harding . . . [r]uns her house; runs the paper . . . runs Warren; runs everything but the car, and could run that if she wanted to." At the same time, Warren Harding pursued a political career. He became senator from Ohio in 1914 and in 1920 accepted the Republican nomination for president.

The Hardings moved into the White House in 1921, and the new first lady made the mansion into a prime location for social gatherings. During the day, the grounds were open to the public; at night, the Hardings and their friends relaxed by playing poker, listening to jazz, and drinking alcohol (although the Eighteenth Amendment made alcohol consumption illegal).

In 1922, evidence began to appear that some of the Hardings' friends, who held high governmental positions, had been guilty of bribery and graft. Before the scandal hit, the Hardings, both in poor health, left for a vacation in Alaska. Warren Harding died on the way back, in San Francisco in August, 1923. Returning to Washington, D.C., Florence Harding destroyed all of the papers that she believed might have humiliated Warren Harding. She passed away the following year.

HARLEM RENAISSANCE

A cultural movement by **AFRICAN AMERICANS** in Harlem in the 1920s and 1930s. The movement was predicated on revising African-American racial identity by exploring vernacular cultures and spinning them into new forms. The brightest African-American writers, artists, and intellectuals, dubbed the "Talented Tenth" by historian W. E. B. DuBois, flocked to New York's Harlem neighborhood to participate in this powerful rebirth, although the cultural revival flourished in other cities across the country as well.

Two magazines associated with African-American organizations served as mouthpieces and chronicles of the movement: the National Urban League's *The Opportunity* and the National Association for the Advancement of Colored People's *The Crisis*. Although the more high-profile leaders of the movement were men such as Alain Locke, a Howard philosophy professor and poet Langston Hughes, women were an important driving force.

One of the first books associated with the Harlem Renaissance, *There Is Confusion,* was written by a woman, Jessie Fauset, in 1924. Fauset also edited *The Crisis* and nurtured the careers of Hughes and Jean Toomer. Another woman, Dorothy West, won second place in *The Opportunity*'s first writing contest.

One of foremost authors of the Harlem Renaissance was **ZORA NEALE HURSTON**, who wrote prolifically about identity and Southern African Americans, though to mixed reception. Playwright and writer Marita Bonner was another important voice for Southern African Americans. Her essay, "On Being a Young Woman and Colored" is also well known for its discussion of race and gender.

Like Bonner, many women of the Renaissance felt a special responsibility to address the particular challenge of being both African American and women. Elise Johnson McDougald wrote an essay entitled *The Task of Negro Womanhood* that contrasted race and gender struggles. Not all women addressed gender issues, however. Many of the poets wrote traditional romantic poetry, such as Anne Spencer and Georgia Douglas Johnson. Other writers of note were novelist Nella Larsen, poet Gwendolyn Bennett, and Angelina Weld Grimké (the mixed-race great-niece of **ANGELINA GRIMKÉ WELD**—see Volume 2).

The Harlem Renaissance was not only a literary movement; singers like **BILLIE HOLIDAY** and Bessie Smith and sculptor Augusta Savage each captured the spirit of the Renaissance with their unique styles of art and performance.

FURTHER READING

Lewis, David Levering. *The Portable Harlem Renaissance Reader.* New York: Viking, 1994.

HARVEY GIRLS

Young, single women who worked as waitresses for the Fred Harvey chain of restaurants located at major stops on the Santa Fe Railway. Between 1880 and 1950, approximately 100,000 women left their families and friends to "go West," earn a decent wage, and have a little adventure. Nearly half of them stayed in the Southwest after their work for Harvey was over.

Until the 1930s the railroad was the main way Americans traveled long distances across the country. Accommodations were rough until Fred Harvey started his chain of hotel-restaurants. To create the image he wanted, Harvey insisted that the women employed in his restaurants be called Harvey Girls rather than waitresses. Reminiscent of the **LOWELL MILL WORKERS** (see Volume 2), they lodged together, kept a strict schedule, and followed detailed dress codes. Very few women of color became Harvey Girls and held jobs in the public eye. They did worked in the kitchens and housekeeping departments, however. Harvey wanted his "girls" to not only serve meals to travelers but also create an image of a hospitable and safe West that would enhance tourism.

Eventually, automobile and air travel began to replace trains in the 1920s and 1950s, respectively, and Harvey's customer load dropped, leaving entire communities with little employment. Harvey's food service business continued in the dining cars of trains, but the era of Harvey Houses and Harvey Girls ended forever.

HEALTH

At the beginning of the twentieth century, many companies made unsafe products, and progressive and reform-minded women used their roles as guardians of their families' health and welfare to justify their involvement in the political process. Mothers, teachers, social workers, nurses, and concerned citizens worked tirelessly to ensure standards for food and drugs: Women wanted to buy flour that actually contained flour, not talc, calcium carbonate, or wood shavings; meat that was not chemically treated to disguise spoilage; and drugs without alcohol or addictive substances. When President Theodore Roosevelt signed into law the 1906 Pure Food and Drug Act and the Meat Inspection Act, he credited the women of this country for making these laws reality.

Throughout the twentieth century, patients, particularly women, became more active in their own health care and sought to improve health and health services for themselves, their families, and others. Their efforts, paired with technological advances and scientific breakthroughs changing how we understand the body and health led to improved health care for all, and each succeeding generation has had a longer life expectancy than the previous generation.

Advances in medical knowledge affected women's reproductive health perhaps more than any other area. An emphasis on scientific study coupled with technology utilizing the new scientific knowledge led to improved medical treatment. This occurred first in larger urban areas and gradually became the norm. In childbirth, for example, doctors (but not midwives) had access to equipment such as medical forceps, which could aid in the delivery process. This in and of itself was not enough to convince women to give birth in a sterile, clinical, and isolated hospital setting rather than the comfortable and familiar home environment. When childbirth remained in the home, it was part of the life cycle, something that could be done without technological intervention, and was seen as a "natural" process in that is was nonmedicalized. In 1902, however, a new drug, scopolamine, was developed in Germany. For many women, the drug promised to make childbirth less painful and prolonged. To get access to scopolamine, women needed to give birth in a hospital.

Scopolamine caused several cases of death and paralysis and was eventually withdrawn from the market. Despite this, more and more women gave birth in hospitals. As with all health care, there were geographic and racial variations: Middle- and upper-class women and women who lived in or near cities of some size were more likely to go to a hospital to give birth.

In the 1950s, at the height of the baby boom, the approach to childbirth shifted again. Childbirth stayed in hospitals but new attitudes emerged regarding pain medications. The publication of Dick Grantly-Read's *Natural Childbirth;* approaches to childbirth, such as Lamaze and controlled breathing; and a reemphasis on breast-feeding rather than reliance on formula encouraged women to try to experience "natural" or drug-free childbirth. In the 1970s and 1980s, there was an increase in the use of **MIDWIFERY.** In response to financial concerns from insurance and managed care companies and patient demand, hospitals built birthing suites as an alternative to traditional delivery rooms. Midwives, once fully outside the purview of accepted medical practice, are now often part of an obstetrical practice.

The twentieth-century focus on pregnancy has also had other health implications for women. German scientists in the 1930s determined women's hormonal cycles, which had implications for our understanding of menstruation, menopause, and birth control. Medical opinion on physical activity shifted from the 1940s view that women should avoid activity during menstruation to the 2000 view that they should exercise throughout the month. Ailments such as premenstrual syndrome ceased being thought of as psychosomatic illnesses and gradually became accepted medical diagnoses. Menopause and the physiological consequences for a woman's body as hormone levels shift has received scientific attention as well; drugs are now formulated expressly for women to combat potential medical problems caused by the onset of menopause, such as heart disease. Accurate information about hormonal cycles has made reliable contraceptive birth control: Pharmaceutical discoveries make it possible to induce an artificial pregnancy state in the body, thus preventing contraception and implantation of a fertilized egg.

One of the most notable features of health care in the twentieth and early twenty-first centuries has been the increasing role the patient has played in medical decisions. In the early 1970s, a self-health movement swept parts of the country. Patients started to question physicians, read more about medical procedures, and learned about their own bodies. At a time when many people were questioning authority and authority figures, patients became informed consumers who were unwilling to blithely accept what a medical (or any other) authority told them was the "right" treatment. Patients wanted to be involved in their medical decisions. This change in perceptions about health care can be seen in the publication of ***OUR BODIES, OURSELVES*** (see Documents), written by the Boston Women's Health Book Collective; in the growth of natural or health food stores replete with natural remedies;

in a resurgence of interest in alternative medicines, including homeopathy and chiropractic; and, indirectly, in a shift in how health care is provided.

Women's involvement in the health care system and their willingness to question and challenge traditional assumptions about health care, research, and proper medical treatment is visible in the fight against breast cancer. The activism and organization of women to push for better treatment, less radical surgery, and earlier diagnosis has led to increased federal funding, increased awareness, numerous foundations awarding research monies, and, hopefully, a drop in the number of women diagnosed with late-stage cancers each year. In addition, the cadre of women involved in women's health issues has changed some federal policies regarding drug trials. Where women were once excluded from drug trials because of changing hormonal levels over the course of a month (which would render them unstable participants in tests for new drugs), the National Institutes of Health (NIH) now mandates that women be included in studies for promising drugs. If women are to be recipients of these drugs, the NIH and others have argued, they need to be part of the trial period as well.

FURTHER READING

Apple, Rima. *Women, Health and Medicine: A Historical Handbook*. New Brunswick, NJ: Rutgers University Press, 1994.

Leavitt, Judith Walzer, ed. *Women and Health in America: Historical Readings*. Madison: University of Wisconsin Press, 1999.

HEARST, PHOEBE APPERSON (1842–1919)

Philanthropist. Phoebe Elizabeth Apperson was born in Missouri in 1842 to a wealthy farming family. At age 20, she married her cousin, George Hearst. Because he was a miner who had made his fortune in the West, the couple settled in San Francisco in 1862. Hearst shared her wealth generously. Her charitable work began on her honeymoon, when she agreed to sponsor a young painter, Orrin Peck. She also donated money to the YWCA, the University of California at Berkeley, and the San Francisco Children's Hospital. Hearst was the founder of the Children's Milk Fund and sponsored free kindergarten in California before kindergarten was part of the public school system. In all, it is estimated that by the time she died in 1919, Phoebe Hearst had donated an estimated $25 million to charity.

Phoebe Hearst is the woman behind the success of publishing tycoon William Randolph Hearst, her son. During his youth, she surrounded him with prominent artists and leading politicians to foster in him a sense of culture. When he wanted to start his publishing company, Hearst sold her husband's Anaconda mine for $7.5 million and gave the money to her son.

HEIGHT, DOROTHY IRENE (b. 1912)

Civil rights leader. Dorothy Irene Height was born on March 24, 1912, in Richmond, Virginia. Her mother, Fannie, was a nurse and her father, James, was a builder. As a young girl, Height became involved in volunteer activities through her church. She won a scholarship to New York University because she was such a good speaker and graduated in 1932 with both bachelor's and master's degrees in educational psychology.

During the 1930s Height became an active member of the **Young Women's Christian Association** (YWCA), focusing her efforts on improving wages for black domestic workers. Shortly afterward, she joined the **National Council of Negro Women (NCNW)** and worked to obtain equal pay and employment for women. In 1957, Height became president of the organization, a position she held until 1998.

As head of the NCNW, Height was a leader in the civil rights movement during the 1960s, spearheading the struggle to register black voters in the South. She also lobbied Congress to acquire funding for women who needed job training or wanted to open their own businesses. During the 1970s, the NCNW began programs to provide food, housing, and child care to the poor. Meanwhile, Height served as a member of the national staff of the YWCA, initiating its Center for Racial Justice in 1965.

In 1989, Height received the Citizens Medal Award from President Ronald Reagan for her community work. Five years later she was awarded the Presidential Medal of Freedom by President Bill Clinton.

HELLMAN, LILLIAN

(1906–1984)

Playwright and writer. Born on June 20, 1906, in New Orleans, Lillian Hellman moved to New York City with her family at age six. She studied at both Columbia University and New York University but did not earn a degree. She worked in publishing, occasionally reviewing books and publishing short stories. In 1925, she married Arthur Kober and moved with him to Hollywood, where she became a reader for MGM.

> ***"I cannot and will not cut my conscience to fit this year's fashion."***
>
> **—Lillian Hellamn, letter to the House Committee on Un-American Activities, 1952**

Hellman hated Hollywood and began to drink heavily. In 1930, she met mystery writer Dashiell Hammett, 11 years her senior. She divorced Kober in 1932 and continued what would be a tumultuous affair with Hammett until his death in 1961. They moved back to New York, and Hellman published more stories before completing her first dramatic work, *The Children's Hour*, in 1934. Filled with irony, the play was well reviewed. It is still performed.

Hellman and Hammett were both politically radical. Hellman participated in Marxist study groups while writing her play *The Little Foxes* in 1938 and was included on Hollywood's blacklist of suspected communist sympathizers. In 1951, Hammett was jailed for communist activity, and in 1952, Hellman appeared before the House Un-American Activities Committee, refusing to answer questions about Hammett and others.

Hellman often staged revivals of her plays to earn money. In 1960, she regained popularity with *Toys in the Attic*, a play about two Southern sisters and their relationship with their difficult brother. She also began work on her memoir trilogy, which eventually produced three volumes, *An Unfinished Woman*, *Penitmento*, and *Scoundrel Time*. In 1964, she was awarded the Gold Medal for Drama by the National Institute of Arts and Letters. Hellman continued to write and teach until her death on June 30, 1984.

Lillian Hellman, playwright and writer, was known for her politically radical ideas.

HEPBURN, KATHARINE HOUGHTON (b. 1907)

Actress. The eldest of six children, Katharine Houghton Hepburn was born to Thomas Hepburn, a urologist, and Katharine Houghton Hepburn, a feminist, in Hartford, Connecticut, on May 12, 1907.

Although Hepburn was shy in her early years at Bryn Mawr College, she became involved in campus drama productions. Immediately after graduating with honors in English, she lined up a job acting in Baltimore. In 1932, she appeared as an Amazon in *The Warrior's Husband* on Broadway.

That same year, Hepburn arrived in Hollywood aggressive and determined, and negotiated her first paycheck, for David O. Selznick's *Bill of Divorcement,* up from $500 to $1,500 a week. The film would be the first of many collaborations with director George Cukor. In 1933, Hepburn starred in *Morning Glory*, for which she won the 1934 Oscar for Best Actress. This was the first of 12 Oscar nominations. Hepburn would win three more times, for *Guess Who's Coming to Dinner?* (1967), *The Lion in Winter* (1968), and *On Golden Pond* (1981). She also won an Emmy for a television production of *Love Among the Ruins*. Hepburn was known for her crisp New England accent and commanding presence on-screen. True to her off-screen personality, Hepburn often played strong, independent, stubborn women who came to terms with their flaws.

Intensely private, Hepburn shielded from the public her 1928 marriage to Ludlow Ogden Smith until they divorced in 1934. Hepburn would carry on a lifelong affair with actor Spencer Tracy from their first meeting in 1941, before they co-starred in *Woman of the Year*, until Tracy's death in 1967, through nine co-starring roles. Today, Hepburn lives in New York City.

Hispanic-American children celebrate their heritage.

HISPANIC AMERICANS

In the late nineteenth and early twentieth centuries thousands and thousands of Mexicans emigrated to the United States, pushed by poverty and the Mexican Revolution and drawn by opportunities in mining, transportation, farming, and other industries. In the Southwest they found Mexican-American communities that dated from as early as the late sixteenth century.

Unlike the newcomers—mostly young men—these communities were dominated by families. Mexican-American women of the Southwest enjoyed substantial status and power. In New Mexico, brides were as likely to live with their parents as with their husbands' families. Molesting a woman or whipping a wife were punishable crimes. Women often kept property separately from their husbands.

The poverty that dogged most Mexican-American families required flexible gender roles. Women often headed households while men traveled to find work. A Latino from the vicinity of the New Mexican and Colorado border later recalled that "when the men came back, they were kind of like guests."

The **GREAT DEPRESSION** and **WORLD WAR II** profoundly affected Mexican-American communities. During the Depression of the 1930s, about one-third of the nation's Mexican Americans went to Mexico, including many U.S. citizens. Some were forced to leave so that they would not compete with Anglo Americans for jobs that had become scarce. Then, during the labor shortages of World War II, the federal government and private employers drew Mexicans northward. Both of these movements affected men more than women, as single males were the most likely to cross the border. Among those who stayed in the United States, a second generation of more independent Mexican Americans arose who struggled for more autonomy from their parents, created a vibrant, consumer-oriented subculture, and formed labor **UNIONS**.

The Hispanic community became much more diverse in the last half of the twentieth century as immigrants from Puerto Rico, Cuba, and many other parts of Latin America settled in the United States. In 2000, people of Latin-American descent constituted 13 percent of the nation's population. The Hispanic community also became more militant. A **CHICANA** feminist movement appeared around 1970, even though some Hispanics argued that it threatened family stability and ethnic solidarity. Many Latinas have led the way to a more prosperous and stable future. By the 1990s Hispanic women outnumbered Hispanic men in both colleges and professions.

FURTHER READING

Ruiz, Vicki L. *Cannery Women, Cannery Lives: Mexican Women, Unionization, and the California Food Processing Industry, 1930–1950*. Albuquerque: University of New Mexico Press, 1987.

HOLIDAY, BILLIE (1915–1959)

Influential jazz vocalist. By most accounts, Eleanora Holiday was born to a young mother

Billie Holiday struggled against racism and other personal trials but is remembered for her remarkable voice.

in Baltimore on April 7, 1915. Although her childhood was unhappy and filled with abuse and exploitation, she was close to her struggling and devoted mother and maintained contact with her absent guitarist father.

Born into a hard life, Holiday was blessed with a remarkable voice. She adopted the name Billie after her favorite movie star, Billie Dove, and began performing at age 15. She had her first professional engagement at a club known as Pod's and Jerry's. At a running engagement at this club, many important events occurred: She earned the nickname "Lady," had her first love affair (with resident pianist Bobby Henderson), and was discovered by critic John Hammond, who effectively launched her career.

Holiday's career spanned both incredible highs and heartbreaking lows. Her legendary recordings with tenor-saxophonist Lester Young are still noted today for their perfectly complementary sound, as is her potent rendering of "Strange Fruit," the song about the horror of **LYNCHING** (see Volume 2) chosen especially for her voice. However, Holiday struggled against pervasive racism in the entertainment industry and personal trials with drug and alcohol addiction, as well as a number of highly publicized and disastrous romantic relationships.

Beloved by her fans but frequently betrayed by managers, lovers, and friends, Holiday died nearly destitute on July 15, 1959, from complications to her liver and heart. As a testament to the impact of her music, a crowd of 3,000 attended her funeral in New York.

HOLLANDER, NICOLE

(b. 1940)

Writer, cartoonist. Nicole Hollander, the daughter of a carpenter and a hospital administrator, was raised in Chicago, Illinois, and attended the University of Illinois, majoring in art. She also received a masters in fine arts from Boston University. Married in 1962 to Paul Hollander, she was divorced four years later. Hollander's first job was as a graphic designer in Chicago, where she began creating illustrations that she eventually turned into a comic strip.

Hollander is best known for her cartoon character Sylvia, who sprang to life in 1979. Sylvia is a quick-witted feminist who smokes cigarettes and wears outlandish clothes. Hollander's first book of cartoons featuring Sylvia was titled *I'm in Training to Be Tall and Blonde* (1979). This was followed by other books, such as *Ma, Can I Be a Feminist and Still Like Men?* (1980) and *Mercy, It's the Revolution and I'm in My Bathrobe* (1982).

Hollander has also created other characters as part of the strip, including "The Love Cop," and "The Woman Who Does Everything More Beautifully Than You." Her cartoon strip is syndicated in newspapers throughout the United States, including the *Washington Post* and the *Chicago Tribune*. In 1991, Hollander's musical about Sylvia opened in Chicago to "enthusiastic" reviews from audiences. She also creates humorous books about cats, like *Everything Here Is Mine: An Unhelpful Guide to Cat Behavior*.

HOME ECONOMICS

Also known as "domestic science," the scientific study of all aspects of homemaking and child rearing. The field of home economics was founded by **ELLEN SWALLOW RICHARDS** (see Volume 2). Richards organized a conference in Lake Placid, New York, in 1899, from which emerged standards for teacher training and certification in a new field of study she dubbed "home economics." Those who attended the conference founded the American Home Economics Association in 1908 and named Richards its first president. Richards also established the *Journal of Home Economics* in 1910.

The idea behind home economics was to improve home life in America through the application of scientific principles to homemaking. Although many women today regard home economics as part of an effort to confine women to the domestic sphere, the field has made an impressive contribution to research in subjects ranging from nutrition to child development, from fiber science to consumer economics. From its founding, the field of home economics was part of a progressive movement to improve life in cities, especially for poor and immigrant women. Outreach programs helped women in rural settings. The field of home economics also opened up many educational and employment opportunities for women. Graduates of home economics programs found jobs in agricultural extension services, the government, hospitals, restaurants, and teaching. Activists in the woman **SUFFRAGE MOVEMENT** worked closely with leaders of the home economics movement for their allied goals.

From 1914 through the Great Depression, several federal laws influenced the development of the field of home economics. In 1914, the **SMITH-LEVER ACT** encouraged home economics instruction through the provision of federal funds to colleges. The Purnell Act of 1925 provided federal money to study vitamins and rural home-management. In 1935, the Bankhead-Jones Act provided funding to study nutritional needs.

Home economists influenced how women managed homes and children through magazine articles in popular women's magazines, "how-to" pamphlets, and radio broadcasts. Their research influenced health and hygiene practices in rural and urban homes, helped set social welfare practices, and became the basis for many federal policies dealing with women and children. Home economists researched such topics as nutrition, food storage, stain removal, and household design.

Throughout the century, home economists helped when the nation was in crisis. During the influenza epidemic of 1917, women trained in home economics served as hospital dietitians. During **WORLD WAR I**, nutritionists helped to design food rationing programs. During the **GREAT DEPRESSION**, home economists helped poor women learn how to feed and clothe their families inexpensively. Home economists planted "victory gardens" during **WORLD WAR II** to help families ensure a supply of fresh fruits and vegetables despite rationing.

The Vocational Act of 1963 provided funds for secondary and vocational schools to make the study of home economics more widely available. By the 1970s, however, the field of home economics had fallen out of favor with many women because it seemed to support traditional gender stereotypes. Many home economics departments renamed themselves in an effort to reflect new attitudes toward women and homemaking. Today graduates from colleges of "Human Ecology" across the country work in such fields as textile design, nutrition, interior design, journalism, and child development. Departments today often focus less on "how to" than on the "why" of the various subject areas included in home economics. Students also study global issues including poverty, domestic life in developing countries, and overpopulation.

FURTHER READING

Matthews, Glenna. *"Just a Housewife": The Rise and Fall of Domesticity in America.* New York: Oxford University Press, 1987.

Ogden, Annegret S. *The Great American Housewife: From Helpmate to Wage Earner, 1776–1986.* Westport, CT: Greenwood Press, 1986.

HOMEMAKER

The role of the homemaker changed drastically from the beginning of the twentieth century to the end. First among the factors that led to change was the ability to limit the number of children a woman bore, thanks to modern methods of contraception. While Americans once viewed a wife's primary role in a marriage as procreation, birth control led to a different notion of marriage and a woman's role. The ideal of marriage changed from one based on children, according to Marilyn Yalom, to one based "on the ideal of a union based on love, companionship, and the enjoyment of sex."

Another change came with **WORLD WAR II**, when women were needed in the workforce. When the war was over, some women found that they enjoyed the freedom they earned with their pay checks. Nevertheless, most women quit their jobs to make room for returning soldiers, and the 1950s saw most women back home keeping house and raising children. The ideal homemaker of the era worked to stay beautiful and alluring for her husband, entertained to advance his career, kept a spotless house, and raised 2.5 clean-cut, obedient children.

Of course, reality did not always correspond to the ideal. Many women found this role stifling, and they were ignited to action when **Betty Friedan**'s *Feminine Mystique* (1963; see Documents) exposed the frustrations that many homemakers experienced.

Thanks to the "second wave of feminism," sparked by Friedan's book, women began to enter the workforce in larger numbers in the 1970s, a trend that continues to the present day. Although most homemakers now work outside the home, studies suggest that women still perform most of the homemaking duties they did when husbands were the primary breadwinners.

FURTHER READING

Yalom, Marilyn. *A History of the Wife*. New York: Harper Collins, 2001.

HOOVER, LOU HENRY (1874–1944)

First lady, wife of Herbert Hoover, the thirty-first president of the United States. She was an advocate for physical fitness and the **Girl Scouts of America**.

Born in Iowa in 1874, Lou Henry moved with her family in 1884 to California and settled in Monterey a few years later. Both parents encouraged her interests in outdoor activities and intellectual pursuits. She attended Stanford University and became the first woman in the United States to receive an A.B. degree in geology in 1898. While at Stanford, she met Herbert Hoover. They married in 1899.

Over the next two decades Herbert Hoover's work as a mining engineer took them around the globe. They were in London when England entered **World War I**. They moved back to the United States in 1917. That year, President Woodrow Wilson asked Herbert to head the U.S. Food Administration and take charge of the flow of food to Europe from the United States. Lou Hoover worked on a parallel project, speaking on food conservation to women's groups during wartime shortages.

Although Lou Hoover advocated traditional family roles, she believed that women should participate in civic life. She supported the social and political equality of women, yet she did not participate in **suffrage** activities and disagreed with the tactics, such as hunger strikes, civil disobedience, or getting arrested, used by radical suffrage groups. Her major voluntary activities revolved around the National Amateur Athletic Federation (NAAF) and the Girl Scouts of America.

In 1923, as the vice president of NAAF, Hoover established a women's division to set policy for women's involvement in **athletics**. A number of debates surrounded women's participation in competitive sports, and the organization opposed women's involvement in the Olympics. Hoover also served on the national board of the Girl Scouts of America from 1917 to 1944 and was elected president twice.

Lou Hoover presided as the first lady of the White House between 1929 and 1933 and continued her voluntary activities. When she left the White House, she spent her time in Palo Alto and New York. She died in New York City on January 7, 1944.

HORNE, LENA (b. 1917)

Actress and singer. Born June 30, 1917, in Brooklyn, New York, Lena Horne was raised by her grandmother, a civil rights and woman suffrage activist. Because of financial difficulties, she left school to work as a chorus dancer at Harlem's Cotton Club at age 16.

Horne developed her voice through singing lessons and in 1934, performed in *Dance with Your Gods* on Broadway. She then moved to Philadelphia to sing with Noble Sissle's Society Orchestra, where she was reunited with her estranged father and met Louis Jones, the son of a minister, whom she married in 1937. After two children, the couple divorced in 1941. Horne appeared in another Broadway show before becoming the lead singer in 1940 in Charlie Barnett's Band and a performer at Cafe Society Downtown. During this time, she met activist and scholar Paul Robeson and became involved in the National Association for the Advancement of Colored People.

Horne moved to southern California to perform and signed a movie contract with MGM Studios. Conscious of the pervasiveness of negative stereotypes of **African Americans** in films, Horne stipulated in her contract that she would not play stereotypic roles. In 1942, she won her first lead role in *Cabin in the Sky*, a musical about an African-American woman who is intent on her husband's salvation in church.

In 1947, she appeared in her landmark role in *Stormy Weather*. It was during the filming that she met her second husband, Lenny Hayton, whom she married the same year. Because **ANTI-MISCEGENATION** sentiment prevailed at the time, they did not make their marriage public until 1950. Horne continued to be active in the civil rights movement in the 1960s. In 1956, she took a break from Hollywood to concentrate on Broadway and singing. She returned to Hollywood in 1969, in *Death of a Gunfighter*, and again in 1978, in *The Wiz*.

Horne captured and performed the highlights of her legendary song and dance career in the Broadway one-woman musical, *Lena Horne: The Lady and Her Music*, which began in 1981 and became the longest-running one-woman show on Broadway.

HOYT v. FLORIDA

A 1961 U.S. Supreme Court case in which the justices upheld arbitrary classifications of people based on gender. The U.S. Supreme Court had a long history of allowing states to pass laws that were based on gender classifications. As far back as 1873, for example, it refused to overturn an Illinois statute that prohibited women from obtaining licenses to practice law. *Hoyt v. Florida* concerned the issue of jury duty. It arose when a Florida woman named Hoyt was convicted of murder by an all-male jury and argued that she had not been judged by a jury of her peers. Under Florida statute, every man was eligible for jury duty unless he requested an exemption. Women, however, were automatically granted an exemption from jury duty unless they waived the exemption. The distinction was based on the belief that men were better suited than women to participate in civic affairs.

In its decision the Court did not address the issue of whether a state could constitutionally restrict jury duty to males. Instead, it addressed the narrower question of whether the exemption for women was based on a reasonable classification. The Court found that the Florida statute was, saying that "despite the enlightened emancipation of women from the restrictions and protections of bygone years, and their entry into many parts of community life formerly considered to be reserved to men, woman is still regarded as the center of the home and family life." The Court concluded that the Constitution did not prohibit a legislature from exempting all women, even those without family responsibilities, from jury duty. It would be another ten years before the Court would finally strike down arbitrary gender classifications in ***REED v. REED***.

HUERTA, DOLORES FERNANDEZ (b. 1930)

Mexican-American labor leader and activist. Born in Dawson, New Mexico, on April 10, 1930, Huerta was raised by her mother in Stockton, California. Although separated from her father, she stayed in touch with him as he went from being a migrant worker to a union activist to an elected member of the New Mexico state legislature. After graduating from the University of the Pacific's Delta Community College, she taught elementary school in Stockton. Discouraged by the poverty of her students, she decided to concentrate her efforts on improving the lives of their parents, most of whom were farm workers.

Huerta went to work for the Community Service Organization (CSO), a social service agency for the Mexican-American community in Stockton, in 1955. She managed a number of community empowerment projects and later acted as the group's lobbyist in Sacramento, the state capital. Around 1960, she joined the Agricultural Workers Association, and met the CSO director for California and Arizona, Cesar Chavez. Frustrated by the lack of attention given to the treatment of migrant farm workers, the two founded the National Farm Workers Association (later the United Farm Workers [UFW]) in 1962.

Since then, Huerta has been a union leader and champion of migrant workers' rights, lobbying against the use of toxins and pesticides, leading strikes, and organizing boycotts. One of her greatest achievements came when California governor Jerry Brown signed the Agricultural Labor Relations Act in 1975. It was the first bill of rights for farm workers in the United States, granting them the right to form unions.

Huerta is known for her uncompromising and tenacious style, but has always advocated nonviolence as a means to effect change. In 1988, she was injured by San Francisco police officers during a protest against labor policies. It was one of more than 20 arrests during her career. She has received numerous awards for her contributions to labor and women's rights. She holds high positions in the UFW, the California AFL-CIO, the Labor Coalition of Women, and the Feminist Majority, and is the mother of 11 children.

HURSTON, ZORA NEALE

(1891?–1960)
African-American writer who portrayed Southern black culture. Hurston grew up in in the all-black township of Eatonville, Florida, in stable conditions until, when she was 13, her mother died. She shuttled among relatives after her father's remarriage, but left Eatonville at 14 with a traveling theatrical troupe. Over the next 15 years she managed to get a high school diploma and took courses at Howard University, where she published her first stories in the literary journal. In 1925 Hurston moved to New York City and became involved in the **HARLEM RENAISSANCE.** Her stories were published in Charles Johnson's journal *Opportunity* and in Alain Locke's anthology *The New Negro*, and won her a scholarship to Barnard College, which she entered in 1925 as its first African-American student. After graduating in 1928 she went on to graduate studies in anthropology at Columbia University under Franz Boas, who encouraged her to return to Eatonville to collect folklore. She traveled throughout the South, collecting material that was published in her 1935 book, *Mules and Men*. She later took two collecting trips to the Caribbean, funded by Guggenheim Fellowships, and published her findings in *Tell My Horse* (1938).

Hurston's personal life took a backseat to her career; two marriages were short-lived. She worked as a dramatist, teacher, and writer. She published four novels, *Jonah's Gourd Vine* (1934), about an adulterous Southern Baptist preacher; *Their Eyes Were Watching God* (1937), considered her best novel, a tribute to the independence and vitality of African-American women; *Moses, Man of the Mountain* (1939); and *Seraph on the Suwanee* (1948), in which she defied expectations by focusing on a white protagonist, a woman who strives for a sense of self.

Her autobiography, *Dust Tracks on a Road* (1942), is more folklore than fact, containing proven inaccuracies and omitting whole areas of her life, such as her marriages. It was well received and won the Anisfield-Wolf Award for its contribution to race relations. It is notable for refusing to focus on the negative side of black experience in America—a refusal running through all her work, which drew criticism from African-American contemporaries.

Hurston suffered public humiliation in 1948, when she was accused of child molestation. Although she disproved these charges, she left New York and spent her final years in Florida, living off odd jobs and infrequent sales of magazine articles. After suffering a stroke in 1959, she entered a public nursing home and died on January 28, 1960, penniless and alone.

Hurston was forgotten until the 1970s, when writers such as **ALICE WALKER** began rediscovering her writing. Today she remembered as the most accomplished African-American woman writer of her period.

FURTHER READING

Walker, Alice, ed. *I Love Myself When I Am Laughing—and Then Again When I Am Looking Mean and Impressive: A Zora Neale Hurston Reader.* Old Westbury, NY: Feminist Press, 1979.

HYDE AMENDMENT

Passed by Congress in 1976, it denied funding for abortions in health-care services provided to low-income people by the federal government through Medicaid. Part of the legislative battle over **ABORTION**, the Hyde Amendment immediately came under fire from organizations like the **NATIONAL ORGANIZATION FOR WOMEN** and the **AMERICAN CIVIL LIBERTIES UNION**. These organizations argued that such legislation discriminates against low-income women and makes it too difficult for them to control and protect their bodies. After a series of court cases, the Supreme Court upheld the constitutionality of the Hyde Amendment in 1980.

In 1997, Congress altered the amendment by allowing Medicaid funds for abortions in cases of rape, incest, or if the woman's life is endangered from illness or injury. In step with the national government, most state legislatures have also banned abortions from their medical funding. At present, 35 of the 50 states refuse public funding for abortions except in cases of rape, incest, and physical danger.

I

IMMIGRATION AND NATURALIZATION

Coming to another country to live and becoming a citizen. In the final decades of the nineteenth century, immigration legislation began to place limits on who could enter the United States. The first restrictive immigration legislation, the **PAGE ACT** of 1875 (see Volume 2), attempted to discourage Chinese women suspected of "immoral purposes" from entering the country. In the early years of the twentieth century, further restrictions were added, which in some cases placed women at a disadvantage. Immigration legislation passed in 1917, for example, excluded, among others, people who could not read, making immigration more difficult for many women and members of the peasant class. In 1924, a quota system was established that ranked immigrants by country of origin.

Before 1930, more men than women emigrated to the United States. Since then women have accounted for a little more than half of all the immigrants coming into the United States. The increase in the number of female immigrants can be attributed to three factors. First, many more American men than women marry foreign brides. Many women have entered the United States as "mail order brides" or "war brides." In fact, the **WAR BRIDES ACT** made it easy for the foreign-born brides of American servicemen to become citizens. Second, as immigration laws began to promote the unification of families, many foreign-born women were able to join husbands and children who had immigrated some years earlier. Third, as women gained political and economic freedom around the world, they were able to emigrate on their own instead of coming with husbands or fathers.

Until women were granted the right to vote, there was little incentive for married immigrant women to naturalize, or apply for citizenship. Legislation enacted in 1855 provided that a "woman who is . . . married to a citizen of the United States . . . shall be deemed a citizen." While this made citizenship automatic for many women, this law also had negative consequences in that if a husband chose not to apply for citizenship, his wife could not apply on her own. After 1907, the reverse situation held for native-born women who married foreign men; these women lost their U.S. citizenship. Thus, for the first two decades of the twentieth century, a married woman's citizenship depended on her husband.

These laws were changed only when they began to create disadvantages for men. When women were granted the right to vote, some judges began to refuse citizenship to men because their wives could not read or speak English and yet would automatically become citizens when their husbands were naturalized. In 1922, Congress passed the Married Women's Act, or **CABLE ACT**, legislation that for the first time allowed women to naturalize on their own and allowed women who married foreign men to retain their citizenship.

FURTHER READING

Seller, Maxine Schwartz. *Immigrant Women.* 2nd ed. Philadelphia: Temple University Press, 1995.

INFANT AND CHILD HEALTH

As woman reformers began to effect social change in the United States in the late 1800s, they focused increasing attention on the well-being of children. The idea for a government agency devoted to children's issues has been attributed Lillian Wald, whose plans and lobbying efforts ultimately resulted in the establishment of the **CHILDREN'S BUREAU** in 1912. The first director of the agency was Julia Lathrop, who chose infant and maternal mortality rates as her first area of study. Initial studies revealed that the United States had one of the highest rates of infant and maternal mortality of any industrialized nation. The major cause, the bureau demonstrated, was poverty. Realizing there was little the agency could do to increase wages, it focused its efforts on education. Lathrop published a series of easy-to-read pamphlets to teach mothers how to take care of themselves during pregnancy and how to care for their newborn babies. The pamphlets were immensely popular and were still being distributed in the 1950s. (See Documents for letters from mothers to the bureau.)

The next major advance in infant and child health was the **Maternity and Infancy Protection Act** of 1921, which provided federal matching funds for state services on behalf of pregnant women and new mothers. States that chose to participate typically hired public health nurses who traveled from town to town, often on horseback, to educate pregnant women and to persuade local doctors to volunteer their services. These nurses also established permanent clinics.

The Children's Bureau and the Maternity and Infancy Protection Act were largely responsible for a major decline in infant mortality in the 1920s. To combat child labor, meanwhile, Congress had passed the Child Labor Act of 1916; but it was declared unconstitutional six years later. In 1924, Congress passed a constitutional amendment to make child labor illegal, but it failed to be ratified by the states. Finally, in 1938, the **Fair Labor Standards Act** struck a successful blow at child labor—and for child health—by prohibiting manufacturing and mining companies that engage in interstate commerce from employing workers under the age of 16, or under 18 in hazardous conditions.

A variety of federal programs and initiatives in recent decades have focused specifically on infant and child health. The Medicaid program, enacted in 1965 as an extension of the **Social Security Act** of 1935, provided medical services for indigent children and later was expanded to include preventive health services. In 1972, the Special Supplemental Food Program for Women, Infants, and Children (WIC) provided the first major nutritional support for mothers and children. And in 1998, federal legislation provided states with $48 billion over ten years to broaden efforts to provide children with health insurance.

Advances in medical science and general improvements in living conditions have contributed most directly to improvements in infant and child health. From 1940 to 2000 alone, the infant mortality rate in the United States dropped from 47 per 1,000 to about 7 per 1,000.

TRAILBLAZERS

As a prominent physician once said, "Every baby born in a modern hospital anywhere in the world is looked at first through the eyes of Virginia Apgar." This is because Apgar developed the system that is used around the world by obstetricians to evaluate the health of newborn babies. Until Apgar pioneered her method, newborn babies were assumed to be healthy unless they showed obvious signs of distress. Unfortunately, doctors often missed subtle signs of circulatory or respiratory problems. Apgar's method helps doctors discern internal problems right away. The maximum Apgar score is ten points, with up to two points assigned for each of the following five factors: heart rate, muscle tone, reflexes, color, and respiration. Infants are evaluated at one minute after birth and at five minutes after birth. The maximum score of ten is almost never given; an infant with a score of 7 is generally considered to be healthy. Apgar's scoring system has saved many lives since she first introduced it to physicians in 1953.

Virginia Apgar graduated from MOUNT HOLYOKE College (see Volume 2) in 1929 and received her medical degree from Columbia University in 1933. She studied surgery but switched to anesthesiology after two years of surgical internship. She was eventually appointed the first full professor of anesthesiology at Columbia. She completed a master's degree in Public Health at Johns Hopkins University in 1959. That same year she was appointed Director of the March of Dimes, and she devoted the rest of her life to the work of preventing birth defects. She died in 1974.

J

JAZZ

Since the early 1900s, many musical styles have been called "jazz," and all of them have benefited from the labor, artistry, and contributions of women. Socially acceptable roles for women in jazz have been primarily restricted to vocalists, sometimes pianists; it is in these areas that women musicians have received greatest recognition. Yet woman musicans have played every instrument, in every style and era of jazz history.

The earliest manifestations of the diverse musical lineages we now call jazz emerged in the early 1900s from a number of musical sources, including African-American forms, such as spirituals, work songs, and blues, as well as African, European, and Latin-American influences. These combinations took place in contexts of African-American social, cultural, and economic life in the years following the demise of **RECONSTRUCTION**, the rise of segregation, and African-American urban migration.

African-American women were prominent actors in the musical forms that influenced jazz, including vodun (voodoo) chants and drumming in New Orleans; spirituals and gospel; and the blues. African-American and white women were among the pianists and composers of the ragtime craze of the early 1900s, and many women played piano, as well as brass, reeds, bass, and drums (instruments traditionally associated with men) in family bands—in circuses, carnivals, and minstrel and tent shows.

In the 1920s, African-American female vocalists made the earliest blues records. "Blues queens," such as Mamie Smith (singer on the first vocal blues recording, "Crazy Blues," 1920), **BESSIE SMITH**, and **GERTRUDE "MA" RAINEY**, recorded with well-known jazz instrumentalists, mostly men, but sometimes women, including pianist Lovie Austin.

Austin, as well as Emma Barrett and Lil Hardin (later Armstrong) were among the most highly regarded pianists in early jazz bands. Less remembered, but celebrated in their day, were female cornetists, trumpet players, and saxophonists, including the trumpet-playing mother and daughter team, Dyer and Dolly Jones. Women instrumentalists often played in "all-girl" bands such as the Fourteen Bricktops.

In the 1930s, female jazz vocalists, and some pianists, continued to garner notoriety, but women played other instruments as well. Arguably the most highly regarded vocalist in jazz history, **BILLIE HOLIDAY** gave some of the most celebrated live and recorded performances. Pianist and composer Mary Lou Williams brightened the swinging Kansas City sound. Jazz trumpeter Valaida Snow played to international acclaim. All-woman bands of the 1930s included Ina Ray Hutton's Melodears, the Harlem Playgirls, and in the later part of the decade, the International Sweethearts of Rhythm, whose popularity would increase during **WORLD WAR II**. The Sweethearts' inclusion of Asian-American, Latin-American, and Native American, as well as African-American women, reflected the ethnic variety that existed on the "colored" side of Southern segregation. After 1943 the Sweethearts and several other African-American all-woman bands sometimes broke the color line by covertly traveling through the South with one or two white members. Other all-woman bands of the 1940s included the Darlings of Rhythm, the Prairie View Co-eds, and Ada Leonard's "All-American" Girls. The war opened opportunities for women in men's bands: Woody Herman hired trumpet player Billie Rogers and vibist Marjorie Hyams; Gerald Wilson hired trombonist/arranger Melba Liston.

As in other industries, not all American women jazz musicians had the option or desire to leave paying jobs behind after the war ended. Female vocalists, whose artistry could be more easily imagined as reflecting domesticity of postwar gender ideology, continued to be popular. Some women who had played big band instrumental jazz throughout the war spent the 1950s working in nightclubs in solo acts or all-woman combos. Some found music-related employment in fields thought to be more "feminine", such as music education, or traded their horns for piano or Hammond organ. The emergence of television brought employment for some white women musicians in the show bands of Ina Ray Hutton and Ada Leonard.

Jazz played a key role in the **CIVIL RIGHTS** and Black Power movements of the transformative 1960s, and included powerful contributions by vocalists Abbey Lincoln and Nina Simone, pianist/harpist/percussionist/composer Alice McLeod Coltrane, and pianist/organist Amina Claudine. The **WOMEN'S LIBERATION MOVEMENT** in the 1960s and 1970s brought new interest in women's achievements, and thus, a new audience for women in jazz. The first Women's Jazz Festival was held in Kansas City in 1978, followed by the first New York Women's Jazz Festival. All-woman groups founded in the 1970s include Sisters in Jazz (New York, 1974–1977) and Maiden Voyage (Los Angeles, 1979–present).

Despite high profiles and multiple recordings of contemporary women musicians in the 1980s and 1990s, including drummer Teri Lyne Carrington, saxophonist Jane Ira Bloom, violinist Regina Carter, and the all-woman big band, Diva, there remains overwhelming evidence that women jazz musicians do not receive the same encouragement or opportunities as do men of their skill levels. Organizations attempting to correct these inequalities include the International Association of Jazz Educators, Sisters in Jazz, International Women in Jazz, and the Mary Lou Williams Jazz Festival.

Sherrie Tucker

FURTHER READING

Davis, Angela Y. *Blues Legacies and Black Feminism: Ma Rainey, Bessie Smith, and Billie Holiday*. New York: Pantheon Press, 1998.

Gourse, Leslie. *Madame Jazz: Contemporary Women Instrumentalists*. New York: Oxford University Press, 1995.

Handy, D. Antoinette. *The International Sweethearts of Rhythm*. rev. ed. Metuchen, NJ: Scarecrow Press, 1998.

JEFFERSON, MILDRED

(b. 1927)

A leader in conservative political and social causes and founding member (in 1973) of the **NATIONAL RIGHT TO LIFE COMMITTEE**. Mildred Faye Jefferson received her A.B. from Texas College, her M.S. from Tufts University, and in 1951 became the first African-American woman to be granted an M.D. by the Harvard Medical School. From 1973 to 1995 she was assistant clinical professor of surgery at Boston University. In 1994 Jefferson waged an unsuccessful campaign in the Republican primary in Massachusetts, hoping to unseat Democratic senator Edward Kennedy.

In addition to being a former president and cofounder of the National Right to Life Committee, Jefferson is former chairperson of the National Right to Life Crusade. She is one of the *Conservative Digest*'s Ten Most Admired Women and the only woman to receive the Lantern Award for patriotism from the Massachusetts Council of the Knights of Columbus.

JEWISH AMERICANS

Jewish Americans comprise one of the smallest ethnic groups in the United States; however, their contributions to American culture, politics and industry far outweigh their numbers. Throughout their history in the United States, Jews, like other minority groups, have had to find ways to balance the push toward assimilation with their desire to preserve a distinct identity. Notable Jewish American women have resolved this problem in a variety of ways.

In the early part of the century, the identities of many Jewish American women were still closely linked to their immigrant origins, and many women settled in the cities of the East Coast where they could find jobs in the garment industry. Most of the families who settled in the cities of the East Coast traced their roots back to Eastern Europe, and their European ancestry deeply affected their lives in the United States. Living in urban poverty and under the shadow of the persecution and hardship they had experienced in Russia and Eastern Europe, many Jewish women became politically radicalized and chose to express their commitment through their political work. J. Edgar Hoover called **EMMA GOLDMAN**, the garment worker, activist and anarchist the "most dangerous woman in American" during her deportation hearings in 1919. Ethel Rosenberg (1915–1953), a labor organizer, was sentenced to death along with her husband for giving atomic secrets to the Soviet Union during World War II. Golda Meir (1898–1978), an educator and labor activist, became Israel's fourth prime minister in 1969. Meir emigrated with her family from Russia to Milwaukee in 1906. Childhood memories of Russian pogroms influenced Meir to become a Zionist, and by 1921 her Zionism and socialism compelled her to settle in Palestine.

Beginning at mid-century, Jewish Americans began leaving the urban centers where they had lived, and joined other Americans in the movement toward **SUBURBANIZATION**. As opportunities for women and Jewish Americans broadened, the linkages with their Eastern European past weakened, and the impulse toward assimilation strengthened. The events of **WORLD WAR II** and the Holocaust, however, brought to the fore the situation of Jewish groups all over the world, and Jewish Americans were forced to consider their role in the sphere of world politics. In the 1950s, more and more Jewish American women attended prestigious educational institutions and went on to occupy powerful positions in the government. Jewish American **RUTH BADER GINSBURG** attended Harvard and Columbia law schools in the 1950s and was appointed a Supreme Court justice by President Bill Clinton in 1993. In the mid-1990s, U.S. Secretary of State **MADELEINE ALBRIGHT** held a press conference to announce the discovery of her Jewish roots. **BETTY FRIEDAN**, author of the groundbreaking book *The Feminine Mystique* (see Documents), was a founder of the **WOMEN'S LIBERATION MOVEMENT.** Feminist activist **GLORIA STEINEM** founded ***MS.* MAGAZINE** in 1972.

Jewish Americans have also made their mark as pioneers in the sphere of arts and culture. Theda Bara, one of the most glamorous and successful silent film stars of the 1910s, was born in a largely Jewish suburb of Cincinnati. Born in 1901 in Russia, author Ayn Rand emigrated to the United States in her twenties and went on to become famous for her novels and her Objectivist philosophy. Cosmetics mogul Estée Lauder was born in New York City in 1910 and opened her first office in 1946. World famous entertainer **BARBRA STREISAND** has won innumerable awards for her work in music, screen, and stage. Goldie Hawn, Roseanne Barr, and Bette Midler have been recognized for their contributions to film and television. Contemporary poet **ADRIENNE RICH** has published more than 20 volumes of poetry and was a recipient of a MacArthur fellowship.

JOHNSON, CLAUDIA (LADY BIRD) ALTA TAYLOR (b. 1912)

Wife of Lyndon Baines Johnson, the thirty-sixth president of the United States. Claudia Alta Taylor was born on December 22, 1912, near Karnack, Texas, the daughter of a wealthy businessman. Her nursemaid gave her the childhood nickname "Lady Bird." After earning two bachelor's degrees in liberal arts and journalism from the University of Texas, she married Johnson in 1934. They had two daughters.

Outgoing, intelligent, and ambitious, Johnson was a vital asset to her husband's rise in politics. With her support, he was elected as a congressman from Texas in 1937. She managed his congressional office during his service in **WORLD WAR II** and purchased a radio station in Austin, Texas, that they developed into a multimillion-dollar broadcasting corporation.

Lady Bird Johnson first campaigned for her husband in the 1948 Senate election and assisted his staff in 1955 when he suffered a heart attack. In 1960, when her husband was the Democratic vice presidential nominee, she campaigned for the ticket throughout the country. As wife of the vice president, Johnson visited 33 foreign countries.

After the assassination of President John F. Kennedy in 1963, Johnson helped with the transition to her husband's administration and his reelection in 1964. As first lady, she promoted the Head Start program for preschoolers and became best known for her national beautification program. Originally focused on the nation's capital, her plans soon expanded to the national level. The program included federal legislation for highway beautification. Returning to Texas when her husband's term expired in 1969, Johnson wrote a book and was the subject of documentary and television movies. She established the National Wildflower Research Center in 1982.

JOHNSON, SONIA (b. 1936)

A member of the Church of Jesus Christ of Latter-day Saints, Sonia Johnson began speaking out in support of the **EQUAL RIGHTS AMENDMENT** (ERA, see Documents) in 1977. She became known nationally with her 1978 testimony in front of the U.S. Senate's Constitutional Rights Subcommittee. At the congressional hearing,

Senator Orrin Hatch (R-UT) squared off against Johnson, a **HOMEMAKER**, who had been born and raised in Logan, Utah, and was an active Mormon. Her strong testimony in support of the ERA caught media attention and she became a lightning rod for Mormon and other religious supporters of the amendment.

She also spoke out against Mormon groups that opposed the ERA. A well-publicized church trial in 1979 led to Johnson being excommunicated from the Mormon Church. She then became president of the Mormons for ERA group. After being married for 20 years, she announced she was gay. Her book about her embrace of feminism, *From Housewife to Heretic*, was published in 1981. She went on to write several other books about feminism and lesbianism.

Janis Joplin is remembered for her folk and blues music.

JOPLIN, JANIS (1943–1970)

Singer. Born in Port Arthur, Texas, Janis Joplin grew up in a traditional home, but never felt that she fit in at her high school. She flaunted a bohemian, wild, and original style. The "bad girl" reputation she gained at that time would later become an asset in the world of the 1960s acid rock.

After training as a secretary, Joplin moved to Los Angeles. She returned to Texas but soon grew bored with small-town life. She experimented with drugs and sex, moved to Austin with her high school boyfriend, and eventually enrolled at the University of Texas at Austin. She was at the center of the 1960s counterculture at the conservative campus and soon became popular as a local folk singer.

After several trips between Texas and California, Joplin joined a band called Big Brother and settled in San Francisco. By 1967, she played regularly on the city circuit with the Grateful Dead, the Paul Butterfield Blues Band, and Jefferson Airplane. In 1968, Joplin and Big Brother signed with Columbia Records, but the band split up soon after. Joplin then formed the Kozmic Blues Band and enjoyed relative success, but in 1970 they also disbanded.

Throughout her life, Joplin was insecure about her looks and was vulnerable in her love relationships with men and women. Infidelity, jealousy, and passion characterized those relationships. She also struggled with drug and alcohol addiction. In 1970, Joplin went to Rio to get clean. When she returned, she formed a new band, Full Tilt Boogie, reunited with Big Brother, and toured the East Coast. She performed what would be her last live concert at Harvard Stadium in Massachusetts. After attending her high school reunion, she recorded *Pearl* in Los Angeles. On October 3, 1970, she was to record the vocal of the album's final track, but she died at 1:40 a.m. on October 4 of a heroin and alcohol overdose.

Joplin is remembered for her passionate personality and folk- and blues-influenced rock in songs such as "Me and Bobby McGee" and "Piece of My Heart" even more than for her tragic end.

JORDAN, BARBARA (1936–1996)

Lawyer, Congresswoman. Barbara Charline Jordan was born on February 21, 1936, in Houston, Texas, to Benjamin and Arlyne (Patten) Jordan. As a high school student, Jordan excelled in speech and debate, winning first place in a national speech contest in 1952. Her senior year she decided to become an attorney after hearing a lawyer speak at a career day assembly.

Jordan earned a B.A. in political science and history from Texas Southern University in 1956 and an LL.B. from Boston University Law School in 1959. Her first legal office was her parents' dining room, where she worked at the table until she could afford an office in downtown Houston.

Jordan's interest in politics began in 1960, when she campaigned for presidential candidate John F. Kennedy. Eager to hold a seat in the Texas House of Representatives, she ran unsuccessfully in 1962 and 1964. When she was finally elected in 1966, she became the first African-American state senator in Texas since 1883. While in the Texas senate, Jordan served on the first Fair Employment Practices Commission to fight discrimination in the workplace. She was also instrumental in the passage of Texas's first minimum wage law and organized a department to deal with urban affairs. When she was elected president pro tem of the Texas legislature in 1970, she became the first African-American woman in U.S. history to preside over a legislative body.

In 1973, Jordan was elected to the U.S. House of Representatives. At the federal level, she continued to focus on humanitarian and racial issues as she had in Texas. But she did not gain national renown until she made a compelling speech at President Nixon's impeachment hearing in 1974. As a member of the House Judiciary Committee, Jordan argued that the evidence against Nixon was so powerful that if he were not impeached, the "Eighteenth Century Constitution should be abandoned in the Twentieth Century paper shredder." When casting her vote for his impeachment, she stated, "My faith in the Constitution is whole, it is complete, it is total."

Jordan left Congress in 1979 to teach political science at the University of Texas in Austin. Although she denied it, she retired from public office because of her health. She suffered from both multiple sclerosis and leukemia. She was the keynote speaker at the Democratic National Convention in 1992 (as she had been in 1976, when she was the first African American to be selected to deliver such a speech). She remained in Austin until her death, caused by viral pneumonia, on January 17, 1996.

FURTHER READING

Rogers, Mary Beth. *Barbara Jordan: American Hero.* New York: Bantam Books, 2000.

JOURNALISM

The art and profession of writing for newspapers, magazines, and the broadcast media to inform and educate the public. Journalism in the twentieth century underwent a major transformation from purely print-based media to instantaneous global transmission of electronic text and images. Women played a central role in this evolution throughout the century.

In the late 1800s and early 1900s, as American women were fighting for equal rights, higher pay, and access to higher **EDUCATION**, coverage of their plight was still largely confined to specialized publications with limited readership. One such publication was the *Woman's Journal*, a newspaper founded in 1870 and edited by Alice Stone Blackwell until 1916. Its articles and editorials helped give the women's rights movement the exposure sought by its leaders, leading to passage of the **NINETEENTH AMENDMENT** (granting the right to vote) in 1920.

Other woman journalists, meanwhile, had been influential in the general press. **NELLIE BLY** (see Volume 2) had become a star newspaper reporter in the 1880s and 1890s, writing on such subjects as slum life, divorce, and conditions inside insane asylums. Following her tradition, **IDA TARBELL** became a prominent muckraker. Her magazine articles and book on the Standard Oil Company (1904) led to federal action limiting the operations of that giant corporation. Dorothy Thompson earned acclaim as a foreign newspaper correspondent in Europe during the years leading up to **WORLD WAR II**. Martha Gellhorn and Marguerite Higgins were award-winning journalists who earned their stripes covering the war in Europe. And Margaret Bourke-White pioneered the field of photojournalism in the 1930s and 1940s. From Dorothy Dix, Hedda Hopper, and Liz Smith to Ann Landers, Abigail Van Buren, and Erma Bombeck, women have also won vast newspaper audiences with advice and society columns.

The achievements of women in newspaper journalism have come despite professional and social barriers, including limited placement in schools of journalism and a distinctly male culture in many offices and newsrooms. **KATHARINE GRAHAM** took over the reins of the *Washington Post* after the death of her husband in 1963, but she soon gained the respect of the entire industry for her independent editorial judgment. Gradually, more and more newspaperwomen, such as *New York Times* executive editor Gail Collins, rose to top positions on the strength of their talent and experience.

MAGAZINE journalism is one field in which women have been especially prominent during the twentieth century—from writers and editors to publishers and owners. Notable figures include Clare Booth Luce, a top editor at *Vanity Fair*; **HELEN GURLEY BROWN**, the longtime chief editor of *Cosmopolitan*; **GLORIA STEINEM**, a cofounder and the editor of ***MS.* MAGAZINE**; and Tina Brown, head of the venerable *New Yorker* from 1992 to 1998.

Although the prominent figures in early television journalism were men, the opportunities for women opened up significantly—along with those in other professional fields—beginning in the 1970s. Led by **BARBARA WALTERS**, Charlayne Hunter-Gault, Cokie Roberts, and other women broadcasters, coverage of major events, primetime broadcasts, and editorial comment were increasingly handled by women.

See also: Photographers; "Women and the Media," p. 27.

K

KELLER, HELEN (1880–1968)

Activist. Helen Keller was born in Alabama on June 27, 1880. When she was just 19 months old, she was struck deaf and blind by an illness. She went untutored until age seven, when **ANNIE SULLIVAN** became her teacher in 1887. Sullivan taught Keller by outlining the shapes of letters on her hands; within three months, Keller knew the alphabet and obtained basic spelling skills. Within three years, Keller was lipreading and learning to speak, as well as learning to read and write using Braille. Keller, with Sullivan's assistance, completed her schooling and attended Radcliffe College, graduating with honors in 1904.

Keller is best known for her lectures and writings. Her writings were initially shunned, because many people believed that the ideas of a deaf and blind woman had to be intellectually worthless. She proved them wrong. In addition to writing, Keller advocated women's rights and was a spokesperson for the American Foundation for the Blind. She was also a member of the Socialist Party and promoted labor unions and aid to the disadvantaged. She is noted for her fund-raising efforts for blind people. Keller died on June 1, 1968.

Helen Keller, a deaf and blind woman, lectured and wrote, advocating women's rights.

KELLEY, FLORENCE
(1859–1932)

Labor activist and socialist, born in Philadelphia to an activist family. Kelley's father was a congressman and abolitionist, and her great-aunt, Sarah Pugh, was the president of the Philadelphia Female Anti-Slavery Society and a close friend of **LUCRETIA MOTT**'s (see Volume 2).

Kelley entered Cornell University in 1876 at age 16 but contracted diptheria in 1879 and was unable to return. She still completed her senior research project on the correlation between women's rights and the legislative history of children in the United States. The resultant thesis was published in the *International Review*. After graduation, Kelley taught history and published articles addressing how health affected working women's labor prospects, and asserting women's rights to protection from exploitative labor.

She left the United States for the University of Zurich after the University of Pennsylvania denied her admission to graduate school because of her gender. She often corresponded with women's rights leader **SUSAN B. ANTHONY** (see Volume 2) regarding working women. Her growing anger over the condition of women in the United States pushed her toward socialism and its egalitarian tenets. She married a Russian-born member of the Socialist Labor Party, Lazare Wischnewetzky, in 1884, and together they joined the Social Democratic Party. Kelley collaborated closely with Friedrich Engels and translated his famous tract *The Condition of the Working Class in England* into English in 1887.

Shortly thereafter, Kelley moved to New York with her family, and then to Chicago in 1891 without Wischnewetzky, who was abusive. She took refuge in **JANE ADDAMS**'s **HULL HOUSE** (see Volume 2), and quickly became involved in labor reform work. She pushed for legislation to combat the horrifying conditions of Chicago's sweatshops, and was appointed by the governor of Illinois to be the first chief factory inspector in 1893. In 1894, she scored a major victory when the state legislature passed labor laws ensuring the eight-hour workday for women and children.

Kelley continued to work for her **PACIFIST**, egalitarian, and socialist beliefs and lobbied for a minimum wage and the eight-hour workday. She helped found the **NATIONAL CONSUMERS LEAGUE**, the Intercollegiate Socialist Society, and, in 1909, the National Association for the Advancement of Colored People. She also served as the president of the Socialist Party of America and the National American Woman Suffrage Association. Kelley died in Germantown, Pennsylvania, on February 17, 1932.

KING, BILLIE JEAN (b. 1943)

Tennis champion and outspoken advocate of the rights of women tennis players. King was born in Long Beach, California. At a young age, she showed exceptional skill in softball, but there was no significant career for a woman in that sport, so her parents introduced her to tennis. In 1962, at the age of 18, King won the Wimbledon Championship in lawn tennis in London, upsetting Margaret Smith Court, the leading women's tennis player in the world at that time. King went on to become the first woman player since 1939 to win the triple crown of singles, doubles, and mixed doubles in both American and British tournaments. In 1967, King was named Outstanding Female Athlete of the World, and five years later she was named *Sports Illustrated* magazine's Sportsperson of the Year, the first female to receive that honor. In 1971, she became the first woman athlete to earn $100,000 in a single year.

King is perhaps best known for her victory in 1973 over former men's tennis star Bobby Riggs in a much-hyped exhibition match called the "Battle of the Sexes." This was in the early days of the **WOMEN'S LIBERATION MOVEMENT**, and King had long advocated equal payment for women players. Riggs had beaten Margaret Smith Court earlier the same year and declared that he wanted a match with Billie Jean King saying, "I want the women's lib leader." That match set a record for the largest tennis audience and called attention to women's **ATHLETICS.**

King was one of the founders of the Women's Tennis Association and served as its first president. In 1984, she retired from competitive tennis and became the commissioner of the World Team Tennis League, the first woman commissioner in professional sports.

KING, CORETTA SCOTT
(b. 1927)

African-American activist. Coretta Scott was born in Marion, Alabama. She attended Antioch College, where, despite the college's liberal origins, she still faced discrimination and racism as the first **AFRICAN-AMERICAN** woman to major in elementary education. After graduation, she studied voice at the New England Conservatory.

It was through a conservatory classmate that she met Martin Luther King, Jr., then in graduate school at Boston University. They married in 1953 and moved to Montgomery, Alabama, after completing their studies. King worked alongside her husband and made significant contributions to women and civil rights. She gave Freedom Concerts which chronicled the civil rights movement through intertwined narrative and song and eventually raised over $50,000 for the Southern Christian Leadership Conference (SCLC). King was also a member of the Women's International League for Peace and Freedom, and in 1962, was a delegate to the Women's Strike for Peace's Geneva conference on atomic test-bans.

After her husband was fatally shot before a march in Memphis on April 4, 1968, King continued in his spirit, marching in Memphis four days after his death. She continued to work for the SCLC, and later, for the Martin Luther King Jr. Center for Social Change. A passionate activist in her own right, today King continues to lobby for peace and against the death penalty.

KINGSTON, MAXINE HONG (b. 1940)

Writer. Maxine Hong was born on October 27, 1940, the oldest of six children to Chinese immigrant parents. In 1958, she entered Berkeley on a full scholarship. She majored in English and was active in campus politics. In 1962, she graduated and married Earll Kingston. Hong Kingston taught high school and gave birth to a son in 1963. The Kingstons were active in California's counterculture and Hong Kingston actively opposed the Vietnam War. However, in 1967, they became disillusioned with the movement and moved to Hawaii. There, she continued to teach and began writing.

In 1976, Hong Kingston wrote her first book, *Woman Warrior: Memoir of a Girlhood Among Ghosts*. The book was based on her mother's life and addressed issues of racial and gender identity. The book won critical acclaim and is considered a seminal work in Asian-American literature. In 1979 *Time* magazine named it one of the top ten books of the decade.

She continued to write books that portrayed the human victims of racial and gender inequalities. *China Men* (1980) looked at Chinese immigration from the male perspective. In 1989, she wrote her first novel, *Tripmaster Monkey: His Fake Book*. She also published several other works of nonfiction.

Hong Kingston has won many awards for her work, including the National Book Critics Circle Award, the American Book Award, and the National Humanities Medal. She is also politically active, teaching writing workshops for Vietnam veterans.

KIRKPATRICK, JEANE JORDAN (b. 1926)

First woman to serve as permanent U.S. Representative to the United Nations. Born on November 19, 1926, in Duncan, Oklahoma, Jordan was the daughter of an oil drilling contractor. She transferred from Stephens College in Missouri to graduate from Barnard College. She earned a masters and Ph.D. from Columbia University. There, she studied European war refugees, and developed a deep opposition to totalitarianism, which she held responsible for the refugees' appalling condition.

Before receiving her Ph.D., she worked in the research and intelligence bureau at the State Department, where she met and married a colleague, Evron Kirkpatrick, in 1955. After receiving her doctorate and having three children, she taught at Georgetown University, where she eventually received an endowed chair. She published a number of scholarly works, including *Political Woman*, a study of women in state legislatures. However, it was an article for *Commentary* that changed the course of her life. When Ronald Reagan read her article urging the United States to carefully distinguish between totalitarian and authoritarian states in determining its foreign policy, he asked Kirkpatrick, then a Democrat, to join his campaign as foreign policy adviser. He later appointed her ambassador to the United Nations, the first woman to hold the job.

Although Kirkpatrick met with fierce opposition from administration insiders, her principled handling of foreign affairs at the end of the Cold War era earned her the respect of others. After resigning from the post in 1985, she continued to work in politics, serving as advisers to both Bob and Elizabeth Dole's campaigns for president. Currently, she is a senior fellow at the American Enterprise Institute, a conservative think tank.

KUHN, MARGARET
(1905–1995)

Social activist who organized the Gray Panthers. Margaret Eliza Kuhn was born on August 3, 1905, in Buffalo, New York, the daughter of an office manager. In 1926, she graduated from Case Western Reserve University where she had organized a chapter of the **League of Women Voters**.

Kuhn worked for the **Young Women's Christian Association** in Cleveland for 11 years and became familiar with members' problems. Because many of the members held low-paying jobs with few benefits, Kuhn assisted them in forming **unions** to address their concerns.

Kuhn next worked as associate secretary and editor of the *Social Progress* magazine for the United Presbyterian Church in New York City. Angry that the church's policy required her to retire at age 65, Kuhn directed her energies toward combating ageism in society. She met with retirees to discuss their experiences with geriatric discrimination. In 1971, Kuhn organized the Consultation of Older and Younger Adults for Social Change, which a journalist nicknamed the "Gray Panthers." The group, based in Philadelphia, Pennsylvania, joined with others in protesting the **Vietnam War** but soon focused its efforts on ending housing and employment discrimination against the elderly.

Margaret Kuhn was a social activist who organized the Gray Panthers.

Kuhn campaigned for a national **health** care system and sought legislation assuring free care for the elderly. She demanded protection for Social Security benefits and implementation of federal nursing home reform. She also defended the image of senior citizens by criticizing the media for bias and stereotypes in its portrayals. Kuhn died on April 22, 1995, in Philadelphia.

See also: Old Age and Mortality.

L

LEAGUE OF WOMEN VOTERS

Founded in 1920, the successor to the **National American Woman Suffrage Association** (see Volume 2), the league (LWV) is a nonpartisan political organization that informs citizens and encourages them to participate in government.

With the ratification of the **Nineteenth Amendment**, the old suffrage organizations shifted their attention to the needs of the new woman voter. Having gained the right to vote, women needed to use it wisely, and local leagues assumed the duties of educating women about the political process. They published booklets describing the structure and function of local government. They held candidate forums around elections. As a nonpartisan organization, they advocated for issues that they believed benefited women. The League was one of several national women's organizations to form the **Women's Joint Congressional Committee** and to support passage of the **Maternity and Infancy Protection Act**. For a brief period, it was among the most influential lobbies in Washington, D.C.

The LWV not only provided voters with information on issues and candidates, but also became the training ground for women to run for political office. During the years after **World War II** and before the Second Wave of the women's movement, many female officeholders said it was the League of Women Voters that gave them their initial political education.

Among the guiding principles of the modern organization are universal protection of the right to vote, free public **education**, and equal opportunity free from discrimination. Over the past 80 years, it has also developed positions on broad, national issues through a process of research, discussion, and consensus. Local and state chapters have put these principles into action by supporting projects such as campaign finance reform, environmental cleanup, civil rights, and the **Equal Rights Amendment** (see Documents).

LESBIANS

Women whose sexual preference is other women. Lesbians have played influential roles throughout the history of the United States, although their sexuality was often kept a secret. Lesbians entered the twentieth century as members of a taboo underground and emerged as a diverse and powerful lobbying force, promoting freedom of sexual preference and frequently, women's rights.

By the 1920s, lesbians had articulated an identity based on sexual difference and the idea of sexual choice. **Feminist** groups such as Heterodoxy had formed, and many of its members were openly lesbian. A lesbian counterculture began to emerge. In popular culture, lesbian characters began appearing in plays and novels. These representations were not always created by lesbians or gay-friendly individuals, and reception was mixed.

Lesbian bars provided space for lesbians to build a community. Mona's, which opened in 1936 in San Francisco, is thought to be one of the first. Also, publications serving the lesbian community emerged. The first was Edythe Eyde's *Vice Versa*, published under the pseudonym Lisa Ben, in 1947.

It was not until the 1950s that lesbian and gay organizations gained higher visibility. One of the first groups to promote a homosexual collective history and identity was the Mattachine Society, founded in 1950. In 1955, Del Martin and Phyllis Lyon formed the **Daughters of Bilitis** (DOB) in San Francisco. Originally a social club, the DOB quickly became political. Its goal was to fully integrate lesbians into society and to fight stereotypes and discrimination.

As the 1960s liberalizing mood prevailed, a gay rights movement emerged alongside the civil rights movement. The first mass lesbian and gay public protest was by the New York League for Sexual Freedom in 1964, against recent military discharges for homosexuals. A watershed in lesbian and gay rights were the Stonewall riots. When police raided a Greenwich Village gay bar in New York City called the Stonewall Inn on June 27, 1969, the crowds fought back and smaller riots flared up afterwards.

Today, there are lesbian groups to advocate on behalf of a diverse population. From militant lesbian groups to organizations for lesbians of color, they aggressively lobby for exposure, resources, and rights. Openly lesbian entertainers, politicians, religious leaders, and other public figures push for recognition and equality. Despite continued prejudice, homosexuals have won small legislative victories. Hawaii and Vermont now allow same-sex marriage, and many companies and corporations have adopted antidiscrimination policies against gays and lesbians, as well as domestic partnership policies.

LITERATURE

The literature of the United States in the twentieth century can be characterized overall as a break from traditional themes and writing conventions, influenced by the perceived disorder of the world. As a result of **World War I** and the **Great Depression**, American culture turned from idealism to cynicism where people questioned tradition and the "American Dream." Whereas the United States had once been perceived as a land of opportunity where anyone who worked hard could gain wealth, status, and a higher standard of living, this optimism was crushed under disillusionment.

The literature of the early twentieth century was dominated by male writers and mirrored changes in American values, philosophies, and lifestyles. **PROHIBITION** in the 1920s gave rise to gangsterism and moral corruption. F. Scott Fitzgerald's novel *The Great Gatsby* summed up "The Jazz Age" and criticized a society obsessed with wealth and status, neither of which seemed to bring anybody happiness. Fitzgerald's wife, Zelda, was also a capable writer but was unrecognized for her talents until the 1970s. The stock market crash of 1929 and the rise of Marxist socialism threatened the capitalistic ideal. As a result, more and more writers began to question industrialization. With the rise of the "protest novel," authors like John Steinbeck (*The Grapes of Wrath,* 1939) questioned the quality of life in a country where the lives of working-class people were reduced to poverty. In psychology, Sigmund Freud's theory of the subconscious caused anxiety that people might not be in complete control over their minds. Its influence on literary form is most notable in the use of stream of consciousness narration and nonchronological plots, which forced the reader to piece together fragments of perception and time. Such techniques were used by fiction writers such as Katherine Ann Porter and William Faulkner, whose stories focused on the disintegration of the American South, a society both unable to grasp Northern industrialism and unable to let go of traditional customs.

In poetry, the focus moved away from traditional metrics, stanza patterns, and themes. Imagist poets, led by Ezra Pound, felt that imagery alone could carry a poem's emotion and message, and attempted to outline an exact visual image through use of precise language and

TRAILBLAZERS

The first African-American woman to have a play produced on Broadway with *A Raisin in the Sun* (1959), Lorraine Vivian Hansberry brought to the American stage a realistic perspective on black life that began a vigorous movement in the nation's theater arts. The success of her play also opened the way for black writers, actors, and producers in unprecedented numbers. The story of a family in Chicago that attempts to move into a white neighborhood, *A Raisin in the Sun*—with Sidney Poitier, Claudia McNeil, Diana Sands, Ruby Dee, and Louis Gossett—won the New York Drama Critics Circle Award as the best play of 1959. It was later made into a movie (1961) and a stage musical (1973). Hansberry's only other finished work, *The Sign in Sidney Brustein's Window,* had a brief run in 1964.

While never militant, Lorraine Hansberry was committed to civil rights throughout her life. Born on the South Side of Chicago in 1930, she was the daughter of a real estate broker and banker who challenged the city's discriminatory housing policies. When Lorraine was eight years old, the family moved into a formerly segregated neighborhood and was subjected to ridicule, violence, and, finally, eviction. Her father sued and eventually prevailed in a landmark Supreme Court ruling against restrictive covenants, *Hansberry v. Lee* (1940). Lorraine studied drama at the University of Wisconsin and moved to New York to pursue her career as a playwright. She was married to the songwriter and music publisher Robert Nemiroff, who edited her autobiographical writings for the posthumous *To Be Young, Gifted, and Black* (1969). Hansberry died of cancer in 1965 at age 34.

Lorraine Hansberry's *A Raisin in the Sun* (1959) was the first play by an African-American woman to be produced on Broadway. It was released as a motion picture in 1961.

poetic images. Other notable imagists include Marianne Moore, Hilda Doolittle, and **Gertrude Stein**.

At the same time, Modernism was rising in popularity with its experimental forms and themes, and the **Harlem Renaissance** was occurring, giving African Americans a voice in American literature. The stories of **Zora Neale Hurston**, including her most famous work, *Their Eyes Were Watching God* (1937), borrowed heavily from African-American folk traditions. Themes in the literature of Lorraine Hansberry (*A Raisin in the Sun*, 1959) often focused on feelings of alienation.

After **World War II**, disillusionment turned to a fascination with the chaotic and irrational. Writers turned to dark humor and absurdism to convey the times in which they lived. Flannery O'Connor, a writer of the Southern Gothic genre, wrote about violence and the grotesque in collections such as *A Good Man is Hard to Find*. Also following the gothic tradition is contemporary writer Joyce Carol Oates (*Where Are You Going, Where Have You Been?*, 1993), whose stories analyze the sociopathy and psychology of everyday life in the United States.

TRAILBLAZERS

In 1993, Toni Morrison (b. 1931) became the first African-American woman to win the Nobel Prize for Literature. Morrison's characters struggle to find their own cultural identities within the confines of an unjust society. The Swedish Academy of Letters, in awarding Morrison the Nobel Prize, described her style as poetic, an exploration of "the language itself, a language she wants to liberate from the fetters of race."

Morrison's Pulitzer Prize-winning novel *Beloved* (1987) relies on the supernatural and African-American folklore to convey the story of a runaway slave who, at the point of capture, kills her newborn daughter to spare the child a life of slavery. Morrison's use of violence to communicate the black struggle in a racist society is also used in her first novel, *The Bluest Eye* (1970). The protagonist, a young girl victimized by her father, is obsessed with white standards of beauty; her only wish is to have blue eyes. Yet while Morrison's work always contains the rage and despair that accompany social determinism, it also embraces hope.

Toni Morrison earned her B.A. in English from Howard University in 1953 and her M.A. in English from Cornell University in 1955. She currently teaches creative writing at Princeton University, and was named the Robert F. Goheen professor in the Council of Humanities in 1989. She has also held teaching positions at Yale University and the University of New York at Albany. Her many works also include *Sula* (1973), *Song of Solomon* (1977), *Tar Baby* (1981), *Jazz* (1992) and *Paradise* (1998).

The 1960s saw a rise in confessional poetry, in which authors such as **Sylvia Plath** and Anne Sexton penned frank poems about their own lives. It also saw a rise the amount of published literature written by women, and by the 1980s, women of various cultural backgrounds were thriving in the book industry. Today, some of the best-known woman authors include **Amy Tan** (*The Joy Luck Club*, 1989); Jamaica Kincaid (*Annie John*, 1986); Louise Erdrich (*The Bingo Palace*, 1994); **Sandra Cisneros** (*The House on Mango Street*, 1984); and Toni Morrison (*The Bluest Eye*, 1970). The writings of these and other women have increased awareness of multicultural issues in the United States.

Overall, the literature of the twentieth century reflected a constant flux in economic, social, scientific, and personal issues. Its pioneers depicted the world as they knew it; irrational, unpredictable, and in need of reform.

See also: Brown, Rita Mae; Cather, Willa; Kingston, Maxine Hong; Walker, Alice; Wharton, Edith.

LOPEZ, JESSIE DE LA CRUZ

(b. 1919)

Labor organizer. Born in 1919 to a single mother in Anaheim, California, Jesusita Lopez was unable to attend school. Instead, she worked year-round as a migrant worker to support her family.

In 1938, she married another migrant worker, Arnold de la Cruz. Together they had five children and followed crops for work in

California. In December 1964, they met with labor organizer Cesar Chavez, who recruited Arnold to join the farm workers organizing movement. Chavez occasionally used Jessie's home to hold meetings, and she eventually became an organizer for the farm workers union also, traveling to promote it and collect dues. Between 1965 and 1972, Lopez signed more members than any other organizer. In September 1965, Lopez joined Chavez's American Farm Workers (AFW) in a Filipino grape farm workers' strike in Delano, California. In 1966, after grape growers sprayed striking workers with agricultural poisons, Chavez organized a 250-mile march from Delano to Sacramento in protest, which Lopez also joined.

In 1966, Lopez began teaching practical engineering to help grow better crops and hosted a show on Fresno public television. She also continued to organize for the AFW. In 1971, **Dolores Fernandez Huerta** asked for her help to negotiate with Christian Brothers growers. In 1972, Lopez represented the growers at the first convention of the United Farm Workers of America (UFW) in Fresno. That same year, she was a delegate to the Democratic national convention.

Lopez and her husband purchased their own acres for a cooperative farm that supported equitable practices and fair payment for labor in 1974. Arnold died in 1990 and Chavez in 1993, but Lopez continues to support and organize for the UFW while sitting on the Board of California Rural Legal Assistance and living in Fresno.

LORDE, AUDRE

(1934–1992)

African-American feminist writer. Audre Geraldine Lorde was born in New York City on February 18, 1934, to immigrants from Granada. She attended Manhattan Catholic schools and graduated from Hunter College in 1959. She received a masters in library science from Columbia in 1961. While working as a librarian, she married Edward Ashley Rollins in 1962. They had two children but divorced in 1970.

In 1968, Lorde's life changed dramatically when she was awarded a grant from the National Endowment for the Arts. She became the poet-in-residence at Tougaloo College a small **African-American** college in Mississippi. There, she published her first book of poems, *The First Cities*, in 1968. Her most popular volume is the 1978 *The Black Unicorn*, poems of empowerment for African-American women that draw on images of African goddesses. Another volume, *From a Land Where Other People Live*, was nominated for a 1974 National Book Award.

Lorde described herself as a black, feminist, lesbian, mother poet. This characterization indicates her strong commitment to exploring her various identities while fighting against the marginalization of each. She wanted to give a voice to African-American women and lesbians, and fight against racism and sexism.

Lorde chronicled another battle, her fight against breast cancer, in 1980 in *The Cancer Journals*. Although she survived breast cancer, she died of liver cancer on November 17, 1992, in New York.

LOVING v. VIRGINIA

A 1967 Supreme Court case reversing the ruling against interracial marriage by a Virginia court. In June 1958, neighbors and teenage sweethearts Mildred Jeter, an **African-American** woman, and Richard Loving, a white man, married in Washington, D.C., because Virginia law banned interracial marriage.

Shortly after they returned home to Virginia, they were arrested for "unlawful habitation" and charged in the circuit court with violating Virginia's **anti-miscegenation** law. They were sentenced to one year in prison in 1959 by presiding Judge Leon Basile who based his ruling on an alleged separation of the races as ordained by God. Later, Basile suspended the sentence, providing that the Lovings left the state of Virginia and not return for 25 years.

The Lovings moved to Washington, D.C., but returned to Virginia and were forced to live apart. In 1963, the Lovings filed a motion to vacate their sentences in the Virginia Supreme Court, which upheld the previous court's ruling.

With the help of the **American Civil Liberties Union**, the Loving case went to the U.S. Supreme Court. When Chief Justice Earl Warren delivered the opinion reversing the decision, he wrote that the Lovings were deprived their due process rights and that the freedom to marry was protected under the Fourteenth Amendment. The *Loving* case led to 16 states abolishing their anti-miscegenation laws, and states who did not were unable to enforce such laws in light of the Supreme Court's ruling.

LYND, HELEN MERRELL
(1894–1982)
Sociologist. Lynd and her partner husband were the first to apply the methods of cultural anthropology to the study of urban life. During the 1920s, Helen M. and Robert S. Lynd examined the social makeup and traditions of Muncie, Indiana. As part of their survey, they looked at the changing roles of women and men in marriage and family life. They reported that all of the social classes they studied believed that romantic love was the only basis for marriage, but that after marriage husbands and wives typically had few interests in common and were as emotionally distant as married couples of the 1800s. The Lynds wrote about their Muncie research in *Middletown: A Study in Contemporary American Culture* (1929)—what they called an examination of "pure" American life "unpolluted" by racial and religious minorities. Later, they studied the social changes that took place as a result of the **GREAT DEPRESSION** of the 1930s and the advent of the automobile in *Middletown in Transition: A Study in Cultural Conflicts* (1937). These books became classics.

Lynd taught at Sarah Lawrence College in New York from 1929 to 1964. She also wrote, independently of her husband, such books as *On Shame and the Search for Identity* (1958) and *Toward Discovery* (1965).

M

McCLINTOCK, BARBARA
(1902–1992)
Scientist. Barbara McClintock was born in Hartford, Connecticut, and attended Cornell University, from which she received her bachelor's degree in 1923 and a doctorate in Botany in 1927. She taught and conducted research at Cornell from 1927 to 1931 and from 1934 to 1936. In between she was a fellow at the National Research Council and the Guggenheim Foundation. In 1936, she became an assistant professor at the University of Missouri.

During these years, McClintock was studying genes in maize kernels. In 1942, she joined the staff of Cold Spring Harbor Laboratory in New York. Her continued genetic research there proved that genes can move on chromosomes and between them. At first, other scientists did not believe her findings, but eventually further research proved them true.

McClintock's work, which helped researchers understand how genetic traits are inherited, won her a Nobel Prize in 1983. She was the first American woman to win the prize on her own, not as part of a scientific team. McClintock continued working as a member of the staff at Cold Spring Harbor until she died in 1992.

McDANIEL, HATTIE
(1895–1952)
Singer, composer, radio performer, and actress. She was the first African American to receive an Oscar. Hattie McDaniel became one of the most widely recognized and controversial American entertainers.

McDaniel was born on June 10, 1895, in Wichita, Kansas. She was the thirteenth child of Henry McDaniel, a Baptist minister and minstrel performer, and Susan Holbert McDaniel. In 1908, when she was 13 years old, McDaniel began her professional career. She performed in minstrel shows, a popular form of vaudeville that depicted African-American songs and dances in stereotypical ways. She dropped out of high school in 1910 to perform full time with minstrel groups throughout the Western states, often with her father's "Henry McDaniel Minstrel Show."

During the 1920s McDaniel developed her singing career through the Theater Owners Booking Association (TOBA) and recorded her original compositions on the Okeh and Paramount labels. After the 1929 stock market crash the TOBA folded, leaving McDaniel without work. In 1931 she moved to Los Angeles.

In California McDaniel worked washing dishes while she picked up radio show and movie parts playing housemaids, almost the only roles available to African-American actresses at that time. At first she earned just $5.00 per film and radio show. McDaniel's talents earned her the parts of Mom Beck in *The Little Colonel* (1935) with Shirley Temple, Malena Burns in *Alice Adams* (1935) with Katharine Hepburn, and Queenie in *Showboat* (1936). These roles in major Hollywood movies gave McDaniel national prominence. By 1937 she had appeared in more than 50 feature films and shorts.

In 1939 McDaniel received the part of Mammy, a loyal house slave, in David Selznick's film adaptation of the best-selling novel, *Gone with the Wind*, by **MARGARET MITCHELL**. The role earned McDaniel $500 a week, an Academy Award for Best Supporting Actress, and a high-profile position in Hollywood's romanticized depiction of racial oppression during slavery. Her Mammy role typecast McDaniel and made her a prime target for African-American leaders' criticism of actors who perpetuated racist stereotypes.

During the 1940s McDaniel struggled to maintain her professional success and improve her reputation among African-American leaders. She achieved both with "The Beulah Show," a nationally broadcast radio program that aired from 1947 to 1952 and later became a television show. In Beulah, the first starring role on radio for an African-American woman, McDaniel had a chance to play a complete character instead of a racial stereotype.

Throughout her life, McDaniel's success was tempered by professional and personal difficulty. She appeared in over 300 films, but most often in housemaid roles. McDaniel defended her career by saying that she would rather play a maid than be one. She endured four failed marriages and serious depression in 1944 following a false pregnancy. McDaniel died of breast cancer on October 26, 1952.

MAGAZINES, WOMEN'S AND GIRLS'

Throughout the twentieth century, women's mass-circulation magazines played a major role in the lives of millions of American women. Advertisers realized that women made many of the buying decisions in their households, and publishers realized that there were few publications aimed at women. Two of the most popular magazines early in the century were the *Ladies' Home Journal*, which began in 1883, and *Good Housekeeping*, which began in 1885. The *Delineator*, which ran from 1863 to 1937, introduced the fashion magazine.

In the second half of the twentieth century, seven titles (known as the Seven Sisters) became the largest circulators: *Better Homes & Gardens, Family Circle, Good Housekeeping, Ladies' Home Journal, McCall's, Redbook*, and *Women's Day*. These magazines published reliable service departments, fiction, and investigative reporting.

In 1963, Betty Friedan published *The Feminine Mystique* (see Documents), which examined the messages found in 1950s women's magazines. She compared these feminine stereotypes with those of the preceding decades, and she discovered what she called "the problem that had no name," an epidemic of unhappiness among largely college-educated women who seemed to have it all. Joanne Meyerowitz has argued that Friedan selectively cited fiction articles, overlooking prewar stories lauding housewifery and postwar stories praising career women.

The dominance of the Seven Sisters came to an end in the late 1970s due to a change in women's lifestyles and the appearance of audience-specific magazines.

The number of girls' magazines grew in the 1980s and 1990s. Magazines like *Teen, Seventeen,* and *YM* had dominated the market. Trying to reach as many girls as possible, media companies launched a new series of magazines aimed at teens such as *Teen People* and *Cosmo Girl!*

Women's and girls' magazines have come under fire for presenting superficial topics and unrealistic body images. Fashion magazines have received the most criticism, although beginning in the late 1970s, more diverse models began appearing on the cover of major magazines.

But for all the negative images of women in the media, the trend is slowly reversing. A growing niche market has meant new publications for women that have rejected sexist images and stereotypes. Magazines like *Jane* and *Marie Claire* have been credited with stretching the boundaries of the traditional women's magazine with more thoughtful articles. In addition, there are more business publications aimed at women, such as *Working Woman*, founded in 1975.

Magazines for women and girls played an important role in American culture throughout the twentieth century.

Mass market magazines aimed at African-American women achieved prominence in the 1970s with *Essence Magazine*. Similar publications were introduced in the 1980s. Feminist publications saw growth in the late 1960s before seeing circulation drop off in the 1980s. **GLORIA STEINEM** founded ***MS.* MAGAZINE** in 1972 as a feminist publication and later converted it to a no-advertising publication to avoid the impact of sexist advertising on its content. After several years of struggling for funding, Steinem took control in 1999 and stopped advertising, relying largely on subscription revenues.

See also: "Women and the Media," p. 27.

FURTHER READING

Zuckerman, Mary Ellen. *A History of Popular Women's Magazines in the United States, 1792–1995.* Westport, CT: Greenwood, 1998.

MANA, A NATIONAL LATINA ORGANIZATION

Founded in 1974 as the Mexican American Women's National Association, this nonprofit advocacy organization has expanded to include all Latinas within its membership and agenda.

Originally, the organization provided a platform for Mexican-American women, but today the organization has a mission that is both more encompassing and better defined. An autonomous organization committed to social activism and self-definition, MANA supports educational opportunities for women and girls, helps develop leadership skills, promotes community service, and shares knowledge about Latin cultures and women's contributions to them.

The organization sponsors a program, "Las Primeras,®" to recognize Latinas who have been the first to achieve recognition in their field. Members also serve as mentors to young women in the program HERMANITAS® (little sisters).

MARRIAGE

When a man and a woman, in a religious or civil ceremony, vow to live together as husband and wife. During the early part of the twentieth century, many women aspired only to be married. Woman had few career options, and finding men to support them was essential to economical survival. Divorce was not common. Married women tended the house and raised their children while husbands worked outside the home.

Today, according to the 2000 Census, only 25 percent of the population is composed of married couples who live with children of that marriage. Blended families, single parents, and people living on their own make up the rest. While the median marriage age for women in 1970 was about 21 years old, by 2000 it was 25.1. Furthermore, 22 percent of women ages 30 to 34 have never married. In 1970 that figure was only 6 percent. Many women are opting to stay single because they have more education and career options than previous generations and can, therefore, support themselves financially.

Attitudes about marriage and the role of women changed gradually and are still evolving, but one person credited for bringing the topic of marriage to the world's attention is **BETTY FRIEDAN**, author of *The Feminine Mystique* (see Documents). This 1963 book depicted many women who were dissatisfied working as housewives. Many felt they had sacrificed their personal dreams to fulfill family obligations. Friedan criticized advertisers who portrayed women as subservient housewives in television commercials, promoting the concept that women were satisfied with this role. Her book helped start a revolution, and Friedan would become the first president of the **NATIONAL ORGANIZATION FOR WOMEN** (NOW). The organization pushed for equal pay, equal job opportunities, access to birth control, and legalized abortion.

By the latter part of the twentieth century, many married women were working outside the home. But now they found themselves doing everything—going to work for several hours a day, then coming home at night to cook dinner, clean house, and tend to their children as well as their husbands. The changing concept of marriage and its responsibilities created friction in households. Divorce became more common, and therefore more socially acceptable. In 1970 there were 3 million single mothers; in 2000 there were 10 million.

MARTIN, ANNE (1875–1951)

Suffragist, feminist, author. Anne Henrietta Martin was an important leader in the Western campaigns orchestrated by the **NATIONAL WOMAN'S PARTY**. She led Nevada's successful suffrage campaign in 1914 and ran for the U.S. Senate unsuccessfully.

Born in Empire City, Nevada, in 1875, Martin received bachelor's degrees from both the University of Nevada and Stanford University. In 1897, she completed an A.M. in history at Stanford. She founded and led the history department at the University of Nevada. Then in 1909 she departed for Europe to participate in the militant branch of the British **SUFFRAGE MOVEMENT.** After two years, she returned to the United States to continue her work for women's right to vote.

She assumed the presidency of the Nevada Equal Franchise Society in 1912 and led the victorious state campaign in 1914. She coordinated a drive to defeat candidates of "the party in power" as president of the Woman's Party of Western Voters in 1916 and was elected vice chair of the new National Woman's Party in 1917. In 1918 and 1920, Martin campaigned for the U.S. Senate as an Independent from Nevada. She lost but drew 20 percent of the vote with a platform that supported sexual equality, prohibition, and public ownership of utilities.

During the 1920s and 1930s, Martin devoted her time to **PACIFIST** activities and worked with the Women's International League for Peace and Freedom. She moved to California in 1921 and died in Carmel in 1951.

MARTIN, LYNN MORLEY

(b. 1939)

Politician and educator. Judith Lynn Morley was born in Evanston, Illinois, and went to the University of Illinois, from which she graduated Phi Beta Kappa in 1960. That same year she married John Martin and over the next nine years the couple had two children. Martin taught school before entering politics in 1972, when she was elected to the Winnebago County Board. Four years later, Martin, a Republican, won a seat in the Illinois House of Representatives. In 1978, she became a state senator and helped reform conditions in Illinois nursing homes. In 1980, when the congressman in her district retired, Martin won the election to fill his seat in Congress where she served for ten years. In 1991 President George H. W. Bush appointed her secretary of labor. As secretary, Martin helped enlarge vocational training programs and also established the Glass Ceiling Commission to study the barriers to women who sought promotion in corporations and other organizations. After leaving office, Martin became a professor at the J. L. Kellogg Graduate School of Management at Northwestern University in Evanston, Illinois.

MATERNALISM

The belief that motherhood ascribes special rights, responsibilities, and authority to women. The idea gained tremendous popularity during the late nineteenth century and early twentieth century, although strands of maternalism may be found throughout the 1900s.

Maternalism incorporates a set of ideas and corresponding values that reinforce essentialist ideas about the sexes. The primary assumption underpinning maternalist views is the idea that one's sex carries social and cultural characteristics that are specific and different from the opposite sex. For example, if women have the *nat-*

ural potential to give birth, all women are more nurturing than men, better able to care for and raise children, and born with a greater aptitude to understand and conduct the workings of a family. It reinforced ideas that society's interests were best served when women became mothers and used their talents to rear children.

A public aspect of maternalism exists as well. Those who believed that women had innate qualities that made them better qualified to care for children and families would, by extension, find women best suited for jobs as teachers, healers, sanitation directors, and community welfare directors, for example. Similarly, women's organizations or individuals used maternalist arguments to further civic causes, such as clean water and public sanitation, or the benefits of programs such as **MOTHERS' PENSIONS** and **AID TO DEPENDENT CHILDREN**.

During the second half of the 1900s, one could still find maternalist arguments in movements to end nuclear testing, the war in Vietnam, or drunk driving.

See also: National Congress of Mothers.

MATERNITY AND INFANCY PROTECTION ACT

The first federally funded social welfare legislation in the United States. The Sheppard-Towner Maternity and Infancy Protection Act of 1921 was written by Julia Lathrop, the first director of the **CHILDREN'S BUREAU**, and introduced in the House of Representatives by Jeannette Rankin, the first woman to serve in Congress. President Warren Harding signed the act into law in 1921, shortly after taking office in the first election in which women could vote. The purpose of the legislation was to provide federal matching funds to states so they, in turn, could provide services to mothers and their children. States used the funds to establish standards for infant care, education for pregnant women and new mothers, and training for midwives.

The Sheppard-Towner Act was repealed in 1929 as a result of pressure from the American Medical Association and other groups that feared this law was the first step toward socialized medicine. Although short-lived, the law marked the first time the federal government accepted responsibility for the welfare of women and children. Some of the provisions of the law found their way into **NEW DEAL** programs during the Depression. Later efforts by the Children's Bureau led to funding of maternity services for the wives of military men and other public health initiatives aimed at mothers and children.

MENOPAUSE

Often called "change of life," menopause is the cessation of ovulation and menstruation in middle-aged and older women. In a broader sense, menopause is a time when women begin to experience changes in the production of sex hormones, and this frequently begins with a change in menstrual patterns. There may be a significant reduction in monthly discharge, and monthly periods may be skipped or become irregular. Eventually, menstruation stops entirely.

These changes may also be accompanied by other physical characteristics. Some women experience "hot flashes," the sensation of feeling warm when environmental conditions do not warrant it. Others experience mood fluctuations, headaches, dizziness, or weakness. Some symptoms are severe enough to warrant medical attention. Estrogen Replacement Therapy is a treatment in which women are given estrogen, balanced with progesterone, in pill form, to replace the loss of the estrogen hormone and thus alleviate some of these symptoms.

It is important to note that many women who experience menopause do so without any of the problems described above. In fact, some women are relieved to stop menstruating and enjoy the freedom that comes with no longer having to be concerned about getting pregnant.

MERITOR SAVINGS BANK v. VINSON

A 1986 U.S. Supreme Court case that played a key role in the fight against **SEXUAL HARASSMENT** in the workplace. The case was brought by Mechelle Vinson, a teller at Meritor Savings Bank, who claimed that her manager coerced her into having sex with him. In 1986, the Court ruled against Meritor Savings Bank, saying that the bank was responsible for the sexual harassment of its employees. In reaching its decision, the Court relied on guidelines the Equal Employment Opportunity Commission had issued in 1980. The Court noted that there are two types of sexual harassment. One is called *quid pro quo* ("something for something"); for example, a supervisor attempts to trade promotions, higher pay, or more favorable work assignments for sexual favors. *Meritor Savings Bank v. Vinson,* though, strengthened laws protecting workers from another form of sexual harassment: the "hostile work environment." This term refers to an ongoing pattern of verbal or physical sexual conduct that a "reasonable" person would find offensive. Examples include making comments about one's anatomy; displaying pornographic material; telling off-color jokes; referring to women in a derogatory way; or touching, pinching, or slapping. After *Meritor,* employees subjected to a hostile work environment could sue for damages without having to show that they were required to submit to sexual advances as a condition of employment.

MIDWIFERY

From colonial times through the eighteenth century, most babies born in America were delivered by midwives. Beginning in about 1760, doctors became more involved in the birthing process, and by the end of the nineteenth century, most middle-class women chose doctors to deliver their babies. By the first quarter of the twentieth century, only poor and immigrant women continued to use midwives.

In 1925 the Frontier Nursing Service, founded by Mary Breckinridge, introduced the British model of the nurse-midwife in the United States, and in 1931 a program at the Lobenstine clinic was founded to educate nurse-midwives to care for disadvantaged women in New York City. Despite these initiatives, from the 1930s through the 1960s, midwife-assisted births were primarily confined to poor African-American and Hispanic women.

By the early 1970s, though, some women had become dissatisfied with the medical model of childbirth, leading to a renewed interest in midwifery. Today there are two primary kinds of midwives: nurse-midwives, who are medically educated, and lay midwives, who have learned their craft by experience. A number of studies conducted in the 1980s and 1990s confirm that there are no health risks to mothers or babies associated with midwife-assisted deliveries. In fact, midwife-assisted deliveries may even confer certain advantages. For example, recent studies have shown that babies delivered by midwives weigh more at birth and that mothers are less likely to have Cesarean sections.

TRAILBLAZERS

Descended from a distinguished Kentucky family—her father was a congressman and her grandfather, John Cabell Breckenridge, had been vice president of the United States under James Buchanan—Mary Breckinridge (1881–1965) overcame tragedy in her own life to become a pioneer of public-health nursing and midwifery services for rural America. After the deaths of her husband and her two children, she devoted her energies to nursing and "raising the status of childhood everywhere." She studied nursing at St. Luke's Hospital in New York City and traveled to France as a Red Cross volunteer after WORLD WAR I. The success of visiting nursing services for women and children in Europe convinced her that public health and midwifery programs could—and should—be established in the rural United States.

In 1925, Breckinridge started the Kentucky Committee for Mothers and Babies in eastern Kentucky. Introducing family-health, prenatal, and midwifery services to poor, isolated areas in the Appalachian Mountains, the organization sent nurses on horseback to remote outposts, set up district nursing facilities, and eventually built a teaching hospital—today the Mary Breckinridge Hospital in Hyden. Renamed the Frontier Nursing Service (FNS) in 1928, the organization reached more than 1,000 rural families in the first five years. Breckinridge kept careful records on childbirth mortality and demonstrated the success of her services. The rate of death in childbirth for Leslie County, Kentucky, fell from the highest in the country to below the national average. "The glorious thing," she said on her deathbed, "is that it works!"

MILITARY SERVICE

Although women had participated in every American war since colonial days, their formal entrance into the U.S. military began at the start of the twentieth century. In 1901, in the aftermath of the Spanish-American War, Congress created the Army Nurse Corps (ANC). The 1,600 civilian women who had contracted with the military as nurses in that war proved vital, and the War Department recommended the ANC's creation to Congress. Based on the assumption that all nurses are female, the aim of the legislation was to make these women quickly available to the military command when the next emergency occurred.

The peacetime planning for war and the inclusion of women continued with the 1908 authorization of the Navy Nurse Corps (NNC). The NNC differed significantly from the ANC in that the women had greater responsibility and higher status; instead of carrying bedpans and changing sheets, NNC women supervised male paramedics who did the menial tasks. Nurses spent their time as administrators and especially as teachers; they trained the young men who would work on combat ships where women were not allowed.

Members of both the ANC and NNC were treated as officers, but equality with men was far from complete. Nurses had to meet more stringent educational and age requirements; they were not officially commissioned, did not receive full benefits, and faced many rules that did not apply to men. Nor did the women who had the difficult assignment of creating these unprecedented corps receive the support they merited. Neither Dita H. Kinney, the first head of the ANC, nor Esther Vorhees of the NNC had any official rank; instead, both were genteelly addressed as "director."

WORLD WAR I began less than a decade later. Although it was little noted, a number of women joined the military itself during this war. The Navy, desperate for clerical workers in Washington, D.C., researched its enlistment law and discovered that there was no legal barrier to recruiting women. The call went out, and some 12,500 women quickly enlisted, beginning in August 1918. The war ended that November, but the women worked on clearing the paperwork through 1919.

The Navy's law also applied to the Marine Corps, and thousands of women applied; the corps accepted only 305. Both these "Marinettes" and the Navy's "Yeomen" (females) dressed in skirted khaki uniforms and performed in marches and drills. This highly visible training, which took place on parade grounds in Washington, was not necessary to the women's jobs but was used as a recruiting ploy to lure men into enlisting.

Both the Marine and Navy groups were dissolved after the war ended, but the two **NURSING** corps continued. With the onset of **WORLD WAR II**, the model for non-nursing women was quickly revived by those who remembered it from the previous war, including first lady **ELEANOR ROOSEVELT** and several congresswomen. Representative Edith Nourse Rogers of Massachusetts introduced legislation to create the Women's Army Auxiliary Corps (WAAC); Maine Representative **MARGARET CHASE SMITH** would become known as the mother of the Navy's **WOMEN ACCEPTED FOR EMERGENCY VOLUNTEER SERVICE (WAVES)**; and Representative Frances Bolton of Ohio functioned in the same role for the nursing corps.

Rogers introduced her bill to create the WAAC in May 1941, but it was not until Japan's attack on Pearl Harbor in December that the War Department took it seriously. Congressional hearings were held in March 1942 and, after extensive debate, both the House and Senate passed the bill by May. The new law preserved the auxiliary status of the corps, a serious flaw in the eyes of many, but that did not deter the thousands of women eager to join. By mid-1943, when Congress reconsidered its decision and renamed it the **WOMEN'S ARMY CORPS** (WAC), tens of thousands of women had enlisted. The woman appointed to head the new institution was Oveta Culp Hobby of Texas, who was heavily scrutinized and highly praised for her efforts.

Benefiting from the Army's experience, the Navy bypassed the auxiliary status of its women and the pejoratives associated with Army term "wack." The Navy's female unit would be called **WOMEN ACCEPTED FOR VOLUNTARY EMERGENCY SERVICE (WAVES)**.

The third women's military unit was the Coast Guard's SPARS, which began November 22, 1942. (SPARS is an acronym of the first letters of the Coast Guard motto, "Semper Paratus," and its English translation, "Always Ready.") Like the Coast Guard itself, the SPARS remained small, with fewer than 10,000 members, compared with more than 100,000 each in the WAC and WAVES.

Like the Coast Guard, the Marine Corps was a subdivision of the Navy. The Marines were the last U.S. military service to create a unit for women. Called simply the Women's Marines, it was launched on January 28, 1943. Some 20,000 women enlisted, despite notoriously tough training requirements.

The WAVES and SPARS did not accept black women until late in the war and the Women Marines never did, but Oveta Hobby assured a place for them in the WAC immediately on its formation; moreover, she saw to it that black WACs were assigned to occupational, rather than menial, categories.

Navy women were not permitted to go abroad until late in the war, when they were sent to relatively safe areas, but WACs were on the beachheads of North Africa as early as 1942. Some landed in Italy with the men, while others moved from camps in Great Britain to the Normandy invasion; still others served in the Pacific theater. WACs worked as radio transmitters, translators, air controllers, mechanics, photographers, cartographers, and other specialists, often only a few miles from front lines. The women most likely to be closest to battle, of course, were the Army Nurse Corps, who served throughout the world. Almost 100 ANC women spent the war fighting off starvation in a Manila prisoner-of-war camp; they had been captured early in 1942, when Corregidor fell.

The Air Force was still part of the Army during World War II, and the two units that used the skills of female fliers had only a quasi-military status. The Women's Auxiliary Ferrying Squadron (WAFS) began in September 1942 under veteran pilot Nancy Harkness Love; it was eventually absorbed by the Women's Airforce Service Pilots (WASP) under aviation legend Jacqueline Cochran (who won several major races in the 1930s).

By the spring of 1944, WASPs had flown 30 million dangerous miles. The requirements for joining this elite group were so high that there were never more than about 2,000 WASPs, but more women died in this unit than in any other. Thirty-eight were killed in the line of duty; their families received no benefits, and in at least one case, WASPs had to take up a collection to pay for a comrade's funeral. The War Department canceled the program at the end of 1944. With victory in sight, male pilots sought the most prestigious flying assignments.

Most Americans expected that all non-nursing women's units would be disbanded when the war was over, but military commanders found repeatedly that while they wanted to discharge women in general, there was a reason why this or that particular woman was an asset to the task at hand. By 1948, three years after the war's end, Congress passed the **WOMEN'S ARMED SERVICES INTEGRATION ACT**, formalizing the place of non-nursing women in the peacetime military. At the same time, the Air Force separated from the Army, and its female unit was renamed the Women's Air Force (WAF).

Although the 1948 legislation was a milestone, women were limited to 2 percent of total U.S. armed forces, and their rank and occupational choices were restricted. Women's place in the military was to be a narrow one, and few noticed President Harry S Truman's 1950 appointment of Anna Rosenberg as assistant secretary of defense.

Nevertheless, military women continued to push for an expansion of their service opportunities. The Korean War set a precedent. For the first time in U.S. history, women were called to involuntary duty like men, and 13 platoons of Women Marines were mobilized. Between 1950 and 1955, 120,000 women served. Most were stationed on U.S. soil, but nurses assigned to Korea saw tremendous action. This was especially true for Air Force nurses who worked evacuation units.

The **VIETNAM WAR** was the last in which women served in a clearly secondary, gender-segregated capacity. To have women killed in this highly unpopular war would have been politically damaging. Most of the approximately 11,000 women who went to Vietnam were nurses; about 250,000 women served elsewhere during the war.

At the same time, the women's movement was creating far-reaching change in civilian society, and the military followed suit during the 1970s and 1980s. The first visible change was in the rank of commanders. Hundreds of thousands of women had served in the ANC since its creation in 1901, and the chiefs of the WAC and the WAVES during World War II had each commanded 100,000 women. Still, no women had been promoted beyond colonel, a rank sometimes held by officers who command as few as 500 men. On June 11, 1970, ANC chief Anna Mae Hayes and WAC commander Elizabeth P. Hoisington were promoted to brigadier generals. The Air Force followed the next year by promoting Jeanne Holm to director of the WAF and in 1973 to major general. The Navy was last, promoting Alene Duerk, commander of the Navy Nurse Corps, to the rank of admiral in 1972. The Marine Corps did not promote a woman to its highest ranks but did set a precedent in 1971 when barracks were gender-integrated and the first women were allowed to remain on active duty during pregnancy.

When the draft ended in 1972, the need for recruits led to many changes beneficial to women. Women no longer had to meet higher standards than men to enlist and, for the first time, their dependents became eligible for benefits. The Navy, which had long recognized the need for nurses on ships, now allowed other women to serve at sea. Women also became eligible for Reserve Officer Training Corps (ROTC), which paid expenses for college students who received formal training and were commissioned at graduation.

In 1973, the Coast Guard's SPARS unit was abolished and women were merged into the regular corps; Captain Eleanor L'Ecuyer became the first woman to command a Coast Guard division. That same year, Marine Colonel Mary E. Bane took command of a nearly all-male battalion at California's Camp Pendleton, despite what a journalist called "astonishing furor." New precedents followed rapidly in subsequent years, with the first woman to pilot a helicopter, the first female aviator in the Navy, and so forth. The year 1978 was especially meaningful: The Marine Corps became the last service branch to promote a woman to general; the Navy Nurse Corps gained its first African-American captain; and, most significantly, the Army abolished the WAC and integrated women into its regular forces.

The 1980s began with the first admissions of women to the prestigious military academies at West Point, Annapolis, and Colorado Springs. Prodded by Representative **PATRICIA SCOTT SCHROEDER**, the House Armed Services Committee held its first hearings on sexual harassment in the military in 1980. The public also recognized Admiral Grace Hopper, the nation's oldest military officer, when she finally retired in 1986 at age 79; the Navy had found Hopper's pioneering computer work so valuable that it routinely exempted her from mandatory retirement rules.

The Panama invasion in 1989 and especially the Persian Gulf War two years later finally featured a military in which women were allowed to work to capacity. Women flew planes, won medals, and gave their lives. More than 40,000 women, many of them young mothers, were deployed with Operation Desert Shield/Desert Storm.

Among the milestones of the 1990s were the cancellation of the official ban on women in combat aviation positions and the Navy's deployment of women on combat ships. In 1993, President Bill Clinton appointed Sheila A. Widnall as secretary of the Air Force, the highest Pentagon position a woman had ever held. As the century drew to a close, a monument and museum built by Women in Military Service to America was opened at Arlington National Cemetery outside Washington, D.C. Its location in America's most sacred military burial ground serves as enduring testimony to the fact, as well as the recognition, of the role of women in U.S. military service.

FURTHER READING

DePauw, Linda Grant. *Battle Cries and Lullabies: Women in War from Prehistory to the Present.* Norman: University of Oklahoma Press, 2000.

Herbert, Melissa S. *Camouflage Isn't Only for Combat: Gender, Sexuality, and Women in the Military.* New York: New York University Press, 1998.

MILLETT, KATHERINE MURRAY (b. 1934)

Feminist author and artist. Katherine Murray Millett was born in St. Paul, Minnesota. A graduate of the University of Minnesota in 1956, she received a master's degree from the University of Oxford, England, in 1958. In Harlem, New York, she worked as a kindergarten teacher, then taught English at the college level in Tokyo, Japan. In 1965, she married sculptor Fumio Yoshimura. They were divorced 20 years later. In 1970, Millett received a doctorate from Columbia University and published her doctoral thesis, *Sexual Politics,* which examined how women had been systematically exploited in a society run by males. *Sexual Politics* rapidly became one of the most influential books in the feminist movement.

In 1974, Millett published *Flying,* an autobiography in which she revealed she was a **LESBIAN**. Later books included *Going to Iran* (1982) and a memoir of her own psychiatric treatment, *The Loony Bin Trip* (1990). As an artist, Millet has displayed her works throughout the world.

MISS AMERICA PAGEANT

One of the best-known beauty pageants in the world. It has been an American institution since 1921. It has helped to define the nation's definition of beauty, identity, and the roles of women, as well as created controversy. It began as an East Coast business marketing campaign to attract tourists to Atlantic City. During the 1940s, pageant organizers wanted to expand the influence of the contest and help contestants go to college as a scholarship program for winners. Bess Myerson, the first and only Jewish winner of the crown, won the first scholarship in 1945. In 1954, the pageant reached a nationwide audience, appearing on television for the first time.

The Miss America beauty pageant in Atlantic City, New Jersey, has been a cultural institution since 1921.

Over the years, the pageant came under fire for reducing women to sexual objects. Opera singer Yolanda Betbeze, Miss America 1951, refused to wear a bathing suit in public after her crowning. In 1968 feminists demonstrated at the pageant, dumping items such as girdles and padded bras into a "freedom trash can." The pageant has defended its position by focusing on its role as a scholarship provider. In the early 1990s, the swimsuit competition was debated. A call-in vote was conducted in 1995 to decide whether to keep the competition. The callers voted to keep swimsuits.

The 1974 Miss America, Rebecca King, used her winnings to go to law school, and Miss America 1975 earned a doctorate with her award. In 1970, the first African-American state winner, Cheryl Brown of Iowa, competed in the pageant. The first African-American Miss America, Vanessa Williams, was crowned in 1983 only to lose the crown soon after when it was revealed that she had posed for sexually explicit photos. The same year, Suzette Charles was named the first African-American runner-up. Heather Whitestone, who is hearing impaired, was the first disabled woman to win the title, when she won in 1994 after performing a ballet routine to music she could not hear.

MITCHELL, JONI (b. 1943)

Singer-songwriter and artist. Joni Mitchell, considered to be one of the most influential singer-songwriters in popular music, was born Roberta Joan Anderson in Fort MacLeod, Alberta, Canada, on November 7, 1943. She began her folksinging career in 1963, when she performed in coffeehouses. In 1964, after leaving the Alberta College of Art, she wrote her first song, "Day After Day."

In 1965, Anderson met and married folksinger Chuck Mitchell and moved with him to Detroit, where they performed together. There, she had her first commercial release with "Urge for Going," performed by George Hamilton IV. In 1967, after divorcing Chuck, Joni met musician David Crosby and moved to New York City. Crosby helped Mitchell release her first album, *Song to a Seagull*, which was distinguished by the high, lilting voice, intricate melodies, and poetic verse that would become her trademarks. Mitchell's career took off, and in 1969, she played at Carnegie Hall and in 1970, her album *Ladies of the Canyon* went gold (sold more than 500,000 copies). Her next album, *Blue,* in 1971, is one of her most famous. In 1975, with *The Hissing of Summer Lawns,* she began to move toward a much jazzier sound, an experimentation that culminated in her 1979 collaboration with jazz composer Charles Mingus on *Mingus.*

Mitchell has continued to experiment with her style and has collaborated with a diverse range of musicians to achieve different sounds. She has also painted many of her album covers.

MITCHELL, MARGARET (1900–1949)

Novelist. Born in Atlanta, Georgia, Margaret Mitchell began writing at age 12. She wrote her first story at age 16, based on an early love. It was recently rediscovered and published as *Lost Laysen*.

Mitchell entered Smith College in 1918, but withdrew upon her mother's death and that of her fiancé, Clifford Henry, in World War I. She began feature writing at the *Atlanta Journal Sun Magazine* in 1922 and married Red Upshaw that same year, but divorced in 1924 after a short and abusive marriage. In 1925, she married Upshaw's best man, John Marsh.

In 1926, Mitchell quit her job to research the Civil War for a novel she wished to write. That novel was completed in 1932. Margaret was secretive about the novel and was reluctant to let an editor see it. It was eventually accepted by a

Macmillan editor in 1935. *Gone With the Wind*, Mitchell's story of a woman's experience of the Civil War and the aftermath of Reconstruction, would be her only novel. It was published in 1936 to rave reviews and tremendous fanfare. Mitchell received the Pulitzer Prize in 1937.

In 1939, David O. Selznick released the screen adaptation of *Gone With the Wind*. Beginning in 1940, Mitchell devoted her life to community service and philantrophy, donating time and money to hospitals and other charities. She died at 49 when she was hit by a car.

MONROE, MARILYN (1926–1962)

Actress. Born Norma Jean Baker Mortensen on June 1, 1926, Marilyn Monroe was the daughter of a Los Angeles film cutter. Monroe's father was never positively identified, and her mother was unstable. Therefore, from the time she was two weeks old, young Norma Jean lived mainly in orphanages and foster homes. Lack of stability left her with a lifelong sense of insecurity and fear of abandonment. In 1942, at 16, she escaped another orphanage by marrying James Dougherty. She dropped out of high school, and when Dougherty went off to **WORLD WAR II**, she took a job inspecting parachutes in an arms factory.

In 1946, the year she and Dougherty divorced, she had her first screen test. She signed with 20th Century Fox and took on the pseudonym Marilyn Monroe. Her roles were small until the 1950s. She was usually typecast in "dumb blonde" roles such as her character Lorelei Lee in *Gentlemen Prefer Blondes* (1953). This bothered her and she strove to act in more serious roles. When 20th Century Fox failed to take her talent seriously, she ended her contract in 1955.

Monroe's life was engulfed in controversy. In 1954, she married and quickly divorced baseball star Joe DiMaggio. From 1956 to 1961, she was married to playwright Arthur Miller. In addition, she suffered chronic health problems and could not conceive a much desired baby. These stresses, along with her life long psychological problems, may have contributed to her death on August 5, 1962. Officially, Monroe's death is listed as a suicide. However, some argue that she may have accidentally overdosed on drugs prescribed by her psychiatrist or been murdered.

Marilyn Monroe may be most widely known as a sex symbol, but she wanted to be known as a serious actress. In her final interview with *Life* magazine, she said to the reporter, "Please don't make me a joke." A few of her many films include *The Seven Year Itch* (1955), *Some Like It Hot* (1958), and *The Misfits* (1961).

MORENO, LUISA (1907?–1992)

Labor organizer. Luisa Moreno was born in Guatemala and emigrated to the United States. During the 1930s, she organized other Latino immigrants in New York City to protest brutality by the police. In 1937, she moved to San Diego, California, where she joined the United Cannery, Agricultural, Packing and Allied Workers of America (UCAPAWA). Moreno wrote articles for the union newspaper and helped organize workers in the fish canneries in San Diego and Los Angeles. During **WORLD WAR II**, as American workers enlisted in the armed forces, many Mexicans came across the border to work in the canneries. However, the United States would not allow them to become citizens. Moreno protested this treatment. As she told an interviewer many years later in 1971, "California has become prosperous with the toil and sweat of Mexican immigration attending to its number one industry, agriculture. Now they have sustained a true and lasting patriotism to a democratic country that refuses to give them citizenship or even basic civil rights."

During the 1940s, Moreno became a labor consultant and continued to champion the cause of Mexican civil rights. However, as the Cold War began between the United States and the Soviet Union after the end of World War II, some labor leaders were suspected of being communists. As a result, Moreno was deported in 1950. She died in Guatemala on November 4, 1992.

MORGAN v. VIRGINIA

A 1946 U.S. Supreme Court case that helped end legal racial segregation in the United States. At the time, Virginia law segregated passengers by color on public transportation. To avoid friction between the races, a bus driver could instruct any passenger to change seats to prevent adjoining seats from being occupied by white and "colored" passengers. Irene Morgan, an African-American woman, refused to change her seat and was found guilty of a misdemeanor. The Supreme

Court of Appeals in Virginia affirmed her conviction, but the U.S. Supreme Court reversed it.

The Court, however, did not base its decision on the belief that racial discrimination was unconstitutional. Rather, it relied on a clause in the U.S. Constitution that gives Congress the power to regulate interstate commerce. The Court concluded that the Virginia law placed an "undue burden" on transportation, for it required bus drivers to constantly shuffle people around as the passenger makeup changed during the bus's journey, leading to delays. While the Court's decision did not outlaw racial discrimination, it was one success on the part of an African American to resist a Jim Crow law in the South. Later, in 1955, **ROSA PARKS**, an African-American woman, refused to give up her seat to a white person on a Montgomery, Alabama, bus. Her action touched off a 381-day boycott of the city bus system and helped set in motion the modern civil rights movement.

MOSELEY-BRAUN, CAROL

(b. 1947)

Democrat from Illinois, and first African-American woman elected to the U.S. Senate. Raised on Chicago's South Side, where she attended public schools, Moseley-Braun received her B.A. from the University of Illinois at Chicago in 1969, and her J.D. from the University of Chicago in 1972. She served three years as a prosecutor in the Office of the U.S. Attorney, and then was elected to the Illinois House of Representatives.

Moseley-Braun ran for the U.S. Senate in 1992 and was among several women elected in what was described as "The Year of the Women." While a senator from 1993 to 1999, Moseley-Braun served on the Special Committee on Aging, the Senate Judiciary Committee, and the committees for Finance, Banking, and Housing and Urban Affairs. She is particularly well known for her arguments against the display of the Confederate flag. Defeated in her attempt at reelection in 1998, she was named by President Bill Clinton as U.S. Ambassador to New Zealand.

MOTHERS' PENSIONS

Also called Mothers' Aid, the first publicly funded welfare policy to recognize the value of a mother's work to raise her children. In the early 1900s, advocates compared the services given by soldiers to their country with those services given by mothers in time, dedication, and sacrifice. In 1911, Illinois passed the first state law authorizing counties to spend public funds to subsidize the income of mother-only families. Other states rapidly adopted the policy, but not all counties in these states dispersed mothers' pension funds. Local control allowed significant discretion in the way the policy actually worked.

Most of the women who received mothers' pensions were widows who lived in urban areas and were either native-born or Western European immigrants. Local programs frequently rejected the applications of unmarried mothers or women whose husbands had deserted the family. African-American and Mexican-American women rarely received these funds because of local prejudices and dependence on their wage labor as servants or field workers.

Scholars credit women's organizations for building popular support for mothers' pension laws. National organizations with local and state branches such as the **GENERAL FEDERATION OF WOMEN'S CLUBS** (see Volume 2) and the **NATIONAL CONGRESS OF MOTHERS** lobbied for these provisions. Essential support also came from juvenile courts and the budding social work community.

During the **GREAT DEPRESSION**, funding for the state-level programs dried up, but the policy of **AID TO DEPENDENT CHILDREN**, Title IV of the federal **SOCIAL SECURITY ACT** continued the policy.

MOTHERS, UNMARRIED

A major change in family structure during the twentieth century was the large increase in unmarried women with children. By the year 2000, 7.5 million American families were headed by unmarried females, an increase of 25 percent since 1990. Almost one-third of all children were born to unmarried mothers at the beginning of the twenty-first century, approximately a tenfold increase since 1940.

For decades, the stereotype of an unmarried mother was a teenage girl pregnant out of wedlock. However, that stereotype accounts for only about 13 percent of children born to single mothers, or approximately 375,000 births annually.

By the beginning of the twenty-first century, the average unmarried mother was in her late twenties. Some had never been married. Approximately 40 percent of these unmarried mothers were living with a man. Some of these men were the fathers of the children. The 2000 Census showed a 72 percent increase since 1990 in couples living together outside of marriage.

Some single women have adopted one or more children or been artificially inseminated, while others have been married and divorced. The divorce rate in the United States is approximately one out of every two marriages.

Experts explain the increase in the numbers of unmarried mothers in various ways. Throughout the twentieth century, there was a steady rise in the divorce rate. The stigma attached to divorce gradually disappeared, and state laws made divorce easier to obtain. The average age of marriage for women increased from 20 in 1960 to 25 in 2000. Some sociologists believe that this change is due to women's fears of divorce and their hesitancy to enter into marriage. As a result, more women are cohabiting with men until they determine whether the relationship will work. Almost 40 percent of births to unmarried women occur during the period of cohabitation. Adoption laws have also changed, making it possible for single women to raise children.

Some studies show that children raised by single mothers may be at greater risk than children in two-parent families. According to a report by the Heritage Foundation, these children are more likely to experience emotional and disciplinary problems. Approximately 35 percent of single-parent families, usually headed by women, are living in **POVERTY**—more than twice the overall poverty rate for the general population. In addition, the children of unmarried mothers are more likely to drop out of school and find themselves on **WELFARE** as adults.

FURTHER READING

Worth, Richard. *Poverty.* San Diego: Lucent Books, 1997.

———. *Single Parent Families.* New York: Franklin Watts, 1992.

MOVIES

Motion pictures. In 1896, Alice Guy Blache, secretary to photography equipment salesman Leon Gaumont, shot a short film sample to demonstrate a new invention to the world: the motion picture. The first motion pictures were black and white silent comedies filled with slapstick and fast-paced action, and often took **ACTORS** from the vaudeville stage and made them into movie stars.

But prior to 1920, acting was not the primary role for a woman in the film industry; there were

TRAILBLAZERS

In 1922, film found its first sex symbol in a 16-year-old Brooklyn girl. Clara Bow (1905–1965) would be emulated for decades, most notably by MARILYN MONROE and MADONNA.

Bow's mother was mentally ill, and her father was seldom around. Hoping to flee home, she entered her picture in a magazine contest and won. Her prize was a role in the 1922 film *Beyond the Rainbow.* When the film was edited, however, her performance had been cut. Fortunately, another film director cast her in *Down to the Sea in Ships* (1922). This time, she did not end up on the cutting room floor.

In 1923 Bow signed with Preferred Pictures. Her films *The Plastic Age* and *Mantrap* transformed her into the model of sexual moral freedom of the 1920s, and by 1926 she was receiving over 40,000 fan letters a day. But Bow's greatest fame came from the 1927 film *It.* "It," defined by the screenwriters as "general sex appeal," described Bow perfectly, and she became "The *It* Girl." Women plucked their eyebrows to look like hers, stores sold Clara Bow style hats, and America's flappers wanted to *be* Bow.

By 1930, Bow had made 52 films. But the onset of "talkies" sent her into a nervous breakdown. Bow, who had suffered a slight speech impediment as a child, was nervous about speaking on screen. Additionally, she had become notorious for being a "wild" woman who hosted poker parties, bootleggers, and various suitors. The 1931 trial of her former secretary for misappropriating funds furthered her despair, and soon she became known as "Crisis-a-Day Clara." The media exploited her personal affairs, and that year she was fired by Paramount studios because of her unsavory reputation.

Bow acted in a few "talkies" in the mid-1930s but retired soon afterward. Like her mother and grandmother, she suffered mental breakdowns for the rest of her life. She died of a heart attack in 1965.

Clara Bow, one of the very first movie stars, has been emulated by many over the years.

more women behind the scenes of motion pictures in the early 1900s than at any other time in movie history. Women worked as producers, directors, screenwriters, and editors, while some even owned movie studios. In the 1920s, Mary Pickford became the first woman president of a motion picture studio, Lois Weber was the highest paid director of silent film, and Mabel Normand was the woman behind the genius of silent film star Charlie Chaplin—she taught him many of his routines and directed many of his comedies. After 1920, if they could not act, women were pushed out of the movie business. Male-dominated unions placed men in positions formerly held by women. The only female director in Hollywood in the 1930s and 1940s was Dorothy Arzner, who also invented the boom microphone and the movie crane.

Among the actresses who dominated the "silver screen" in the 1930s and 1940s were **Mae West** and **Rita Hayworth**. West, known for her humor and her sex appeal, wrote her own comedy routines. Hayworth's success arrived after she performed a "striptease" (which merely involved her removing her gloves) in *Gilda* (1946), which was directed by Virginia Van Upp. Because of the success of *Gilda* and Van Upp's portrayal of female characters in positions of social power, Van Upp was promoted to vice president of Columbia Pictures in 1945.

From 1940 to 1970, the woman's role in the film industry remained primarily in the field of acting. Some of the most famous women of film were **Marilyn Monroe**, **Bette Davis**, **Katharine Hepburn**, **Judy Garland**, and **Betty Grable**. However, by the 1970s women were again welcomed behind the scenes of Hollywood pictures. In 1971, Elaine May directed *A New Leaf* and more women began directing films. Other actresses who gained popularity during the 1970s were Jane Fonda and **Barbra Streisand**, who eventually moved into the production and directing fields. Today, as in the early days of motion pictures, women work in various fields both in front of and behind the camera.

MS. MAGAZINE

A national magazine by, for, and about women. In December 1971, *Ms.* made its first appearance as an insert in *New York* magazine. The insert was followed by 300,000 test copies in January 1972 that sold out in eight days. This success allowed **Gloria Steinem**, Pat Carbine, Letty Cottin Pogrebin, and the other founders to publish the first regular issue in July 1972.

The **women's liberation movement** had helped create an audience for serious coverage of feminist issues. *Ms.* answered to this audience. The magazine ran articles about **abortion**, the **Equal Rights Amendment**, domestic violence, and other issues that received little coverage elsewhere. All the articles were written by women. In addition to its regular contributors, over the years *Ms.* has featured writers such as **Alice Walker**, Barbara Ehrenreich, and Susan Faludi.

Despite its early success, rising publication costs and advertiser resistance have at various times forced *Ms.* to the brink of folding. After being briefly suspended in 1989 and again in 1998, a group of women dedicated to keeping *Ms.* alive formed Liberty Media for Women. Liberty Media for Women included founding editor Gloria Steinem, current editor Marcia Gillespie, as well as feminist activists and businesswomen. The consortium purchased *Ms.* and began to publish the magazine again in 1999.

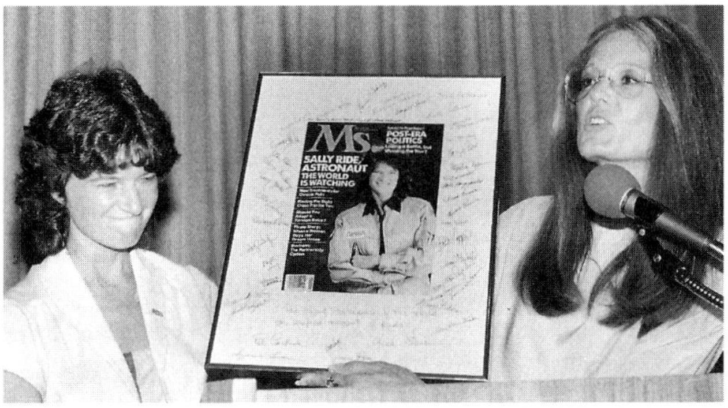

Gloria Steinem and *Ms.* magazine honor Sally Ride.

Currently, *Ms.* is published bimonthly and remains dedicated to examining the lives and struggles of women throughout the world. Since 1990, *Ms.* has been free of advertising. Readers alone support the publication.

See also: Magazines, Women's and Girls'; "Women and the Media," p. 27.

MULLER v. OREGON (1908)

U.S. Supreme Court case that upheld the right of the state of Oregon to pass a minimum wage law for women (see Documents). In 1903 Oregon had passed a law establishing a ten-hour workday for women in laundries and factories. Business owners opposed the law, saying that it was not needed to protect the health or safety of women. The case arrived at the Supreme Court after the state in 1905 fined Curt Muller, a laundry owner, for allowing a supervisor to require a woman to work more than ten hours. To defend the law before the Supreme Court, Oregon hired a noted Boston attorney Louis D. Brandeis, who later would serve as a Supreme Court justice. Attached to his legal brief were more than 100 pages of sociological, economic, and physiological data about the effects of long working hours on the health of women.

The Supreme Court heard *Muller v. Oregon* at a time when the nation was trying to deal with some of the worst effects of industrialization. After the **CIVIL WAR**, many Americans worked long hours under dangerous conditions, and business generally remained free of government and court regulation. But between the end of the nineteenth century and **WORLD WAR I** the Progressive movement in American politics enjoyed increasing success in fighting for laws that protected consumers, the environment, and especially workers. Reformers persuaded state legislatures to pass factory-safety and minimum-wage laws, create workers' compensation programs for persons injured on the job, and regulate the maximum number of hours employees could be required to work. Many of these laws were passed over stiff opposition from business owners who believed that the laws interfered not only with private property rights but with the ability of workers to enter freely into contracts with employers.

An earlier Supreme Court case, *Lochner v. New York* (1905), set the stage for *Muller v. Oregon.* In that case, the Supreme Court ruled that a New York law limiting bakery workers to a ten-hour workday was unconstitutional. The Court, however, did say that any similar law *could* be constitutional if the state could show that the law was necessary to protect the health and safety of workers. That opening led to the Court's decision in *Muller v. Oregon.*

Brandeis, and the state of Oregon, won the case. In its decision the Court referred to the "proper discharge" of women's "maternal functions" and the "well-being of the race." The Court concluded that a woman "is properly placed in a class by herself, and legislation designed for her protection may be sustained, even when like legislation is not necessary for men, and could not be sustained."

At the time Progressives felt that they had won a major victory: The Court had upheld a state law passed to protect the health and safety of workers. *Muller v. Oregon* was also one of the earliest cases in which the Court considered not only the law but other information about the effects of its decisions in the real world and on the lives of everyday people. Later reformers relied on the case in efforts to change social and political conditions—for example, laws affecting the health and safety of workers. Many feminists, though, were troubled by the decision, because the Court had extended protection to women by reinforcing gender stereotypes. They believed that the decision would ultimately restrict economic and professional opportunities for women.

MURRAY, PAULI (1910–1985)

Activist, author, lawyer, priest. Murray grew up an orphan and poor but aggressively pursued an **EDUCATION** and civil rights. She lived with her grandparents in Durham, North Carolina, and graduated from the city's segregated black high school in 1926. Despite a poor high school education, she took additional coursework to be admitted to Hunter College in New York City.

Murray wanted to be a lawyer and pursue a career working for social justice and civil rights. In 1941, Howard University Law School admitted her with a scholarship. It took only a few months for Murray to discover that racial prejudice would not be the only limit on her opportunities. At the historically black law school, as with other private law schools of the era, discrimination on the basis of sex was common practice. Murray repeatedly said that although she entered law school to fight for racial justice, she left law school an avowed feminist. During her legal career, she had many opportunities to advance the cause of equality. In addition, she served as a consultant to the **PRESIDENT'S COMMISSION ON THE STATUS OF WOMEN** for its landmark 1963 report. She also cofounded the **NATIONAL ORGANIZATION FOR WOMEN**.

Murray wrote about her remarkable life and that of her family in two books. *Proud Shoes* (1954) tells the story of her family's heritage as descendants of slaves, freeborn **AFRICAN AMERICANS**, slaveholding whites, and Cherokee Indians. *Song in a Weary Throat: An American Pilgrimage* (1987) recounts her personal struggles and accomplishments. Her other publications include a volume of poetry and a massive reference work on state laws relating to race.

In 1977, Murray was ordained as one of the first women Episcopal priests.

TRAILBLAZERS

Singer Marian Anderson (1897-1993) made her first public singing appearance in 1903 at age six. Twenty-seven years later, she was performing at Carnegie Hall. Although she was heralded as one of the world's greatest contraltos, Anderson repeatedly faced and overcame racial prejudice. In high school, she tried to enroll at a local music school but was rejected because she was an African American. In 1938, while negotiating for a concert at Constitution Hall in Washington, D.C., the venue, owned by the Daughters of the American Revolution (DAR), threw in a contractual clause stating that only white artists could perform there. But Anderson did not give in easily; with the help of first lady ELEANOR ROOSEVELT, who resigned her DAR membership in protest, Anderson sang on the steps of the Lincoln Memorial instead.

Critics didn't know how to describe Anderson's distinctive vocal style, so they labeled it "The Negroid Sound," a classification that was as nebulous as it is unacceptable today. Later, critics described her voice, which spanned a range of five octaves, as mysterious and a wonder of nature. One thing was certain: Her audience loved her voice. When she became the first African American to perform at the Metropolitan Opera House in New York in 1955, she answered eight curtain calls.

Anderson accumulated many awards and honors in her lifetime. In 1921 she won the National Association of Negro Musicians competition. From 1940 to 1946, she was named U.S.A. Radio's foremost woman singer every single year. She won the Spingarn Medal (NAACP), the Handel Medallion, the Page One Award (Philadelphia Newspaper Guild), and the National Medal of the Arts. In addition, she received 24 honorary doctorates, and a 750-seat theater at the City College of New York was named in her honor. Her autobiography, *My Lord, What a Morning* (1956), serves as an inspiration to aspiring singers who face difficult odds.

MUSIC

American women in the twentieth century, especially singers, made a mark on every variety of music. **MARIA CALLAS** thrilled opera lovers; **MA RAINEY** was for many the embodiment of the blues; **BILLIE HOLIDAY** contributed to the golden age of **JAZZ**; **ARETHA FRANKLIN** pioneered the sixties soul sound; **JOAN BAEZ** was a leader of the folk revival; **JANIS JOPLIN** was the queen of rock; and Patti Smith mixed spoken word performance with punk rock. In the nineties, Queen Latifah, Salt 'n' Pepa, and Jill Scott became especially visible as part of a second wave of rap and hip-hop artists. Some women sought a less commercial, independent scene—like the fusion of feminism and punk known as "riot girl."

Throughout the century, it was difficult for women who were not singers to achieve recognition in any genre. In the field of classical music, the compositions of such women as Amy Beach, Peggy Glanville Hicks, and Ruth Crawford Seeger were respected but not played as often as they deserved, and it was hard for woman conductors to gain exposure. The Women's Philharmonic orchestra of San Francisco was founded in 1981 to address this problem.

Because men have dominated the recording industry, it was and remains difficult for women to retain control over their work. Annual conventions such as the Michigan Womyn's Festival, started in 1976, became an important way for women artists and bands to develop their fan bases. The nineties saw the development of many independent woman-owned recording labels, such as Ani DiFranco's Righteous Babe Records and Madonna's Maverick Records.

See also: Anderson, Laurie; Entertainment; Fitzgerald, Ella; Garland, Judy; Horne, Lena; Mitchell, Joni; Smith, Bessie; Streisand, Barbra; West, Mae.

FURTHER READING

Betrock, Alan. *Girl Groups: The Story of a Sound.* New York: Delilah Books, 1982.

Citron, Marcia J. *Gender and the Musical Canon.* New York: Cambridge University Press, 1993.

O'Brien, Lucy. *She Bop: The Definitive History of Women in Rock, Pop and Soul.* New York: Penguin, 1995.

Whiteley, Shelia. *Women and Popular Music: Sexuality, Identity, and Subjectivity.* New York: Routledge, 2000.

N

NATIONAL ABORTION AND REPRODUCTIVE RIGHTS ACTION LEAGUE

Political organization devoted to securing and defending women's **REPRODUCTIVE RIGHTS**. Founded in 1969, the National Abortion Rights Action League (NARAL) publicized the effects of abortion laws—dangerous back-alley abortions and unwanted births—and helped build grassroots support for change in the law, which came in 1973 with ***ROE V. WADE***.

The passage of the **HYDE AMENDMENT** in 1977 restricted Medicaid funds for abortion, with the result that though abortions were still legal they were no longer available for poor women. Women who could not afford legal abortions turned again to the back alleys. The first woman known to have died from an illegal **ABORTION** because of the Medicaid cutbacks was Rosie Jimenez, who died in 1979 at age 27. NARAL set up a fund in her honor to help provide abortions for low-income women.

Kate Michelman, NARAL's president since 1985, experienced the difficulties of a pre-Roe abortion in 1970. She had to get the written consent of the husband who had deserted her and their three young children, as well as the approval of an all-male hospital panel. This degrading experience motivated her to work to ensure that other women responding to crisis pregnancies in a responsible way were not humiliated. She spearheaded NARAL's 1988 "Silent No More" campaign, which featured women telling their own stories about dealing with unintended pregnancies.

NARAL, under its new name, the National Abortion and Reproductive Rights Action League, and with nearly 300,000 members and state affiliates across the nation, now divides its efforts among three arms. NARAL, Inc., is an advocacy group that lobbies legislators. NARAL-PAC is a political action committee that works to help elect prochoice candidates for political office. The NARAL Foundation is a charitable organization that performs research on reproductive issues, mounts public education campaigns, and provides leadership training for activists, working to keep abortion legal and available and also to make it less necessary.

NATIONAL ASSOCIATION OF COLORED WOMEN

The NACW began in 1896 as a self-help organization focusing on issues related to employment, including job training, equal pay, and child care for working mothers. Its first president was **Mary Church Terrell** (see Volume 2).

Unlike white women's organizations in the early 1900s, the NACW did not separate issues of race and gender, as they believed the two were inseparable. Most members also believed that women had a special place in society rooted in the home and based on the supposed moral superiority of women. These beliefs did not, however, keep them from active public roles.

With the motto, "Lifting as we climb," the middle-class African-American women who belonged to the NACW were convinced that the lower social classes needed to adhere to middle-class standards for their people to advance. The NACW therefore founded schools and provided scholarships and loans for African-American women to attend college. Members founded settlement houses to aid in job placement and provide training for African Americans. They also worked to improve the conditions in many poor African-American neighborhoods, spoke out against segregated transportation, and advocated black pride.

The NACW continued to serve the needs of its community through the twentieth century. At present, it is the oldest African-American secular institution in existence. The women of the organization continue to work to lift the standards of home and community.

NATIONAL ASSOCIATION OPPOSED TO WOMAN SUFFRAGE

Organization founded in 1911 by Josephine Dodge, who was married to Arthur M. Dodge, to fight the women's **suffrage movement**. The National Association Opposed to Woman Suffrage (NAOWS) was organized in New York City during an antisuffrage convention. Members included women, political leaders, and Catholic clergy. The group's opposition to suffrage was ostensibly based on the belief that equal rights, including the right to vote, would diminish women's ability to affect social reform, and that suffrage should be considered a state's rights issue. The organization moved its headquarters to Washington, D.C., in 1918, and disbanded in 1920 after passage of the **Nineteenth Amendment**. NAOWS published a newsletter called *Woman's Protest,* later renamed *Woman Patriot. Woman Patriot* continued to be published through the 1920s as an antifeminist periodical.

NATIONAL COMMITTEE TO STOP ERA

Organization founded in 1972 to oppose passage of the **Equal Rights Amendment** (ERA). The National Committee to Stop ERA was founded and led by **Phyllis Schlafly**, who described the **women's liberation movement** as an assault on American women's roles as wives and mothers, as well as an assault on the family. Together with political and commercial allies on the right, including the Christian Coalition, the Moral Majority, and insurance and service industries for whom discrimination was profitable, the organization gained ground in the 1970s and 1980s by arguing not about the merits of equal rights for women, but that the ERA would result in gay rights, women in combat, and unisex toilets. The Republican Party joined the movement in 1982 (after supporting the ERA for decades) and despite much public support, the ERA was defeated that same year.

NATIONAL CONGRESS OF MOTHERS

Formed in 1897 to improve home life, child rearing, and the status of mothers in society. The National Congress of Mothers (NCM) worked toward these goals by establishing thousands of local mothers' clubs to study the latest scientific and psychological research on child development. Eventually, they saw the merit of extending "mother-work" into the public sector and formed committees at the state and national level to pass new legislation such as **mothers' pensions** and the **Maternity and Infancy Protection Act**. Their efforts to reassert the value of traditional mothering had tremendous appeal at the turn of the twentieth century. Membership reached 190,000 by 1920.

NCM founders Alice Birney and **Phoebe Apperson Hearst** attracted to the group men and women who believed in distinct and separate roles for men and women in society. As mothers, women had *natural* skills and talents best suited for the home and family. This did not diminish women's role but rather should elevate it because of the importance of a stable family to a secure society. Women's authority and power came from their child-rearing practices and their ability to shape their children's lives. The NCM leadership worked to elevate these maternal skills rather than to eliminate barriers to women's opportunities outside the home.

NATIONAL CONSUMERS LEAGUE

Founded in 1899, the National Consumers League (NCL) sought to use the power of the pocketbook to promote the sale of healthy and quality goods. At the same time it used its members' purchasing power to lobby for improved working conditions, better wages, and limited working hours. Social reformer **FLORENCE KELLEY** led the organization and helped create the "white label." Only employers who passed the NCL standards received this seal of approval. The organization continues today as a membership group offering consumer advocacy on issues of child labor, food safety, and medical information. It operates a National Fraud hotline and monitors fraud on the worldwide web through the Internet Fraud Watch.

NATIONAL COUNCIL FOR RESEARCH ON WOMEN

Founded in 1982 as a working alliance of nearly 80 centers, the focus of which is research, policy analysis, and educational programs for women and girls. University research centers are well represented on the council, as are educational coalitions and policy organizations. In addition, 1,700 organizations in 15 countries have become affiliate members.

The collaborative research fostered by the National Council for Research on Women (NCRW) has produced new information on some of the most vital issues faced by women during the late twentieth century. Among these issues are the balance of work and family, **SEXUAL HARASSMENT**, advances in higher **EDUCATION**, and providing educational and employment opportunities across all social groups. In the early years of the council's work, numerous projects focused on "mainstreaming" the new research into university courses in **WOMEN'S STUDIES**.

The NCRW distributes research and other news in a variety of formats. The publication *Women's Research Network News* provides brief overviews of center news, policy issues, and research in progress. More in-depth analysis may be found in *Issues Quarterly*.

NATIONAL COUNCIL OF AMERICAN INDIANS

Based in Washington, D.C., the National Council of American Indians (NCAI) is the oldest, largest, and most representative national organization serving the needs of both American Indian and Alaska Native governments. Founded in 1944, it revived a group by the same name established by **GERTRUDE SIMMONS BONNIN** in 1928.

The NCAI stresses the need for unity and cooperation among 250 tribal governments. It serves to secure for the original members and their descendants the rights and benefits to which they are entitled; to enlighten the public toward better understanding of the Indian people; to preserve rights under Indian treaties or agreements with the United States; and to promote the common welfare of American Indians and Alaska Natives.

NATIONAL COUNCIL OF NEGRO WOMEN

A nonprofit membership organization dedicated to improving the quality of life for African-American women, their families, and the community, founded in 1935 by educator **MARY MCLEOD BETHUNE** and headquartered in Washington, D.C. The motto of the National Council of Negro Women (NCNW) is "Commitment, Unity, Self Reliance" and it sponsors a variety of self-help projects on a national level as well as educational, social, economic, and scientific projects in communities throughout the United States. Under the leadership of **DOROTHY IRENE HEIGHT**, the NCNW focused on issues critical to African-American families.

The NCNW receives its funding from membership dues, private donations, and grants from foundations, corporations, and the federal and state governments. It consists of 38 affiliated national organizations, 250 community-based sections chartered in 42 states, 20 college-based sections, and 60,000 individual members. Some of its affiliates include the National Assembly of Voluntary Health and Social Welfare Organizations, the National Council of Women of the United States, the International Council of Women, the National Women's Business Council, the Alliance for Volunteerism, the Black Leadership Forum, and the National Committee on Concerns for Hispanics and Blacks.

NATIONAL EDUCATION ASSOCIATION

The world's largest and oldest professional organization for teachers, school administrators, and other educators. The National Education Association (NEA) was established in 1857 in Philadelphia as the National Teacher's Association (NTA). In 1870 the NTA merged with two other education organizations and became the NEA. Since then, the group has worked to increase the professionalism of teaching and protect the welfare of its members. Anyone who works for a public school district, college, or university is eligible for membership.

The purpose of the NEA is to promote public education in the United States. At the local level, affiliates organize professional workshops and negotiate contracts for school district employees. At the state level, affiliates lobby legislators for school resources and campaign for higher professional and academic standards. At the national level, the NEA conducts research, develops new projects, and fights federal attempts to privatize education.

Membership in the NEA, which exceeds 2.5 million as of the year 2001, far outweighs that of its parallel organization, the **AMERICAN FEDERATION OF TEACHERS**. The two unions, which essentially serve the same purposes, proposed an unsuccessful merger in the 1990s.

NATIONAL FEDERATION OF BUSINESS AND PROFESSIONAL WOMEN'S CLUBS

A group dedicated to improving the lives of working women through economic empowerment, pay equity, focus on women's health and family issues, and insurance reform. The National Federation of Business and Professional Women's Clubs (BPW) was founded in May 1918 when the War Department invited two representatives from each state to plan a national committee that would coordinate the efforts of the numerous women's groups organized in response to **WORLD WAR I**. Despite the end of the war six months later, the committee continued as a support for peacetime endeavors. In July 1919, the first national BPW convention was held in St. Louis, Missouri.

During the 1920s the BPW was influential in the enactment of **CHILD LABOR** laws; it assisted government relief agencies and helped create employment opportunities during the **GREAT DEPRESSION**; and in May 1937, it was the first women's organization to endorse the **EQUAL RIGHTS AMENDMENT**. During **WORLD WAR II**, it supported the establishment of women's branches of the armed services; during the 1960s it led the fight for the Equal Pay Act; and in the 1970s it worked for the passage of **TITLE IX** and the prohibition of sexual harassment.

Based in Washington, D.C., the BPW strives to improve the future of women in the workplace through community awareness, legislation, education, and personal and professional development. The BPW includes 3,000 local organizations in 53 state federations, including the District of Columbia, Puerto Rico, and the U.S. Virgin Islands.

NATIONAL ORGANIZATION FOR WOMEN

Women's rights organization. The National Organization for Women (NOW) was founded in 1966 by **BETTY FRIEDAN**, **ANNA PAULI MURRAY**, and 26 other women. Its main purpose is to battle sexual discrimination in education, the workplace, and wages, and to support such measures as child-care laws and pregnancy leave to enable women to compete with men in the workforce. In addition, for decades NOW has supported the ratification of the proposed **EQUAL RIGHTS AMENDMENT**, which would make all sexual discrimination unconstitutional.

From its earliest days, NOW has been involved in political lobbying. It has consistently supported awareness about violence against women. Its other causes include the eradication of **SEXUAL HARASSMENT** and the promotion of multiculturalism, affirmative action, and **WELFARE** rights.

NOW's first campaign began in 1967, when NOW members demanded the legalization of **ABORTION**, which was realized in the landmark Supreme Court decision ***ROE v. WADE*** in 1973. The March for Women's Lives, the largest abortion rights demonstration in U.S. history, was organized by NOW in 1992. Over 750,000 people attended the protest in Washington, D.C.

In 1971, NOW became the first general women's organization to support **LESBIAN** rights. NOW was also influential in the 1979 *Belmont v. Belmont* case, which defined lesbian partners as a family with the right to the custody of children. The plaintiff of this case, Rosemary Dempsey, was NOW's Action Vice President from 1989 to 1997.

In addition to lobbying for legal action, NOW also advocates women's rights by promoting the election of women to government offices. By lending financial support to female candidates who support its goals, NOW hopes to equalize power in government so that women's issues will receive greater attention than in the past.

At over 250,000 members nationwide, the National Organization for Women is the largest feminist organization in the United States as of the year 2001.

NATIONAL RIGHT TO LIFE COMMITTEE

Lobbying organization working to ban **ABORTION** and some forms of contraception, as well as euthanasia. The National Right to Life Committee (NRLC) began as a predominantly Catholic organization, founded in 1973 in response to the U.S. Supreme Court ruling in ***ROE v. WADE***. Together with fundamentalist and evangelical groups, it became part of "The New Right" that rose to prominence in American politics during the 1970s and 1980s. Today the NRLC is the nation's largest and most influential anti-abortion group, with more than 3,000 local chapters.

NATIONAL WOMAN'S PARTY

Women's rights organization founded in 1916 by Quaker lawyer and social reformer Alice Paul (1885–1977). The first goal of the National Woman's Party (NWP) was **SUFFRAGE** (see Volume 2) for American women—the right to vote. In pursuit of this goal, NWP members engaged in speaking tours to educate both men and women and employed a strategy of dramatic, nonviolent protest that included parading, picketing, civil disobedience, and hunger strikes. Participants faced brutal attacks, arrest, and unpleasant prison conditions. Alice Paul was jailed for obstructing traffic on Pennsylvania Avenue in front of the White House. The NWP achieved its first goal in 1919 with the ratification of the **NINETEENTH AMENDMENT**.

In 1923, the NWP under Paul's leadership launched a campaign to pass the **EQUAL RIGHTS AMENDMENT**, an effort to win full equality for women. This divided women's organizations between those supporting **PROTECTIVE LABOR LEGISLATION** and those supporting equal treatment under the law.

From the beginning, the organization has wielded considerable influence on elections—in 1928, for instance, the NWP endorsed presidential hopeful Herbert Hoover, who became known as "the women's candidate"—and has also led the fight for international women's rights, assisting suffrage campaigns in Puerto Rico and Cuba. Paul and the NWP were instrumental in ensuring the inclusion of language regarding women's equality in the United Nations Charter and were an influential force in establishing a permanent U.N. Commission on the Status of Women.

Today, the NWP continues its efforts to wipe out all forms of discrimination so that all people may achieve full legal, economic, and social equality. The group's headquarters are in the Sewall-Belmont House in Washington, D.C., purchased in 1929 when Congress demolished the Old Brick Capitol, their original headquarters, to make way for the construction of the U.S. Supreme Court. The house is named for Robert Sewall, who built it in 1799, and for Alva Vanderbilt Belmont (1853–1933), a major supporter of the NWP. When it was designated a National Historic Landmark in 1972, it was the only site in the United States dedicated to the contemporary women's movement.

NATIONAL WOMEN'S CONFERENCE

The National Women's Conference (NWC) was first held in November 1977 in Houston, Texas. Established by the federal government and chaired by former congresswoman **BELLA ABZUG** (D-NY), the conference, which was attended by approximately 20,000 women and men, assessed the legal and social status of American women, identified impediments to women's full participation in public and private life, and made recommendations to the U.S. Congress and the president.

The NWC grew largely out of action taken by the United Nations in 1972 when it declared 1975 International Women's Year and the years 1975 to 1985 the Decade for Women. The United Nations World Conference on Women, held in 1975 in Mexico City, established goals for achieving gender equity in member countries. In 1975 President Gerald Ford established the bipartisan National Commission on the Observance of International Women's Year, and in 1976 Congress passed Public Law 94-167 to extend the commission and have it organize a national women's conference. President Jimmy Carter expanded the commission in 1977, and named Abzug chair.

As a follow-up to conventions held in the states and territories, the National Women's Conference convened in Houston and presented its findings that American women suffered as a result of discriminatory practices and a lack of representation in politics, law, business, and media. The NWC adopted a national plan of action designed to eliminate violence against women and children, end discrimination against women in education and employment, establish quality child care, and move toward more equitable representation in all fields by 1985. While some goals established in 1977 have been achieved, such as moving toward more equitable representation, many have not, including eliminating gender-based violence and establishing quality child care. The NWC continues to hold annual meetings to assess progress, as well as to train activists and facilitate networking among organizations working to improve the status of women.

TRAILBLAZERS

Wilma Mankiller's great-grandfather was one of the thousands of Cherokees who walked the Trail of Tears to Oklahoma during the INDIAN REMOVAL (see Volume 2). By 1945, when Mankiller was born in Tahlequah, the Cherokee capital, the Cherokees were settled in Oklahoma, but the struggle with poverty was hard, and when she was ten Mankiller's father, Charlie Mankiller, moved his family to California. Mankiller graduated high school and went to San Francisco State College, where she met and married Hugo Olaya de Bardi; their daughters were born in 1964 and 1966.

The occupation of the prison island of Alcatraz by Richard Oakes and his "All Tribes" group in 1969–1971 awakened Mankiller's sense of Native American pride. She became involved in activism for California's Native Americans. In 1971 her father died, and the family took his body back to Oklahoma for burial. Though she returned to California, Mankiller determined to go back to her native soil to live. Her marriage had suffered from her new sense of independence and purpose, and when she finally went back to Oklahoma in 1976 it was as a single mother. Despite personal tragedies and health problems, she became active in the Cherokee community. In 1983 she ran successfully for deputy chief of the Cherokee Nation of Oklahoma on a ticket with Principal Chief Ross Swimmer. When Swimmer moved to Washington to head the Bureau of Indian Affairs, Mankiller took over as principal chief, the first woman in modern history to head a major tribe. She was reelected in 1985 and 1991, but resigned in 1995 because of her health. She has worked tirelessly to develop the economy of the Cherokee Nation and to raise awareness across the United States of Native American issues and achievement.

NATIONAL WOMEN'S POLITICAL CAUCUS

The National Women's Political Caucus (NWPC) was established in 1971 to recruit, train, and support pro-choice women seeking political office regardless of political party. The caucus agenda seeks to help end sexism, racism, poverty, and violence. It also works to provide quality dependent care and reproductive choice. The organization also advocates for women to be named to public offices and policy-making posts. It is a membership organization open to anyone who agrees with the mission and goals. Among its accomplishments, the NWPC points to the dramatic increase in women officeholders.

NATIVE AMERICANS

In the early twentieth century, the longstanding policy of assimilating Native Americans and expunging

Four generations of Native American women from the Arapaho tribe

their traditions began to change, and in fact was reversed under President Franklin D. Roosevelt with the "Indian New Deal" of the 1930s. Among the groups calling for change was the **NATIONAL FEDERATION OF WOMEN'S CLUBS** (see Volume 2). Efforts were made to restore independence and self-determination for the different tribes.

One result of the new attitude to Native American culture was a flowering of traditional crafts; rugs, basketry, and pottery, mostly made by women, brought new income and a renewed pride to Indian reservations. Among the more famous craftswomen of this revival was Maria Martinez, whose black on black pottery can be found in museums worldwide.

Native American self-awareness grew throughout the century. Evidence of this is found in the decennial census counts of the last half of the century, which show almost double the number of self-defined Native Americans from the previous decade's counts. (In 1990, the figure was 190,000.)

The 1960s saw the rise of the Red Power movement, spearheaded in many cases by women such as Cherokee Wilma Mankiller and Menomonee Ada Deer. Cheyenne Susan Harjo has been an effective lobbyist for Indian interests in Washington.

Women writers have contributed much to the new awareness of Native American identity and strength, among them the Creek poet Joy Harjo and the Chippewa novelist Louise Erdrich.

See also: Bonnin, Gertrude (Zitkala-Sha); Silko, Leslie Marmon.

NEVELSON, LOUISE

(1900–1988)

Sculptor. Born Louise Berliawsky in the Ukraine, Nevelson came to the United States in 1905 with her parents and settled in Rockland, Maine. Her father was in the lumber business, and her first art works were made of lumber scraps.

At 20, she married Charles Nevelson and moved to New York, where she studied singing and drama as well as drawing and sculpture, and gave birth to a son, Myron. The marriage failed in 1931. Nevelson took Myron to her parents in Maine, and went to Europe to continue her art studies in Munich; after six months the Nazi government closed her school. Before returning to the United States she saw in Paris an exhibition of African masks and sculpture that greatly influenced her.

From 1932 to 1933 she worked as an assistant in Diego Rivera's New York City studio and worked with him on WPA mural projects. Shortly after that she turned to sculpture. In the 1950s she became the first artist to use discarded materials to create large-scale works, using scrap wood to create large wall sculptures and painting the whole work in one color, usually black or white.

Nevelson always devoted herself full time to her art, even when it brought in barely enough money to eat. She later suggested that her flamboyant personal style and flair for clothes, combined with her gender, may have made it hard for the art world to take her seriously. But recognition began to reach her. In 1959 she participated in her first important museum exhibition at the Museum of Modern Art, and the Martha

Jackson Gallery gave her a solo show. Her first major museum retrospective took place in 1967 at the Whitney Museum of American Art. Nevelson was actively engaged in making art out of a wide range of materials until her death in 1988.

NEW DEAL

Term for the social programs created in the 1930s by President Franklin D. Roosevelt and Congress to combat the devastating effects of the **GREAT DEPRESSION**. The New Deal was a turning point in twentieth-century history because it laid the foundations of many of the social programs that continue today. Perhaps the most well known New Deal program is Social Security.

Roosevelt first used the term *new deal* while campaigning for president in 1932. After winning the election, he began his legislative program with a flurry of activity. In the first three months of office—known as the "First Hundred Days"—he pushed through Congress a vast number of bills that formed the foundation of the New Deal. Among these were laws that reformed banking, legalized the sale of alcohol, established the Tennessee Valley Authority (TVA), and created a series of public-works programs. Other laws reformed American industry to create a more productive and more humane economy and still others set up relief programs to aid the unemployed. Women directly benefited from these aspects of the New Deal.

The cornerstone of the New Deal's social insurance program was the **SOCIAL SECURITY ACT** of 1935. It provided a federal system of insurance based on contributions for those unable to work, the elderly, and the unemployed. **FRANCES PERKINS**, Roosevelt's secretary of labor and the first woman cabinet member, played a key role in the development and writing of the social security bill. Amendments passed in 1939 extended benefits to the spouse and minor children of a retired worker (dependents benefits), and survivors' benefits were paid to the family in the event of the premature death of a covered worker, thus providing more benefits for women. Other important New Deal legislation included unemployment insurance, a minimum wage, and the right of workers to join unions.

The New Deal fundamentally changed the federal government by expanding its role in society. With the passage of New Deal programs, many people came to believe that the federal government had the responsibility to take an active role in solving the nation's problems. Although the New Deal was created to end the Great Depression, it was only mildly successful. It was not until 1939 and 1940, with the onset of heavy defense spending before **WORLD WAR II**, that prosperity returned.

See also: Bethune, Mary McLeod; Children's Bureau; Perkins, Frances; Roosevelt, Eleanor.

THE NEW WOMAN

From the 1890s through the 1920s, the term *New Woman* referred to a woman who sought new roles in American society. While there was no simple definition of a New Woman, she asserted her independence and her abilities in many spheres. No longer believing that marriage and family was the ultimate goal in her life, she could be found in many places. She might be a reformer, a political activist, or a professional. While she might marry, many New Women remained single or even divorced. Some New Women were most concerned with changing society and the way it looked at gender; others were more focused on achieving personal freedom and happiness. However, all New Women recreated Americans' perceptions of the concept of womanhood. As writer Margaret Deland described her, the New Woman "occupies herself passionately, with everything, except the things that used to occupy the minds of girls."

New Women attended college in greater numbers. By the end of nineteenth century, close to 20 percent of all bachelor's degrees awarded were to women; that percentage rose to close to 35 percent by 1920. These women often applied their newfound knowledge outside of the family circle. They began to make modest entries into professional jobs, particularly teaching, **NURSING**, and **SOCIAL WORK**.

Many women used their education to further their efforts for social reform. Working as volunteers and careerists, these women formed clubs and organizations to contribute to the betterment of society. Some women sought to reform the workplace and campaigned successfully for laws that restricted child labor and improved conditions for women workers. Others focused on moral reform, particularly prohibition. Still others were most concerned with making urban areas healthier, and worked to improve housing and public health standards.

The SUFFRAGE MOVEMENT was perhaps the largest reform movement in which New Women participated. The National American Woman Suffrage Association, founded in 1890, attempted to achieve woman suffrage through laws enacted at the state level. Suffragists began fighting for a constitutional amendment in 1914, and the NINETEENTH AMENDMENT giving all women the right to vote was ratified in 1920. In the initial years following the amendment's passage, the newly enfranchised formed political groups like the LEAGUE OF WOMEN VOTERS to lobby for specific causes of particular concern to women.

Some New Women, however, were less interested in bringing about social or political changes than in enjoying and even flaunting their personal freedom. New Women did so by exchanging restrictive Victorian garments for looser-fitting, more androgynous clothing. New Women also challenged traditional ideas of proper behavior. They smoked in public, drank alcoholic beverages, wore makeup, and bobbed their hair. They became more active in ATHLETICS. Many sought sexual freedom. The New Woman who embraced these lifestyle changes culminated in the image of flapper of the 1920s.

NINETEENTH AMENDMENT

Added to the Constitution in 1920, this amendment guarantees women's right to vote. Although some localities allowed women to vote in school board elections as early as the 1830s, full voting rights came much later. The SENECA FALLS CONVENTION of 1848 (see Volume 2) included woman SUFFRAGE (see Volume 2) on the list of rights women sought. During the debates over the Fourteenth and Fifteenth amendments in the 1860s—designed to prevent states from abridging the rights of former slaves—suffragists tried unsuccessfully to include women. In 1869 Wyoming became the first territory to grant women equal voting rights with men, which were extended upon statehood in 1890.

Male and female champions of voting rights for women worked tirelessly and used a variety of strategies. Since the eligibility of voters was determined by each state, some advocated a state-by-state approach, which achieved some success as nine Western states adopted woman suffrage legislation by 1912. Others, such as SUSAN B. ANTHONY (see Volume 2), challenged male-only voting laws in the courts. More militant suffragists used tactics such as parades, silent vigils, and hunger strikes. Often supporters met fierce resistance. Opponents heckled, jailed, and sometimes physically attacked them.

Male and female champions of voting rights for women worked tirelessly and used a variety of strategies.

> ***Section 1. The right of citizens of the United States to vote shall not be denied or abridged by the United States or by any State on account of sex.***
>
> **—Nineteenth Amendment to the U.S. Constitution (1920)**

By 1916 most suffrage organizations united behind the goal of a constitutional amendment. After New York adopted woman suffrage in 1917, and President Woodrow Wilson changed his position to support an amendment in 1918, the political balance tipped. On May 21, 1919, the House of Representatives passed the amendment, and two weeks later the Senate followed. When Tennessee became the thirty-sixth state to ratify the amendment on August 18, 1920, it pushed the amendment over its final hurdle of obtaining ratification by three-fourths of the states. Secretary of State Bainbridge Colby certified the ratification on August 26, 1920. Women nationwide voted for the first time in the election of 1920.

FURTHER READING

Dubois, Ellen Carol. *Feminism and Suffrage: The Emergence of an Independent Women's Movement in America, 1848–1869.* Ithaca: Cornell University Press, 1999.

NINETY-NINES

Founded in 1929, an organization of women aviators started for mutual support and advancement in the field of aviation.

In 1929 only 117 women held pilot licenses in the United States. Twenty-six of those pilots met in November of that year to discuss the needs of women pilots. After recruiting additional members, the group adopted the name Ninety-Nines in recognition of the original number of its members. One of the cofounders, **AMELIA EARHART**, served as the group's first president. Other members included Louise Thaden, who, in 1936, received the Harmon Trophy recognizing her as the world's outstanding flier. Another notable member, Jacqueline Cochran, supervised hundreds of women pilots during **WORLD WAR II** as part of the Air Transport Auxiliary, Women's Division and the **WOMEN'S AIRFORCE SERVICE PILOTS (WASPs)**. A third member, Ruth Cheney Streeter, became the director of the Women's Marine Corps.

Today, the Ninety-Nines continues to support women in aviation with scholarships and programs. Approximately 6,500 international members support the group.

NIXON, PATRICIA RYAN (1912–1993)

First lady of the United States (1969–1974) and wife of Richard Nixon, the nation's thirty-seventh president. Thelma Catherine Ryan was born in Ely, Nevada, on March 16, 1912, the day before St. Patrick's Day. When her father came home from his job as a miner early the next morning and heard that he had a new daughter, he said, "St. Patrick's babe in the morn." She was thereafter called Pat.

The Ryans moved to California. When Pat Ryan was 13, her mother died and she thereafter ran the family household for her father and her two older brothers. She lost her father five years later. She put herself through the University of Southern California, graduating in 1937, and became a teacher in Whittier, California. She met Richard Nixon when they performed together in an amateur theater. The couple married on June 21, 1940, and had two children.

Mrs. Nixon campaigned with her husband, helping him win election to Congress in 1946 and to the U. S. Senate four years later. In 1952, Nixon was elected vice president of the United States and served for eight years. Although defeated for president in 1960, Nixon ran again and won his race for the presidency in 1968. As first lady, Mrs. Nixon lent her strong support to volunteering, which she called "the spirit of people helping people." She also invited a wide range of artists, from pop to classical, to perform at the White House. She accompanied her husband to China and traveled to Africa.

Mrs. Nixon left the White House in 1974 after her husband resigned from the presidency during the Watergate crisis. She suffered strokes in 1976 and 1983, and died on June 22, 1993, in Park Ridge, New Jersey.

NORTON, ELEANOR HOLMES (b. 1938)

A nonvoting delegate since 1991 to the U.S. House of Representatives from the District of Columbia. Norton helped achieve the first (ultimately failed) congressional vote on statehood for the District in 1993 and a restructuring of the financial relationship between Congress and the District.

> ***"As commissioner, I will attempt to see that no man is judged by the irrational criteria of race, religion, or national origin. And I assure you that I use the word 'man' in the generic sense, for I mean to see that the principle of nondiscrimination becomes a reality for women as well."***
>
> **—Eleanor Holmes Norton, on becoming head of New York City's Commission on Human Rights, 1970**

After graduating from Antioch College in Ohio in 1960, Norton attended Yale Law School, from which she earned her law degree in 1964. Norton holds a tenured law professorship at Georgetown University. She has fought for her constituents in the District of Columbia, which is not accorded all the rights and privileges of the 50 states. People living in the District pay federal taxes without having full representation in the Senate and the House. In 1993, Norton achieved the first right to vote on the House floor for the District representative, but the vote was rescinded in 1995 when the Republicans gained control of Congress. Also a civil rights advocate, Norton was appointed by President Jimmy Carter as chair of the Equal Employment Opportunity Commission.

NOVELLO, ANTONIA (b. 1944)

The first woman and the first Latina to hold the position of surgeon general of the U.S. Public Health Service. Appointed U.S. surgeon general in 1990 by President George Bush, Dr. Novello held that position until June 1993.

Born in Fajardo, Puerto Rico, Novello graduated from the University of Puerto Rico with a B.S. degree in 1965 and an M.D. degree in 1970. She held her internship and residency at the University of Michigan, Ann Arbor. She also received a M.P.H in public health from The Johns Hopkins University in 1982. In addition to a private pediatric practice, Novello worked as a project officer at the National Institutes of Health and as Coordinator for AIDS research in the National Institute of Child Health and Human Development. In 1984, she contributed to the draft of the Organ Transplantation Procurement Act.

Her tenure as surgeon general drew attention to the health issues of women, children, and minorities, but her most important legacy may be in her campaign against underage smoking. She challenged the tobacco industry's use of cartoon images, Joe Camel for example, to attract children; a campaign that ended with the removal of such images. In 1999, she was appointed as the New York State Health Commissioner.

NURSING

The nurses of the early twentieth century were an impressive group, fervently committed to bettering society through education and caring. They included such women as Lillian Wald, the founder of New York's Henry Street Settlement; **MARGARET SANGER**, who, like the other public health nurses of the period, climbed tenement stairs to bring not only care but also education and hope to the desperately poor; and the radical suffragist Lavinia Dock. In 1901 Dock wrote in an editorial in *American Journal of Nursing*, "Nothing . . . is more trying to one's toleration than to see men—most of whom never did and never can comprehend what a woman's work really is, what its details are, or how it ought to be done—undertaking to instruct and train women in something so unquestionably her own special field as nursing. . . . Medicine and nursing are not the same; and how-ever [sic] much we may learn from the physician about disease and its treatment, the whole field of nursing—as nursing is realized by the *patient* (the centre of the question)—is unknown to him." Dock's words encapsulate the tension that existed throughout the twentieth century between the sense of nursing as essentially women's work and the sense of its being at least as important as medicine to the patient's well-being. Dock believed nurses deserved professional recognition and pay.

The gender divide between doctors and nurses became less rigid in the course of the century. Early in the century a woman who was interested in health care was likely to be barred from entering medical school—most medical schools would not allow more than 5 percent of their classes to be women—so she might fall back on nursing. At the end of the twentieth century little stood in the way of a woman who wanted to become a doctor, but the battle for recogni-

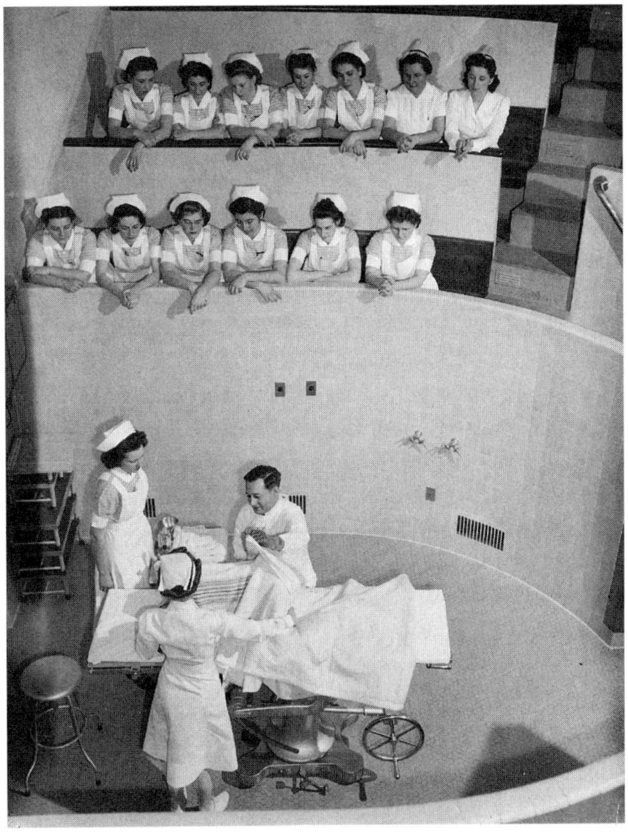

Nursing was among the first professional opportunities available to women in America.

tion of the unique value of a nurse's work was far from over.

Nursing changed a great deal in the course of the century as health care moved more into hospitals and as technology became more important. In 1903 a nurse might spend hours coaxing a dehydrated patient to take liquid from a spoon. In 1953 she would be more likely to open a vein, attach an intravenous drip, and move on to the next patient. The patient of 1953 might be more effectively rehydrated, but the human connection between nurse and patient was in danger. The 1950s were a time when great efforts were made to streamline nursing; the most highly trained nurses were appointed "team leaders," often responsible for managing the care of 50 patients, and it was the student nurses and aides who did the intimate bed care that patients experienced as "nursing." Nurses tended more and more to be seen as merely executing a doctor's orders. A backlash against this was the "primary nursing" movement of the 1960s, articulated by Lydia Hall at Montefiore Hospital in New York, which aimed to set up the nurse as the primary factor in patient care, who coordinates the efforts of the patient and family to solve problems that might hinder recovery, and who brings in the help of doctors as needed.

Ironically, the successes of twentieth-century medicine gave rise to a greater need for traditional nursing care. Fewer patients died of acute infections, and advances in pharmaceuticals and surgery allowed more to survive with potentially fatal conditions. AIDS is the most dramatic example. The rise in the numbers of patients with chronic illness has reemphasized the importance of "caring" as opposed to "curing"—and most people associate curing with doctors, caring with nurses.

As the twentieth century drew to a close, women had many other career choices open to them, and men had yet to turn to nursing in significant numbers—in 1999, less than 6 percent of nurses were men, and the average age of a registered nurse was 48. Some experts predicted that by 2020 there would be a significant shortage of nurses. Perhaps the law of supply and demand will gain nurses greater recognition and compensation for their work.

See also: Military Service.

FURTHER READING

Donahue, M. Patricia. *Nursing: The Finest Art.* 2nd ed. St. Louis: Mosby, 1996.

Sandelowski, Margaret. *Devices and Desires: Gender, Technology, and American Nursing.* Chapel Hill: University of North Carolina Press, 2000.

Schorr, Thelma M. *100 Years of American Nursing: Celebrating a Century of Caring.* Philadelphia: Lippincott, 1999.

O

O'CONNOR, SANDRA DAY

(b. 1938)

First woman to serve as a justice on the U.S. Supreme Court. Sandra Day was born on March 26, 1930, in El Paso, Texas, and grew up on her family's cattle ranch in Arizona. She attended Stanford University, where she earned a bachelor's degree in 1950 and a law degree two years later. In 1952 she married John Jay O'Connor, III, and eventually gave birth to three sons. After graduating from law school she could not find a job in private practice because few law firms at the time were willing to hire women, so she turned to government service, eventually becoming assistant attorney general for Arizona in 1965. During those years she was active in civic affairs and Republican Party politics, and in 1969 the Arizona governor appointed her to a vacant seat in the state senate. She won election in her own right in 1970, and after her reelection in 1972, became the first woman in U.S. history to serve as a majority leader in a state senate.

In 1974 O'Connor was elected a county superior court judge. Five years later she was appointed to the Arizona Court of Appeals. While on the court, she remained active in the Republican Party and was an early supporter of Ronald Reagan for president. When Supreme Court Justice Potter Stewart retired, President Reagan nominated her for the vacant seat, and in 1981 the U.S. Senate overwhelmingly confirmed her. During her early years on the Court, her voting record was consistently conservative, but in later years she became more centrist and was regarded as a crucial "swing vote" in closely decided cases, sometimes voting conservatively, sometimes joining a more liberal majority. She showed her moderation in a pivotal 1989 case when she wrote a controversial majority ruling that the guaranteed channeling of city funds to minority-owned public works contractors is discriminatory and unconstitutional.

OLD AGE AND MORTALITY

Because women live an average of seven years longer than men, the majority of the elderly are women. Thus the problems and challenges of aging are, in large measure, women's issues. For a variety of reasons, aging women have been and are still regarded more negatively than aging men. While an older man with graying temples—especially if he is powerful or wealthy—is still considered sexually attractive, for example, an older woman is generally regarded as almost "gender neutral"—unless, like some models and movie stars, she has managed to preserve the *appearance* of youth with plastic surgery. Old women also tend to be more impoverished than older men. Because of cultural attitudes that kept most women in the home or in low-paying jobs throughout the first 70 years of the twentieth century, many older women today do not have pensions and are entitled to less Social Security than men who earned more throughout their lives. Since women live longer, they must make what pensions they do have "stretch" over a longer period of time.

In seventeenth-century America, many historians assert, the old were revered for their wisdom. But during the eighteenth century, respect for the elderly eroded. Historians are still debating about when the transformation occurred and what caused it, but it is clear that the economic power of the elderly was substantially reduced when retirement became the norm in the world of work. While an old farmer might continue to work for many years, factory workers were often retired at a specified age—sometimes with no pension. Also, America was a place of rapid change, and Americans came to value change over stability. Especially in a world driven by technology, the knowledge of the old became simply outdated, the ideal of wisdom replaced by the ideal of being modern. Americans value energy, vitality, and physical prowess, all characteristics that seemed to decline with age.

The **SOCIAL SECURITY ACT** of 1935 was designed to help older Americans economically, but it also had a negative impact, in that it helped to create a perception of the elderly as dependent and unable to care for themselves. In fact, the Social Security Act, according to Brian Gratton, actually served to encourage retirement, something the elderly in earlier periods may not have considered.

The study of aging evolved in the twentieth century. Scientists have redefined what is and is not "normal" in the aging process. Senility, once seen as an inevitable part of the aging process, is now regarded as the exception, rather than the rule. In the last decade of the twentieth century, medical studies focused on wellness issues, and researchers discovered that resistance training, for example, can strengthen muscles at any age and allow individuals to be more mobile and active as they age. Hormone replacement therapies and medication for osteoporosis have mitigated age-related medical problems for some women.

FURTHER READING

Cole, Thomas R. *The Journey of Life: A Cultural History of Aging in America.* New York: Cambridge University Press, 1992.

Doress-Worters, Paula B., and Diana Laskin Siegal. *The New Ourselves, Growing Older.* New York: Simon & Schuster, 1994.

Haber, Carole, and Brian Gratton. *Old Age and the Search for Security: An American Social History.* Bloomington: Indiana University Press, 1994.

ONASSIS, JACQUELINE KENNEDY (1929–1994)

First lady of the United States from 1961 to 1963 and wife of the nation's thirty-fifth president, John F. Kennedy. Onassis was born in Southampton, New York, and raised in wealthy, cultured surroundings. She attended Vassar College and graduated from George Washington University in 1951. While working for the Washington *Times-Herald* in 1952, Onassis interviewed Senator John F. Kennedy of Massachusetts. They married a year later, and Kennedy ran for president in 1960. Perhaps because Kennedy was the youngest person ever elected president, he, his wife, and their two small children—Caroline and John Jr. (another child died two days after birth)—brought to the office the idealism of youth.

As first lady, Onassis devoted much time to making the White House a showplace and gave the first televised tour of the house in 1962. She turned traditional state dinners into elegant but more casual affairs, with guests that included artists, writers, and musicians. The way she dressed, especially the pillbox hats she wore, became fashionable. Most important of all, Onassis was relaxed conversing with people from a variety of backgrounds and cultures, and her charm was instrumental in contributing to the popularity of her husband's presidency.

Onassis was beside her husband in an automobile when he was assassinated on November 22, 1963. In 1968 she married Aristotle Onassis, a Greek shipping magnate 23 years older than she. He died in 1975, and Onassis moved to New York. Working as an editor at Doubleday, she fought hard to keep a low profile, but the public was always intrigued by her style and inner strength. She died May 19, 1994, and is buried in Arlington National Cemetery, next to John Kennedy.

O'REILLY, LEONORA

(1870–1927)

Born in New York City, labor organizer Leonora O'Reilly began working in a collar factory when she was 11 years old. At 16 she joined the Knights of Labor and later she organized a female chapter of the United Garment Workers of America. Through the aid of wealthy reformers, she attended Brooklyn's Pratt Institute. Her training led to a teaching position at the Manhattan Trade School for Girls, where she taught from 1902 to 1909. She became vice president of the New York chapter of the National Women's Trade Union League in 1909. She was involved in the shirtwaist workers' strike in 1909 in which nearly 30,000 sweatshop workers walked out to protest labor conditions. She helped lead an investigation into the **TRIANGLE SHIRTWAIST FACTORY FIRE** that killed 146 workers.

In later years, she was involved in the suffrage movement as president of the Wage Earners' League. She helped to publicize International Women's Day to recognize the contributions of women. She was also a founder of the National Association for the Advancement of Colored People and a member of the Socialist Party of America.

OUR BODIES, OURSELVES

A groundbreaking book about women's health published by the Boston Women's Health Book Collective in 1970. (See Documents.)

The idea for *Our Bodies, Ourselves* grew from a 1969 **WOMEN'S LIBERATION** conference. At a workshop about women's bodies, a number of women shared their frustrations with the largely male-dominated medical profession. After a series of meetings, this group published the first version of the book as a course booklet titled *Women and Their Bodies.*

The renamed first edition of *Our Bodies, Ourselves* was published in 1973 and sold 250,000 copies in its first three years of publication. It focused on reproductive health and sexuality, and also provided feminist critiques of women's oppression. The authors urged women to take control of their bodies and their health. They also candidly addressed lesbianism, masturbation, abortion, and other issues of sex and sexuality that were then considered taboo.

For many women, *Our Bodies, Ourselves* remains a valuable resource. The Boston Women's Health Book Collective has continued to publish updated versions, the most recent edition titled *Our Bodies, Ourselves for the New Century: A Book By and For Women.*

P

PACIFISM

The belief that disputes between nations should be settled peacefully. Perhaps because of their roles as mothers, women have long been leaders in movements to limit war and promote peaceful settlements to conflicts. In the twentieth century, American women founded a number of organizations that promoted the cause of peace at home and abroad.

Shortly after the outbreak of **World War I** in 1914, more than 3,000 women met in Washington, D.C., to form the first independent women's peace group, the Woman's Peace Party (WPP). **Jane Addams** (see volume 2) was elected the group's first chair, and she was joined in her efforts by such prominent women as Jeanette Rankin, **Carrie Chapman Catt** (see Volume 2) and Sophonisba Breckinridge. In alliance with the International Congress of Women, the Woman's Peace Party called for mediation to end the war and opposed the United States' entry into the conflict. Former President Theodore Roosevelt attacked the WPP in the press, labeling members "hysterical pacifists." Once the United States actually entered the war in 1917, many of the 40,000 WPP members dropped their opposition and instead worked to help victims of the war and conscientious objectors.

After World War I, women established four organizations promoting peace: the Women's International League for Peace and Freedom, the Women's Peace Society, the Women's Peace Union, and the National Committee on the Cause and Cure of War (NCCCW). The NCCCW successfully supported ratification of the 1928 Kellogg-Briand Pact, an international treaty that condemned "recourse to war for the solution of international controversies," but the agreement never had any real impact on world peace. In the years between World War I and **World War II**, some of the women who led peace organizations were denounced as communists and spied on by the newly created Federal Bureau of Investigation (FBI). There were, for example, extensive FBI files on both Jane Addams and Carrie Chapman Catt.

After World War II, Women Strike for Peace (WSP) was founded in opposition to nuclear testing. This organization was responsible for a one-day strike that occurred on November 1, 1961, when approximately 50,000 women protested radioactive contamination of milk and other hazards associated with nuclear testing. When investigated by the House Un-American Activities Committee, WSP members brought babies in cribs and nursed their infants during the hearings. This group was also instrumental in persuading President John F. Kennedy to sign the Nuclear Test Ban Treaty in 1963. During the **Vietnam War**, WSP worked with draft resisters, counseling more than 100,000 men on their rights. A small organization called Another Mother for Peace also lobbied against the war, coining the famous slogan "War Is Not Healthy for Children and Other Living Things."

In 1980, a group called Women's Pentagon Action marched on the Pentagon with huge life-sized puppets and posters shaped like gravestones to demand "no more amazing inventions for death." Many women were arrested when they attempted to block entrances to the building by weaving brightly colored strands of yarn across the doorways. This group and others that followed have been labeled "ecofeminists," because their concerns include not only issues of war and peace but also of the environment. Many

WOMEN'S FIRSTS

A legislator, lifelong pacifist, and advocate of women's rights, Jeannette Rankin (1880–1973) stood alone on political and social issues throughout her six decades in public life. In 1916, when few states allowed women to vote, she ran as a Republican for Montana's at-large seat in Congress and won—becoming the first female member of the U.S. House of Representatives. She served only one term but won reelection 25 years later, representing Montana again from 1941 to 1943 before losing a bid for a U.S. Senate seat.

Born in Missoula, Montana, on June 11, 1880, Rankin graduated from the University of Montana and spent the next several years doing social work and participating in the woman SUFFRAGE movement. As a member of Congress, she sponsored legislation to provide federal voting rights and health services to women. Ever committed to the cause of peace, she voted against U.S. entry into WORLD WAR I. During her second term, she was the only member of the House of Representative to vote against the declaration of war on Japan at the start of WORLD WAR II.

Rankin devoted the rest of her life to the causes of peace, feminism, and disarmament. Her extensive travels abroad included the study of nonviolence with Mohandas Gandhi in India. At age 86 she headed the Jeannette Rankin Brigade in the 1965 March on Washington to protest U.S. involvement in the VIETNAM WAR. Rankin died on May 18, 1973, in Carmel, California.

ecofeminists maintain that there are parallels between male domination of women, imperialism, and male domination of the environment. From the mid-1980s forward, women's groups have called for more women to be involved at the highest levels in decisions about war, peace, economic development, and the environment. In 1995, at the Fourth World Congress on Women, the Women's Environment and Development Organization (WEDO), led by former congresswoman **Bella Abzug**, called for 50-50 participation of men and women in all governmental bodies.

FURTHER READING

Alonso, Harriet Hyman. *Peace as a Women's Issue: A History of the U.S. Movement for World Peace and Women's Rights* (Syracuse Studies on Peace and Conflict Resolution). Syracuse, NY: Syracuse University Press, 1993.

PARKER, DOROTHY

(1893–1967)

Writer and humorist. Dorothy Rothschild was born on August 22, 1893, in West End, New Jersey. After attending private schools, Dorothy took a job as a piano player to accompany students who were enrolled in a dance school. At the same time she was writing poetry, and in 1915 her poem "Any Porch" was published by *Vanity Fair* magazine. A year later she was hired by the magazine as one of their writers.

In 1917, Dorothy married Edwin Pond Parker, but the couple divorced 11 years later. Meanwhile, she had become the first female drama critic in New York, and in 1919 she helped found the famous Algonquin Round Table at the Algonquin Hotel. There she joined other writers, such as Robert Benchley and James Thurber, in literary discussions.

During the 1920s, Parker cowrote her first play *Business Is Business* and published poetry and short stories. She was awarded the O.Henry award for her story "The Big Blonde" in 1929. During the 1930s, Parker wrote screenplays for Hollywood movies and won an Academy Award in 1937 for coauthoring *A Star Is Born*. She married Alan Campbell in 1933.

Above all, Parker was known for her sharp wit. "Wit has truth in it," she once wrote, "wisecracking is simply calisthenics with words."

Parker continued publishing plays, stories, and poems during the 1940s and 1950s. She was also a book reviewer for *Esquire* magazine. She died on June 7, 1967.

PARKS, ROSA McCAULEY

(b. 1913)

Civil rights activist. When she was born in Tuskegee, Alabama, on February 4, 1913, Rosa Louise McCauley's parents had no idea that their daughter would one day be credited with beginning a major civil rights movement. Growing up in the South, Rosa witnessed frequent Ku Klux Klan activity in her own neighborhood. It was a childhood of constant fear that prepared her for adult fearlessness.

Rosa McCauley attended the Montgomery Industrial School for Girls; she cleaned classrooms to pay tuition. After graduating from Alabama State College (now University), she married Raymond Parks, a barber and activist, in 1932. Like her husband, Rosa was active in various black rights organizations. In 1943, she became the secretary of the Montgomery branch of the National Association for the Advancement of Colored People (NAACP).

But it was a bus ride on December 1, 1955, that made Rosa Parks the "Mother of the Civil Rights Movement." At that time, the buses in Montgomery had segregated seating. The first ten seats on the bus were reserved for white riders, whether or not there were whites on the bus. Blacks who sat there—knowingly or not—were threatened by white bus drivers. On that particular morning, Parks and three other blacks were seated in the first seat behind the white section. A white rider entered the bus, but there were no more white seats. Parks and the other blacks were told to move so the white rider could sit down. Recognizing the driver as one who had evicted her from a bus a year earlier, Parks refused to move. The driver called the police, and Parks was arrested, fingerprinted, booked, jailed, and fined $14.00. Her bail was posted by her husband, and she was released the same day.

This incident prompted the Montgomery bus boycott, which lasted until December 21, 1956. Because 70 percent of the ridership was black, and so many African Americans refused to ride the buses, the bus company lost revenue and went bankrupt. In addition, bus segregation was banned, and the Montgomery Improvement Association was founded with Martin Luther King, Jr., as its first president.

Her refusal to give up a bus seat made Rosa Parks a pioneer of civil rights in America.

Following the bus incident, Parks moved to Detroit, Michigan, in 1957 to work with Martin Luther King's Southern Christian Leadership Conference. In 1965 she became administrative assistant to Congressman John Conyers, Jr. Additionally, Parks founded the Institute for Leadership and Career Training for young blacks in 1987.

She continues to live in Detroit and lectures approximately 25 times per year.

FURTHER READING

Parks, Rosa. *Rosa Parks: My Story.* New York: Dial Books, 1992.

Siegel, Beatrice. *The Year They Walked: Rosa Parks and the Montgomery Bus Boycott.* New York: Maxwell Macmillan International, 1992.

PARSONS, ELSIE CLEWS

(1875–1940)

Sociologist and anthropologist. Elsie Clews was born on November 27, 1875, in New York City. Her father was a successful banker, and her mother was a descendant of President James Madison. Elsie Clews became one of the early women graduates from Barnard College in New York City in 1896, then attended Columbia University, where she received a Ph.D. three years later in sociology.

Over the next six years, Clews taught at Barnard. In 1900, she married Herbert Parsons. Even after the couple had their first child, Parsons wrote and published books on sociology. Each of them examines the impact of society on the behavior of individuals. She published *The Family* in 1906, *The Old Fashioned Woman* in 1913, and *Social Freedom* in 1915. In her books she proposed that women should be the social and political equal of men. She also wrote about the controversial idea of trial marriage for couples.

Parsons also conducted anthropological studies of various American cultures. Among her major interests were the Pueblo Indians. In 1939 she published *Pueblo Indian Religion.* In addition she studied Mexican village culture and African-American folklore, and conducted fieldwork in the Caribbean. Beginning in 1933, she published a three-volume work, *Folk-Lore of the Antilles.* Parsons died in December 1940 in New York City.

PERKINS, FRANCES

(1882–1965)

American reformer, and the first woman to hold a Cabinet-level post in the U.S. government. Perkins grew up in a middle-class family in Worcester, Massachusetts, and got her A.B. from **Mount Holyoke College** (see Volume 2) in 1902. For a few years she taught at various girls' schools in Massachusetts and then Illinois; she volunteered at a settlement house in Worcester, and then at Chicago's **Hull House** (see Volume 2). In 1909 she went to New York to study political science at Columbia University, completing her master's degree in 1910. While working for the New York Consumers League and living in Greenwich Village she witnessed the **Triangle Shirtwaist Factory fire**, which painfully confirmed her commitment to fighting the conditions that allowed such a tragedy to happen.

1913 she married Paul Caldwell Wilson, a progressive economist who agreed that Perkins should continue to use her own name. Their home became a gathering place for reformers. Of their two daughters, only one survived infancy. In 1918 Wilson suffered a nervous breakdown, and for the rest of his life Perkins was the family's main breadwinner. Shortly afterward Alfred E. Smith, the newly elected governor, invited Perkins to become a member of the New York State Industrial Commission. She was a key member of Smith's team throught his three-term administration. When Smith was succeeded as governor by Franklin D. Roosevelt, in 1929,

Frances Perkins was the first woman appointed to a cabinet position.

Perkins was appointed to head the Industrial Commission, the first woman to serve in any governor's cabinet, and she had the task of leading the state's response to the onset of the **GREAT DEPRESSION**. Upon Roosevelt's election to the presidency, he asked Perkins to serve as his labor secretary. Despite the objections of labor, who wanted a male union activist, and of businesspeople, who thought she was too pro-labor, she took the job (stipulating only that she must be free to spend weekends with her family), and held it for 12 years—longer than any other U.S. cabinet member. She developed many of Roosevelt's **NEW DEAL** programs to help workers through the Depression. The **SOCIAL SECURITY ACT** of 1935 was her most important achievement. She also rooted out corruption the the Labor Department and revitalized offices such as the **WOMEN'S BUREAU** and the **CHILDREN'S BUREAU**.

Her record and her insistence on communicating directly with workers about their rights eventually won labor leaders over, as they confirmed the enmity of the right-wing business community. In 1939 the House Un-American Activities Committee brought an impreachment proceeding against her. It failed for lack of evidence, and she served six more years. In 1945 she led the U.S. delegation to the International Labor Conference in Geneva. In her last years she taught at Cornell University's School of Industrial and Labor Relations. She died at 85.

PETERSON, ESTHER EGGERTSEN (1906–1997)

Teacher, union organizer, consumer advocate. Esther Eggertsen was born on December 9, 1906, in Provo, Utah. She graduated from Brigham Young University in 1927 then moved to New York City where she received a master's degree from Columbia Teachers College. In 1932, she married Oliver A. Peterson, who was a member of the Socialist Party in the United States.

Esther Peterson taught school in Boston from 1932 to 1937 then became a union organizer for the American Federation of Teachers. In 1938, she took a similar position in New York with the Amalgamated Clothing Workers of America (ACWA). During the 1940s, she served as a union lobbyist, urging Congress to increase the minimum wage. During the 1950s, she continued her lobbying activities with the **AMERICAN FEDERATION OF LABOR AND CONGRESS OF INDUSTRIAL ORGANIZATIONS (AFL-CIO)**, arguing for the rights of workers.

President John F. Kennedy named Peterson assistant secretary of labor and director of the **WOMEN'S BUREAU** in 1961. She led efforts to secure equal pay for equal work for women. During the 1960s and 1970s, she served as special assistant for consumer affairs in the administrations of Lyndon Johnson and Jimmy Carter. As a consumer advocate, Peterson helped achieve such improvements as truthful advertising for food products and nutritional labeling on food packages.

In 1981, Peterson was awarded the Presidential Medal of Freedom. She died on December 20, 1997.

PHOTOGRAPHERS

Since the invention of photography in 1839, women have played leading roles in the advancement of the art.

Gertrude Käsebier (1852–1934) and Anne W. Brigman (1868–1950) made impressionistic images including interiors, landscapes, and portraits. Called "Pictorialists," they were part of the avant-garde art circles in New York City during the first years of the twentieth century.

Imogen Cunningham (1883–1976) first worked in the Pictorialist style as well. In 1930 however, as a founding member of the f/64 group in San Francisco, she was among the first to promote a new approach to photography. Her sharply detailed, close-up images of flowers bring together a range of tones from the brightest whites to the most velvety blacks. She received many awards during the course of her long career.

From the 1930s onward, Dorothea Lange (1895–1965) and Margaret Bourke-White (1906–1971) were pioneers of documentary photography and **JOURNALISM**. Lange's image of a tired woman surrounded by her small children, the *Migrant Mother, Nipomo, California* (1936), has become an icon of the hardships of the **GREAT DEPRESSION**. Berenice Abbott (1898–1991) belonged to the circle of surrealist artists working in Paris in the 1920s. She returned to the United States in 1929 and began to produce the photographs that both documented and celebrated the rapidly changing appearance of New York City. Diane Arbus (1923–1971) concentrated on the social "misfits," photographing the many unusual people she encountered. Contemporary documentary photographers such as Mary Ellen Mark (b. 1940) continue to be inspired by their examples.

Women have also made great contributions to contemporary art and advertising. Olivia Parker (b. 1941) works in both black-and-white and color, creating dreamlike still lifes of ordinary objects. Cindy Sherman (b. 1954) produces enormous Polaroid photographs of herself disguised as famous actresses, stereotypical American women, and even homeless or abused women. Carrie Mae Weems (b. 1953) brings art and journalism together, saying, "my primary concern in art, as in politics, is with the status and place of Afro-Americans in our country." Annie Liebowitz (b. 1949) is best known for the portraits of celebrities she made for magazines like *Rolling Stone* and *Vanity Fair.*

TRAILBLAZERS

Prior to the 1930s and before the work of photographer and social activist Margaret Bourke-White (1904–1971), the journalistic "photo-essay," a group of photographs accompanied by short texts, did not exist. A photo-essay combines words with pictures, placing the news into context and providing readers with more personal access to events in the world around them.

Born in 1904, Bourke-White studied biology and technology before attending the Clarence White School of Photography at Columbia University in New York City in the 1920s. She worked first as a freelance photographer of architecture and industrial structures, later joining the staff of publisher Henry Luce.

On November 23, 1936, the first issue of *Life* magazine hit the stands. On its cover was a dramatic image of the Fort Peck Dam in Montana. The "first" was but one of many that Bourke-White would go on to claim. She was the first woman photographer hired by *Fortune* magazine (in 1929) and was one of the first four staff photographers hired by *Life.* She was the first American photographer permitted to take pictures in the Soviet Union, in 1930, the first female war correspondent in World War II, and the first to be allowed to work in combat. Bourke-White was there to record the horrors when American soldiers liberated the prisoners at the Buchenwald concentration camp in Germany on April 11, 1945.

Margaret Bourke-White died on August 27, 1971, after a 19-year battle with Parkinson's disease. She published a number of books of her photographs, including six about her international travels. Her photographs are in the permanent collections of numerous museums and archives.

Margaret Bourke-White, photographer and social activist, was one of the first to create a photo-essay.

PLANNED PARENTHOOD

An organization founded as the Birth Control League in 1921 to provide women with information about their sexual health and reproductive choices.

Although women have shared information with each other on ways to prevent pregnancy for centuries, the organized and scientifically-informed dissemination of birth control information took an enormous step forward in 1916 when **MARGARET SANGER** opened a clinic in Brooklyn, New York, to provide the poor and largely immigrant women of the neighborhood with information about preventing an unwanted **PREGNANCY**. Providing such information was considered obscene at the time and against the law. The clinic was closed and Sanger spent a month in jail for the "crime." Twenty years later, a United States Circuit Court of Appeals removed the classification of birth control information as obscene. Thirty years after that (1966) the Supreme Court case ***GRISWOLD v. CONNECTICUT*** (1965) found in favor of married couples who wanted to obtain contraceptives from their doctor.

Sanger had never stopped her work to support research and education on birth control. Many joined her in the work. The Birth Control League, which became the Planned Parenthood Federation of America in 1942, funded research that led to the development of the birth control pill in 1960 and supported clinics around the country.

Planned Parenthood has been at the center of political controversy because of its pro-choice position on **ABORTION**. During the 1980s and 1990s, the Right to Life movement held vigils outside Planned Parenthood offices in an attempt to discourage women from getting abortion information. The more radical anti-abortionists attacked clinics and doctors and in a few cases murdered clinic workers and doctors. In 2001, President George W. Bush restricted the funding for international Planned Parenthood because it provided women with information about abortions.

The world's largest and oldest family planning organization, Planned Parenthood today serves more than 5 million women and men in the United States and developing countries. It operates 875 affiliate health centers in 49 states and the District of Columbia.

See also: Reproductive Rights.

TRAILBLAZERS

Influenced by Sylvia Plath, her friend, and Robert Lowell, with whom she studied, the poet Anne Sexton (1928–1974) is often regarded as a member of the "confessional school" for her intimate, unsentimental portrayals of personal anguish in verse form. Her first book, *To Bedlam and Part Way Back* (1960), is a harrowing account of her depression, mental breakdown, and partial recovery. *All My Pretty Ones* (1962) pursues the themes of personal anguish and collapse. *Live or Die* (1966), widely considered her best work, was awarded a Pulitzer Prize for its stark evocation of mortal truths. Yet Sexton's interest as a poet, she said, was less rooted in personal confession than in her experience as a woman—her loves, children, parents, breakdowns, and physical existence. Among the subjects treated in her poems are menstruation, abortion, and drug addition—"reality and its hard facts," as she put it.

Born Anne Gray Harvey in Newton, Massachusetts, she was sent to prep school at age 17 for her undisciplined behavior; it was there that she began writing poetry. After attending Garland Junior College for one year, she married Alfred Muller Sexton at age 19 and gave birth to the first of their two daughters in 1953 (the second two years later). She suffered her first breakdown in 1954 and battled depression throughout the rest of her life. Amid frequent hospitalizations and several suicide attempts, she found an outlet in her poetry and the support of mentors and friends (Plath, Lowell, W. D. Snodgrass, Maxine Kunin, and others). Her last book, *The Awful Rowing Toward God* (1975), was published after her final, successful attempt at suicide at age 46. Although her poetry was criticized in some circles for its raw subject matter, its skillfulness and power have earned her a place among the enduring voices of modern American poetry.

PLATH, SYLVIA

(1932–1963)

Poet, whose work is known for its painful imagery and its themes of self-destruction.

As a young girl growing up in Massachusetts, Plath was popular and bright. She entered Smith College in 1950 and before graduating *summa cum laude* had published many poems and stories. Plath demonstrated signs of depression early on, however, even attempting suicide, an experience later described in her 1963 autobiographical novel, *The Bell Jar*. She received a Fulbright scholarship to attend Cambridge University in England, and while there married the English poet Ted Hughes.

Plath's first book of poems *The Colossus* was published in 1960, the year her daughter, Frieda Rebecca Hughes, was born. Their son, Nicholas Farrar Hughes, arrived in January 1962, by which time the two had formally separated. Plath's story was one of hardship. She wrote incessantly, often completing a poem a day.

In 1963 Plath attempted suicide again, this time successfully. Her posthumous publications include a collection of poems called *Ariel* (1965), *Crossing the Water,* and *Winter Trees* (1971). Other works include a selection of letters written to her mother, *Letters Home* (1975), and the Pulitzer Prize-winning *Collected Poems* edited by Ted Hughes (1981).

Sylvia Plath is buried in Heptonstall Churchyard in Yorkshire, England. On her tombstone is written words from a sixteenth-century Chinese story: "Even amidst fierce flames—the golden lotus can be planted."

PORNOGRAPHY

The representation of erotic behavior in writing, visual arts, or media intended to cause sexual excitement. The word *pornography*, derived from the Greek *porni* ("prostitute") and *graphein* ("to write"), was originally defined as any work of art or literature depicting the life of prostitutes. Gradually, pornography began to refer to a much broader range of erotic representations, and in the contemporary United States, debates continue over the definition of pornography and its role and function in the public sphere.

The current judicial guideline for determining whether material is obscene was established by the U.S. Supreme Court in *Miller v. California* (1973). Material is obscene, the Court held, if the average person, applying contemporary "community standards," finds that it appeals to prurient interest.

Public attitudes toward and legislation on pornography in the United States, however, have not been consistent over the past century. Instead, attitudes have wavered depending on the nature of the material and the political climate. Books widely regarded as classics, such as James Joyce's *Ulysses* (1922) and Henry Miller's *Tropic of Cancer* (1934), were at one time or another banned from publication in the United States based on passages defined as pornographic. Some critics have accused contemporary photographer Sally Mann of child pornography based on the nude photos of her preadolescent children in her book *Immediate Family* (1992).

Prior to the nineteenth century, pornographic representations were limited to the written word and the visual arts of sculpture, painting, and drawing. The nineteenth-century inventions of photography and film had a profound impact on sexual representations, allowing for a kind of accuracy and immediacy previously unavailable, and allowing pornography to reach an unprecedented mass audience. The expansion of pornography in the nineteenth century was accompanied by increasing attempts at controlling its publication and consumption. The first raid on a pornographic film occurred in Pennsylvania in 1915 because the movie contained images of a pregnant woman.

Despite the moral condemnation of pornography, it has continued to proliferate in American society. In 1953, Hugh Hefner challenged prevailing standards when he began *Playboy* magazine. Hefner, who produced the debut issue in his kitchen, eventually built Playboy Enterprises, into a leading player in the multi-billion-dollar pornography industry. By the 1970s, *Penthouse* and *Hustler* appeared, offering readers even more risqué images.

As the **WOMEN'S LIBERATION MOVEMENT** gained momentum in the 1960s, some women began to speak out against the development of pornography. **GLORIA STEINEM** gained attention in 1963 with her article "I Was a Playboy Bunny," which recounted her experience as a waitress at Hugh Hefner's Playboy Club. Steinem's concern with pornography focused on the industry's attempt to control and demean women.

In 1972 the adult film *Deep Throat* debuted and made a star of female actress Linda Lovelace. Although *Deep Throat* was her only feature, Lovelace became a widely recognizable figure in the world of pornography. *Deep Throat* became the target of censorship throughout the United States in the 1970s on the grounds of obscenity. In 1979, the group Women Against Pornography was organized by feminist author **Susan Brownmiller**, who also authored the widely anthologized article "Let's Put Pornography Back in the Closet," in which she insists that she is opposed not to sex and desire but to any sexual representation that humiliates, degrades, or dehumanizes men and women.

A decade after *Deep Throat*'s debut, Lovelace spoke out against the film industry that created her fame, and revealed years of abuse and exploitation. Interviewed by **lesbian** scholar Andrea Dworkin in her classic anti-pornography treatise, *Pornography: Men Possessing Women* (1981), Lovelace is quoted as saying, "Every time someone watches that film, they are watching me being raped."

Lovelace's claim has been reinforced by the feminist lawyer, author, activist, and professor Catherine MacKinnon, who argues that pornography not only represents violence but is violence. In the mid-1970s, MacKinnon pioneered the legal claim for **sexual harassment** as a form of sex discrimination, and later formulated laws, with the help of Dworkin, recognizing pornography as a violation of civil rights.

Aided in part by twentieth-century media such as video and the Internet, pornography is more widely available for private use than ever before. There are many men and women who defend the existence of pornography as a manifestation of the American right to choice and free speech. Some go further and advocate the visibility of sex in society in the form of pornography and fantasy as a natural and healthy element of human life. Some pornography actresses insist that the pornography industry is free from coercion and note that jobs related to pornography offer one avenue to financial independence for women.

Apart from figures in the mainstream pornography business, radical feminists, lesbian feminists, and sex radicals such as Susie Bright, Carol Queen, and Pat Califia have long defended the right of individuals to read and view explicitly sexual material, irrespective of the type of activity portrayed. These women have chosen to reject the idea of pornography as inherently patriarchal and have instead created erotic material that more closely reflects their audience's needs and desires. *On Our Backs,* an erotic magazine by and for lesbians, published its first issue in 1984. Lesbian author, activist, journalist, and sex educator Pat Califia (b. 1954) has written sex-positive essays since the 1970s and has promoted pornography for the liberation of human sexuality.

See also: Feminism, Radical; *Ms.* Magazine; Rape; Sexual Revolution; Women's Liberation Movement; Women's Studies.

FURTHER READING

Slade, Joesph W. *Pornography in America: A Reference Handbook.* Santa Barbara: ABC-CLI0, 2000.

POVERTY

The vast majority of Americans who can be classified as poor are women. The causes of poverty among women are many and complex, but most of them are related to gendered stereotypes and expectations. Women are expected to take care of young children, but if there is no father in the house, the mother must also earn a living. Because women are typically paid less than men, many working women are hard pressed to pay for child care, which can take up to half of a low-wage worker's salary. If single women stay home to take care of their children and collect **welfare**, they are branded as lazy—and even then often do not have enough to live decently. Elderly women are also confronted with poverty. When a single woman who has worked a low-wage job all her life retires, her benefits are significantly less than those of high-paid workers, leaving her to face an impoverished old age. Many widows live on pension amounts that do not bring them above the poverty line. The threat of poverty and the structure of the welfare system make it clear that society expects women to marry and stay married if they want economic security. Many women remain in abusive marriages because they are frightened by the economic consequences of not having access to their husband's income.

The poor in America have long been regarded as completely unlike those who have the good fortune not to be poor. As Susan Holloway and her colleagues point out, "Even though about 60 percent of welfare recipients leave the rolls within two years, they are frequently identified as laggards or portrayed as eager to have more babies and lacking motivation to piece together a better life." This point of view was given scholarly support in the 1950s by anthropologist

Poverty and homelessness among women remains a problem in contemporary America.

Oscar Lewis. He coined the term "culture of poverty" to describe his theory that poverty is not caused by economic difficulties alone. He believed that families evolved norms, or ways of behaving, that kept them in poverty generation after generation. According to this theory, a mother who believes there is little hope of doing better passes this view on to her children, who simply assume they will always be poor and on welfare. Michael Harrington, whose book *The Other America* (1963) had a profound influence on President Johnson's War on Poverty, held essentially the same view: "Poverty in the United States is a culture, an institution, a way of life." Americans did not always see the poor through this lens. When women's **BENEVOLENT SOCIETIES** (see Volume 2) began to organize and help poor women in the 1800s and after, many made the point explicitly that anyone could find themselves in economic difficulties. "There but for the grace of God go I," was the motivating principle for many charitable actions undertaken by these groups. But as the theory of the culture of poverty took hold and as more minority women entered the ranks of the poor, people began to treat the poor as being different from, and inferior to, people who were more affluent. Thus programs designed to help poor women, and especially poor women with children, were stigmatized and resented by many Americans. The most significant welfare program, Aid to Families with Dependent Children (AFDC), ended in 1996 with the passage of the Personal Responsibility Act, which placed time limits on how long a person could collect welfare and reduced federal protection for poor people, leaving many women in extremely difficult situations.

FURTHER READING

Abramovitz, Mimi. *Regulating the Lives of Women: Social Welfare Policy from Colonial Times to the Present.* Boston: South End Press, 1992.

Holloway, Susan D., et al. *Through My Own Eyes: Single Mothers and the Cultures of Poverty.* Cambridge: Harvard University Press, 1997.

PREGNANCY

Until the late 1930s, most pregnant women in the United States gave birth at home without pain medications. Other women usually attended the birth. By the 1940s women began giving birth at hospitals with male physicians attending the births. Women were often anesthetized. In the 1950s, the Lamaze method became popular in the United States. The method, developed by Dr. Ferdinand Lamaze, was based on a series of breathing patterns to use during labor. Another method popular at this time was the natural childbirth technique, the Bradley Method. This method, also known as Husband-Coached Childbirth, emphasized education, controlled breathing and relaxation, breastfeeding, and no drugs.

Natural childbirth and medication-free childbirth became popular in the 1970s. Although more women were giving birth naturally, physicians were making advances in pain control during labor. The development of the epidural altered the birth experience for mothers who used medications. By 2000, more than 90 percent of American women delivered in hospital settings and most women use obstetricians. A small number of women use midwives and deliver in birthing centers or at home.

PRESIDENT'S COMMISSION ON THE STATUS OF WOMEN

A group of 20 legislators and philanthropists who were active in women's rights issues, organized to study the work status of women. President John F. Kennedy established the President's Commission on the Status of Women in December

1961. Former first lady **ELEANOR ROOSEVELT** chaired the commission until her death in 1962.

The primary goal of the commission was to examine public policies and their impact on the ability of women to achieve full participation in American life. Among the practices examined by the group were labor laws relating to hours and wages, the quality of legal representation for women, the obstacles to education for women, and federal insurance and tax laws that affected women's economic status and income.

In a report to the president, the commission documented widespread discrimination against women in the workplace and recommended several charges, including provision of affordable child care for all income levels, hiring practices that promoted equal opportunity for women, and availability of paid maternity leave. The report also called for the establishment of a Citizens' Advisory Council on the Status of Women. The council would recommend coordination of activities with private institutions and organizations, review the progress of women's participation in American economic life, and consider new methods of advancing the status of women.

Though the report itself did not bring about immediate changes, many states set up similar commissions on the status of women, and these state-level commissions played a critical role in promoting more equal economic opportunities. The president's committee was terminated in October 1963 after the submission of the final report.

PROSTITUTION

The performance of sexual acts in exchange for money. Prostitution is often associated with the sexual exploitation of women. It is a result of economic dependency. In the early 1800s, moral reform crusaders began pushing to end prostitution. At the turn of the twentieth century, the progressive reformers also campaigned to end prostitution. One criticism of the bias in state laws made throughout the century is the prosecution of prostitutes while their male customers were allowed to go free. In the United States, only part of Nevada permits legal prostitution.

In 1949, the United Nations adopted a resolution to decriminalize prostitution. Fifty countries ratified the resolution, although the United States did not. In 1973 the **NATIONAL ORGANIZATION FOR WOMEN** passed a resolution supporting the decriminalization of prostitution. The National Task Force on Prostitution (NTFP), founded in 1979, serves as an umbrella organization for prostitutes and prostitutes' rights organizations across the United States. It expanded its purpose in 1994, to involve organizations and individuals who support the rights of prostitutes and other sex workers. Prostitutes' rights organizations, such as COYOTE and the NTFP, have advocated for unionization.

Poverty, drugs and violence are often associated with prostitution. The women's movement has been split on the topic. Some, like legal scholar Catharine MacKinnon and author Andrea Dworkin, believe that prostitution perpetuates the victimization of women. Others follow the principle of "a woman's body, a woman's right," and insist that the choices a woman makes about her own body must be accorded full legal protection.

FURTHER READING

Hobson, Barbara Meil. *Uneasy Virtue: The Politics Prostitution and the American Reform Tradition.* Chicago: University of Chicago Press. 1990.

Seagraves, Anne. *Soiled Doves: Prostitutes in the Early West.* Hayden, ID: Wesanne Publishers. 1994.

PROTECTIVE LABOR LEGISLATION

Legislation requiring such worker protections as minimum wages or maximum legal hours in a workweek. Protective labor legislation first appeared in England in the early 1800s and was designed to limit the hours worked by children. In the 1840s protective legislation was extended to women to limit the number of hours they could work for pay, and bar them from working in certain jobs. These measures purportedly aimed at protecting women's health and morals, but they also limited women's employment opportunities. Many of the jobs from which women were barred tended to be relatively high paying.

The U.S. Supreme Court upheld a maximum-hours law for male mine workers in 1898 (*Holden v. Hardy*) but seven years later struck down a similar law in *Lochner v. New York* on the basis that such laws impinged on individual liberty by restricting the freedom to contract.

In 1905, the United States began passing protective legislation aimed at women, often under the guise of protecting the nation's reproductive forces. The resulting restrictions increased women's reliance on lower-paid service-sector jobs and work that could be done in the home (legislators did not restrict the hours women could spend on unpaid domestic labor). Most men and many **LABOR UNIONS** supported the restrictions. Women's rights advocates were divided. Some supported minimum wages for women, since employers tended to pay women less than men; others opposed them out of the belief that laws should treat women and men equally.

In 1908, the U.S. Supreme Court upheld a maximum-hours law for women in ***MULLER v. OREGON*** (see Documents), on the basis that fundamental differences between women and men (i.e., women's "delicacy") warranted the restrictions, but in 1923 it struck down a minimum-wage law for women in ***ADKINS v. CHILDREN'S HOSPITAL***, arguing that freedom of contract was protected under the Due Process Clause of the Constitution. Again, in 1936, the Court struck down a minimum-wage law covering female laundry workers in *Morehead v. New York*, but within a year reversed itself and upheld a minimum-wage law in *West Coast Hotel v. Parrish* on the basis that reasonable regulations did not violate due process and that government could protect workers' health and safety. Today's protective labor laws generally cover men and women equally, and those that focus on women are more likely to bar differential treatment than to mandate it.

Q

QUILTS

A form of the textile arts that is centuries old and most often created by women.

A quilt is distinguished from other textile forms by a fabric top (pieced or appliqué), a filler referred to as batting, and a backing. The three layers are held together with stitching that secures the fabric layers and enhances the pattern of the overall piece. For those who view quilts as an art form, the artistry of the overall design and the mastery of the quilted stitch size and pattern determine the quality of the piece. Some quilt makers simply tie the layers together with colored thread using a blanket or similar piece of solid fabric as the batting. Tying was frequently used in the fancy quilts of the early 1900s.

Quilts provide historians with information about the daily lives of average women, **HOMEMAKERS**, and community life in various regions of the country. This is particularly true for the first half of the twentieth century. Women made the majority of quilts for practical purposes: to warm their families' beds and to recycle worn clothing in an efficient use of domestic resources. Women saved pieces of fabric from men's shirts and ties, women's housedresses, children's clothes, kitchen toweling, and flour sacks for the piecework of quilt tops. They used spare moments of "rest" to cut the patterns and piece the tops. Many women brought their quilts to quilting bees where they were assisted by neighbors, relatives, or friends. Women of privileged classes made parlor quilts pieced of velvet and silk, and stitched together with fancy embroidery that emphasized their handiwork skills.

Quilting became less common during **WORLD WAR II** and the postwar decades. The increase in married women workers and the wide availability of low-priced goods diminished the production of quilts as objects of necessity. Yet these trends also produced two reactions that reignited the interest of Americans. Collectors began acquiring and preserving the finest examples of American quilts. As quilts began to move from domestic craft to contemporary textile, artists reinvented this traditional art form.

FURTHER READING

Cooper, Patricia, and Norma Bradley Buferd. *The Quilters: Women and Domestic Art.* New York: Doubleday and Company, 1977.

Dewhurst, C. Kurt, et al. *Artists in Aprons: Folk Art by American Women.* New York: E.P. Dutton, 1979.

Ferraro, Pat, et al. *Hearts and Hands: The Influence of Women and Quilts on American Society.* San Francisco: The Quilt Digest Press, 1987.

R

RAINEY, MA (1886–1939)

Known as the "Mother of the Blues" for her influential role in shaping the genre of blues music. At the beginning of the twentieth century, Rainey was among the first black performers in the emerging black entertainment industry.

She was born Gertrude Pridgett to parents who performed in minstrel shows, and first appeared on stage in 1900. In 1904, still a teenager, she married Will Rainey and toured with him as "Ma and Pa Rainey, the Assassinators of the Blues." By the 1920s she had become a solo star on the vaudeville circuit.

Rainey was signed by Paramount in 1923 and recorded 100 songs for them between 1923 and 1928. Like the female blues singers who followed her, Rainey explored the themes of race and gender in her music. Her songs reflected the experiences of many African-American women, and, like many other blues songs, often focused on violent relationships with men.

Despite the fact that many of Rainey's songs focused on relationships with men, she also sang about her attraction to women. Rainey's colleagues knew that she was sexually involved with women. She sang about this involvement in "Prove It on Me Blues," a song she composed.

See also: African Americans; Holiday, Billie; Lesbians; Music; Smith, Bessie.

RAPE

Forced sexual intercourse. In many jurisdictions, the term "sexual assault" has replaced the term "rape" in statutes and includes forced sodomy (oral or anal sexual acts), child molestation, incest, and fondling. Rape laws changed significantly throughout the twentieth century. The concept of rape in marriage, for example, was dismissed as something imagined by the wife. It was not until the 1970s that society began to acknowledge that rape in marriage could occur and that laws were passed to criminalize marital rape. Another reform included rape shield laws that prevented the accuser's sexual history from being presented at trial. Prior to this law, jurors and judges could use previous sexual history as justification for the rape. Also, the invasion of privacy made women reluctant to report rapes.

Public protest against sexual assault has led to important changes in law and institutional policies.

Part of the credit for the increased public attention and assault legislation in the 1970s goes to the WOMEN'S LIBERATION MOVEMENT. Authors such as Susan Griffin argued that rape was a crime of control rather than passion; and Susan Brownmiller hypothesized that acts of rape, much like acts of terrorism, created a "rape culture" that kept women in fear.

Date rape was also recognized in the late 1970s. Rape prevention programs now are used on many college campuses, and rape counseling centers are available across the country. In 1974, Ann Burgess and Lynda Lytle Holmstrom developed a model called the Rape Trauma Syndrome to describe some of the experiences sexual assault victims may go through following an assault. Enactment of the federal Violence Against Women Act in 1994 (see Documents) helped to strengthen rape laws.

REAGAN, NANCY DAVIS (b. 1921)

Actress, first lady (1981–1989), and wife of U.S. President Ronald Reagan. Nancy Davis Reagan was born Anne Frances Robbins in New York

City. Her father left the family and Nancy spent her early years with her grandmother while her mother, Edith Luckett, toured as an actress. When her mother married neurosurgeon Loyal Davis, she became Nancy Davis.

Davis earned a drama degree from Smith College in 1943, then acted on Broadway until signing with the MGM movie studios in 1949. In 1952, her name showed up erroneously on a list of communist sympathizers, and Davis was referred to Ronald Reagan, then president of the Screen Actor's Guild. The two met, fell in love, and married in 1952.

When Ronald Reagan was elected governor of California in 1966, Nancy Reagan began her role as the politician's wife—a role that would extend all the way to the White House. She was very involved in her husband's 1980 campaign for U.S. president and had a significant influence on his presidency.

During her time in the White House, Nancy Reagan sponsored various social programs. The best-known was the "Just Say No" foundation, an antidrug program for juveniles for which she won various honors and awards. Her memoir, *My Turn*, was published in 1989.

REED v. REED

U.S. Supreme Court case in 1971 that overturned a state law because the law discriminated on the basis of gender. In March 1967 a child named Richard Lynn Reed died in Idaho. Richard died intestate, meaning that he did not leave a will. Since there was no will, there was no one to ensure that any money or property he owned was distributed as he would have wished. About seven months after his death, his adoptive mother, Sally Reed, filed a petition with the probate court (the court that deals with cases involving wills, estates, and the like), asking to be named administrator of the boy's estate. Before the court could act on her petition, the boy's adoptive father, Cecil Reed, who had separated from Sally Reed before their son's death, filed a competing petition. The probate court would have to decide between the two.

At the time, Idaho law listed several classes of people who might be entitled to administer an estate. One of those classes was "the father or mother" of the deceased. Both Sally and Cecil Reed qualified. But the code went on to state, "Of several persons claiming and equally entitled to administer, males must be preferred to females." Therefore, the court named Cecil Reed administrator of his son's estate. The court did so without conducting a hearing to decide whether he was the more capable of the two to carry out the responsibilities of administrator.

Sally Reed appealed the probate court's decision to the district court of Idaho. She argued that the Idaho legal code violated the Equal Protection Clause of the Fourteenth Amendment to the U.S. Constitution. The basis of her argument was that the code treated similarly situated men and women differently. She won the appeal, but Cecil Reed appealed to the Idaho Supreme Court, which ruled in his favor, citing the "mandatory" provision of Idaho law. The case then went to the U.S. Supreme Court.

In 1971 the Supreme Court ruled unanimously in Sally Reed's favor. Chief Justice Warren Burger wrote the decision that declared the Idaho code unconstitutional: "To give a mandatory preference to members of either sex over members of the other . . . is to make the very kind of arbitrary legislative choice forbidden by the Equal Protection Clause of the Fourteenth Amendment."*Reed v. Reed* was thus an important case in the use of the Fourteenth Amendment to combat gender discrimination. It was also one of the first gender-discrimination cases in which the Court refused to uphold a state law.

RELIGION

The history of religion in America, as historian Ann Braude points out, is the history of women's involvement. From the colonial period on, women have constituted the majority of churchgoers in America. Braude also notes that it is primarily women who raise the next generation of churchgoers, thus keeping religion alive. Although women have loyally supported religions, most denominations largely excluded them from positions of authority until the 1970s.

In the nineteenth century women began to assert moral authority. By founding a variety of **BENEVOLENT SOCIETIES** (see Volume 2) women promoted religious values. They moved from the domestic into the public sphere to work for the **ABOLITION** of slavery and for **TEMPERANCE** (see Volume 2). And they formed **MISSIONARY** organizations that exerted considerable influence, especially in Protestant denominations. In fact, women's missionary societies were so successful

TRAILBLAZERS

In 1989, Barbara Clementine Harris was named a bishop of the Episcopal Church, the first women elevated to such a position in any of the three largest Christian branches—Anglicanism, Roman Catholicism, and Eastern Orthodoxy.

While many people, including many women, were delighted with Harris's appointment, other church members were very unhappy. Traditionalists labeled the ordination "sacrilegious," while others were concerned because Harris's background was so unusual. A divorced woman without a college education, Harris had been a businesswoman for most of her life. She was, however, active in her church for many years before she chose the religious life.

Harris's business career began after her high school graduation in 1948. She took a position with a public relations firm, where her job was to help white-owned companies market their products and services in black communities. She was so successful that she was eventually named president of the firm. In 1968, she went to work for Sun Oil and ultimately became head of community relations. Throughout her business career, Harris was active in her church as a volunteer and civil rights advocate.

Harris began to study for the priesthood in 1976, taking classes in the evenings and on weekends. She was ordained a deacon in 1979 and a priest in 1980, among the first women to be ordained in the Episcopal church. She served as a parish priest for four years and then was appointed director of the Episcopal Church Publishing Company. In that role, she edited and wrote for the *Witness*, a church journal known for its liberal leanings. In 1989, after much controversy within the church, Harris was appointed suffragan (assistant) bishop for Massachusetts. In an interview for the *Boston Globe* in 1998, Harris told reporter Alisa Valdes-Rodriguez that she actually got death threats when she was selected. Rodriguez notes that Harris "stopped to grin, and added, 'All in the name of the Lord, of course.' "

Since Harris became a bishop, sixteen other women in the Episcopal church have been named bishops.

that some male church leaders felt threatened by them. Eventually, they brought women's societies under the control of more general groups. Even so, women remained a powerful force in religion in the first half of the twentieth century.

Beginning in the 1970s women began to seek ordination as ministers in greater numbers, and more churches began to accept them. By the 1980s women made up half of all the ministerial students in many denominations. Even in those religions that still do not allow women to join the clergy, women have been able to draw attention to the issue and institute debate and discussion. Women have also influenced change in the language of hymns and the liturgy to reflect the idea that God is not a man but a spiritual being who encompasses both male and female characteristics. Thanks to the efforts of feminists, many religions have begun to refer to God as "mother" as well as "father," emphasizing God's nurturing, forgiving, loving nature. Feminist theologians, such as Catholic feminist Rosemary Radford Ruether, have begun to exert an influence on the nature of religious belief. Ruether emphasizes the relationship of Christian theology to issues of social justice, including sexism. Elisabeth Schüssler Fiorenza examines biblical texts and church history from a feminist perspective and challenges many assumptions about religion, the Bible, and religious authority. In 1989, Barbara Harris became the first woman in any of the major religious denominations to be ordained a bishop. Since then, several others have followed.

While women have been ordained and elevated into positions of leadership in many Protestant denominations, they are still excluded from positions of leadership in the Catholic church. Nevertheless, women have deeply influenced Catholicism. The **Irish immigrants** who swelled the ranks of **Catholics** in the nineteenth century (see Volume 2) and deeply influenced the direction of American Catholicism were largely female. With the establishment of parochial schools in the 1800s, lay women and nuns became the primary educators of Catholic children. Nuns far outnumbered priests and exerted a much greater influence on the day-to-day practice of religion. In addition, in the early days of parochial education, girls were more likely to attend Catholic schools than boys because boys were sent into the workforce. These girls, in turn, raised their children in the faith.

Feminists in Judaism have also worked to change the language of prayers that portray women in a negative light and have feminized certain aspects of the liturgy. Reconstructionist, Reform, and Conservative Jews now ordain women as rabbis. Only the Orthodox do not.

While it has always been true that American women filled the pews while men held sway in the pulpits, a shift seems to be under way as more women are elevated to positions of power and influence in their churches.

FOR FURTHER READING

Braude, Ann. "Women's History *Is* American Religious History." In Thomas A. Tweed, ed., *Retelling U.S. Religious History*. Berkeley: University of California Press, 1997.

Schüssler Fiorenza, Elisabeth. *In Memory of Her: A Feminist Theological Reconstruction of Christian Origins*. New York: Crossroad, 1994.

REPRODUCTIVE RIGHTS

The right of a person to decide if, when, and how to have children. Although couples practiced contraception in ancient Greece and Rome, the modern birth control movement began in the late nineteenth century. In 1916, the first U.S. birth control clinic was established in Brooklyn, New York, by **MARGARET SANGER**. At the time, contraception was illegal. State laws essentially forced women who were sexually active to conceive children, whether they wanted to or not. Sanger's clinic was quickly closed by police, and Sanger herself was sentenced to 30 days in jail. In 1917, she founded the National Birth Control League, which eventually became **PLANNED PARENTHOOD**. Sanger and her organization campaigned to legalize contraception and worked to overcome the objections of nearly every major religion. In 1930, the Church of England was the among first organized religions to allow the use of contraception by married couples. Almost all Protestant denominations followed suit, but the Roman Catholic church continued to condemn the practice. Despite years of pressure from Planned Parenthood and many Catholic couples, Pope Paul VI reaffirmed the church's teachings against contraception in his 1968 *Humanae Vitae* (On Human Life).

Margaret Sanger and a friend financed research that led to the first oral contraceptive, the birth control pill, which led to what has been called the **SEXUAL REVOLUTION** of the 1960s. For the first time in history, women could engage in sexual activity without the fear of becoming pregnant. Because they no longer needed to fear unwanted pregnancy, many women felt freer to engage in sex outside of marriage.

In the 1960s and 1970s, several Supreme Court decisions helped void state laws that made contraception illegal. In ***GRISWOLD v. CONNECTICUT*** (1965), the Court ruled that states could not prevent the distribution of contraceptives to married couples. In ***EISENSTADT v. BAIRD*** (1972), it ruled that states could not prevent the distribution of contraceptives to unmarried people. In both cases, the Court based its decision partially on the right to privacy granted by the Fourteenth Amendment. In 1977, the Court extended the right to access contraceptives to minors, in *Carey v. Populations Services*.

Until the middle of the nineteenth century, abortions were performed by women themselves or by midwives and were not illegal in the United States. But after the Civil War, many state legislatures passed laws making **ABORTION** a crime. Thus a pregnant women had no legal choice other than to bear the child, unless her life was threatened by the pregnancy. Laws against abortion did not stop women from terminating pregnancies, but they did force women to obtain the procedure illegally. These "back alley" abortions were often performed by unqualified persons, resulting in permanent physical damage to some women and death to others. By the mid-1960s, some states had liberalized abortion laws, but abortion was still illegal in most of the country. Two landmark Supreme Court cases decided in 1973, ***ROE v. WADE*** and *Doe v. Bolton,* struck down state laws that criminalized abortion. Justice Harry Blackmun, writing the *Roe* decision, declared that the constitutional "right of privacy is broad enough to encompass a woman's decision to terminate a pregnancy."

The debate over reproductive rights continues. Groups who oppose abortion and advocate criminal penalties actively pursue their agenda in the courts and the press.

FURTHER READING

Davis, Susan E. *Women under Attack: Victories, Backlash, and the Fight for Reproductive Freedom*. Boston: South End Press, 1988.

Hartman, Betsey. *Reproductive Rights and Wrongs: The Global Politics of Population Control*. Boston: South End Press, 1994.

RICH, ADRIENNE (b. 1929)

Poet. Adrienne Rich was born in Baltimore, Maryland. In 1951, the year she graduated from Radcliffe College, poet W. H. Auden selected one of her poems for publication in Yale University's Younger Poet Series. It was her first published work, and a huge honor for Rich.

Rich married Alfred Conrad in 1953, and the couple had three children before Rich left her husband in 1970; later that year, he committed suicide. Throughout her marriage, Rich had continued writing poetry, publishing several collections of her works, including *The Diamond Cutters* (1955) and *Necessities of Life* (1966). She published *The Will to Change* in 1971 and in 1974 received the National Book Award for *Diving into the Wreck*, accepting the honor on behalf of all women. Also in 1974, Rich became a professor of English at City College in New York. Her 1976 book *Twenty-One Love Poems* describes her lesbian relationship.

Additional volumes of poetry appeared during the 1970s and 1980s, as did several books of nonfiction, including *Of Woman Born: Motherhood as Experience and Institution* (1986). She has received numerous prizes, including the Ruth Lilly Poetry Prize, the Lenore Marshall Poetry Prize, and the Academy of American Poets Wallace Stevens Award.

RIDE, SALLY (b. 1951)

The first American woman in space. When the National Aeronautics and Space Administration (NASA) put out a call for astronauts in 1976, more than 8,000 men and women applied to the program. Of the 35 who were accepted, six were women, among them Sally Ride. Ride was not the first woman in space—that honor belongs to a Soviet cosmonaut—but she did pioneer space travel for American women, serving as mission-control communications officer during the second and third flights of the space shuttle *Columbia* in 1981 and 1982. In 1983, she became the first American woman in space, flying as a mission specialist aboard the shuttle *Challenger.* She flew again on *Challenger* the following year, and after the 1986 *Challenger* explosion was appointed to the presidential commission that investigated the accident. She resigned from NASA in 1987 and became director of the California Space Institute. In 1999 she joined space.com, a Web site about the space industry.

ROCKEFELLER, ABBY ALDRICH (1874–1948)

Philanthropist. Born in Providence, Rhode Island, Abby Greene Aldrich was the daughter of Nelson Aldrich, a U.S. Senator from 1881 to 1911, and Abby Pearce Chapman. After graduating from Miss Abbott's School for Young Ladies in Providence in 1893, Abby traveled to Europe. A year later, she met John D. Rockefeller, Jr. The couple were married in 1901.

During **World War I**, Mrs. Rockefeller did extensive volunteer work with the American Red Cross, and in 1918 wrote "Suggestions for Housing Women War Workers," which led to the development of federal standards for housing women who worked at American factories during the war. A year later, she began efforts to improve the living conditions for employees at a New Jersey refinery owned by Standard Oil, her husband's company. This led to the building of homes and a community center.

Much of Rockefeller's philanthropic work was focused on the arts. In May 1929, she helped found the Museum of Modern Art in New York City, and in 1935 donated more than 180 paintings to its collection. Four years later, several years after Williamsburg, the former capital of Virginia, had been restored with financial assistance from her husband, Abby Rockefeller donated her collection of American folk art to the city. A museum of folk art at Colonial Williamsburg was subsequently named after her. She died on April 5, 1948.

ROE v. WADE

A 1973 U.S. Supreme Court case that legalized abortion in the first trimester of pregnancy, profoundly changing the lives of women and societal attitudes toward women's reproductive rights. Few decisions in judicial history have been as divisive.

In 1970 "Jane Roe" (a pseudonym designed to protect the identity of a Texas woman named Norma McCorvey) sued Henry Wade, the Dallas County district attorney, in federal court. McCorvey had been pregnant and sought an abortion, a procedure that was illegal in most of the United States and that subjected women and their doctors to arrest. In her suit, McCorvey argued that the Texas law criminalizing abortion was unconstitutional. The lower court agreed, but the state appealed the case to the U.S.

Supreme Court. In its 7-to-2 decision, the Court affirmed the lower court's ruling, saying that the Texas law was unnecessarily restrictive and violated a woman's constitutional right to privacy.

Writing for the Court majority, Justice Harry A. Blackmun stated, "This right of privacy, whether it be founded in the Fourteenth Amendment's concept of personal liberty and restrictions upon state action . . . or in the Ninth Amendment's reservation of rights to the people, is broad enough to encompass a woman's decision whether or not to terminate her pregnancy." Blackmun went on to say that "the detriment that the State would impose upon the pregnant woman by denying this choice altogether is apparent," including a "distressful life and future" and "psychological harm" to unwilling mothers and unwanted children.

The Court, however, declined to say that the right to an abortion was absolute. Any state law restricting abortion had to serve a "compelling state interest." It also had to balance the rights of pregnant women with the state's interest in both the health of the woman and the potential life of the fetus. The Court thus concluded that to protect the health of the mother the state could limit abortions after the first trimester, or three months, of pregnancy; it could assert its right to protect fetuses at the point when the fetus was viable, or had "capability for meaningful life outside the mother's womb."

In the years that followed numerous efforts were mounted to overturn *Roe v. Wade,* including a 1992 case, *Planned Parenthood v. Casey*, or to put in place a constitutional amendment that would prohibit abortions. Nearly 30 years after *Roe v. Wade,* Americans remain deeply divided over the issue of abortion rights.

See also: Griswold v. Connecticut; Planned Parenthood.

FURTHER READING

Faux, Marian. *Roe v. Wade: The Untold Story of the Landmark Supreme Court Decision That Made Abortion Legal.* New York: Cooper Square Press, 2001.

ROOSEVELT, EDITH KERMIT CAROW (1861–1948)

First lady and wife of Theodore Roosevelt, the twenty-sixth president of the United States. Edith Kermit Carow was born in Norwich, Connecticut, the daughter of shipping magnates. Growing up in New York City, she befriended Roosevelt and married him in 1886, after his first wife died. They had five children, in addition to his daughter from his previous marriage.

Roosevelt was first lady from 1901 to 1909, during which time she molded the role expected of modern presidential wives. Overseeing White House social activities and managing the Roosevelt children—with their menageries of pets—she carried out her public and private duties with efficiency and grace. Though the family was under constant public scrutiny, she managed to keep their private lives private. She was responsible for separating family quarters from administrative areas within the White House, ensuring a measure of privacy for all future first families.

Striving to achieve order and professionalism in the White House, Roosevelt was the first presidential wife to employ a personal secretary to assist her with social planning and correspondence, and hire caterers to help with the extensive entertaining required in the White House. She distributed family photographs to the press, scheduled interviews, gave her husband news articles that she considered important, and created a White House portrait gallery of first ladies.

Upon leaving the White House, the Roosevelts returned to the family residence at Oyster Bay, New York. Edith Roosevelt performed charity work, traveled, and wrote several books. A staunch Republican, she publicly opposed her husband's cousin, Democrat Franklin D. Roosevelt, in the presidential campaign of 1932. She died at Oyster Bay on September 10, 1948.

ROOSEVELT, ELEANOR

(1884–1962)

Humanitarian, feminist, first lady (1933–1945), and diplomat. Anna Eleanor Roosevelt was born in New York to an aristocratic family (her father was President Theodore Roosevelt's younger brother), but had an unhappy childhood and was orphaned by the time she was 11. A relationship with Marie Souvestre, a teacher at the boarding school she went to in London when she was 14, gave her a sorely needed emotional connection; in later years she attributed much of her achievement to her three years of contact with Souvestre's "liberal mind and strong personality."

Eleanor Roosevelt was a humanitarian who worked hard to promote the New Deal programs.

Back in New York, even as she embarked on the social life of a debutante and a secret courtship with her distant cousin Franklin Delano Roosevelt, she began her activist career, joining the **National Consumers League** and volunteering in the **settlement house movement** (see Volume 2).

She married her cousin in 1905, and the two settled in New York City in a household dominated by Franklin's mother. Although Roosevelt loved the six children who were born to them between 1906 and 1916 (one of whom died in infancy) it was not a happy time. The beginning of Franklin's political career and the start of **World War I** opened new possibilities for her. She visited wounded soldiers and coordinated Red Cross activities. After the war she joined the **League of Women Voters**. When Franklin contracted polio, in 1922, she became his political representative, speaking in his behalf before women's groups across the state. By 1928 she was speaking on her own account as well, advocating reform issues such as equal pay legislation, and had a rich network of activist friends. Many of these women went with her to Washington when Franklin became the thirty-second president in 1933, and it was largely due to Roosevelt's influence that women achieved an unprecedented level of power in government in Franklin's administration. Roosevelt coordinated the 1936 reelection campaign, and became part of the everyday life of millions through her syndicated column, "My Day" (see Documents).

Although the president and first lady worked together to promote the **New Deal**, and although Franklin respected his wife and relied on her judgment, on a personal level they were at odds. His exuberant personality and her more serious one seemed to conflict. Also, during World War I he had begun a relationship with Eleanor's social secretary, Lucy Mercer, that drove a wedge between them. At the family's Hyde Park, New York, estate, Roosevelt moved out of the main house and settled in a cottage on the grounds with two of her friends. There and in Washington she found emotional support in friendship.

In addition to supporting her husband's political initiatives, Roosevelt mounted her own campaigns, especially on behalf of civil rights for **African Americans**. In the constant visits she made to meet those she was concerned about—striking miners, wounded soldiers, welfare mothers, children in trouble with the law—she had a genius for making those people feel that she cared.

Far from retiring from public life after her husband's death in 1945, she deluged President Truman with advice about civil rights, fair employment practices, and world peace. Truman appointed her a delegate to the United Nations, where she drafted and lobbied for the Universal Declaration of Human Rights, passed in 1948. Her last public office was as chair of the **President's Commission on the Status of Women**, under John F. Kennedy. She died in New York at 78, having played a part in almost every significant social movement of her lifetime.

See also: Music; "Women and the Media," p. 27.

FURTHER READING

Black, Allida M. *Casting her Own Shadow: Eleanor Roosevelt and the Shaping of Postwar Liberalism.* New York: Columbia University Press, 1996.

RUBYFRUIT JUNGLE

First novel by **Rita Mae Brown**, published in 1973. *Rubyfruit Jungle* is the coming-of-age story of smart, funny, and **lesbian** Molly Bolt. Although there had been lesbian novels written before this time, *Rubyfruit Jungle,* unlike many of its predecessors, is filled with humor and positive portrayals of lesbian life, and launched Brown's writing career.

Although the book's protagonist is a lesbian, the work appeals to a broad audience. Brown always insisted that she wanted her novel to be read and enjoyed by everyone. The fact that *Rubyfruit Jungle* is a classic American rags-to-riches story may account for some of its appeal. Molly Bolt, born poor and of uncertain parentage, makes it on her own in a life full of adventure. She has been compared to the quintessential American character Huck Finn.

RUKEYSER, MURIEL

(1913–1980)

Poet, educator, political activist. A prolific poet and author, Rukeyser may have been the most widely published female poet at mid-century. Her writings included biography, children's books, and translations as well as her better-known poetry and prose. Her achievements in poetry were matched by a lifelong interest in and commitment to social justice.

Born in New York City, Rukeyser spent most of her life there and received degrees from Vassar College and Columbia University. She taught at both alma maters and Sarah Lawrence College where she mentored Alice Walker. Although Rukeyser received prestigious awards recognizing her writing, such as the Guggenheim Award and the Yale Younger Poets Prize, she also experienced censorship because of her political support for women's rights, civil rights, and anti-Semitism.

Her commitment to human rights led her to support Spanish loyalists during the Spanish Civil War, oppose the U.S. intervention in Vietnam, and protest the harassment of artists around the world. In 1977, the Academy of American Poets and the Poetry Society recognized her accomplishments by awarding Rukeyser their national poetry awards. She died in New York City on February 12, 1980.

S

SABIN, FLORENCE RENA

(1871–1953)

Medical researcher. Florence Rena Sabin was born in the mining community of Central City, Colorado, on November 9, 1871. She graduated from Smith College in Massachusetts in 1893 and attended The Johns Hopkins Medical School in Baltimore, Maryland. After earning her medical degree, she stayed on to do research and in 1901 published *An Atlas of the Medulla and Midbrain*. It became a standard textbook in the field.

In 1917, Sabin became the first woman to be named a full professor at Johns Hopkins. She conducted research on the body's blood circulation and lymphatic system, and in 1925 became the first woman on the staff of the Rockefeller Institute of Medical Research in New York. Sabin left the institute in 1938 and moved to Denver, Colorado. In 1944, she was asked by the governor to reform the state's public health system, and in 1948 she was named head of the Colorado health department. She served five years in that post, resigning just before her death on October 3, 1953.

SAGE, MARGARET SLOCUM

(1828–1918)

Philanthropist. Margaret Olivia Slocum was born on September 8, 1828, in Syracuse, New York. After graduating from the Emma Willard School in Troy, New York, in 1847, Margaret pursued a teaching career for more than 20 years. She married Russell B. Sage, a wealthy banker and financier, in 1869.

Under Margaret Sage's influence, her husband became a philanthropist, giving financial support to programs in education and health care. After his death in 1906, she used his $63 million estate to continue these philanthropic activities. In 1907, with $10 million, she set up the Russell Sage Foundation, whose goal was "the improvement of social and living conditions" throughout the United States.

Sage also used her wealth to finance new buildings for the Emma Willard School, donate gifts to universities such as Harvard and Yale, and provide financial support to the YMCA and YWCA. At her death on November 4, 1918, she had donated a total of $75 to $80 million to worthy causes.

SAGER, RUTH (1918–1997)

Geneticist. Sager, sometimes called the "High Priestess of the Second Genetic System," was born in Chicago on February 7, 1918. She was educated at the University of Chicago, Rutgers University, and Columbia University, where she received her Ph.D. in genetics in 1948. Her discovery of the non-chromosomal gene composed of DNA revolutionized genetics.

In 1951, Sager was appointed to the research staff at the Rockefeller Institute, where her research debunked the Mendelian genetic theory, which asserted that transmission of inherited characteristics is controlled by chromosomes inside the nucleus of the cell. However, Sager's research with alga Chlamydomonas in 1953 proved that genes outside the chromosome can pass on inherited characteristics. These non-chromosomal genes are resistant to environmental change and can be passed on for generations.

Sager's research proved that every cell contains duplicate genes, one chromosomal and one non-chromosomal, that work in tandem to pass on characteristics. Her discovery that non-chromosomal genes are composed of deoxyribonucleic acid (DNA) changed the face of genetics forever.

Dr. Sager worked with the Dana-Farber Cancer Institute from 1975 until her death from cancer in 1997. She also served as a faculty member at Harvard Medical School from 1975 to 1988. In 1988, she was recognized for her research by the National Academy of Sciences.

SALT OF THE EARTH

A 1954 feature film about a Mexican-American community's response during a prolonged mining strike in New Mexico. Filmed during the height of Cold War anticommunist fervor, the film was banned from theater distribution in the United States in 1954 because of its purported communist propaganda. In retrospect, the Library of Congress recently identified it as one of the nation's top 100 films for posterity.

The film tells the story of labor conflict through the eyes of one family. As the strike wears on, the women of the families replace the men in the picket line. By doing so, the women surprise themselves, challenge their husbands' views of women's roles, and temporarily confuse the mine owners.

Hollywood did in fact view the film's content as communist propaganda. The film was blacklisted from distribution in the United States for nearly 30 years.

The film presents a rare example of a community's successful challenge to dominant sex hierarchies during the Cold War as well as an all too rare depiction of public activism on the part of Latinas.

SANGER, MARGARET (1879–1966)

Founder of the U.S. birth control movement. Margaret Louise Higgins was born in Corning, New York, the sixth of 11 children. Although Higgins was influenced by her father's radical ideals, she resented him when her mother died of tuberculosis and the doctor indicated that frequent pregnancy also contributed to her death.

After attending a progressive boarding school in Hudson, New York, Higgins entered the White Plains Hospital to study NURSING in 1900. In 1902, she met architect William Sanger, whom she married six months later. In 1903, she gave birth to a son. The Sangers moved to Hastings-on-Hudson, New York, where Margaret had two more children, but they tired of suburban life and returned to New York City in 1910. They immersed themselves in bohemian culture by attending Liberal Club meetings, organizing for the Socialist Party, and meeting intellectuals such as EMMA GOLDMAN. Margaret worked as a nurse in Lillian Wald's Visiting Nurse Service. Her experiences tending to pregnant women who could not afford children and women who died from self-induced ABORTIONS reinforced her belief in the need for birth control.

In 1912, Margaret began writing a column entitled "What Every Girl Should Know" for *The Call*, a Socialist daily. Because it was illegal under the 1873 COMSTOCK LAW (see Volume 2) to disseminate any information about birth control through the media or mail, she avoided direct

Margaret Sanger believed women should have accurate information about birth control.

mention of birth control, but discussed the reproductive process. In 1914, she published a feminist magazine, *The Woman Rebel* (see Documents), and was arrested for publishing obscene material.

Sanger viewed birth control both as a health issue and a social issue. She believed that poor women were economically oppressed by unwanted pregnancies and that birth control would liberate them. After printing a pamphlet entitled "Family Limitation" under an alias, she fled to Europe, where contact with radical intellectuals expanded her argument on birth control as a means for women's sexual liberation and enjoyment.

In 1916, Sanger opened the first birth control clinic in Brooklyn, New York, which also resulted in her arrest. A year later, she published a new journal, *Birth Control Review*. In 1921, she established the American Birth Control League. Estranged from her husband, she had a number of affairs before marrying oil magnate James Noah Slee in 1922. Sanger continued to fight for support for her cause from the medical community and make legislative strides. She met with leaders around the world, including Mohandas Gandhi. More conservative members joined the movement and eventually Sanger was seen as too radical. By 1942, she had effectively retired from the movement. Months after ***Griswold v. Connecticut*** made contraception legal in Connecticut, Sanger died in Tucson.

FURTHER READING

Kennedy, David M. *Birth Control in America: The Career of Margaret Sanger.* New Haven: Yale University Press, 1970.

Sanger, Margaret. *Margaret Sanger: An Autobiography.* New York: Norton, 1938.

SCHLAFLY, PHYLLIS STEWART (b. 1924)

Writer, conservative activist. Phyllis Stewart was a studious child from a conservative St. Louis family. Well educated, she earned a J.D. from Washington University Law School and an M.A. in political science from Radcliffe College.

Schlafly entered politics in the 1940s with her first job as a researcher in Washington, D.C. She also worked as a congressional campaign manager and as the editor of a financial institution's newsletter. After marrying lawyer John Fred Schlafly, Jr., in 1949, she took time off from her job to do volunteer work for various Christian organizations. However, she reentered politics in the 1950s, conducting research for Senator Joseph McCarthy.

In 1952 and 1970, Schlafly ran unsuccessfully for the U.S. Congress. During that time, she published several books on conservative issues and held the position of first vice president of the National Federation of Republican Women. She also established a women's organization now known as the **EAGLE FORUM**. In 1972, Schlafly made her first attack on the **EQUAL RIGHTS AMENDMENT** and founded the **NATIONAL COMMITTEE TO STOP ERA**, arguing that the ERA would destroy the traditional family structure.

Schlafly published *The Power of the Positive Woman*, her response to feminism, in 1977. In 1985 President Ronald Reagan appointed her to the Commission on the Bicentennial of the U.S. Constitution. She was voted Illinois Mother of the Year in 1992. Schlafly continues to be one of the leading conservative activists in the country.

SCHROEDER, PATRICIA SCOTT (b. 1940)

Member of the House of Representatives for 24 years and the first woman to serve on the House Armed Services Committee. As chair of the House Select Committee on Children, Youth and Families from 1991 to 1993, she was responsible for the passage of Family and Medical Leave Act.

Schroeder was born in Portland, Oregon, in 1940. During World War II, she and her family moved frequently as they followed her father, a flight instructor for the Army Air Corps. She went on to attend the University of Minnesota and Harvard Law School, where she was one of 15 women in a class of more than 500 men. While at Harvard, she met and married classmate Jim Schroeder. After graduation, they moved to Denver to raise their two children.

She challenged an incumbent Republican for Colorado's First Congressional District seat in 1972. While she was recruited by a group of Democratic liberals in Denver, the Democratic National Committee refused to support her campaign that year. Her grassroots campaign led to her victory with 52 percent of the vote. She was an early supporter of legalized abortion and sponsored legislation making it a federal crime to prevent access to abortion clinics. She considered running for president in 1987 but then withdrew from the race. After leaving Congress in 1997, she went on to become president and chief executive officer of the Association of American Publishers, a national trade organization for U.S. book publishers.

TRAILBLAZERS

"Amazing Grace" Brewster Hopper, mathematician and an officer in the United States Navy, has been described as a futurist in the world of computing. She was born in New York City in 1906, the eldest of three children, and received her Ph.D. from Yale University in 1934. She married educator Vincent Foster Hopper in 1930, and took a job teaching mathematics at VASSAR COLLEGE (see Volume 2). In 1943 she joined the WOMEN ACCEPTED FOR VOLUNTEER EMERGENCY SERVICE (WAVES) where she was assigned to the Bureau of Ordnance Computation Project at Harvard University. Hopper's first job was to learn how to program the electromechanical Mark I computing machine; she later produced the first manual that outlined the operating principles of computers.

Hopper worked with early machines that were crude by twenty-first-century standards, yet she anticipated in her programming most of the capabilities that digital computers now have. She was one of the first software engineers and her best-known contribution to computing was the invention of a program or "compiler" that translates English language instructions into the language with which the computer is programmed. She is credited with coining the term "bug" when she traced an error in the Mark II computer to a moth trapped in a relay.

After the end of WORLD WAR II and the death of her husband, Hopper joined the Harvard faculty as a research fellow and worked concurrently for a series of high-technology firms. She also remained in the Navy where, in December 1983, she was promoted to commodore and later admiral.

Admiral Hopper was buried at Arlington National Cemetery with full military honors on January 7, 1992.

SCIENCE AND TECHNOLOGY

In fields historically dominated by men, women have numbered among the leaders in the twentieth century. The past few decades, moreover, have seen a new emphasis on science and technology education for girls.

Fanny Cook Gates, Ph.D. (1872–1931), was an educator as well as physicist, and advanced understanding of radioactivity through her discoveries about the exact nature of radioactive materials. Anna J. Harrison, Ph.D. (1912–1998), became the first female president of the American Chemical Society in 1978.

Surgeon and anesthesiologist Virginia Apgar, M.D. (1909–1974), made a mark on the field of INFANT AND CHILD HEALTH in 1959 by inventing the system now called the "Apgar Score." This score, still in use today, evaluates the developmental status and health of newborn infants. The chemist Gertrude Belle Elion, M.S. (1918–1999), eventually held 45 patents on processes and materials connected to her research. Best known for her discovery of a number of antiviral and cancer drugs, in 1988 she shared with two others the Nobel Prize in medicine.

Women have been important participants in the American space program as well. In 1983, astrophysicist turned astronaut, writer, and educator **Sally Ride**, Ph.D. (b. 1951), became the first woman to go into space. Women have also accepted the same dangers in the field as have men. Judith A. Resnick, Ph.D. (1949–1986), was a biomedical engineer with NASA and went to space on two missions; she was among the seven who died in the explosion of the space shuttle *Challenger* in 1986. Currently, more than two dozen women are qualified astronauts or candidates undergoing training.

Engineer, industrial psychologist, and mother of 12, Lillian Moller Gilbreth (1878–1972) was called the "Mother of Modern Management" and helped pioneer the field of "efficiency engineering." In 1926 Gilbreth also became the first woman member of the American Society of Mechanical Engineers. As a consultant she worked with firms like General Electric to improve the design of kitchens and household appliances; she also created new techniques to help disabled women accomplish common household tasks.

According to the Society for Women Engineers, the percentage of women among those who earned doctoral degrees in engineering rose from 2 percent in 1975 to 12 percent in 1997, and the women among employed engineers rose from 5.8 percent in 1983 to 10.6 percent in 1999. Significant numbers of women now work as aerospace, chemical, civil, electrical, industrial and mechanical engineers. Organizations like the Advocates for Women in Engineering, Science and Mathematics (AWESM) founded in 1994 work to improve opportunities for women in all branches of mathematics and science.

See also: Aviation and Space; Business and Industry; McClintock, Barbara; Sager, Ruth; Taussig, Helen Brooke.

FURTHER READING

Gornick, Vivian. *Women in Science: Portraits from a World in Transition.* New York: Simon & Schuster, 1983.

Wasserman, Elga. *The Door in the Dream: Conversations With Eminent Women in Science.* Washington, DC: Joseph Henry Press, 2000.

SEXUAL HARASSMENT

A form of sex discrimination that violates Title VII of the Civil Rights Act of 1964. It is defined as unwelcome sexual advances; requests for sexual favors; and other conduct of a sexual nature that explicitly or implicitly affects an employee's employment, interferes with an individual's work performance or creates an intimidating, hostile, or offensive work environment. Women did not have a term to describe the experience of sexual harassment until 1976, although the fight against sexual harassment began with the women's movement in the early 1960s. Women fought to be hired in positions that had been reserved for men and to be paid the same as men for equal work. As more women entered the workforce, new positions were established that challenged gender roles.

Many feminists, including Catherine MacKinnon, fought for legal remedies for harassment. In the 1980's, the courts ruled that sexual harassment was unacceptable in the workplace. Supreme Court Justice Clarence Thomas' 1991 confirmation hearings brought national attention to the issue. During the hearings, law professor Anita Hill came forward with allegations that Thomas had sexually harassed her during his tenure as head of the Equal Employment Opportunity Commission. Despite outrage from women's groups, he was later confirmed.

The nationwide discussion uncovered instances of sexual harassment in schools, although the Education Amendments of 1972 (Title IX) prohibits sex discrimination, including sexual harassment. Many universities established rules prohibiting harassment. The military also set new standards after studies found instances of sexual harassment.

FURTHER READING

Altbach, Philip, ed. *Sexual Harassment and Higher Education: Reflections and New Perspectives.* New York: Garland Publishing. 1998.

Shaw, Victoria. *Coping with Sexual Harassment and Gender Bias.* New York: Rosen Publishing. 1998.

SEXUAL REVOLUTION

A movement that changed American society in the 1960s and 1970s. The invention of the birth control pill, the rise of feminism, and the growing acceptance of commercial pornography stimulated an unprecedented period of sexual openness and experimentation in American society.

The most influential of these changes for women was the Food and Drug Administration's approval of the contraceptive pill. The pill came on the market in 1961, priced between $10 and $15, making it affordable for most women. By reducing the possibility of pregnancy, women could plan pregnancy and enjoy sex as men had been able to do. The 1960s refrain "Make Love, Not War" symbolized the approach to the complicated events of the time, as well as the beginning of the sexual revolution. The combination of student protests, counterculture movements, and the emerging women's movement created the context for a break with the values of the past that confined women's sexual pleasure to heterosexual marriage. It was not until the 1970s that women's sexuality outside marriage became widely accepted.

The sexual revolution reduced barriers and spawned the political mobilization of the gay and lesbian movements. Reforms in the legal and medical regulation of sexuality kept the revolution alive, including the legalization of abortion in 1973 with ***Roe v. Wade***. Society and the media began to incorporate the changes. Fashion, television, music, and movies changed, and sexuality became more visible than before. Women's **MAGAZINES**, such as *Cosmopolitan*, began printing sex tips for women in the 1960s, which would have been unheard of in the past.

SHALALA, DONNA (b. 1941)

United States secretary of health and human services under President Bill Clinton. Born in Cleveland, Ohio, Shalala received her Bachelor's degree from Western College for Women in 1962, and volunteered for the Peace Corps. After spending two years teaching in Iran, she began graduate studies at Syracuse University, and got her Ph.D. in Public Affairs in 1970. Over the next ten years she divided her time between college teaching (at New York's Baruch College and Columbia University) and public service, serving as the director and treasurer for New York City's Municipal Assistance Corporation during the city's economic crisis of the 1970s and working in the Carter administration from 1977 to 1980 as assistant secretary at the Department of Housing and Urban Development.

In 1980, Shalala was appointed president of New York City's Hunter College. From there she moved, in 1988, to be chancellor of the University of Wisconsin-Madison—the first woman to head a major state university. She served as secretary of Health and Human Services for Bill Clinton's entire eight-year term, the longest anyone has held that post. She was in charge of Clinton's **WELFARE** reform process; she also extended health insurance for children, raised child immunization levels to the highest level in history, and brought about reforms at the Food and Drug Administration and the National Institutes of Health.

SIEBERT, MURIEL (b. 1932)

Financial analyst, first woman to purchase a seat on the New York Stock Exchange. Born in Cleveland, Ohio, Siebert attended Western Reserve University briefly, and in 1954 moved to New York with $500 to look for a job. Hired at first as a trainee, she quickly proved herself at several brokerage firms and rose to partnership at one. Yet when, in 1967, she decided to apply to purchase a seat on the Stock Exchange, she was laughed at by many brokers, and nine of the first ten she asked refused to sponsor her application. She would not give up, and was finally elected to membership on December 28, 1967. For the next ten years she remained the only woman on the exchange. In 1969 she started the first brokerage firm to be headed by a woman, Muriel Siebert and Company, which is still flourishing. In 1975 she announced its transformation into one of the first discount commission houses. Wall Street reacted with hostility, but Siebert led her company to remarkable success.

In 1977 Siebert became New York's first woman Superintendent of Banking. While many banks nationwide were going bankrupt, Siebert implemented new measures, and no New York banks failed. In 1982 she resigned to campaign for U.S. Senate; she placed second of three candidates in the primary, and returned to the leadership of her company.

In 1990 Siebert started the Siebert Entrepreneurial Philanthropic Plan (SEPP) to share with charities half her firm's net profits from new securities underwitings. In the next ten years SEPP's donations to charities across the nation totaled $4 million dollars.

Siebert has received offers from companies interested in purchasing her firm, but she feels that as long as it is the only woman-owned firm on Wall Street she must hold on to it.

SILKO, LESLIE MARMON (b. 1948)

NATIVE AMERICAN poet and novelist whose writing illuminates the images and beliefs of her Laguna Pueblo heritage.

Silko grew up at Laguna Pueblo with a mixed heritage of Laguna Pueblo, Mexican, and Anglo cultures. Her father managed the Marmon Trading Post, a business established generations earlier by her Anglo relatives who moved to the area after the Civil War and married Laguna women. Silko grew up listening to family stories of her people and learning about Laguna culture from her great-grandmother. She graduated with honors in English from the University of New Mexico in 1969 and began the American Indian Law Program there. She soon switched to the school's Creative Writing Masters program.

Silko began to receive wide public attention when she published *Ceremony* in 1977. The novel describes a returning veteran's path to recovery with the assistance of a tribal healer. The book communicated Laguna ideas on health, war, healing, and cosmology without romanticizing or victimizing the subjects. Her poetry, short stories, and other novels have continued these and other native themes. Silko received a MacArthur Foundation Fellowship to support her writing. She has also held a variety of teaching positions. Today she is a Professor of English at the University of Arizona in Tucson.

SMEAL, ELEANOR CUTRI

(b. 1939)

Feminist leader. Eleanor Marie Cutri was born in Astabula, Ohio. She graduated from Duke University in 1961, and in 1963 earned a master's degree in political science from the University of Florida. That same year she married Charles R. Smeal, an engineer.

During the 1960s, she became active in the women's movement for equal rights in Pennsylvania, campaigning for equal opportunity for girls in **ATHLETICS**. In 1970, she joined the **NATIONAL ORGANIZATION FOR WOMEN** (NOW) and served two terms as president of the organization (1977–1982). She became president for a third term from 1985 to 1987.

As president of NOW, Smeal led the fight for ratification of the **EQUAL RIGHTS AMENDMENT**. The amendment was eventually defeated, but Smeal had more success with her campaign to ensure that women continued to have the right to an **ABORTION**. This right was recognized by the U.S. Supreme Court in 1973, although it is still under attack by many conservatives.

In 1987 Smeal cofounded the Feminist Majority Foundation, which is dedicated to securing leadership roles for women in government, education, and business. The foundation helps organize feminist groups on campuses to support choices for women, including reproductive choices, career choices, and leadership choices.

SMITH-LEVER ACT

A federal law that created a partnership between the U.S. Department of Agriculture and colleges in order to provide instruction and practical demonstrations in agriculture and home economics. Signed by President Woodrow Wilson in 1914, the Smith-Lever Act created the Cooperative Extension Service, the function of which was to provide informal education that would help people help themselves. This education was focused on finding solutions for the various problems people—particularly residents of rural areas—encounter on a daily basis. The Smith-Lever Act was named for two congressmen, Senator Hike Smith of Georgia and Representative A. F. Lever of South Carolina.

The Smith-Lever Act provided significant resources and opportunities for advancement to women. The science of **HOME ECONOMICS**, far from focusing only on homemaking skills, provided an avenue for women into higher **EDUCATION** and positions of leadership in education, government, and industry.

SMITH, BESSIE (1894–1937)

Blues singer, born in Chattanooga, Tennessee. Her parents died when Bessie was a child, and she was raised by her sister. Eventually she joined the vaudeville show in which her brother Clarence performed and began dancing and singing. The great blues singer **MA RAINEY** was a member of the same show and probably influenced Smith's singing style.

Smith became a singing sensation in the South and, in 1921, traveled to Philadelphia, Pennsylvania. Two years later she made a recording for Columbia Records that featured two songs: "Gulf Coast Blues" and "Down Hearted Blues." The record became a hit and made Smith a star. During the 1920s she was earning as much as $2,000 a week, making her the nation's most successful black star. She sang with jazz great Louis Armstrong and others.

During the 1930s, blues began to decline in popularity and Smith's career went downhill. She began a comeback, but in 1937 was killed in an automobile crash.

SMITH, MARGARET CHASE

(1897–1995)

Political leader. Margaret Madeline Chase was born on December 14, 1897, in Skowhegan, Maine. She completed high school in 1916, became a schoolteacher, and in 1930 married Clyde H. Smith, a newspaper owner. Mrs. Smith served on the state Republican committee in Maine, then became her husband's secretary after he was elected to the U.S. House of Representatives in 1936.

Congressman Smith died in 1940, and Margaret Smith won a special election to take his seat in Congress. She served until 1948, when she was elected to the U.S. Senate. Smith is best known for her denunciation in 1950 of the campaign waged by fellow Republican Senator Joseph McCarthy of Wisconsin to brand many government officials, writers, and artists as communists. Smith issued her declaration of conscience in a speech in the Senate. It said, in part, "I think that it is high time for the United States Senate and its members to do some soul-searching . . . on the manner in which we are using or abusing our individual powers and privileges."

In 1964, Smith became the first woman to have her name placed in nomination for president by the Republican Party at its convention. She lost to Senator Barry Goldwater. During her long career, Margaret Smith was admired for her outspokenness and courage. She retired from the Senate in 1973 and was awarded the Presidential Medal of Freedom in 1989. She died on May 29, 1995.

SOCIAL SECURITY ACT

In early 1935, President Franklin D. Roosevelt introduced his proposed Social Security bill, a key part of the **NEW DEAL**, to both houses of Congress. **FRANCES PERKINS**, Roosevelt's secretary of labor, played a key role in the writing of the bill that would become the Social Security Act. President Roosevelt signed the act into law on August 14, 1935. In addition to several provisions for general welfare, the new act created a social insurance program designed to pay workers age 65 or older a continuing income after retirement.

Grace D. Owen of Concord, New Hampshire, received the lowest social security number, 001-01-0001. She applied for her number on November 24, 1936, and was issued the first card, typed in Concord. On January 31, 1940, the first monthly retirement check was issued to Ida May Fuller of Ludlow, Vermont, in the amount of $22.54. Miss Fuller, a legal secretary, retired in November 1939 and started collecting benefits in January 1940 at age 65. She lived to be 100 years old, dying in 1975.

The original act provided only retirement benefits, and paid them only to the worker. In 1939, two amendments made a fundamental change in the program, adding two new categories of benefits: payments to the spouse and minor children of a retired worker (dependents' benefits) and survivors' benefits paid to the family in the event of the premature death of a covered worker. This change transformed Social Security from a retirement program for workers into a family-based economic security program.

Today, nearly every American has Social Security protection, either as a worker or as a dependent of a worker. When the program began in 1935, most women did not work outside the home. The role of women is far different now. Nearly 60 percent of all women are in the nation's workforce, and many women work throughout their adult lives. Thus, although Social Security always has provided benefits for women, it has now taken on added significance. More women work, pay Social Security taxes, and earn credit toward a monthly income for their retirement. Working women with children earn Social Security protection for themselves and their families. This means monthly benefits for a woman and her family if she becomes disabled and can no longer work. If she dies, her survivors may be eligible for benefits.

Although some women choose lifetime careers outside the home, many women work for a few years, leave the labor force to raise their children, and then return to work, and some women choose not to work outside their homes. They usually are covered by Social Security through their husbands' work and can receive benefits when he retires, becomes disabled, or dies. Whatever a woman's situation, it is important that she knows exactly what Social Security coverage means to her.

SOCIAL WORK

The organized activities intended to improve the social conditions of a community and its disadvantaged members. The term itself was coined in 1890 to describe professionals who conduct investigations, secure treatment for the ill, provide care for abused or neglected children, and extend material aid to the poor, disabled, and elderly. While social workers concentrated at first on short-term solutions to specific problems, they soon expanded their focus beyond practical action. Academic researchers began to identify and analyze the ongoing social and economic structures that underlay problems, and activists agitated for new state and federal legislation.

Today, social work is rooted in the philanthropic activism of such nineteenth-century figures as **JANE ADDAMS** (See Volume 2). **WELFARE** became a federal program in 1935 during the **GREAT DEPRESSION** when Congress enacted **AID TO DEPENDENT CHILDREN** (ADC), a program focused primarily on widows, orphans, divorced or deserted mothers, and their children. **EDITH ABBOTT**, an economist and the dean of the School of Social Service and Administration at the University of Chicago from 1924 to 1942, stressed the responsibility of the state in relation to social problems and helped create generations of professional social workers. Her sister, **GRACE ABBOTT** was an advocate for children as director of the Child Labor Division of the United States **CHILDREN'S BUREAU** from 1931 to 1934.

The professional organization of social workers is the National Association of Social Workers, headquartered in Silver Spring, Maryland, which publishes the quarterly magazine *Social Work Journal* and the *Encyclopedia of Social Work*.

TRAILBLAZERS

In 1946 Emily Greene Balch (1867–1961), peace advocate, social reformer, and economist, was awarded the Nobel Peace Prize for her service to world peace and woman suffrage, the first Bostonian to be so honored.

Balch graduated from BRYN MAWR COLLEGE (see Volume 2) with its first graduating class, in 1889. She went on to study poverty alleviation policy in France, on a European Fellowship from Bryn Mawr. On her return, in 1892, she became involved in the SETTLEMENT HOUSE MOVEMENT (see Volume 2). She founded Denison House, Boston's first settlement house, and lived there as its head for several months. In 1896, convinced of the need to recruit for the social reform movement among the new generation of femal college students, she joined the faculty of WELLESLEY COLLEGE (see Volume 2), to teach economics and sociology. An outstanding teacher who insisted on the importance of firsthand observation she was also active in the SUFFRAGE MOVEMENT and in the campaigns for racial justice and against CHILD LABOR.

After the outbreak of WORLD WAR I she was among the delegates from 12 countries attending an International Congress of Women in 1915 at The Hague, Netherlands. She campaigned aggressively against America's entry into the war, and along with JANE ADDAMS helped to found the Women's International League for Peace and Freedom in 1919. Her activism cost her her position at Wellesley. She took an editorial position at the liberal weekly *The Nation*, and continued to work for peace. During WORLD WAR II, however, Balch's fundamental commitment to human rights overcame her PACIFISM. She spoke out against Hitler's anti-Semitism and domination of Europe, and supported America's entry into the war after the bombing of Pearl Harbor in 1941.

STEIN, GERTRUDE (1874–1946)

Writer, art collector, critic. Although Gertrude Stein was born in Allegheny, Pennsylvania, she spent the first five years of her life traveling in Europe with her parents. She moved several times upon returning to the United States, finally settling in Baltimore with her grandmother. Stein graduated from Harvard Annex (now Radcliffe College) in 1898 and attended Johns Hopkins Medical School until 1902, but decided against becoming a doctor. Her writings from this time reveal depression caused by her inability to fit into traditional women's roles.

Stein and her brother, Leo, moved to Paris in 1903. In Europe, they began collecting modern art. Their home became a meeting place for artists and intellectuals such as Pablo Picasso, Ernest Hemingway, and Mabel Dodge Luhan, the woman who published Stein's early poems. Eventually Stein moved into a new home with her partner, Alice B. Toklas. The couple remained together until Stein's death from cancer in 1946.

The poetry, drama, and prose of Gertrude Stein attempted to do for writing what cubism and abstraction did for painting. Her unique style is characterized by unconventional plot and dialogue, elimination of punctuation and capitalization, and repetition of words and phrases, as exemplified through her most famous poem, which states: "A rose is a rose is a rose." Her numerous works included fiction, poetry, biography, nonfiction, and opera.

STEINEM, GLORIA (b. 1934)

Feminist, author, editor, and public speaker. Gloria Steinem gained prominence in the **WOMEN'S LIBERATION MOVEMENT** in 1971 as a cofounder of ***Ms.*** magazine with Dorothy Pitman Hughes and co-founder of the **NATIONAL WOMEN'S POLITICAL CAUCUS** with **BELLA ABZUG**, Shirley Chisholm, and **BETTY FRIEDAN**.

Born in Toledo, Ohio, Steinem spent her early childhood traveling with her family through the Midwest as her father bought and sold antiques. Her mother, who suffered from depression, remained a distant figure. At the age of ten, Steinem's parents split up, and she assumed the role of primary caretaker for her mother. Despite this early adversity, Steinem did well in school and read voraciously. Her diligence paid off when Smith College accepted her for undergraduate work in 1952. The college shaped Steinem's intellectual development and provided a secure and stable environment in which to thrive. She studied politics and developed her writing skills with the student newspaper. She graduated from Smith College in 1956, spent the next two years in India, and then returned to the United States to look for work as a journalist.

Steinem found employers reluctant to hire women, but she persisted, and by the early 1960s she published articles as a freelance writer. It took several more years to establish her reputation in political reporting. In 1968, she was one of the few women in television writing when the political assignment she had been working for came through. She was assigned to follow George McGovern's presidential campaign. That work led to her next position as an editor with *New York* magazine. From that point forward, she selected her own stories to cover the political movements of the decade. She also began to identify herself as an activist for women's rights.

Steinem wanted to bring the issues of racial justice and sexuality to the forefront of the women's movement. Her friend and colleague, Dorothy Pitman Hughes, an African-American activist, had profoundly influenced her ideas on feminism. They traveled the country together on speaking tours and raised the central issues of the women's liberation movement: legalized abortion, equal pay for equal work, and passage of the **EQUAL RIGHTS AMENDMENT**. By 1971, they began to plan the publication of their own magazine and in January 1972 the first issue of ***Ms.*** magazine—a forum for feminist issues—was published.

Steinem also published several books including a collection of her essays *Outrageous Acts and Everyday Rebellions* (1983), a biography of Marilyn Monroe, and *Revolution from Within: A Book of Self-Esteem* (1992) that examined the critical role of self-esteem in young girls' development. She continues to write and speak on women's issues today.

STREISAND, BARBRA (b. 1942)

Singer and actress. Barbra Streisand was born in Brooklyn, New York, to Diana and Emmanuel Streisand in 1942. Just a year and a half later, Emmanuel died, leaving Diana to care for Barbra and her brother, Sheldon.

Streisand left home as soon as she graduated from high school to pursue her dream of being a singer and actress. Her big break came when she was cast as Miss Marmelstein in the Broadway show *I Can Get It for You Wholesale.* She was such a hit that the part was expanded for her, and new songs were added. In 1963, she married Elliott Gould, who was the male lead in *Wholesale.* The couple had one son and divorced in 1971. In 1964, Streisand opened on Broadway in the musical *Funny Girl* and released *The Barbra Streisand Album,* which remained at the top of the popular music charts for 18 months and sold more than a million copies.

In 1968, Streisand starred in the movie version of *Funny Girl,* for which she won an Academy Award as best actress. In 1983, with the film *Yentl,* Streisand became the first woman to produce, direct, write, and star in a major motion picture. Since then she has produced, directed, and starred in three other films, *Nuts, Prince of Tides,* and *The Mirror Has Two Faces.*

Streisand is one of only a few individuals to win an Oscar, a Tony, an Emmy, and a Grammy.

In 1998, Streisand married actor James Brolin. Four concerts in September 2000 were promoted as "the end of her concert career."

SUBURBANIZATION

The development of residential areas beyond city centers that increasingly took place after the end of **WORLD WAR II**. The creation of suburbs was a central part of late-nineteenth century urban planning. The "baby boom" of the 1950s and 1960s, however, along with the prosperity of the postwar years, contributed to their explosive growth in the United States.

The growth of the suburbs was fueled by the promise of a middle-class lifestyle. Americans envisioned well-educated people living in comfortable, single-family homes surrounded by lawns, gardens, and trees. Suburbanites had easy access to good schools and shopping, as well as to city employment opportunities and cultural attractions.

The social impact of the suburbs has long been the subject of debate. Some argue that the suburbs developed as close-knit, supportive communities, and others argue that they enforce a stultifying sameness and destroy cultural diversity.

In the suburbs of postwar America, the women tended typically to be **HOMEMAKERS**, staying at home, caring for their breadwinner husbands and their children, and building a social structure largely comprised of other women like themselves. Volunteerism in schools, churches, and youth groups was the norm rather than the pursuit of a career. More recently, with the rise in numbers of women working outside the home, this stereotype is no longer as prevalent. In the 1990s, the traditional suburban housewife took on a new identity as a political force, as "soccer moms" ran for elective office and fought for environmental and educational causes.

SUFFRAGE MOVEMENT

The movement to guarantee women the right to vote. It may have begun with **ABIGAIL ADAMS**'s 1776 appeal to her husband John to remember the ladies' in the laws he was writing for the second Congressional Congress (see Volume 1). But the appeal for woman **SUFFRAGE** did not become a battle until the **SENECA FALLS CONVENTION** of 1848 (see Volume 2). The battle was waged through many disappointments for the rest of the nineteenth century. The only real successes were achieved in the West: By 1900, women had the vote in Wyoming, Colorado, and Utah.

In 1890, the movement, which had split over the strategy question of whether to pursue suffrage state by state or work at the national level for a constitutional amendment, found unity by

TRAILBLAZERS

A daughter of suffragist ELIZABETH CADY STANTON and abolitionist Henry Brewster Stanton, Harriot Eaton Stanton Blatch (1856–1940) was a leading women's rights activist and, in 1907, founder of the Equality League of Self-Supporting Women (later renamed the Women's Political Union).

After graduating from Vassar College in 1878, she traveled and studied in Europe and assisted her mother in compiling the monumental *History of Woman Suffrage* (1881). She married an Englishman, William Henry Blatch, in 1882 and lived in England for the next 20 years. Inspired by the success of women's rights organizations among factory workers and mill hands there, she returned with her family to the United States in 1902 and immediately began working for the political enfranchisement of women. The Equality League attracted some 20,000 women workers and launched a massive drive for a New York state constitutional amendment for woman SUFFRAGE. Their efforts in New York inspired suffragist campaigns in a number of other states.

As Blatch and her organization shifted their attention to the drive for a federal suffrage amendment, the Women's Political Union became the nucleus of the NATIONAL WOMAN'S PARTY. Working as an administrator of government agencies during WORLD WAR I, Blatch enlisted the support of American women on behalf of the U.S. military effort. After the war, she continued her work for women's rights and was active in the Progressive and Socialist parties. Her autobiography, *Challenging Years*, was published in 1940. She died later that year, on November 20.

America's first large-scale suffrage parade took place in New York City in 1913.

merging into the National American Woman Suffrage Association (NAWSA), with **Elizabeth Cady Stanton** as president and **Susan B. Anthony** as vice president (see Volume 2). Stanton retired in 1900, and was succeeded by **Carrie Chapman Catt**. But a new generation of suffragists called for new tactics. Harriot Stanton Blatch, Stanton's daughter, returned from a trip to England inspired by the militance of the "suffragettes," and founded the Equality League of Self-Supporting Women in 1907 to reach out to the working class. In 1910, the League (now renamed the Women's Political Union) organized America's first large-scale suffrage parade, in New York City. In 1913 another militant, Alice Paul, organized a parade in Washington that drew 8,000 women. Later suffrage demonstrations led to arrests and to hunger strikes by jailed activists.

The Western states had continued one by one to grant woman suffrage, Nevada and Montana in 1914. In 1916, Montana elected suffragist Jeannette Rankin to the House of Representatives, its first woman member.

The entry of the United States into **World War I** in 1917 changed the situation. Grateful for the support of women's organizations for the war effort, President Woodrow Wilson became more favorably disposed to their cause. In 1918 he issued a statement supporting a federal amendment, and Jeanette Rankin opened debate on the amendment in the House of Representatives. The amendment passed in the House relatively easily, but it did not pass in the Senate until 1919. The suffragists began their ratification campaign, which finally bore fruit with the ratification of the **Nineteenth Amendment** in 1920.

T

TAFT, HELEN HERRON

(1861–1943)

Wife of William Howard Taft, the twenty-seventh president of the United States. Helen "Nellie" Herron was born in Cincinnati, Ohio, to Harriet and John Herron.

Herron met William Taft in 1883 and married him three years later. They had three children. William always credited his wife with pushing him into politics and encouraging him to strive for more prestigious appointments and political offices. While he would have been content to pursue a career in the law, Taft encouraged him to accept various political appointments, including the governorship of the Philippines. She pushed him to make his successful run for the presidency in 1908.

Taft was delighted to be first lady, and immediately began a round of entertaining. Soon after moving into the White House, however, she suffered a stroke that left her partially paralyzed. Still, during her term as first lady, Nellie was responsible for importing the Japanese cherry trees that surround the Reflecting Pool in Washington, as well as for constructing a bandstand in Potomac Park where the Marine Band gave regular concerts.

After serving one term in office (1909–1913), the Tafts retired to New Haven, where William taught constitutional law at Yale University. They returned to Washington in 1921, when he was appointed chief justice of the Supreme Court. William died there in 1930 and Helen in 1943.

TAN, AMY (b. 1952)

Novelist. Amy Tan was born in Oakland, California, in 1952, to Chinese immigrants John and Daisy Tan. During Tan's adolescence, she and her mother were in almost constant conflict because Amy wanted to be as American as possible, while her mother wanted her to behave like a good Chinese daughter.

Tragedy struck the Tan family when Amy was fourteen years old. Both her father and her brother Peter died of brain tumors. After her father's death, Tan discovered that she had three half sisters living in China, children of her mother's first marriage. Tan was surprised to find that she felt jealous of her sisters. "Three obedient daughters, beautiful girls who could speak Chinese. I was crushed. I didn't see them as anything but competition."

In 1986, Daisy Tan was hospitalized with heart problems. During her stay in the hospital, she and Amy had an argument during which Daisy told her daughter, in broken English, "You don't know little percent of me." Tan promised herself that if her mother survived, she would try to get to know her better. In 1987, the pair traveled to China to visit Daisy's other daughters. Tan was delighted to find that she and her half sisters had a great deal in common.

Amy Tan's novel *The Joy Luck Club* was a *New York Times* best-seller longer than any other Chinese-American novel.

Out of this trip came Tan's first novel, *The Joy Luck Club* (1989), a series of interconnected stories about four Chinese mothers and their four American daughters. The novel stayed at the top of the *New York Times* best-seller list longer than any other Chinese-American novel had before. Since then, Tan has written three other novels: *The Kitchen God's Wife* (1991), *The Hundred Secret Senses* (1995), and *The Bonesetter's Daughter* (2001). She has also written children's books.

TARBELL, IDA MINERVA (1857–1944)

Journalist who exposed business corruption. Ida Minerva Tarbell was born in Hatch Hallow, Pennsylvania, the daughter of an oil producer and a teacher. The family moved to Titusville, a booming oil town, where Ida attended public school and, as a teenager, became enamored of the women's rights movement. In 1880 she earned a bachelor's degree in biology from Allegheny College, where she was one of only five women students.

Unable to secure employment as a biologist, she worked as a teacher and began her career in **JOURNALISM** on the staff of *The Chatauquan* monthly. While studying feminist history in Paris, she supported herself by writing for several American **MAGAZINES AND PERIODICALS** (see Volume 2). Her articles came to the attention of the young publisher Samuel S. McClure, who asked Tarbell to write for his new publication, *McClure's*. Excelling at the brand of scholarly journalism promoted by McClure, she penned a serial biography of Napoleon that was a success for the magazine and was later published as a book. Her biographical articles on Abraham Lincoln, collected in book form in 1900, were based on new documentation that separated fact from myth.

In 1900, Tarbell began researching the Standard Oil Company, and her investigative reports on company practices began appearing in the magazine two years later. Embittered because Standard Oil's practices had forced her father out of business, Tarbell scoured legal documents and interviewed oil industry executives in building her case against the company. Her indictment,

TRAILBLAZERS

The first English-language woman writer to be awarded the Nobel Prize for literature (1938), Pearl S. Buck was cited by the Swedish Academy for "her rich and truly epic descriptions of peasant life in China and for her biographical masterpieces." Of her more than 70 books—including novels, story collections, biographies, poetry, drama, children's literature, and translations from Chinese—the most popular was *The Good Earth* (1931). The first novel of her "House of Earth" trilogy, it recounts the changing fortunes of the peasant family of Wang Lung. Awarded a Pulitzer Prize in 1932 and made into a major motion picture in 1937, the best-selling book introduced traditional Chinese life and customs to mainstream American audiences.

Pearl Comfort Sydenstricker was born on June 26, 1892, in Hillsboro, West Virginia. Her parents were Southern Presbyterian missionaries on furlough from their station in China at the time of her birth. The family returned to China three months later, and Pearl spent most of the next 40 years of her life there. She was taught at home by her mother and a Chinese tutor, and spoke English and Chinese from childhood. After four years at Randolph-Macon Women's College in Lynchburg, Virginia, she returned to China in 1915 and married an agricultural economist, John Lossing Buck, two years later. The couple moved to a village in rural Anhui Province, which was the inspiration for *The Good Earth* and other works; they had one daughter and adopted another. From 1920 to 1934 they lived in Nanjing, where they both held university teaching positions.

In the 1920s, Buck began publishing stories and articles in such magazines as *Nation* and *Atlantic Monthly*. Her first novel, *East Wind, West Wind*, appeared in 1930, followed by *The Good Earth*. Twin biographies of her mother, *The Exile*, and father, *Fighting Angel: Portrait of a Fighting Soul*, appeared in 1936 and contributed to the reputation that earned her the Nobel Prize. The Bucks moved permanently to a farm in Green Hills, Pennsylvania, in 1934, where they adopted six more children. She published her autobiography, *My Several Worlds*, in 1954 and died on March 6, 1973.

which appeared in book form as *The History of the Standard Oil Company* (1904), revealed how the company had manipulated rates and policies to dominate the oil industry. Tarbell's work, a classic of "muckraking" journalism, increased public awareness of company practices and convinced Congress to pass antitrust legislation to break Standard Oil's monopoly. In 1911, the U.S. Supreme Court ordered the dissolution of the Standard Oil holding company.

Later, writing for *The American Magazine*, Tarbell focused her attention on the subject of tariffs, which she opposed as another advantage for corporate trusts. In a series about the women's movement, Tarbell stressed her disapproval of the **SUFFRAGE MOVEMENT**. Her many books include an autobiography, *All in the Day's Work* (1939). Tarbell died on January 6, 1944, in Bridgeport, Connecticut.

TAUSSIG, HELEN BROOKE (1898–1986)

Physician best known as the pioneer of a surgical technique that saves the lives of "blue babies." Helen Brooke Taussig was born into an academic family in Cambridge, Massachusetts, on May 24, 1898. After earning her B.A. from the University of California at Berkeley in 1921, she attended Harvard Medical School but left because of gender discrimination; she earned her M.D. from Johns Hopkins University in 1927. In 1930, the same year in which she went deaf, Taussig became head of the Johns Hopkins pediatric heart clinic, a position she held until her retirement in 1963.

In the early 1940s, Taussig began studying an infantile heart malformation called pulmonary stenosis (constriction of an artery), which prevents the baby's heart from pumping oxygen into the blood, causing the fatal "blue baby" syndrome. In collaboration with surgeon Alfred Blalock, Taussig developed an artificial duct—called the Blalock-Taussig shunt—that could be surgically implanted to carry blood past the constricted part of the artery. The surgery, which the team first performed in 1944, would save thousands of lives. Taussig's research spurred the development of other surgical treatments for heart disorders.

Throughout her life, Taussig worked to protect the health of woman and children. In 1962 she began alerting doctors to the dangers of thalidomide, a tranquilizer prescribed for pregnant women that was later proved to cause serious deformities in newborns. Her efforts led the United States to ban the drug.

In recognition of her lifelong achievements, Taussig received numerous honors, including the Medal of Freedom in 1964 and election as the first female president of the American Heart Association in 1965. She was killed in an automobile accident on May 21, 1986.

TAYLOR v. LOUISIANA

A 1975 Supreme Court case that affirmed the right to trial by a jury that fairly represents the population of the community. In 1971, Billy J. Taylor was tried and convicted of aggravated kidnapping in St. Tammany Parish in Louisiana. He appealed his conviction because there were no women on the jury that convicted him. At the time, few women in Louisiana served on juries because of a state law that removed a woman from the jury pool unless she had submitted a written declaration agreeing to serve.

When Taylor's case reached the Louisiana Supreme Court, the judges ruled that the state law was constitutional and refused to overturn Taylor's conviction. Taylor appealed this decision to the U.S. Supreme Court. The case was heard in October 1974 and decided in January 1975. The Supreme Court ruled 8 to 1 in Taylor's favor, saying that a system based on the idea "that it would be a special hardship for each and every woman to perform jury service" was not justifiable. The Court further ruled that Taylor had been deprived of his Sixth Amendment right to trial "by an impartial jury drawn from a fair cross section of the community."

The Court noted that Taylor did not have to be a member of the affected group (women) to bring a case alleging discrimination against that group. The Court added that while juries must be drawn from pools that fairly represent the community, any particular jury of 12 did not have to be representative.

TELEVISION AND RADIO

Communications media that changed the way people learned about news and the ways they were entertained. Early radio programs included some targeted to the female listener. The National Broadcasting Company (NBC) became the first radio network in 1926. By the 1930s, household product advertisers sponsored serialized dramas, or soap operas, in the daytime hours. The narratives of these shows often revolved around female characters. By 1932, radio networks had begun their own news gathering operations. In local news radio of the 1940s and 1950s, women's voices were seldom heard except on specific "women's news programs," which included mostly housekeeping tips.

Television sets went on sale in New York in 1938. By 1941, the first year of television's commercial operation, 10,000 sets had been sold. The Federal Communications Commission (FCC) put news experimentation on hold during World War II, although by 1945, NBC created an organization for production of news film. By the early 1950s, the networks produced 15-minute news programs.

In the 1940s, the radio soap operas made the transition to daytime television. Another program format that proved popular with women was the call-in talk show, most often associated with *Donahue,* which started in 1967 in Dayton, Ohio. Aired during a time of political and social unrest and change, by 1980 it was carried on 218 stations around the country. In 1986, *The Oprah Winfrey Show* went national, not only beating *Donahue* in the ratings, but also becoming the third-highest rated show in syndication.

Prime-time programming did not appeal to women in the same way. Most 1950s and 1960s comedy shows focused on the family, where women were seen mainly as wives, mothers, and daughters. Programs in the 1970s introduced independent, working women. Some of the programs continued into the 1980s and 1990s, yet many television producers during this period created family sitcoms that banished women to roles as mothers. Feminist Susan Faludi has suggested that the programming of network television in the 1980s was an attempt to get back to those earlier stereotypes of women, thereby countering the effects of the women's movement. In 1970, the **NATIONAL ORGANIZATION FOR WOMEN** formed a task force to study and change the derogatory stereotypes of women on television, and in 1972 it challenged the licenses of two network-owned stations on the basis of their sexist programming and advertising practices. In

TRAILBLAZERS

Comedic actress and businesswoman Lucille Ball was one of the first women to ever run a multimillion dollar corporation. While she was successful in business, she is better known for her comedic timing which became the model for other female comedians to follow.

Ball was born in 1911 in suburban New York. She left high chool at 15 to attend a New York City drama school and befan modeling under the name Diane Belmont. This lead to her appearance in more than 60 films by the late 1940s. During that time, she performed in the musical "Too Many Girls," with popular Cuban band leader, Desi Arnaz. The two married and in 1950, they formed their own production company, Desilu Productions. Its first production was "I Love Lucy," which starred the couple. By the end of the 1950s, Desilu had became a powerful corporation, producing such hit TV shows as "Star Trek" and "Mission Impossible."

Ball and Arnaz divorced in 1960 and Ball bought out her husband's half of their business. She starred in "Here's Lucy," from 1962 until 1974. In 1967, she sold Desilu Productions for $17 million. Ball married again in 1968 to Gary Morton. Morton, a former comedian, worked with Ball to help create Lucille Ball Productions. In the late 1970s and early 1980s, Ball made sporadic, guest-star appearances on television. She died in 1989.

1984, the first cable network for women, Lifetime, was launched.

When it came to television news operations, few women were seen on-air prior to 1970. This changed due to the FCC's affirmative action rule which required women be treated equally as employees. More women were hired as news reporters and anchors through the 1980s and 1990s, although few rose into management ranks.

See also: Walters, Barbara; Winfrey, Oprah; "Women and the Media," p. 26.

TENAYUCA, EMMA

(1916–1999)

Labor organizer who raised the political awareness of Mexican-American workers. Tenayuca was one of 11 children born to a poor family in San Antonio, Texas. She grew up in her grandparents' home in an integrated neighborhood on San Antonio's West Side, where she learned about the struggles of working people. Tenayuca joined the Communist Party in 1937 and was active in the Worker's Alliance of America, an organization founded in 1933 to aid those unemployed during the **Great Depression**.

In 1938, San Antonio's pecan shellers went on strike when their wages were cut in half. At the time, pecan shelling was the city's largest industry. Because of her prominence in several labor organizations, Tenayuca was asked to represent the shellers in negotiations with company owners. The strike lasted several months and turned violent. Eventually the Texas Industrial Commission held hearings on the strikers' grievances, and wages were returned to prestrike levels.

On August 25, 1939, during Tenayuca's appearance at a meeting at San Antonio's Municipal Auditorium, about 5,000 anticommunist protesters attacked the building. The police kept Tenayuca safe, but afterward she was the victim of death threats and was unable to find work. Tenayuca left San Antonio, ending her activity in the labor movement, and settled in California, where she received her teacher certification from San Francisco State College in 1952. In 1974, Our Lady of the Lake University awarded her a master's degree in education. Tenayuca taught reading until her retirement in 1982.

TITLE VII

The section of the Civil Rights Act of 1964 that prohibits discrimination in employment based on race, color, religion, sex, or national origin. The original text of Title VII did not include the word "sex." The ban on employment discrimination was added almost as an afterthought, just before the bill was voted on in the House of Representatives. In fact, many historians have noted that the addition of the word "sex" to the text of Title VII was part of an attempt to scuttle the Civil Rights Act, not an attempt to gain equality in the workplace for women. Representative Howard W. Smith of Virginia, an opponent of the Civil Rights Act, acting at the behest of the **National Women's Party**, proposed that the word "sex" be added because he assumed that more people would vote *against* the legislation if equal employment for women was at issue. A debate followed, which was later referred to as "ladies day in the House" because some of those present treated the idea of employment equality for women as a joke.

Opponents of equal employment opportunity for women included people who regarded women as inferior or unfit for the world of business. But labor unions, many politicians, and many women also opposed workplace equality because they feared it would end protective legislation. During the early years of the twentieth century, reformers had fought long and hard to pass legislation that limited the hours women could work and the amount of weight they could be required to lift. While these laws did protect many women from exploitation by unscrupulous employers, they were also used to prevent women from taking higher-paying jobs.

Despite the addition of the word "sex" to Title VII, the legislation did pass, helped along by Congresswoman Martha Griffiths (D-MI). Title VII was signed into law by President Lyndon Johnson on July 2, 1964.

After the passage of the Civil Rights Act, the **Equal Employment Opportunity Commission** (EEOC), which was created to enforce its provisions, did not enforce the ban on gender discrimination. Representatives of state commissions on the status of women were so dissatisfied with the EEOC and the national commission that they created an organization to work for equality in other ways. As a result, the **National Organization for Women** (NOW) was formed to put pressure on the EEOC to enforce the law.

Over the past four decades, Title VII has helped women on the journey toward equity in career advancement. It has also been interpreted as prohibiting sexual harassment, allowing women redress behavior in the workplace that demeans or threatens them.

See also: Weeks v. Southern Bell.

TITLE IX

A section of a federal law, passed in 1972, that bars discrimination in federally funded educational programs, including **athletics**.

> ***No person in the United States shall, on the basis of sex, be excluded from participation in, be denied the benefits of, or be subjected to discrimination under any educational program or activity receiving federal financial funds.***
>
> —Title IX (1972)

When this legislation was before Congress, colleges, coaches, and some members of Congress warned that the law would lead to such "evils" as unisex locker rooms and the destruction of sororities and fraternities. After the law was passed, high schools and colleges complained that boys' sports would be penalized if athletic programs for girls received equal funding.

Under presidents Ronald Reagan and George H.W. Bush, Title IX enforcement was lax. A Supreme Court decision in *Grove City College v. Bell* (1984) also weakened the law by ruling that Title IX did not cover entire institutions but only programs that were federally funded. However in 1988, Congress passed the Civil Rights Restoration Act, which outlawed sexual discrimination for the entire institution if any part of the institution receives federal funds, and restored Title IX to its original scope. In 1992, the U.S. Supreme Court ruled in *Franklin v. Gwinnett County Public Schools* that victims of sexual discrimination could be awarded monetary damages. This decision put teeth into Title IX and led to many changes in funding, admissions policies, and educational choices that benefit women.

Although there are still inequities, Title IX has had a very positive impact on opportunities for women. Many more women participate in sports today—nearly ten times more than before Title IX. Women's enrollment in law schools has increased from 6.9 percent to nearly 50 percent at many colleges, and pregnant students are allowed to remain in school.

TOMLIN, LILY (b. 1939)

Actress and comedian. Lily Tomlin was born Mary Jean Tomlin in Detroit, Michigan, in 1939. She attended Wayne State University, where she was a premedical student until she discovered the theater, at which point she began acting and first developed one of her signature characters,

"The Tasteful Lady." Lily left college in her junior year and moved to New York City, where she worked in cabarets and clubs. In 1969 she joined the cast of the television series *Rowan & Martin's Laugh-In*. Characters such as the child Edith Ann and the adenoidal telephone operator Ernestine made Tomlin a star.

After *Laugh-In* Tomlin did several television specials, for which she won Emmy Awards in 1973, 1975, and 1981. Tomlin has also won two Tony Awards, one in 1977 for *Appearing Nitely*, her first Broadway show, and one for *The Search for Signs of Intelligent Life in the Universe* in 1985. She has appeared in several films, including *Nashville, 9 to 5, All of Me,* and *The Kid*.

Tomlin is recognized as a supporter of feminist causes and gay rights.

TRAILBLAZERS

Pauline Newman emigrated from Lithuania to the United States in 1901, when she was just 11 years old. She got a job at the Triangle Shirtwaist Factory but left before the deadly fire. Her letters detailed conditions at the factory and explained why workers were willing to accept such unpleasant conditions.

When Newman got her job at Triangle, the foreman told her that she was lucky to work in a place with plenty of business year-round. The workday began at 7:30 A.M. and was supposed to end at 6:00 P.M., but on most days workers were required to put in as many as three hours of overtime. Newman noted with irony that the company gave workers "a piece of apple pie for supper instead of additional pay" for the extra hours they worked. The workweek was often seven days long, and Pauline earned only a dollar and a half a week. She pointed out that it did no good to protest against these conditions—anyone who objected was fired and replaced by another willing immigrant who needed the money to support a hungry family. Newman also noted that friendships among the workers kept people at exploitative jobs.

Like many other young children, Newman worked as a "cleaner," trimming threads off shirtwaists. The shirts were stored in high cases, tall enough for all the underage children to hide in when the inspectors came by to check on working conditions. Employees were constantly watched by supervisors and penalized with deductions from their paychecks if they stayed too long in the rest room or came to work a minute late.

Newman's account of her experiences in the factory was eventually published in a Jewish newspaper called *The Forward*. "In a small way," she said, "I became the voice of the less articulate young men and women with whom I worked and with whom later I was to join in the fight for improved working conditions and a better life for us all."

By the time of the fire, Pauline had become an organizer for the International Ladies' Garment Workers Union and was no longer working in the factory. She became the ILGWU's first full-time organizer, founded the union's health center and served as its first director, and acted as an advisor to the U.S. Department of Labor.

TRIANGLE SHIRTWAIST FACTORY FIRE

On Saturday, March 25, 1911, at 4:40 in the afternoon, a fire broke out at the Triangle Shirtwaist Factory, located on the eighth floor of a ten-story building at the corner of Greene Street and Washington Place in New York City. Many of the workers in the building had gone home by that hour, but there were still about 600 people in the building, mostly girls and young women working as seamstresses making shirtwaists, a popular ladies' garment. A spark from one of the sewing machines may have set fire to the oil that was used to lubricate the moving parts, but no one is sure. However the fire started, it spread with deadly speed, igniting the garments hanging from the ceiling and the fabric scraps that littered the floor.

The building did not have enough staircases, and the elevator cables soon burned through. Only one fire escape existed—which melted during the fire; the doors opened inward (which made opening them difficult amid the crush of people), and none of the young women had ever practiced a fire drill. Within minutes, desperate young women began hurling themselves out of windows on the eighth, ninth, and tenth floors onto the pavement below. Others were pushed by coworkers who were trying to escape.

The Triangle Shirtwaist Factory fire caused more than 100 deaths, but it led to reforms that improved safety in the workplace.

Many of the bodies fell to the ground wrapped in flames. When the fire department arrived, they held blankets and nets for the women to jump into, but these proved too weak to hold the weight of bodies falling from such a height—the victims simply fell through to their deaths. Because the fire department's ladder only reached to the sixth floor, women threw themselves out the windows trying to reach the ladder.

The fire department extinguished the fire within a half hour. In addition to the 50 or 60 bodies that lined the streets, firemen found many people horribly burned inside the building, some still sitting at their machines. The elevator shaft alone held 30 bodies. Experienced firefighters and police officers said they had never witnessed such a scene. The dead numbered 146, including 125 young women.

The Triangle fire has gone down in history as one of the worst industrial fires of the century, but it also led to reforms that improved workplace safety. The commission established to investigate the fire advocated new laws that gave greater power to the New York fire commissioner to enforce safety codes.

TRUMAN, ELIZABETH VIRGINIA WALLACE (1885–1982)

First lady, wife of Harry S Truman, the thirty-third president of the United States. Elizabeth Virgina "Bess" Wallace was born in Independence, Missouri, the daughter of David and Madge Wallace. She met Harry Truman in the fifth grade and graduated with him from Independence High School in 1901. They were married in 1919, just after Harry's discharge from the army following **WORLD WAR I**. They had one child, Mary Margaret.

The young family moved to Washington, D.C., in 1934, when Harry Truman was elected senator from Missouri. When he was appointed chairman of the Senate Special Committee to Investigate the National Defense Program, Bess joined his staff as a clerk.

In 1944, Harry Truman was elected vice president. When President Franklin Roosevelt died in office in April 1945, Truman became president. Bess was unprepared for the role of first lady, but she is remembered as one of the hardest working White House hostesses. She was scrupulous about answering all her mail and was much loved for her down-to-earth attitudes. She served as first lady from 1945 to 1953.

When Bess Truman was asked by a reporter what she and the president would do after he retired, she said, "Return to Independence." This was exactly what they did. After he died in 1972, she continued to live in the same house until her own death at the age of 97.

U

UAW v. JOHNSON CONTROLS

A 1991 U.S. Supreme Court case that was important in the history of American law for banning discrimination against women in the workplace. It began in 1982, when the Johnson Controls Corporation, which manufactured batteries, announced a "fetal protection policy" for its workforce. Under this policy, all women except those who could provide medical evidence that

TRAILBLAZERS

At the beginning of the twentieth century, many of the women working in the garment industry were Jewish immigrants; most of these were between 16 and 25 years old. The women worked in terrible conditions for 12- and 15-hour days. Often, the factories where women cut cloth, sewed buttons, hems and trimming were filthy, and it was easy to contract communicable diseases. Many women, paid a paltry wage, would take work home and work into the night, often with the help of their children and other family members.

Conditions were terrible across the garment industry, and on June 3, 1900, the United Brotherhood of Cloak Makers New York union made a public call for a convention to improve conditions. Only 11 delegates showed up to represent seven East Coast unions, but the International Ladies' Garment Workers Union was established with Herman Grossman as the first president. The first years were ineffective and lifeless, and membership was unremarkable.

However, this changed in 1909 when female garment workers went on strike. The women were exploited under a subcontracting system in which wages were paid to a man in charge of a group of women, who would then distribute the wages to the women under him. Many women earned less than three dollars a week in this system. Women were docked for broken needles, and sometimes for the cost of electricity in the factory. In addition, sexual harassment was rampant. At a meeting organized to address the shirtwaisters' grievances, a working girl named Clara Lemlich stood up and called for a general strike. From November 15 to December 25 of 1909, the women of one of the largest shirtwaist factories, the Triangle Shirtwaist Factory, went on strike. In the course of the strikes, women were harassed and abused on the picket line and 723 women were arrested. This strike rejuvenated the garment labor unions.

In 1920, David Dubinsky, one of the best-known of the ILGWU's presidents, fought communist takeover of the union. He won, but membership dipped. However, under President Franklin Roosevelt's labor policies, the membership swelled again to 300,000 in 1942. Later, the ILGWU fought against issues like the mass exportation of labor to other countries and illegal sweatshops with inhumane conditions.

In 1995, the ILGWU's 125,000 members merged with the Amalgamated Clothing and Textile Workers' Union to form the Union of Needletrades, Industrial and Textile Employees (UNITE).

they could not bear children were barred from jobs that exposed them to high levels of lead, an element known to cause birth defects. The United Auto Workers (UAW), the labor union representing the women, challenged the policy, arguing that it violated **TITLE VII** of the 1964 Civil Rights Act because it discriminated against women in the workplace.

The problem faced by Johnson Controls and its employees was a difficult one. On the one hand, the company could be sued if employees' children were born with birth defects caused by the company's manufacturing processes. On the other hand, the jobs from which the women were excluded were relatively high-paying ones that traditionally had been held by men. Further, male workers exposed to high levels of lead ran the risk of fathering children with birth defects, yet the company did not exclude them from the jobs in question. In sum, the company's policy seemed to suggest that women were marginal workers whose primary role was to bear children. The U.S. Supreme Court agreed and in its 1991 decision struck down the Johnson Controls policy, saying that it violated laws against gender discrimination.

UNIONS, LABOR

Much as it had in the last decades of the nineteenth century, the participation of women in the labor movement during the early twentieth century was centered in the textile and clothing industries. Mainstream unions, representing skilled and industrial workers, were established chiefly for the benefit of white men. The **AMERICAN FEDERATION OF LABOR** (AFL), formed in 1886, excluded women, blacks, and immigrants for decades. Nevertheless, women made major contributions to the rise of unions in America.

The establishment of the International Ladies' Garment Workers

Union (ILGWU) in 1900 and the International Workers of the World (IWW), a socialist union for unskilled workers (many of them immigrants), in 1904 helped provide the organizational strength to force labor reforms on behalf of women. The ILGWU negotiated the settlement of a strike by New York City shirtwaist workers in 1909–1910—called the "Uprising of the 20,000"—that raised wages, reduced working houses, and provided for the resolution of disputes by impartial arbitration. The **TRIANGLE SHIRTWAIST FACTORY FIRE** of 1911, which killed 146 workers, led to additional reforms and stricter building codes. Both events attracted new union members, many of them women. In 1912, the IWW took control of a walkout by textile workers—many of them women and immigrants—in Lawrence, Massachusetts, and organized the famous "Bread and Roses" strike. The job action forced union recognition and also attracted many new members.

Another important organization in the twentieth-century women's labor movement was the Women's Trade Union League (WTUL), established in 1903 to educate women about the advantages of union membership, raise awareness about the exploitation of women workers, and support demands for reform. Founders included **JANE ADDAMS** (see Volume 2), Sophinisba Breckinridge, **ALICE HAMILTON**, **FLORENCE KELLEY**, and **MARY KENNEY O'SULLIVAN** (see Volume 2). The WTUL was a major participant in the American labor movement until its demise in 1950.

Today, women make up nearly half of the U.S. labor force and represent a powerful voice in the labor movement. Millions belong to industrial, trade, and white-collar unions in the **AMERICAN FEDERATION OF LABOR AND CONGRESS OF INDUSTRIAL ORGANIZATIONS (AFL-CIO)**, including the **AMERICAN FEDERATION OF TEACHERS**, the **AMERICAN ASSOCIATION OF UNIVERSITY WOMEN**, and the Union of Needletrades, Industrial and Textile Employees. Among the many prominent women in the contemporary labor movement are **LINDA CHAVEZ-THOMPSON**, elected executive vice-president of the AFL-CIO in 1995, and **DOLORES FERNANDEZ HUERTA**, a cofounder (with Cesar Chavez) and leader of the United Farm Workers of America. The specific interests of women in unions and the labor force are addressed by such organization as the Coalition of Labor Union Women, founded in 1973 and comprising women from more than 60 U.S. and international unions, and the **NATIONAL ORGANIZATION FOR WOMEN**.

URBANIZATION AND IMMIGRATION

Each time there has been a wave of immigration to the United States, the results have been most visible in urban centers. As the immigrants' geographic point of origin shifted throughout twentieth century, the urban areas most affected shifted as well. Most immigrants have chosen to locate either in their port of entry or in another city with an established community from their country of origin.

Politics and economics have long driven immigration. People often chose to leave their homeland for life in the United States because of the freedom and opportunities this country seemed to offer. Women who immigrated were critical to keeping family bonds, preserving an ethnic heritage and identity, and oftentimes helping financially to support the family.

The first large influx into the United States in the twentieth century was from southern and eastern Europe, as part of a trend that had begun in the 1880s. This group, unlike previous immigrants, looked distinctly different from most native-born Americans and were considered "less desirable" immigrants by many native-born and first-generation Americans. The sheer volume of new immigrants—40 million arrived between 1880 and 1914—made them easy targets for racial, ethnic, and job discrimination, even as they helped staff factories in an increasingly urban and industrialized economy. Two-thirds of all immigrants were single men between the ages of 14 and 30; the exception was Jewish families fleeing religious persecution and ethnic killings in Russia. For women immigrants, the journey meant an opportunity for a whole new life, free from many of the restrictions of family and community. Female immigrants often found employment in female-dominated surroundings, with many established immigrants eager to share knowledge about their new country.

Although much attention on immigration focuses on the Northeast, there was also significant immigration on the West Coast and across the U.S.–Mexican border. Immigration from Japan and China was extremely difficult: Congress had passed increasingly discriminatory and restrictive rules regarding immigration from these countries in the late 1800s and early 1900s. The San Francisco earthquake and fire of 1906, however, destroyed many official records, thus making it easier for illegal immigrants, particularly women who came as prostitutes or picture brides, to suddenly become "legitimate" citizens.

Immigration declined during **World War I**, and in the early 1920s Congress passed several laws to limit the number of people permitted to enter the country each year. Legislation in 1921 and 1924 set quotas on immigrants, based proportionally on their presence in the United States. To limit immigrants from "undesirable" areas—specifically southern and eastern Europe—quotas were based on 1890 census data, before the big wave of immigration from these areas began. Thus, quotas were highest for countries in northern and western Europe, and lowest for those in southern and eastern Europe. The one loophole was the lack of regulation on migration from other countries on the North American continent. As a result, immigration from Mexico and Canada continued without restriction and cities in the Southwest continued to grow, with a heavy Mexican influence, particularly in border towns in Texas and California.

There was little immigration during the **Great Depression** and **World War II** because of the lack of job opportunities, the cost of travel, and the difficulties and hazards of travel. In addition, during the Depression many immigrants decided to return to their native countries rather than stay in America; in the 1930s more people left the nation than entered it. In World War II, immigration patterns and rules altered. A 1942 agreement between the United States and Mexico, the *Bracero* Program, permitted Mexicans to enter the country for a limited amount of time. Although the hope was that many would find employment as migrant farmworkers, most Mexicans who arrived under this program got factory jobs. For women, the family dynamic began to shift, as women became wage earners even as they sought to retain their native cultures.

The limited immigration during the war was more than compensated for by the internal migration spurred by war production. Companies converted their factory processes for wartime production or increased their size to accommodate defense contrasts. Approximately 10 percent of the population moved during World War II, either because they were searching for better economic opportunities or because they were assigned to one or another base for military service. The war provided a bonanza of job opportunities for women in industries that were never previously open to them, such as automobile and naval construction. Cities such as Los Angeles, Detroit, and Seattle grew quickly as a result of the influx of people working in defense industries. Japanese-American women, with forced internment, found their traditional gender roles subverted in the camp environment.

After the war, immigration picked up again, and migration continued. Quotas were relaxed, partly to atone for the government's refusal to admit Jews during the war. However, given the financial problems of most European countries in the immediate postwar years, most immigration occurred only when American relatives sent money or tickets to their families overseas. Cities and suburbs grew in the early postwar years. The advent of the air conditioner for home use, a national highway system, and continued defense work helped spark a boom in the Southwest.

Immigration quotas were relaxed in the 1960s. Quotas by country shifted to quotas by hemisphere. New laws also created exemptions for people to join their spouses, children, or parents. The biggest shift in immigration occurred in the 1970s, with increased immigration for Mexico, Central America, and Asia, especially from the war-torn countries of Vietnam, Cambodia, and Laos. This wave of immigration affected cities on the West Coast, including Seattle, San Francisco, Los Angeles, and Portland. Like most immigrants at the beginning of the century had, these new immigrants chose to settle where communities had already been established.

Data from the 2000 Census reveal that immigration patterns have, on the whole, remained unchanged. New York, Chicago, Los Angeles, Minneapolis, and other large urban areas continue to attract many immigrants, with ethnic groups migrating to established enclaves—as the Hmong and many West Africans have done in Minneapolis, for example. More immigrants arrive from Central and South America than from Europe, and immigration from Africa and Asia continues to increase, stretching the limits of the country-by-country quota (or lottery system) for a green card.

Gwen Kay

FURTHER READING

Danquah, Meri Nana-Ama, ed. *Becoming American: Personal Essays by First Generation Immigrant Women.* New York: Hyperion, 2001.

Gabaccia, Donna. *From the Other Side: Women, Gender, and Immigrant Life in the United States, 1820–1990.* Bloomington: Indiana University Press, 1995.

V

VANDERBILT, GLORIA

(b. 1924)

Artist, actress, and author. Gloria Vanderbilt, the great-great-granddaughter of the railroad financier Cornelius Vanderbilt, was born in 1924. Her father, the avid sportsman Reginald Claypool Vanderbilt, died when she was just 18 months old, and at the age of ten she became the the subject of a custody battle between her mother, Gloria Morgan Vanderbilt, and her paternal aunt, Gertrude Vanderbilt Whitney. Her aunt won custody by proving that Gloria's mother was an alcoholic who had pilfered her daughter's inheritance. Gloria was taken not only from her mother but also, and perhaps more importantly, from her nurse, Dodo, the only person she really trusted.

Vanderbilt studied drawing and painting, and in 1952 was featured in a one-woman exhibition in New York. Many other exhibits of her paintings followed. Vanderbilt worked as an actress in television plays in the 1950s and also created her own clothing and cosmetics line. She is credited with creating the first designer blue jeans.

Her personal life has been tragic. Her first three marriages ended in divorce, and her fourth, to actor and writer Wyatt Cooper, was happy but brief. Cooper died in 1979, leaving Vanderbilt with two sons. In 1988, her son Carter committed suicide at 24. Eight years after his death, Vanderbilt wrote about her despair and recovery in *A Mother's Story* (1996). She believes now that her son's actions may have been the result of a reaction to an allergy medication.

Vanderbilt has written a two-volume autobiography and has contributed articles to many fashion and women's magazines.

VAN KLEECK, MARY

(1883–1972)

Social researcher and reformer. Mary Abby Van Kleeck was born in New York to Robert and Eliza Van Kleeck. She went to public schools in Flushing, New York, and graduated from Smith College in 1904. Just out of college, Van Kleeck conducted research on young women who worked in New York City factories and on **CHILD LABOR**. In 1908, she joined the staff of the Russell Sage Foundation, which supported her research on women's employment for many years and encouraged her to found and direct a department of industrial studies.

During **WORLD WAR I**, Van Kleeck helped to establish labor standards for women working in war industries and was appointed director of the Department of Labor's Women in Industry Service Agency (later the U.S. Women's Bureau). Van Kleeck returned to the Russell Sage Foundation after the war, where she studied employee relations issues.

By the **GREAT DEPRESSION**, Van Kleeck had become a socialist and supporter of Soviet-style socialism, which advocated state ownership of farms and factories. In 1934, she wrote *Miners and Management,* in which she advocated the socialization of all industry. Van Kleeck became interested in international workers' organizations because she believed that the causes of worker problems were global. From 1928 to 1948, she directed the International Industrial Relations Institute. After her retirement from the Russell Sage Foundation, she made an unsuccessful run for the U.S. Senate from New York as the American Labor Party candidate. Her socialist sympathies resulted in her being subpoenaed to testify before Joseph McCarthy's Subcommittee on Investigations in 1953.

Van Kleeck died in Kingston, New York, in 1972, just before her eighty-ninth birthday.

VIETNAM WAR

An undeclared war between the United States and North Vietnam from the early 1960s to 1975. Women, military and civilian, served in Vietnam in almost all capacities: as support staff, in hospitals, on medical evacuation flights, with Mobile Army Surgical Hospital (MASH) units, in operations groups, in information offices, and in untold other clerical, medical, and intelligence positions. All of these women volunteered for duty, mostly in the early part of the war, since women could not be drafted.

The U.S. military cannot say with certainty how many women actually served in Vietnam, but

TRAILBLAZERS

A 21-year-old architecture student at Yale University, the Chinese-American Ohio native Maya Lin (b. 1959) launched her professional career and earned instant celebrity in 1981, when her design was chosen for the Vietnam Veterans Memorial in Washington, D.C. Prompted by an assignment for her class on funerary architecture, the design was selected by a panel of judges from more than 1,400 submissions. Dedicated on November 13, 1982, the memorial features a V-shaped black marble wall inscribed with the names of more than 58,000 U.S. service personnel who died or remain missing from the war in Indochina. The stark, austere design initially drew protests from several groups, but today it is one of the most visited—and moving—landmarks in the nation's capital.

In the years since, Lin has completed a host of other acclaimed projects. Among these are the Civil Rights Memorial (1989) at the Southern Poverty Law Center in Montgomery, Alabama; the Museum for African Art (1993) in New York City; and a giant elliptical clock with moving shafts of light as the hands (1994) in New York's Pennsylvania Station. The daughter of academics—her father is a ceramist and dean of fine arts at Ohio University, and her mother is a professor of literature—Lin has also exhibited large sculptural installations and smaller-scale studio sculptures at a number of museums and galleries.

the most common estimate is 7,500. The women who served included officers as well as enlisted personnel. They ranged from young women in their early twenties with barely two years in the service to career women over the age of 40. The women who went to Vietnam suffered the same hardships as men and were not sheltered from the dangers of combat. However, they were not allowed to fight, nor could they carry weapons to defend themselves—despite having received basic training with M-16 and M-14 assault rifles.

Women also suffered the same poor treatment and indignities as their male counterparts upon their return to the United States. Like many Vietnam veterans, these women have been haunted by their experiences in fighting an unpopular war; they do not feel officially recognized and have been reluctant to seek help. Some have been plagued by symptoms of posttraumatic stress syndrome and exposure to chemicals. Others have hidden their service like a shameful secret.

In the years following the conflict, the United States desperately tried to put Vietnam behind it. Finally dedicated in 1982, the dramatic black granite Vietnam Veterans Memorial includes the names of the eight military women who died in Vietnam. Believing that the wall and other memorials did not sufficiently honor the women who served, Diane Carlson Evans, a former army nurse, founded the Vietnam Women's Memorial Project in 1984. For the first time in America's history, a memorial that honors women's military service was erected in the nation's capital. The multifigure bronze monument, designed by New Mexico sculptor Glenna Goodacre, portrays three Vietnam-era women, one of whom is caring for a wounded male soldier.

FURTHER READING

Gruhzit-Hoyt, Olga. *A Time Remembered: American Women in the Vietnam War.* Navato, CA: Presidio Press, 1999.

Van Devanter, Lynda, and Joan A. Furey, eds. *Visions of War, Dreams of Peace: Writings of Women in the Vietnam War.* New York: Warner Books, 1991.

W

WALKER, ALICE (b. 1944)

Writer. Alice Walker was one of eight children born to Willie Lee and Minnie Tallulah (Grant) Walker, poor sharecroppers living in Eatonton, Georgia. When she was eight, one of Walker's brothers accidently shot her in the eye with a BB gun. She lost sight in one eye and was disfigured by scar tissue around the wound. Ashamed of her appearance, Walker began to withdraw from social contact. Ironically, this period in her life turned out to be important because it led her to become an avid reader and writer. When she was 14, Walker had surgery to remove the scar tissue.

Walker attended Spelman College in Atlanta, Georgia, and then Sarah Lawrence College in Bronxville, New York. After spending a summer in Uganda, Walker discovered she was pregnant. Terrified of her parents' reaction, she had an **ABORTION**, which was followed by a period of intense depression. Later Walker published the poems she had written during this bleak period in a volume entitled *Once* (1968).

Walker's first novel, *The Third Life of Grange Copeland* (1970), tells the story of two generations of African-American men who, brutalized by society, take out their frustrations on the women in their lives. It is a scenario that is repeated in several of Walker's novels, where her female characters are sympathetic while some of her male characters rape and beat women. Despite the protests of African Americans who believe that Walker betrays her race, she refuses to compromise her vision. "It happens," she says. Walker's best-known book, *The Color Purple,* won the Pulitzer Prize in 1983, making Walker the first African-American women to win the award. The novel was also made into a film by Steven Spielberg.

WALTERS, BARBARA (b. 1931)

America's first regular network anchorwoman. Walters was working as host of NBC's *Today Show* when, in 1976, ABC offered her a record million-dollar salary to become coanchor of the network's nightly news program. The deal drew criticism from some male co-workers. Broadcast journalism was at that time a male-dominated field, and men were not earning this much money. Her contract was viewed by many as evidence of the commercialization of TV news.

Walters is perhaps best known for her candid interviews with entertainment celebrities and political leaders. Conducted in cozy, intimate settings and a personal, conversational style, her interviews often lead her subjects to reveal more about themselves than they had expected to. In 1977, Walters arranged the first joint interview with Egyptian President Anwar Sadat and Israeli Prime Minister Menachem Begin. In 1991, she was the first person to interview General Norman Schwarzkopf, who commanded U.S. armed forces in the Gulf War; during the course of the conversation, Schwarzkopf confided that he believed the war had ended too soon. Walters has interviewed every American president since Richard Nixon, as well as countless foreign leaders, movie stars, musicians, and other celebrities.

A native of Boston, Massachusetts, and a graduate of Sarah Lawrence College, Walters began her broadcast career as a producer at WNBC-TV in New York and a writer for CBS News. She joined the *Today Show* in 1961 as a writer and reporter-at-large, and by 1965 she had become assistant host. From 1971 to 1976, while still with the *Today Show,* she hosted her own syndicated series for NBC, *Not for Women Only.* With ABC in 1984, she joined Hugh Downs as cohost of the weekly magazine show *20/20,* helping make it a prime-time hit for nearly two decades.

Among Walters's many professional honors was her 1990 induction into the Academy of Television Arts and Sciences' Hall of Fame as one of "television's most respected interviewers and journalists."

WAR BRIDES ACT

A federal law that facilitated the immigration process for foreign women who married American servicemen during and after **WORLD WAR II**. Specifically, the act—which was passed on December 28, 1945—waived all immigration requirements except for meeting "physical and mental" standards. The legislation expired after three years, in December 1948.

> New York, February 10: *One of the greatest overseas journeys of women and children in history ended today as the quaint* Queen Mary *docked at Pier 90 with 1,666 wives of American servicemen and their 668 children. . . . The ship was met by a neat white Army Transportation Corps vessel aboard which a band played "Roll out the Barrel" and "Here Comes the Bride."*

As many as one million women from Europe and Asia married American servicemen during the 1940s. In 1946, newspapers across the country printed this Associated Press report, detailing the arrival of one group of war brides:

WEEKS v. SOUTHERN BELL

A 1969 appellate court decision that affected protective labor laws. Lorena Weeks, a clerical employee who worked for Southern Bell Telephone Company, applied for a better-paying job as a switchman. She was denied the job because the company said switchmen had to lift equipment that weighed more than thirty pounds. The company further maintained that only men could lift such heavy loads. Thus, the company said, being male was a "bona fide occupational qualification" (BFOQ) for the job. (A BFOQ is a characteristic or ability that is required to do a particular job.)

National Organization for Women (NOW) attorney Sylvia Roberts took the case to the U.S. Fifth Circuit court in 1969, claiming that keeping women from certain jobs was a violation of **Title VII** of the 1964 Civil Rights Act, which forbids discrimination in hiring, firing, promotion, and the terms and conditions of work based on race, sex, or national origin.

The Court ruled in Weeks's favor in 1969. It rejected Southern Bell's assumption "that few or no women can safely lift thirty pounds, while all men are treated as if they can." The justices held that Title VII "rejects just this type of romantic paternalism as unduly Victorian and instead vests the individual woman with the power to decide whether or not to take on unromantic tasks."

Since this ruling, other courts have invalidated protective laws that were originally enacted to protect women from sweat shop conditions but which in modern times have been used to keep women from fairly competing with men for high-pay or high-prestige jobs.

WELFARE

Aid in the form of money for those in need. Linda Gordon, in her book *Pitied But Not Entitled,* notes that the way welfare is structured and administered in the United States has denigrated and marginalized poor women. She notes that women, especially single mothers, have been the primary recipients of Aid to Families with Dependent Children (AFDC), the program that most people associate with welfare in the United States. But, she points out, the government also gives aid in a number of other ways, which are not labeled as welfare, including "home mortgage tax deductions, business expense deductions, medical expense deductions, farm subsidies, corporate subsidies, government college scholarships and loans, capital gains tax limits, Social Security old-age pensions, and Medicare." These kinds of aid tend to benefit men and the middle class. The distinction between welfare and other social-insurance programs, such as "old-age insurance," has led to stigmatizing welfare recipients and to constant attempts to cut such programs out of the federal budget.

The beginnings of modern welfare programs can be traced to the early days of the twentieth century when women's groups sought to provide aid to single women with children, usually widows. By 1920, 41 states had **mothers' pension** laws designed to keep impoverished mothers from having to give up their children. Those who promoted the legislation convinced states of the need for aid by dividing the poor into two distinct classes: the "deserving" and the "undeserving." These distinctions were never very clear, however, and people tended to think of all poor people as somehow responsible for their own situation. And the vast majority of poor people in America have always been women with children.

There was considerable resistance to a federally funded welfare program until the **Great Depression** of the 1930s. As part of the **Social Security Act** of 1935, however, the program first known as **Aid to Dependent Children** was established. Gordon notes that the social insurance programs established by the Roosevelt administration during the depression covered women only as dependents of husbands and fathers. Only Aid to Dependent Children was designed to help single mothers.

Beginning in the 1950s, women on welfare began to demand better treatment. The National Welfare Rights Organization (NWRO), founded in 1966, fought to improve the lot of welfare recipients. Because AFDC was designed to help only single mothers, it was not unusual for social workers to arrive unannounced at the homes of welfare recipients to search for evidence of a man living in the home. If there was evidence, even if the man living in the home was not the father of the children, welfare could be cut off on the basis of the "man-in-the house rule"—the assumption that any man living in the home could and should support the family. Beginning in 1970, however, the Supreme Court made several rulings that helped mothers on welfare. The Court said that welfare benefits could not be arbitrarily cut off without a hearing, that welfare recipients had a right to privacy and their homes could not be entered without warrants, and that only fathers had the obligation to support children.

Between 1950 and 1990 welfare mothers were caught in a contradiction. On the one hand, welfare rules kept women out of the labor force by punishing anyone who earned money by taking away welfare payments. On the other hand, welfare mothers were stigmatized as lazy because they did not work or as cheaters if they worked and tried to hide the extra income.

Over the years many attempts were made to reform the welfare system. During his administration, Richard Nixon pressed for passage of the Family Assistance Plan (FAP), which would have allowed payments to the working poor. There was a great deal of resistance to Nixon's plan from all sides—some saying that the payments were too little and others objecting to federal money being giving to working people. In 1992, Bill Clinton was elected partly on a promise to "end welfare as we know it." In 1996, he signed legislation that requires welfare recipients to look for work and ended guaranteed cash assistance to the poor.

See also: Poverty.

FURTHER READING

Abramovitz, Mimi. *Regulating the Lives of Women: Social Welfare Policy from Colonial Times to the Present.* Boston: South End Press, 1988.

Gordon, Linda. *Pitied But Not Entitled: Single Mothers and the History of Welfare.* New York: Macmillan, 1994.

WEST, MAE (1893–1980)

Film star and writer. Mae West was born in Brooklyn, New York. She began her theatrical career in burlesque at a very young age. In her twenties, she began writing, directing, and acting. Her first Broadway play, *Sex* (1926), resulted in her arrest on obscenity charges. *Diamond Lil* (1928), which she wrote and performed in, was a big hit and made West into a Broadway star.

In 1932, West signed a contract to act in films for Paramount. She insisted on writing her own material, and she created a character for herself who was brazenly seductive and witty—and who always "got her man." Her dialogue was full of sexual innuendo, and her witty one-liners—such as "It's better to be looked over than overlooked"—are still quoted.

Her first starring role was in in *She Done Him Wrong* (1933), which was such a success at the box office that it saved Paramount from being sold to MGM. Other hit films for West included

Mae West wrote her own material and created characters for herself.

I'm No Angel (1933), *Belle of the Nineties* (1934), and *Klondike Annie* (1936). By the mid-1930s, West was the highest-paid woman in America. She was so popular that sailors named the inflatable life jacket after her.

West's witty sexuality brought her detractors as well as fans. The first motion picture code was established partially to restrict West, and as popular tastes became more conservative, West's career declined. West's autobiography, *Goodness Had Nothing to Do with It,* was published in 1959. She died in 1980.

WHARTON, EDITH JONES (1862–1937)

Novelist. Edith Newbold Jones was the only daughter born to a wealthy and socially prominent New York family. She was educated by governesses and tutors in the skills considered at the time to be appropriate for a young lady, but she also read voraciously in the family's extensive library. In 1885, Jones married Edward Robbins Wharton, a wealthy banker many years older than she. The marriage was not a happy one and the couple had no children. Edith took up writing to help her deal with what she called her "moral solitude."

Edith Wharton wrote about independent women making their way in her novels.

Wharton's first major novel, *The House of Mirth* (1905), placed her among the first ranks of American authors. The story of Lily Bart, an independent young woman caught between the modern world and the old New York society, reflected Wharton's intimate knowledge of this group, as did her best-known novel, *The Age of Innocence* (1920), which was awarded the Pulitzer Prize in 1921. Wharton was prolific, publishing more than 50 books, including travel books, collections of short stories, and criticism.

Wharton divorced her husband in 1913. She was living in France at the time and remained there for the rest of her life. During **World War I**, she worked with refugees, at one time feeding and housing six hundred war orphans.

Wharton died in St. Brice, France, at the age of 75. She was a member of the American Academy of Arts and Letters, as well as the National Institute of Arts and Letters.

WILDER, LAURA INGALLS

(1867–1957)

Writer. Laura Ingalls was born in Wisconsin in 1867 to Caroline and Charles Ingalls. The family moved many times during her childhood as her father searched for better farmland. They finally settled in South Dakota.

Because the family moved so much, Ingalls was not able to attend school regularly until she was nearly 13 years old. Still, two months before her sixteenth birthday, she was certified as a teacher and took a position at a school near her home.

When Almanzo Wilder, a young man who had moved from New York in search of good farmland, proposed to her, Laura was reluctant to accept his offer. Having lived on farms her whole life, she knew how hard farm life was for a woman. But she overcame her reservations, and the couple married in August 1885. Unfortunately, her fears were well founded. In the first few years of their marriage the couple encountered many hardships, including the death of a son and a bout with diphtheria from which Almanzo Wilder never fully recovered.

In 1894, the family, which now included her daughter Rose, moved to Missouri, where they raised chickens and fruit on a large farm. Wilder wrote columns about farm life for a Missouri newspaper and also sold articles to *McCall's* and *Country Gentleman.*

Encouraged by her daughter, Wilder began to write about her childhood. Her first book, *Little House in the Big Woods,* was published in 1932 and was an immediate and enduring success, as were the six other "Little House" books.

Laura Ingalls Wilder died in Missouri in 1957. A television series based on her books, *Little House on the Prairie,* debuted in 1974 and can still be seen in syndication.

WILLIAMS, CLAUDINE

(b. 1921)

First woman to become president and general manager of a casino.

Williams grew up near Shreveport, Louisiana, and took her first job at age 12. She helped her mother in the lunchroom finishing table settings and other odd jobs. She continued to work part-time while attending school to help support her mother and sister. By age 15, she talked her way into a job at a new dinner club and learned the table games from her co-workers. During the Depression a good job took priority over her high school education and she left school. Williams continued to learn the gambling business, moved to Houston, and owned her first club by the time she turned 20. Shortly thereafter, she met Shelby

Williams who became her best friend, business partner, and future husband.

While in Texas, Claudine and Shelby Williams followed the development of the gambling industry in Las Vegas and decided to move there in 1964. They bought the Silver Slipper Hotel and Casino, revitalized its business, and sold it to Howard Hughes in 1969. They built the Riverboat Casino (Holiday Casino), also in Las Vegas, and operated it for ten years (1973–83). The Williamses' partnership ensured that they both understood the business operations. When Shelby's health failed, their decades of experience allowed her to assume greater duties in the casino eventually becoming president and general manager, a first in the industry.

Williams became a pioneer once again in 1981 as the first woman in Nevada history to chair a bank board of directors. Williams, who once received a bank loan to build a club by giving only her word as collateral, now led a venture to provide specialized banking services for Las Vegas businesses. Williams has given back to the community that was good to her and her businesses. She is a generous benefactor to numerous organizations and schools, including the University of Nevada at Las Vegas. She wants to ensure that young people have the opportunities for formal education that she had to forego.

WILSON, EDITH BOLLING GALT (1872–1961)

First lady of the United States (1915–1921) and wife of Woodrow Wilson, who served as twenty-eighth president from 1913 to 1921. Edith Bolling was born on October 15, 1872, in Wytheville, Virginia. She received her early education at home, then attended Martha Washington College in Abington, Virginia. In 1896, she married Norman Galt, a well-to-do jewelry store owner, who died in 1908.

Early in 1915, Galt met President Woodrow Wilson, whose wife had died a year earlier. The president and Galt were attracted to each other, and they married on December 8, 1915, at her home. Wilson was reelected president in 1916, and the following year the United States entered **World War I**.

In 1918, after the war ended, Wilson went to France with her husband to attend the peace conference at Versailles. The president believed strongly that a League of Nations might help prevent future wars. On October 2, 1919, while on a campaign swing across the nation to gather support for U.S. entry into the League, the president suffered a stroke.

Wilson was rushed back to the White House, where his wife helped him through the illness. She read many of the important papers coming before him, decided who should be allowed to see him, and for many months, conducted much of the business of the office. The American public never knew the extent of Wilson's illness.

Wilson left the White House in 1921 and died three years later. Edith Wilson died on December 28, 1961.

WILSON, ELLEN LOUISE AXSON (1860–1914)

First lady of the United States (1913–1914) and wife of Woodrow Wilson, who served as twenty-eighth president from 1913 to 1921. Ellen Louise Axson was born on May 15, 1860, in Savannah, Georgia. She graduated from the Rome Female College in Georgia and attended the Art Students League in New York. A gifted painter, she displayed and sold some of her works.

In 1883, Axson met Woodrow Wilson in Rome and the couple married two years later. They had three daughters, Margaret, Jessie, and Eleanor. Meanwhile, Woodrow Wilson pursued an academic career as a professor at Bryn Mawr College in Pennsylvania and then at Princeton University, of which he became president in 1902. Wilson later resigned, was elected governor of New Jersey in 1910, and was elected president of the United States in 1912.

Mrs. Wilson had been actively exhibiting her paintings since 1910, but after her husband's election in 1912 she devoted herself to her duties as first lady. She worked to improve the housing conditions of the poor who lived in Washington D.C., and also established the Rose Garden at the White House. During her husband's first term, Wilson developed Bright's disease (an inflamation of the kidney) and other health problems. She died on August 6, 1914.

WINFREY, OPRAH (b. 1954)

Talk-show host, publisher, and philanthropist. Oprah Winfrey was born to unwed teenage parents in Kosciusko, Mississippi, on January 29, 1954. As a child, she was uprooted several times, first living with her grandmother, then with her mother, and finally with her father. While living with her mother, Winfrey was sexually molested by male relatives.

In 1968, Winfrey settled down with her father in Nashville, Tennessee. At the age of 19, she became the youngest woman and first African-American woman to anchor the news on a Nashville television station. Her next job was as a news anchor in Baltimore, Maryland. When that did not work out, the station asked Winfrey to host a talk show.

After seven years in Baltimore, Winfrey moved to Chicago to host a morning talk show called *AM Chicago*. She was an immediate success, and before long the show was renamed *The Oprah Winfrey Show*. By 1987, Winfrey was the highest-paid performer in show business; by 2000, her show was the highest-rated talk show ever. Over the years, Winfrey has used her show to advance various causes in which she believes. In 1996, for example, she began a book club designed to get her audiences excited about reading. In 1997, she began the Angel Network, which has collected money to fund college scholarships and now also underwrites $100,000 grants to people who "use their lives" to help others.

In addition to her work as a talk-show host, Winfrey has also worked as an actor. In 1985, she played the role of Sophia in *The Color Purple*, a part for which she received nominations for an Academy Award and a Golden Globe. Since then Oprah has acted in several made-for-television movies and in the film version of Toni Morrison's novel *Beloved*, which Winfrey also produced. Winfrey is also a successful businesswoman. In 1986, she founded Harpo Productions ("Harpo" is Oprah spelled backwards), which owns and produces *The Oprah Winfrey Show* and many of Winfrey's other projects. Thus she became one of the few women to own a major studio. In April 2000, she launched her own successful monthly publication, *O, The Oprah Magazine*.

Winfrey is also an educator, social activist, and philanthropist. She has taught a course called "The Dynamics of Leadership" at the Kellogg Graduate School of Management at Northwestern University. As part of her continuing fight against child abuse, she testified before Congress on behalf of the National Child Protection Act of 1991, which came to be called "Oprah's bill." And she has donated large sums of money to various causes and charities, including her own foundation, called Family for Better Lives.

TRAILBLAZERS

The appointment of Tina Brown (b. 1953) as editor of the prestigious *New Yorker* magazine in September 1992 caused a rare stir in the quiet world of publishing. It was not so much that she was a woman and an English citizen—though certainly that rankled some—but that she had earned a reputation for favoring popular culture, contemporary fashion, and commercial content over "serious" magazine journalism. *The New Yorker*, which had earned its reputation on sophisticated, high-brow articles and humor, had been suffering declines in circulation and advertising revenue that led owner Samuel I. Newhouse to seek new blood.

An Oxford graduate, Brown had gone directly from university to Fleet Street, the heart of newspaper and magazine publishing in London. She wrote for the venerable humor weekly *Punch* and other magazines in the mid-1970s and was named editor of *Tatler*, another British magazine institution, in 1979. Having raised the circulation of *Tatler* by 300 percent, she was hired by Newhouse in 1984 to revive his struggling monthly *Vanity Fair* in New York. With her signature blend of contemporary design and popular, youth-oriented content, she succeeded again in reversing the decline of a major publication.

Declaring herself an editor, not a "curator," Brown brought changes to *The New Yorker* that attracted new readers but alienated many long-time subscribers. Photographs and color art were introduced, younger writers were hired, and coverage of current events, popular culture, and contemporary fashion was expanded. The results were mixed: Circulation and advertising revenues increased, but not to the point of profitability. Brown resigned her editorship in 1998 to become chair of a new media venture by Disney's Miramax Films and edit its magazine, *Talk*. She is married to Harold Evans, a publishing executive.

FURTHER READING

Brooks, Philip. *Oprah Winfrey: A Voice for the People.* New York: Prentice Hall, 2000.

WOMANIST

Term coined by the author **ALICE WALKER** to distinguish the differences of **AFRICAN-AMERICAN** women's experiences from what she perceived to be those of middle-class white feminists. In the preface to her collection of essays, *In Search of Our Mothers' Gardens: Womanist Prose* (1983), Walker described womanist as a "black feminist or feminist of color who possesses strength and persistence for personal development."

The theoretical frameworks developed by feminist theorists and **RADICAL FEMINISTS** to explain sexual inequality during the second wave of feminism became too academic and removed from daily life according to Walker. Furthermore, feminist theory did not address the commitment African-American feminists had to the survival of their community—black men and women. The term womanist derives from the word *womanish* used by U.S. southern blacks to describe a girl who "insists on asking questions, demanding answers, and speaking in her own voice." It is the opposite of girlish, however, indicating a seriousness and boldness learned for survival.

The term *womanist* has been widely adopted by women of color.

WOMAN'S PEACE PARTY

Activist group established in Washington, D.C., in 1915 in response to the beginning of **WORLD WAR I** in Europe. The party grew out of a meeting organized by feminist Jane Addams to call for arms limitations, mediation of the European conflict, a solution to economic issues, and a call for woman suffrage. The organization held a meeting in the Netherlands in April 1915 to call for international peace. As the United States entered the war, the group divided as some members turned to war relief and others opposed the war. Later, the remaining group members formed the new Women's International League for Peace and Freedom (WILPF). It sought to encourage "movements to further peace, internationalism and freedom of women." The U.S. branch of the WILPF is the longest-lasting women's peace organization in the United States.

WOMEN ACCEPTED FOR VOLUNTEER EMERGENCY SERVICE (WAVES)

The U.S. Navy's first body of female members. On July 30, 1942, as World War II got under way in earnest, the Navy began allowing women 20 years of age and older to volunteer. (However, no African-American women accepted until 1944.) The first commander was Mildred McAfee, former president of Wellesley College. Woman volunteers attended military training schools and boot camp.

During World War II, around 100,000 WAVES served in a variety of jobs. While many WAVES were assigned administrative or clerical work, other worked in jobs previously reserved for men, such as pilot or weapon instruction, aircraft repair, cryptology, or air traffic control. The Navy also recruited college-educated women with backgrounds in science, mathematics, and engineering to work on planning bombing operations and on the early efforts at computer programming. However, WAVES were not allowed to serve in combat, or overseas until 1944. The 4,000 WAVES who did serve overseas were mostly in Hawaii.

With the passage of the **WOMEN'S ARMED SERVICES ACT** in 1948, the WAVES became a permanent component of the Navy. The name

WAVES handle many of the traditionally male jobs in the U.S. Navy.

WAVES was dropped as an official title in 1972, when restrictions on the jobs that Navy women could hold were lifted and certain male and female units were combined.

WOMEN AIRFORCE SERVICE PILOTS (WASPS)

A military unit established during **World War II** that included the first women to serve in the United States Airforce. More than 1,000 took part in the program. They flew more than 60 million miles and 38 women lost their lives in service.

WASPs underwent the same training as the male pilots, except for acrobatics and combat flying. WASPs were involved in ferrying aircraft, target towing, training gunners, testing new planes, tracking and searchlight missions, simulated strafing, smoke laying, and other chemical missions, radio control flying, basic and instrument instruction, engineering test flying, administrative and utility flying. When the war came to an end, the program was eliminated over a worry that women would take men's jobs. It was not until 1977 that the women were acknowledged as veterans.

WOMEN'S ARMED SERVICES INTEGRATION ACT

1948 law allowing women to serve permanently in the U.S. armed forces. While some women had served in the U.S. armed forces prior to 1948, they were only allowed to serve when the nation was at war. After World War II, several leaders of all-female units championed a more permanent status for women in the military.

The Women's Armed Services Integration Act was written by Senator Margaret Chase Smith of Maine. While it met little resistance in the Senate, it faced considerable opposition in the House, particularly among members of the House Armed Services Committee. After two years of debate, the bill was passed into law and signed by President Harry S Truman on June 12, 1948. The law authorized regular and reserve status for women in the Army, Navy, Air Force, and Marine Corps. It limited number of women in each branch to 2 percent of the total forces and allowed each branch only one female colonel. In 1967 the two-percent cap was lifted, as were many promotional restrictions. By 1998, when the Act's fiftieth anniversary was celebrated, about 200,000 women were serving on active duty, making up 14 percent of the force.

WOMEN'S ARMY CORPS

A military unit that included the first women, other than nurses, to serve in the United States Army.

In May 1941, Congress began consideration of a bill, introduced by Edith Nourse Rogers, that would establish a women's auxiliary army corps (WAAC). The bill stalled until the Japanese attack on Pearl Harbor raised concerns over a potential manpower shortage. The legislation gave WAACs official status but few of the benefits granted to male soldiers. The Director of the WAAC, Oveta Culp Hobby, was assigned the rank of major. WAAC first, second, and third officers served as the equivalents of captains and lieutenants in the regular Army but received less pay than their male counterparts of similar rank.

In July 1943, the "auxiliary" designation was dropped after thousands of women enlisted. From that time forward members of the Women's Army Corps received full U.S. Army benefits. Enlisted women were ranked as master sergeant through corporal and private, the same as their male counterparts. Much of the Women's Army Corps was demobilized along with the rest of the Army starting immediately after V-E Day in Europe. By December 1946, the number of WACs dropped under 10,000. The majority of those WACs held stateside duty and hoped to be allowed to stay in the Army. More than 150,000 women served in the WAC during **World War II**, in North Africa, Europe, and Asia.

The WAC remained a separate unit of the U.S. Army until 1978, when male and female forces were integrated through the **Women's Armed Services Integration Act**.

WOMEN'S BASEBALL LEAGUE

The All-American Girls Professional Baseball League (AAGPBL) operated from 1943 to 1954. It was started by Philip K. Wrigley, the chewing-gum tycoon who had inherited the Chicago Cubs major league baseball franchise from his father. He believed that famous managers, such as Hall of Fame players, would draw fans to the new league. When the league began, the athletes were actually playing fast-pitch softball using an underhand pitching delivery but with changes to make the game faster. After the 1944 season when it became clear major leagues baseball would not be affected by the war, Wrigley sold the AAGPBL to Chicago advertising executive Arthur Meyerhoff. In the first three years after World War II, between two and three thousand fans attended a single game. The AAGPBL peaked in attendance during the 1948 season, when ten teams attracted 910,000 paid fans. However, attendance declined in the following years and the league eventually disbanded.

WOMEN'S BUREAU

An agency established by Congress in 1920 to address issues concerning working women. One of the agency's first victories was the inclusion of women under the **FAIR LABOR STANDARDS ACT OF 1938** which set minimum wages and maximum working hours. As the bureau gained power, more protection was offered to women. It helped to establish skills training, higher wages, and better working conditions for the growing female workforce during **WORLD WAR II**. In the early 1960s, **ESTHER PETERSON** directed the Women's Bureau and helped the **EQUAL PAY ACT** (1963) pass Congress.

The bureau's early studies and publications addressed unique workplace issues faced by women and continues to do so today. The agency studied contingent female workers in the 1980s and child-care options in the 1990s. The bureau has increasingly focused on workers' concerns over balancing job and family responsibilities. It introduced an initiative to encourage employer-sponsored child care in 1982, the establishment of a multimedia Work and Family Clearinghouse in 1989, and advocated passage of the **FAMILY AND MEDICAL LEAVE ACT** OF 1993. In 1994, the Women's Bureau launched the Working Women Count survey through which more than a quarter of a million women told policymakers what they did and did not like about their jobs. The next year, President Bill Clinton accepted a set of 14 policy recommendations designed to address the concerns women raised, such as **CHILD CARE**. The survey also led the Bureau to create the Working Women Count Honor Roll that encouraged employers, organizations, and individuals to implement new policies and programs in the areas working women said they were most concerned about: improving pay and benefits, building the family-friendly workplace, and valuing women's work through training and advancement.

WOMEN'S EQUITY ACTION LEAGUE

A politically conservative offshoot of the **NATIONAL ORGANIZATION FOR WOMEN** (NOW) founded in 1968 by women who did not wish to confront the issue of abortion rights but sought to work for equal opportunities for women in education and employment. Notable members of the organization include attorney Sonia Pressman Fuentes, a founding member of both WEAL and NOW; Lucy Hargrett Draper, who also served as president; Joline Moore Ohmart; and attorney Elizabeth Boyer.

In 1970, WEAL filed a class-action complaint with the U.S. Department of Labor in support of Bernice R. Sandler, who in 1969 challenged discriminatory hiring practices at the University of Maryland. The action culminated in the passage of **TITLE IX**, which bars gender discrimination in education facilities that receive federal funds.

Based in Washington, D.C., WEAL publishes a number of guides (including *Better Late Than Never: Financial Aid for Re-Entry Women Seeking Education and Training*), regional newsletters, and national periodicals, including the *WEAL Washington Report*, the *WEAL National Newsletter*, and a free quarterly national newsletter, *In The Running*, which focuses on sex discrimination in sports.

WOMEN'S INDEPENDENT FORUM

A politically conservative, nonprofit, nonpartisan organization based in Washington, D.C. Established in 1992, WIF dispels the myth that women exist as a single, united, and politically liberal interest group. Like the **WOMEN'S EQUITY ACTION LEAGUE**, WIF eschews the issue of abortion rights, choosing its causes based on what is "best for society as a whole, and not only for 'women.'"

In the past, WIF has filed briefs in several landmark court cases. It supported the Virginia Military Institute in its claim that single-sex colleges were not discriminatory. WIF also argued, in reference to Brown University's allocation of financial resources between men's and women's athletic programs, that it is counterproductive to require absolutely equal opportunities in sports (and athletic scholarships) without considering the level of interest in and demand for a particular sport.

WIF publishes a journal, *The Women's Quarterly,* and a newsletter, *Ex Femina.*

WOMEN'S JOINT CONGRESSIONAL COMMITTEE

Committee of the U.S. Congress founded by suffragist Maud Wood Park (1871–1955) as a means of exerting influence on the federal legislative process. The Women's Joint Congressional Committee (WJCC) evolved from the congressional committee of the **National American Woman Suffrage Association** as a response to the introduction of the **Equal Rights Amendment** (ERA). The ERA was perceived as a threat to the protective labor legislation that members of the NAWSA had fought for years to secure. Before its demise in the 1930s, the membership of the WJCC peaked at 21 member organizations from the original 17.

Among the early successes of the WJCC was the passage of the Sheppard-Towner Act of 1921, authorizing federal aid to states for maternity, child health programs, and welfare. The WJCC also supported the **Cable Act** (1922), which granted married women citizenship regardless of the status of their husbands. As a result of the efforts of the WJCC, presidents Woodrow Wilson and Warren G. Harding appointed women to positions on federal courts and commissions.

WOMEN'S LIBERATION MOVEMENT

A movement started in the 1960s that is often referred to as the second wave of the women's rights movement that began in the nineteenth century and continued with the right to vote. In the 1960s, the emphasis moved to gaining independence in all areas of women's lives.

Supporters came to the women's movement from a variety of paths. Those involved in the civil rights movement began to challenge their own limitations. They questioned why few women held positions of authority in schools, courts, or businesses. Many middle-class white women were drawn into the movement after reading the 1963 best-seller *The Feminine Mystique* by **Betty Friedan** (see Documents), which described their discontent and sense of underutilization. Working women liked the efforts to increase wages and end segregation in jobs.

As women's liberation became a mass movement, many issues and subgroups spun off. The mainstream sector of the movement that focused on legislative reform was the **National Organization for Women**, organized in 1966. This organization sought equality for women in government, private-sector employment, and throughout society. ***Ms.* magazine** was launched in 1972 by journalist and feminist leader **Gloria Steinem** as a feminist publication designed to reach a mass audience. Other sectors included radical **feminism**, which wanted to change the basic elements of power differences between men and women. They reached a nationwide audience with a demonstration at the **Miss America Pageant** in 1968. Perhaps the most far-reaching impact came out of consciousness-raising groups that concentrated on changing aspects of personal, social, and cultural life and dismantling the patriarchal power structure. These groups focused on issues that had not been previously considered political, such as housework, beauty, reproductive rights, violence, and sexuality.

The introduction of the contraceptive pill in 1961 and the fight to legalize **abortion** brought more women into the women's movement. Equal pay legislation was passed and discrimination in the workplace began to be investigated. The first March for Women's Equality took place in August 1970 in New York, demonstrating that the movement was in full force. By the early 1970s, the movement spread beyond the white, middle-class basis of the formal women's liberation movement. The black feminist initiatives were growing, soon joined by Latina, Asian American, and Native American feminist organizations. Activism was central to the movement. Women's liberation leaders started women's shelters, expanded accessibility to birth control, fought for women's participation in sports, and criticized sexist images in the media. **Women's studies** departments and women's history classes were instituted in colleges across the country. Women's liberation victories included the legalization of abortion in 1973 with ***Roe v. Wade*** and federal guidelines against coercive sterilization. One setback was the **Equal Rights Amendment**, which failed in 1982, just three states short of the required three-quarters majority. No longer referred to today as "women's liberation," the movement has evolved into the wide-ranging, multifaceted pursuit of the "feminist" agenda.

FURTHER READING

Rosen, Ruth. *The World Split Open: How the Modern Women's Movement Changed America.* New York: Penguin Putnam, 2000.

WOMEN'S NATIONAL BASKETBALL ASSOCIATION

The Women's National Basketball Association introduced the United States to women's professional team sports at a level of organization, media support, and popular interest never seen before. Although there had been attempts at women's professional basketball leagues in the past, the WNBA was the first to attract a large following and obtain television coverage. Financial backing by the National Basketball Association and the attention garnered by the U.S. women basketball team's 1996 Olympic gold assured the WNBA a foundation that previous leagues did not have.

Women first played basketball at Smith College in 1892, using rules adapted from the men's game. It wasn't until 1971 that a five-player, full-court game and a 30-minute shot clock were introduced. By 1972, **Title IX** assured female athletes equal opportunities in educational institutions and the Association for Intercollegiate Athletics for Women held its first collegiate basketball championship.

Women's basketball debuted at the Olympics in 1976 and 18-year-old Nancy Lieberman became the youngest basketball player in Olympic history to win a medal when the United States took a silver. A decade later, Lieberman became the first woman to play in a men's professional basketball league when she joined the USBL's Springfield Fame. A year later she joined the Washington Generals, which toured with the Harlem Globetrotters. In 1992, the Women's World Basketball Association (WWBA) was launched in the Midwest with six teams. It folded shortly thereafter. The NBA Board of Governors approved of the Women's National Basketball Association (WNBA) concept in 1995. By October of 1996, the first players, Rebecca Lobo and

The Women's National Basketball Association introduced women's professional team sports to the United States.

Sheryl Swoopes, were signed to play in the eight-city WNBA league. The next spring, the WNBA, overseen by President Val Ackerman, held its draft for college players and unsigned veterans. The inaugural WNBA season began in 1987 and was seen on the NBC, ESPN, and the Lifetime channels. In the first four years, the league averaged about 10,000 fans per game. This was considered a success as it took the NBA 29 years to reach an average attendance of 10,000. The league now has 12 teams: Charlotte Sting, Cleveland Rockers, Detroit Shock, Houston Comets, Los Angeles Sparks, Minnesota Lynx, New York Liberty, Orlando Miracle, Phoenix Mercury, Sacramento Monarchs, Utah Starzz, and Washington Mystics. Each team includes a major star.

WOMEN'S SPORTS FOUNDATION

A charitable and educational organization that focuses on increasing the physical fitness of girls and women, their participation in sports, and creating a more educated public that supports gender equity in all sports opportunities. Founded in 1974 by tennis great **Billie Jean King** and located in East Meadow, New York, the WSF sponsors privately funded programs in participation, education, advocacy, research, and leadership.

The foundation conducts research and publishes reports on a variety of related subjects. It recognizes outstanding journalism in women's sports, coaching, and other significant accomplishments. It provides grants and scholarships to girls and women in sports, as well as information about other sources of funding. The foundation includes a speaker service through which champion female athletes, businesswomen, scholars, and legal and health experts conduct programs and give talks on health, fitness, nutrition, marketing, motivation, and the business and politics of sports.

WOMEN'S STUDIES

Women's studies grew out of the women's movement of the 1960s and 1970s as faculty and students saw that women's social and political experiences were not a part of the curriculum or research priorities in higher education. The first women's studies program was established in 1970 at San Diego State University. The National Women's Studies Association was founded in 1977. The women's studies journal *Feminist Studies* began publication in 1972.

In 1975 there were 150 programs in women's studies. The number of programs doubled in the next five years. By 2000, more than 700 colleges and universities offered women's studies courses. Scholarship in women's studies includes virtually every academic discipline. Interdisciplinary perspectives include English, history, political science, fine arts, psychology, sociology, anthropology, philosophy, and the physical sciences.

Women's studies programs examine women's roles, achievements and experiences, historically and across cultures. Courses in these programs examine the contributions, perspectives, and status of women. The programs usually take diverse approaches to gender studies and the intersection of gender with other social identities such as class, race, sexual orientation, ability, age, and ethnicity. While women's studies began as a political movement, it has developed an intellectual approach and now offers doctoral degrees.

WOMEN'S TRADE UNION LEAGUE

See also: **O'Reilly, Lenora; Unions, Labor.**

WORLD WAR I

A major conflict between the Allies (Great Britain, France, Italy, Russia, and later the United States) and the Central Powers (Germany, Austria-Hungary, and the Ottoman Empire) that raged between 1914 and 1918. The desperate needs arising from this terrible catastrophe spurred the advancement of women's rights.

When the United States entered World War I in 1917, hundreds of thousands of men joined the military, leaving women to fill their jobs, as well as new war-related jobs that were created. Many women were left at home to provide for themselves and their families. Women's roles as employees, volunteers, and military nurses gave them confidence and pride in their work.

A new area of work for women was in the military. Secretary of the Navy Josephus Daniels was a leader in the placement of women in the military, though he had no intention of making women soldiers, but rather clerks. During World War I more than 11,000 women joined the U.S. Navy. The Marines did not open their doors to women until 1918, and the U.S. Army did not enlist women during World War I except as nurses, and then without rank or benefits.

More women served in military-related jobs than in the actual military. American women were employed in munitions plants and factories even before the United States entered the war, but the number increased rapidly once Congress declared war on Germany. As the demand for war materiel increased, *The New York Times* defended the increasing number of working women: "The filtering of the fine screw and the insertion of tiny springs in the assembling of parts of a shell made the sensitive touch perception and delicate handling of a woman's hands . . . really needed."

Volunteer work, certainly not new to women, expanded considerably during World War I. Before the war, women were involved in volunteer work concerning temperance, suffrage, the poor, and other issues. After the United States entered the war, more attention was turned toward aiding soldiers in various ways, such as in the preparation of bandages and "comfort bags." The Red

Cross trained nurses to go to France as well as to work on the homefront. Among them were 1,000 **African-American** women who were trained by the Red Cross, but not allowed to go overseas because "separate but equal" accommodations were not available.

Despite discrimination, World War I provided job opportunities for African-American women and allowed them to gain confidence in their own abilities. Although at the end of the war African-American women suffered setbacks in employment options—they were frequently the first let go from jobs—it was not nearly to the point of prewar discrimination. African-American women's exposure to varied work during the war gave them even more incentive to pursue equal employment rights for African Americans and women.

While there had been a growing trend in female employment before World War I, most of that growth was in the same type of menial positions women had held for centuries. The shortage of men during World War I allowed women to see for themselves that women could perform in jobs previously restricted to men. Once given this taste of economic freedom, many women would never again be satisfied being the domestic property of men.

FURTHER READING

Zeiger, Susan. *In Uncle Sam's Service: Women Workers With the American Expeditionary Force, 1917–1919.* Ithaca: Cornell University Press, 2000.

WORLD WAR II

A major conflict between the Allies (Great Britain, France, the Soviet Union, the United States, and China) and the Axis Powers (Germany, Italy, and Japan) that raged from 1939 to 1945 and was the largest, deadliest, and most violent armed conflict in the history of humanity. More than 150,000 American women served in the **Women's Army Corps** (WAC) during World War II. They were the first women other than nurses to serve within the ranks of the U.S. Army.

At first, both the Army and the American public had difficulty accepting women in uniform. Political and military leaders, however, were faced with fighting a two-front war in Europe and Asia, supplying men and materiel for the war, and sending lend-lease material to the Allies. They quickly realized that women could provide the additional resources so desperately needed by the military and by industry. Given the opportunity to make a major contribution to the national war effort, women seized it.

In 1941, Congresswoman Edith Nourse Rogers of Massachusetts introduced a bill to establish an Army women's corps, separate and distinct from the existing Army Nurse Corps. Rogers remembered that the female civilians who had worked with the Army under contract and as volunteers during World War I were not entitled to the disability benefits or pensions available to veterans. She was determined that if women were to serve again they would receive the same legal protection and benefits as their male counterparts. Although Rogers believed the women's corps should be a part of the Army so that women would receive equal pay, pension, and disability benefits, the Army did not want to accept women directly into its ranks.

A compromise created the Women's Army Auxiliary Corps (WAAC), which was established to work *with* the Army, "for the purpose of making available to the national defense the knowledge, skill, and special training of the women of the nation." The Army would provide food, uniforms, living quarters, pay, and medical care for up to 150,000 "auxiliaries," as the women were known. Women officers would not be allowed to command men. The military ranks of the women were equivalent to that of the men in the regular Army, but women received lower pay than their male counterparts.

Oveta Culp Hobby was appointed director of the WAAC, and she immediately began organizing the WAAC recruiting drive and training centers. Fort Des Moines, Iowa, was selected as the site of the first WAAC training center. Applicants had to be U.S. citizens between the ages of 21 and 45 with no dependents, be at least five feet tall, and weigh 100 pounds or more.

The first auxiliary units and officers to reach the field went to Aircraft Warning Service (AWS) units in the United States. WAACs plotted and traced the paths of every aircraft in their area. Later graduates were sent to Army Air Forces (AAF), Army Ground Forces (AGF), or Services of Supply (renamed Army Service Forces [ASF] in 1943) field installations. Initially, most auxiliaries worked as file clerks, typists, stenographers, or motor pool drivers, but gradually each service discovered an increasing number of positions WAACs were capable of filling.

TRAILBLAZERS

Rosie the Riveter was a fictional American woman featured on posters during WORLD WAR II as part of a government campaign to encourage women to enter the workforce to assist with the war effort and fill jobs left vacant by men. The image was based on Norman Rockwell's famous *Saturday Evening Post* cover of May 1943, showing a strong woman dressed in work clothes and a bandana. Between 1942 and 1945, more than 6 million women responded to the government's appeal to patriotism and joined the workforce. Although most of these women lost their jobs when men returned from the war, a legacy of the campaign was to lessen the stigma of employment for middle-class women.

This woman is drilling rivet holes in airplanes to keep business moving.

The AAF was especially eager to obtain WAACs, and each unit was eagerly anticipated and very well treated. Eventually the Air Force obtained 40 percent of all WAACs. Women were assigned as weather observers and forecasters, cryptographers, radio operators, sheet metal workers, parachute riggers, bombsight maintenance specialists, aerial photograph analysts, and control tower operators. By January 1945, only 50 percent of AAF WAACs held traditional assignments such as file clerk, typist, and stenographer.

A few AAF WAACs were assigned flying duties. Two WAAC radio operators assigned to Mitchel Field, New York, flew as crewmembers on B-17 training flights. WAAC mechanics and photographers also made regular flights. Three were awarded Air Medals, including one in India for her work in mapping "The Hump," the mountainous air route flown by pilots ferrying lend-lease supplies to the Chinese Army.

The first WAAC unit overseas, the 149th Post Headquarters Company, reported in 1943 to General Eisenhower's headquarters in Algiers. One of the most famous WAAC units to serve in the North African and Mediterranean theaters was the 6669th Headquarters Platoon, assigned to Lt. Gen. Mark W. Clark's Fifth Army. This unit became the Army's "experiment" in the use of female units in the field. The 6669th accompanied Fifth Army headquarters from Mostaganem, Algeria, across the Mediterranean to Naples and eventually all the way up the boot of Italy. Unit members remained six to thirteen miles behind the front lines, moved with the headquarters group, and worked in traditional female jobs. The unit included telephone operators, clerks, clerk-typists, and stenographers. Even so, these jobs were vastly different from those in the United States. For example, clerk-typists plotted the locations and movements of the troops and requisitioned and tracked the delivery of crucial supplies. The WAACs' success in the North African and Mediterranean theaters led to an increasing number of requests for WAACs.

Congress opened hearings in March 1943 on the conversion of the WAAC into part of the Regular Army. Army leaders asked for the authority to convert the Women's Army Auxiliary Corps into the Women's Army Corps (WAC), which would be part of the Army itself rather than merely serving with it. The WAAC had been an unqualified success, and the Army received requests for more WAACs than it could provide. Although WAACs were desperately needed overseas, the Army could not offer them the protection that regular soldiers received if captured, or the benefits they received if injured. On July 3, 1943, the WAC bill was signed into law. All WAACs were given a choice of joining the Army as a member of the WAC or returning to civilian life. About 75 percent decided to enlist.

In July 1943 the first battalion of WACs arrived in London. These 557 enlisted women and 19 officers were assigned to duty with the Eighth Air Force. Later, a detachment of 300 WACs served with the Supreme Headquarters, Allied Expeditionary Force (SHAEF). Originally stationed in London, these WACs accompanied SHAEF to France and eventually to Germany. As stenographers, typists, translators, legal secretaries, cryptographers, telegraph and teletype operators, radiographers, and general clerks, these women assisted in the planning of D-day and all subsequent operations up to the defeat of Germany.

In February 1945 a battalion of **African-American** WACs received its long-awaited overseas assignment. Organized as the 6888th Central Postal Battalion and commanded by Major Charity Adams, these 800 women were stationed in Birmingham, England, for three months; moved on to Rouen, France; and finally settled in Paris. The battalion was responsible for the redirection of mail to all U.S. personnel in the European theater of operations, including Army, Navy, Marine Corps, and Red Cross workers—a total of more than 7 million people.

In general, WACs in the European theater, like those in the North African and Mediterranean theaters, held a limited range of job assignments. About 35 percent worked as stenographers and typists, 26 percent were clerks, and 22 percent did communications work. Only 8 percent were assigned jobs considered unusual for women—mechanics, draftspeople, interpreters, and weather observers. By the time of Germany's surrender in 1945, there were 7,600 WACs throughout the European theater, stationed across England, France, and the German cities of Berlin, Frankfurt, Wiesbaden, and Heidelberg.

In the Southwest Pacific Area (SWPA), the need for WACs became acute by mid-1944. Because this was one of the last theaters to request and receive WACs, skilled office workers were scarce. Thus, the women drivers and mechanics were quickly retrained as clerks and typists. Eventually 70 percent of the 5,500 WACs who served in the Pacific theater worked in administrative and office positions, 12 percent were in communications, 9 percent worked in stockrooms and supply depots, and 7 percent were assigned to motor transport.

WACs in the SWPA endured a highly restricted lifestyle. Fearing incidents between the women and the large number of male troops in the area, theater headquarters directed that WACs, as well as Army nurses, be locked within barbed-wire compounds at all times, except when escorted by armed guards to work or to some approved recreation. No leaves or passes were allowed.

Military regulations did not permit women of the Navy, Marines, and Coast Guard to serve overseas until the war was almost over, but Navy nurses were serving on board hospital ships and eventually everywhere in the Pacific theater.

Along with the other women's military groups and the Army as a whole, much of the Women's Army Corps was demobilized starting immediately after the surrender of Germany. Not all the women were allowed to return home immediately, however. In order to accomplish its occupation mission, the Army granted its commanders the authority to retain some specialists, including WACs, as long as they were needed. By December 1946, WAC strength was under 10,000. The majority of these women held stateside duty and hoped to be allowed to stay in the Army.

Earlier in 1946, the Army had asked Congress for the authority to establish the Women's Army Corps as a permanent part of the Regular Army. This is the greatest single indication of the success of the wartime WAC: The Army acknowledged a need for the skills society believed women could provide. Although the bill was delayed in Congress for two years, it finally became law in June 1948. With the passage of this bill, the Women's Army Corps became a separate corps of the Regular Army. It remained part of the U.S. Army until 1978, when its existence as a separate corps was abolished and women were fully assimilated into all but the combat branches of the Army.

FURTHER READING

Keil, Sally V., et al. *Those Wonderful Women in Their Flying Machines: The Unknown Heroines of World War Two.* New York: Four Directions Press, 1994.

Tomblin, Barbara Brooks. *G.I. Nightingales: The Army Nurse Corps in World War II.* Lexington: University Press of Kentucky, 1996.

Y

YALOW, ROSALYN SUSSMAN (b. 1921)

Scientist, second woman to win the Nobel Prize in medicine. Rosalyn Sussman was born in New York City to Clara and Simon Sussman. Neither of her parents had a high school education, but both were determined that their children would get as much education as they could.

Sussman attended Hunter College, where she was inspired to study physics after attending a colloquium given by Enrico Fermi on nuclear fission.

After her graduation from Hunter in 1941, Sussman applied to several graduate schools but assumed she would not be accepted because of her gender, so she took a job as a secretary. She was pleasantly surprised when the University of Illinois not only admitted her but offered her a teaching assistantship in physics. In 1943 she married fellow student Aaron Yalow, with whom she had two children.

In 1945, armed with a Ph.D. in nuclear physics, Yalow returned to New York City and accepted a position at the Bronx Veterans Administration Hospital. There she met Dr. Solomon Berson, who became her research partner and who worked with her until his death in 1972. Together they refined a technique called radioimmunoassay (RIA), a method of using radioisotopes to measure the amount of various substances in the blood. Yalow and Berson's work was primarily devoted to measuring the amount of insulin in the blood of diabetic patients.

In 1977, Yalow became the second woman to receive the Nobel Prize for medicine. (The first was Gerty Theresa Cori in 1947.) In her acceptance speech, Yalow encouraged women to help one another succeed, because "the world cannot afford the loss of the talents of half of its people."

Yalow remained affiliated with the Bronx V.A. Hospital until her retirement in 1991. She had also taught at the Albert Einstein College of Medicine in the Bronx (1979–85) and was chairman of the clinical science department at Montefiore Hospital and Medical Center in the Bronx (1980–85).

YOUNG WOMEN'S CHRISTIAN ASSOCIATION

International social justice organization that began in the United States. The first association in New York City provided a boardinghouse for young women in 1860. The first student association was established in 1873 at Illinois State University. To address racial injustice, institutes on racism were held throughout the country. By 1875 there were 28 YWCAs in cities in the United States, and 15 years later the total of student associations had reached 106. Fighting discrimination has been part of the YWCA'a mission since its beginning. In 1890, the student division of the YWCA organized a program for Native American women at the Haworth Institute (Chilocco, Oklahoma) Indian School after learning about discrimination against Native Americans. By 1936, the YWCA held its first coed, intercollegiate, interracial seminar at Shaw University in Raleigh, North Carolina. During **WORLD WAR II** when many Japanese Amercians faced discrimination and lost their homes, YWCAs in the Midwest opened their facilities and took part in relocation services. In 1965 the Office of Racial Justice was established at the National Board offices. In the 1990s, the YWCA developed resources for communities to eliminate racism. The YWCA has also supported measures to legalize **ABORTION** and to oppose mandatory parental consent. The YWCA defines its purpose as: peace, justice, freedom, and dignity for all people.

YOUTH CULTURE

Term encompassing the popular practices, ideas, values and organizations of young people in society. A valuable method for studying **ADOLESCENTS** is examining their culture and the ways in which they interact with it. During the twentieth century, the study of a distinct set of adolescent values and cultural behaviors that deviated significantly from those of their parents became prevalent. Reasons for interest in youth culture ranged from parental concern for the moral health of their children to a desire to capitalize on consumer marketing to this increasingly powerful demographic group.

Most early studies of youth culture focused on teenage boys, and particularly the link between culture and a high rate of delinquency. Girls were thought to lie outside of this pattern of delinquency and were thus neglected as subjects. However, delinquency is only one consequence of youth culture. The youth cultures of young men and women differ significantly because of gendered notions of self.

As the world changed and opened up for women in terms of political rights, educational opportunities, and careers, a new generation of girls gained a radically different perspective in terms of their possibilities. The traditional formulations of gendered identity and behavior began to lose appeal. In the 1950s, many high school girls still participated in activities geared toward their gender, and held traditional values, such as wanting to get married and raise a family. However, an increasing number of girls began to look outside of these traditional identities and rebelled against them.

Even girls who epitomized feminine qualities and played to gender stereotypes began to demand recognition in their own right as girls. Teenagers became a highly volatile group, frequently alienated from and alien to their own parents. They became associated with fast cars and loud rock and roll, and parents worried about their daughters' chastity.

These phenomena opened up a unique marketing niche. Not only was rock and roll a highly lucrative business, but the culture surrounding it was as well. Consumer companies began to target teenagers and their allowances and after-school jobs.

In the 1960s, some girls joined the political movement of liberal and radical politics. Bohemianism became synonymous with youth. The counterculture that surrounded the politics, including free love and drug use, overturned the restrictive mores of the 1950s. The feminist movement also gained momentum.

In the 1970s, 1980s, and 1990s popular culture and the marketplace fluctuated wildly, sending mixed messages to girls about independence and peer pressure. Despite feminism and the expanding women's rights movement, girls' obsession with their physical appearance reached a fever pitch.

Feminist groups and youth organizations are trying to counteract destructive elements of youth culture, particularly ones that hurt girls' self-esteem. Groups such as the the **GIRL SCOUTS OF AMERICA** present positive options and foster community and strength in young girls. Young feminist magazines, both print and online, also counteract the often harmful effects of the teen consumer market by emphasizing community service, activism, education and independent thought.

Z

ZAHARIAS, MILDRED "BABE" DIDRIKSON (1914–1956)

Athlete, Olympic gold medalist, and a founder of the Ladies Professional Golf Association. Mildred Ella Didrikson was born in Port Arthur, Texas, in 1914. From the time she was a very young girl, she played sports; she played sandlot baseball so well, in fact, that her teammates called her "Babe" after the famous baseball player Babe Ruth, and the nickname stuck.

Didrikson dropped out of high school to work for the Casualty Insurance Company in Dallas, Texas. Although she was hired as a stenographer, her real job was playing for the company basketball team, which went on to win the national championship in 1931. At the same time, she played baseball in the city league and ran for the insurance company's track team. In 1932, Didrikson competed in track and field at the Olympics and won gold medals in javelin and

Athlete Mildred "Babe" Zaharias was an Olympic gold medalist and champion golfer.

hurdles. After the Olympics, she took up golf, the game that made her famous.

In 1938, Didrikson married professional wrestler George Zaharias, who retired to manage his wife's career. In 1946, she won the U.S. Women's Amateur tournament, and in 1947 she won 17 championships. In that same year, she helped to found the Ladies Professional Golf Association (LPGA). Zaharias was the leading money winner in the LPGA in 1949, 1950, and 1951. In 1950, she was voted outstanding woman athlete of the century by the Associated Press.

Zaharias was diagnosed with cancer in 1952. After radical surgery she recovered quickly enough to return to the golf circuit in 1954, winning the United States' Women's Open title that year. But the cancer returned and she died in Galveston, Texas, in 1956.

Part 3

Documents

Excerpts from

Muller v. Oregon (1908)

In a landmark ruling for women workers, the U.S. Supreme Court upheld a 1903 Oregon law that limited the workday of women laundry workers to ten hours. The case involved a laundry owner named Craig Muller (referred to below as the "defendant"), who had been fined $10 for requiring a female employee to work more than ten hours. The conviction was upheld by the Oregon Supreme Court, and Muller appealed the case to the U.S. Supreme Court. His attorneys argued that the ten-hour limit was unconstitutional, because it deprived both laundry owners and women employees of their Fourteenth Amendment guarantees of "life, liberty and property." The rights of employers and employees to agree upon a labor contract are both a liberty and a property right that may not be infringed. But the justices ruled to the contrary, holding that the state's interest in the health of women as potential mothers overrides the right and freedom of a business owner to hire and make contracts with employees. This case ushered in protective labor laws—based on sex—and legitimated different treatment for men and women.

Decided February 24, 1908

MR. JUSTICE BREWER delivered the opinion of the court. . . . The single question is the constitutionality of the statute under which the defendant was convicted so far as it affects the work of a female in a laundry. . . .

Constitutional questions, it is true, are not settled by even a consensus of present public opinion, for it is the peculiar value of a written constitution that it places in unchanging form limitations upon legislative action, and thus gives a permanence and stability to popular government which otherwise would be lacking. At the same time, when a question of fact is debated and debatable, and the extent to which a special constitutional limitation goes is affected by the truth in respect to that fact, a widespread and long continued belief concerning it is worthy of consideration. We take judicial cognizance of all matters of general knowledge.

It is undoubtedly true, as more than once declared by this court, that the general right to contract in relation to one's business is part of the liberty of the individual, protected by the Fourteenth Amendment to the Federal Constitution; yet it is equally well settled that this liberty is not absolute and extending to all contracts, and that a State may, without conflicting with the provisions of the Fourteenth Amendment, restrict in many respects the individual's power of contract. Without stopping to discuss at length the extent to which a State may act in this respect, we refer to the following cases in which the question has been considered: *Allgeyer v. Louisiana*, 165 U.S. 578; Holden v. Hardy, 169 U.S. 366; *Lochner v. New York*, 198 U.S. 45.

That woman's physical structure and the performance of maternal functions place her at a disadvantage in the struggle for subsistence is obvious. This is especially true when the burdens of motherhood are upon her. Even when they are not, by abundant testimony of the medical fraternity continuance for a long time on her feet at work, repeating this from day to day, tends to injurious effects upon the body, and as healthy mothers are essential to vigorous offspring, the physical well-being of woman becomes an object of public interest and care in order to preserve the strength and vigor of the race.

Still again, history discloses the fact that woman has always been dependent upon man. He established his control at the outset by superior physical strength, and this control in various forms, with diminishing intensity, has continued to the present. As minors, though not to the same extent, she has been looked upon in the courts as needing especial care that her rights may be preserved. Education was long denied her, and while now the doors of the school room are opened and her opportunities for acquiring knowledge are great, yet even with that and the consequent increase of capacity for business affairs it is still true that in the struggle for subsistence she is not an equal competitor with her brother. Though limitations upon personal and contractual rights may be removed by legislation, there is that in her disposition and habits of life which will operate against a full assertion of those rights. She will still be where some legislation to protect her seems necessary to secure a real equality of right. Doubtless there are individual exceptions, and there are many respects in which she has an advantage over him; but looking at it from the viewpoint of the effort to maintain an independent position in life, she is not upon an equality. Differentiated by these matters from the other sex, she is properly placed in a class by herself, and legislation designed for her protection may be sustained, even when like legislation is not necessary for men and could not be sustained. It is impossible to close one's eyes to the fact that she still looks to her brother and depends upon him. Even though all restrictions on political, personal and contractual rights were taken away, and she stood, so far as statutes are concerned, upon an absolutely equal plane with him, it would still be true that she is so constituted that she will rest upon and look to him for protection; that her physical structure and a proper discharge of her maternal functions—having in view not merely her own health, but the well-being of the race—justify legislation to protect her from the greed as well as the passion of man. The limitations which this statute places upon her contractual powers, upon her right to agree with her employer as to the time she shall labor, are not imposed solely for her benefit, but also largely for the benefit of all. Many words cannot make this plainer. The two sexes differ in structure of body, in the functions to be performed by each, in the amount of physical strength, in the capacity for long-continued labor, particularly when done standing, the influence of vigorous health upon the future well-being of the race, the self-reliance which enables one to assert full rights, and in the capacity to maintain the struggle for subsistence.

Not upon an equality means at a natural disadvantage.

This difference justifies a difference in legislation and upholds that which is designed to compensate for some of the burdens which rest upon her.

We have not referred in this discussion to the denial of the elective franchise in the State of Oregon, for while it may disclose a lack of political equality in all things with her brother, that is not of itself decisive. The reason runs deeper, and rests in the inherent difference between the two sexes, and in the different functions in life which they perform.

For these reasons, and without questioning in any respect the decision in *Lochner v. New York*, we are of the opinion that it cannot be adjudged that the act in question is in conflict with the Federal Constitution, so far as it respects the work of a female in a laundry, and the judgment of the Supreme Court of Oregon is Affirmed.

In *Lochner v. New York* (1905), the Supreme Court ruled that women were entitled to all the "privileges and immunities" of men and competent to contract for their own employment.

Excerpts from

A New Conscience and an Ancient Evil (1912)

With the rapid growth of American cities in the last decades of the nineteenth century came an increase in the number of women who secured a livelihood by resorting to prostitution. In Chicago, a report by the city Vice Commission in 1900 declared prostitution a rampant "social evil," raising public concern and leading to a major police crackdown. Throughout the Progressive Era, reformers and law-enforcement officials in major U.S. cities targeted prostitution along with such other "vice crimes" as gambling, drunkenness, drug use, and confidence games. But as some feminists argued—and studies confirmed—the problem was directly related to the dire working conditions and meager wages of young women employees. The social reformer and women's rights advocate Jane Addams, founder of Chicago's Hull House settlement, addressed the problem in her 1912 book A New Conscience and an Ancient Evil.

The fifth volume of the report of "Women and Child Wage Earners" in the United States gives the result of a careful inquiry into "the relation of wages to the moral condition of department store women." In connection with this, the investigators secured "the personal histories of one hundred immoral women," of whom ten were or had been employed in a department store. They found that while only one of the ten had been directly induced to leave the store for a disreputable life, six of them said that they had found "it easier to earn money that way." The report states that the average em-

Immoral women refers to prostitutes.

ployee in a department store earns about seven dollars a week, and that the average income of the one hundred immoral women covered by the personal histories, ranged from fifty dollars a week to one hundred dollars a week in exceptional cases. It is of these exceptional cases that the department store girl hears, and the knowledge becomes part of the unreality and glittering life that is all about her.

Another class of young women which is especially exposed to this alluring knowledge is the waitress in down-town cafés and restaurants. A recent investigation of girls in the segregated district of a neighboring city places waiting in restaurants and hotels as highest on the list of "previous occupations." Many waitresses are paid so little that they gratefully accept any fee which men may offer them. It is also the universal habit for customers to enter into easy conversation while being served. Some of them are lonely young men who have few opportunities to speak to women. The girl often quite innocently accepts an invitation for an evening, spent either in a theatre or dance hall, with no evil results, but this very lack of social convention exposes her to danger. Even when the proprietor means to protect the girls, a certain amount of familiarity must be borne, lest their resentment should diminish the patronage of the café. In certain restaurants, moreover, the waitresses doubtless suffer because the patrons compare them with the girls who ply their trade in disreputable saloons under the guise of serving drinks. . . .

Segregated district: In the first years of the twentieth century, authorities in Chicago dealt with prostitution by designating areas in which brothels were permitted but subject to strict controls and limitations.

All girls who work down town are at a disadvantage as compared to factory girls, who are much less open to direct inducement and to the temptations which come through sheer imitation. Factory girls also have the protection of working among plain people who frankly designate an irregular life in harsh, old-fashioned terms. If a factory girl catches sight of the vicious life at all, she sees its miserable victims in all the wretchedness and sordidness of their trade in the poorer parts of the city. As she passes the opening doors of a disreputable saloon she may see for an instant three or four listless girls urging liquor upon men tired out with the long day's work and already sodden with drink. As she hurries along the street on a rainy night she may hear a sharp cry of pain from a sick-looking girl whose arm is being brutally wrenched by a rough man, and if she stops for a moment she catches his muttered threats in response to the girl's pleading "that it is too bad a night for street work." She sees a passing policeman shrug his shoulders as he crosses the street, and she vaguely knows that the sick girl has put herself beyond the protection of the law, and that the rough man has an understanding with the officer on the beat. She has been told that certain streets are "not respectable," but a furtive look down the length of one of them reveals only forlorn and ill-looking houses, from which all suggestion of homely domesticity has long since gone; a slovenly woman with hollow eyes and a careworn face holding up the lurching bulk of a drunken man is all she sees of its "denizens," although she may have known a neighbor's daughter who came home to die of a mysterious disease said to be the result of a "fast life," and whose disgraced mother "never again held up her head."

Yet in spite of all this corrective knowledge, the increasing nervous energy to which industrial processes daily accommodate themselves, and the speeding up constantly required of the operators, may at any moment so register their results upon the nervous system of a factory girl as to overcome her powers of resistance. Many a working girl at the end of a day is so hysterical and overwrought that her mental balance is plainly disturbed. Hundreds of working girls go directly to bed as soon as they have eaten their suppers. They are too tired to go from home for recreation, too tired to read and often too tired to sleep. A humane forewoman recently said to me as she glanced down the long room in which hundreds of young women, many of them with their shoes beside them, were standing: "I hate to think of all the aching feet on this floor; these girls all have trouble with their feet, some of them spending the entire evening bathing them in hot water." But aching feet are no more usual than aching backs and aching heads. The study of industrial diseases has only this year been begun by the federal authorities, and doubtless as more is known of the nervous and mental effect of over-fatigue, many moral breakdowns will be traced to this source. It is already easy to make the connection in definite cases: "I was too tired to care," "I was dog tired and just went with him," are phrases taken from the lips of reckless girls, who are endeavoring to explain the situation in which they find themselves. . . .

Yet factory girls who are subjected to this overstrain and overtime often find their greatest discouragement in the fact that after all their efforts they earn too little to support themselves. One girl said that she had first yielded to temptation when she had become utterly discouraged because she had tried in vain for seven months to save enough for a pair of shoes. She habitually spent two dollars a week for her room, three dollars for her board, and sixty cents a week for carfare, and she had found the forty cents remaining from her weekly wage of six dollars adequate to do more than re-sole her old shoes twice. When the shoes became too worn to endure a third soling and she possessed but ninety cents towards a new pair, she gave up her struggle; to use her own contemptuous phrase, she "sold out for a pair of shoes."

Addams, Jane. *A New Conscience and an Ancient Evil*. New York: Macmillan, 1912.

Excerpts from

The Woman Rebel (1914)

In March 1914, after returning from a trip to Europe to study contraceptive methods, Margaret Sanger began publication of an eight-page monthly newspaper called The Woman Rebel. *A crusader for birth control and a passionate voice for women's rights, Sanger intended for the paper to unite women around the issues of gender and class oppression, sexual and reproductive freedom, marriage, prostitution, and the direction of the feminist movement itself. It was in the pages of* The Woman Rebel *that Sanger coined the term "birth control." Defiant in tone and radical in opinion, the publication was prohibited from mail distribution on the grounds of obscenity because it contained articles on sexuality and contraception. Sanger continued publication and was indicted by federal authorities. She fled to Europe for 13 months and returned home in October 1915 to face trial; the charges were later dismissed. Following are two unsigned articles, presumably written by Sanger, from the inaugural March 1914 issue of* The Woman Rebel.

The New Feminists

That apologetic tone of the new American feminists which plainly says "Really, Madam Public Opinion, we are all quite harmless and perfectly respectable" was the keynote of the first and second mass meetings held at Cooper Union on the 17th and 20th of February last.

Cooper Union is a private, coeducational university in New York City where people often assembled to hear speeches. It was founded in 1859 as a tuition-free night school for the working class.

The ideas advanced were very old and time-worn even to the ordinary church-going woman who reads the magazines and comes in contact with current thought. The "right to work," the "right to ignore fashions," the "right to keep her own name," the "right to organize," the "right of the mother to work"; all these so-called rights fail to arouse enthusiasm because to-day they are all recognized by society and there exist neither laws nor strong opposition to any of them.

It is evident they represent a middle class woman's movement; an echo, but a very weak echo, of the English constitutional suffragists. Consideration of the working woman's freedom was ignored. The problems which affect the working girl who slaves in the home or the nurse girl who spends her days and nights in the care of the babies of the feminists, were not dwelt upon. The freedom which the new feminists expound can only be obtained through a greater enslavement of the already enslaved working-woman, and "where slavery is there liberty cannot be." Instead of launching a movement for woman's freedom the impression gained was that they aimed to combat the contentions of the conventional anti-suffragists.

"Where slavery is there liberty cannot be" is a famous quote from an 1864 speech by Senator Charles Sumner, an ardent abolitionist.

To those who have been on the firing line for woman's freedom for the past several years, the new movement is sadly lacking in vitality, force, and conviction.

Any movement with fear lurking in the background, fear of the press, of public opinion, or our neighbors, or of the enemy, cannot have that spirit which fearlessness of opposition brings. It is not for rights women should ask; all rights are here—rather is it for you to inculcate into her the desire to get these rights.

Feminists—Come out from under the cover of morbid respectability and let's get a look at you!

The Prevention of Conception

Is there any reason why women should not receive clean, scientific, harmless information on how to prevent conception? Everybody is aware that the old, stupid fallacy that such knowledge will cause a girl to enter into prostitution has long been shattered. Seldom does a prostitute become pregnant. The women of the upper middle class have all available knowledge and implements to prevent conception. The woman of the lower middle class is struggling for this knowledge. She tries various methods of prevention, and after a few years of experience plus medical advice succeeds in discovering some method suitable to her individual self. The woman of the people is the only one left in ignorance of this information. Her neighbors, relatives and friends tell her stories of special devices and the successes of them all. They tell her also of the blood-sucking men with M.D. after their names who perform operations for the price of so-and-so. But the working woman's purse is thin. It's far cheaper to have a baby, "though God knows what it will do after it gets here." Then, too, all other classes of women live in places where there is at least a semblance of privacy and sanitation. It is easier for them to care for themselves whereas the large majority of the women of the people have no bathing or sanitary conveniences. This accounts too for the fact that the higher the standard of living, the more care can be taken and fewer children result. No plagues, no famines or wars could ever frighten the capitalist class so much as the universal practice of the prevention of conception. On the other hand no better method could be utilized for increasing the wages of the workers.

As is well known, a law exists forbidding the imparting of information on this subject, the penalty being several years' imprisonment. Is it not time to defy this law? And what fitter place could be found than in the pages of the WOMAN REBEL?

The Margaret Sanger Papers Electronic Edition: Margaret Sanger and *The Woman Rebel*, 1914-1916, Esther Katz, Cathy Moran Hajo, and Peter Engelman, eds. Columbia, SC: Model Editions Partnership, 1999. Electronic version based on the microfilm edition of *The Papers of Margaret Sanger* [accessed: October 8, 2001] Available from http://adh.sc.edu.

Excerpts from

Mothers' Letters to the U.S. Children's Bureau (1916, 1920)

The oldest federal agency dedicated to the welfare of children, the U.S. Children's Bureau was established in 1912 as part of the Department of Labor. (It is now part of the Department of Health and Human Services.) With a mandate to monitor and promote "the welfare of children and child life among all classes of our people," the bureau was headed from 1912 to 1921 by Julia Clifford Lathrop, the social reformer associated with Hull House in Chicago and a moving force in the creation of the first juvenile court in the United States. Among the bureau's efforts to combat infant mortality was the dissemination of information on child care, health, and nutrition. Women from throughout the country sent letters requesting advice on pregnancy, childbirth, and neglectful husbands. Their correspondence underscores the plight of poverty-stricken mothers in the early decades of the twentieth century.

Mrs. M. R., Idaho (January 4, 1916)

Dear Madame.
I would like to know if your people can give me a answer on this. What I am to do I don't know. I am living 25 miles away from any Doctor. We have 4 small children, my husband is only making 1.35 a day, and every thing is so high it takes all he makes to keep our babys in cloths and food, as we have evry thing we put in our mouths to buy. I am looking for the stork about the 19 of aprial, and all I can do is to get a few outing [flannel] slips and a few Dipers. So hear is what I would like for yous to answer if you can: how am I going to get 35 dollar to have a doctor, for he will not come for less and not unless we have the cash. Talk about better babys, when a mother must be like some cow or mare when a babys come. If she lives, all wright, and if not, Just the same. The nearest one that lives is 1 mile and a 1/2 and my oldest child is 9 years old. My husband only come home onest a week, that is on saterday. I have my own wood to cut by my self so how can there be better babys when they must come in to this world like a calf or colt I would like to know.

So please answer me if you can. You may send me a copie of Bulletin and if I live [through] it, then I will try to [follow] it as close as I can. Yours truly, answer at [once].

Mrs. H. B., Illinois (February 28, 1916)

. . . I love my children and willing would have as many as possible but never before have I dreaded the ordeal of child birth, as I am afraid to look upon its little face. How can it be human and a perfect child after all that I have been through this last time? Each place I have asked for advice what to do, or for to compel my husband to work and provide for me and the children, the best I receive is, "why do you live with him and have children for such a man? You deserve no pity." Nice advice to poor mothers, who are nothing but fools for men but to bear their children for them, and then afterwards neglect them to go out to work for to buy their food.

God help the poor mothers of today. The cry is Save the babies, but what about the mothers who produce these babies? Now, Dear Sirs, No hard feeling for what I have written. But would it not be better to enact a law that, when a man marries a woman and she bears his children for him, that he be compelled to provide for the babies he caused to be brought into the world, and permit mothers to properly care for their babies, and give [a man] a life sentence for bringing home disease and inflicting his wife with it. And if possible start an association to protect mothers who are to give birth and after that help them to help themselves, and enable them to do for their babies? Abuse, torture, slurs, that is the best they receive. Men in long service receive their pension. Mothers deserving receive nothing.

Now I hope some evening to pick up a newspaper and be able to read that your department, that you will punish men to severely who neglect their wife and children that their will be less need of advice to *mothers*. Only I beg of you to do something to protect mothers in the pitfall I find myself in. When my baby is born, will I be able to feed it? Or will I be compelled again to leave my infant and work, for to buy for the other 3 as well as the new one—and have to pay some one else to look after the little one I love to put to my breast and let it grow and live? Or will it mean starvation again as before? The time is drawing near, but I would sooner go through the fires of H than the misery I have had to go through. . . .

I also have a little girl 8 years old who is frail, and the school doctor tells her to eat fresh eggs and drink fresh milk and lots of it, but where am I to get it? I can see her going into decline right along, but what am I to do? Think it over gentlemen. See if you cant make men do a little different, and then there will be better babies, better mothers, better grown children, and a better country, and less human beings in the penatentierey.

I trust you will look at this in the right light and excuse for crying out my soul to you. Sincerely yours,

Mrs. H. R., Georgia (June 14, 1920)

Dear Madame

I need advise. I am a farmers wife, do my household duties and a regular field hand too. The mother of 9 children and in family way again. I am quarlsome when tired & fatigued.

When I come in out of the field to prepare dinner my Husband & all the children gets in the kitchen in my way. I quarrel at them for bening in my way. I tell them I will build them a fire if they are cold. I also threaten to move the Stove out on the porch. What shall I do? My husband wont sympathise with me one bit but talks rough to me. I get tired & sick of my daily food & crave some simple article, should I have it? I have [helped] make the living for 20 years. Should I be [de]nied of a few simple articles or money either? Does it make a Mother unvirtuous for a man physician to wait on her during confinement? Is it Safe for me to go through it Without aid from any one? Please give me Some advise. There isent any mid wives near us now. I am not friendless but going to you for advise too keep down gossip.

Yours.

Molly Ladd-Taylor. *Raising a Baby the Government Way: Mothers' Letters to the Children's Bureau, 1915-1932*. New Brunswick, NJ: Rutgers University Press, 1986.

Excerpts from

"My Day" (1939-1962)

From 1935 to 1962, Eleanor Roosevelt wrote a syndicated newspaper column called "My Day." The column appeared consistently six days a week, interrupted only briefly after the death of her husband, President Franklin D. Roosevelt, in 1945. Over the course of those 27 years, she shared her views with millions of Americans in some 2,000 columns. Her subjects ranged from historical events—such as the Depression, the attack on Pearl Harbor, the explosion of the atomic bomb, and the Cold War—to social and political issues and her own life. She was a popular advocate for a wide range of social causes, including civil rights, child care, and the plight of women. Following are some of her columns on this last subject.

Women and Employment

HYDE PARK, JULY 13, 1939 Yesterday, with great interest, I read Mrs. Carrie Chapman Catt's appeal to the National Federation of Business and Professional Women's Clubs. It seems to me so obvious that married women should not be discriminated against, that I cannot imagine anyone who would really consider such a proposition.

It seems this discussion was given impetus by a rule in the federal government during the Depression, forbidding two married people to hold government positions. Now that the emergency is over, that rule has been rescinded, but there is, I think, one consideration in government employment that does not exist in private employment. The government wants to prevent the building up of a family bureaucracy.

It seems to me that if a generous sum is set, on which an adequate standard of living may be preserved for the average family that it might be well, if one member of the family earns that amount, to bar the employment of any other member of the family in government service. If a man and his wife together earn that amount, children who live in the same household should be barred from government employment.

Such a rule would not be directed at women particularly, married or single, but, if adopted by the federal government, it should be very carefully considered for the same pattern might easily be followed by state and local governments.

I see by the morning papers that the Senate Committee has voted for delay on neutrality. One vote makes this important decision. These gentlemen must go on the theory that if you delay making up your mind long enough, perhaps you may never have to, for somebody else may make it up for you. My own experience is that the things you refuse to meet today always come back at you later on, usually under circumstances which make the decision twice as difficult as it originally was. I would not weep over the difficulties of the gentlemen who made this decision, were it not for the fact that the results of their decision may not rest on their heads alone but may affect innocent people in our country and other countries.

Neutrality: Beginning in 1935, Congress had passed a series of acts to restrict U.S. participation in foreign conflicts. In early 1939, as the Nazi threat intensified in Europe, President Roosevelt urged a lifting of the restrictions but was turned down.

Women and Work

HYDE PARK, AUGUST 5, 1939 The other day I was sent a most amusing page from a magazine called "Future: The Magazine for Young Men." An article by Dr. S. N. Stevens, which contains the following quotation, was marked for my attention:

"Women are generally more intuitive than empirical. In other words, they play hunches instead of examining facts in the evaluation of a situation. And I have never yet seen one who, in a tight spot, didn't try to take advantage of the fact that she was a woman."

I am willing to agree to the first part of the paragraph, women have so much intuition and are so much quicker to feel things than men are that they occasionally count too much on that particular gift. However, the woman who has trained herself has the advantage over a man in that she still has her intuition, but to it she has added his gift of examining facts and evaluating all the factors entering into a situation. As to the second half of his statement, I'll grant some women do it, but they are never the women who succeed in their jobs. They are the ones who always preyed on men and always will, for that is a job in itself.

There are so many occasions when a woman is in a tight spot which only she herself can face, that it is rather rare to find her trying to share her burden or ask for assistance on the ground that she is a woman.

What good would it do to try to get someone else to stand by when you are about to have a baby? What good would it do to turn to anyone else if your husband drank and you had to try to collect his wages before they were all spent? A woman may use her womanly wiles to help her in tight spots, but she isn't trading on being a woman, she is just handling the job which is hers, and frequently it is the job of handling a man and making him think he isn't being handled. These doctors and editors who write for magazines like this are very clever, but they should know a little more about women and real life before they venture to write about them.

Equal Rights

HYDE PARK, MAY 14, 1945 I have been getting a good many letters of late about the Equal Rights amendment, which has been reported out favorably to the House by the House Judiciary Committee. Some of the women who write me seem to think that if this amendment is passed there will be no further possibility of discrimination against women. They feel that the time has come to declare that women shall be treated in all things on an equal basis with men. I hardly think it is necessary to declare this, since as a theory it is fairly well accepted today by both men and women. But in practice it is not accepted, and I doubt very much whether it ever will be.

Other women of my acquaintance are writing me in great anxiety, for they are afraid that the dangers of the amendment are not being properly considered. The majority of these women are employed in the industrial field. Their fear is that labor standards safeguarded in the past by legislation will be wrecked, and that the amendment will curtail and impair for all time the powers of both state and federal government to enact any legislation that may be necessary and desirable to protect the health and safety of women in industry.

I do not know which group is right, but I feel that if we work to remove from our statute books those laws which discriminate against women today we might accomplish more and do it in a shorter time than will be possible through the passage of this amendment.

Housewives

NEW YORK, OCTOBER 17, 1955 Recently I received a letter which raised a question of interest to many women. It reads as follows:

> "Reading your article in the August Safeway Magazine gives me the inspiration and opportunity I have long been looking for, namely to 'speak' to you regarding the word 'housewife,' used to define the greatest profession we women perform.
>
> QUESTION: What is your occupation?
> ANSWER: Housewife, wife of a house.
> QUESTIONING A CHILD: What does your father do?
> ANSWER: He is a lawyer on Wall Street, N.Y.C.
> QUESTION: What is your mother's occupation?
> ANSWER: Oh, she is just a housewife.
>
> I have heard this on TV. I am sure other women have cringed at the term. The dictionary defines the word as 'the woman in charge of a household.' 'Wife' is defined as 'a woman joined in marriage to a man as husband.'
>
> Surely there is another name for us. How do you feel about it? Why not write an article which will bring opinions from other married women?"

I must confess that in days gone by I have often entered myself on questionnaires as "housewife" without feeling the slightest embarrassment. Now I put down "writer" or "lecturer," because the major part of my life is taken up in this way rather than in running a home and watching over the daily needs of a household and children plus guests, as it used to be in earlier days. I am not sure, however, that I did not feel more useful when I had to be home the greater part of the time. I had to make very careful plans when I left home so that all would go on in the same way while I was gone. I was limited in my free time. One could never be sure that there would not be sudden illness which would make a change in plans inevitable, or that home tasks would not clash with some demands outside my family—and of course, the demands outside the family were always secondary.

Those were the days when on a questionnaire I would put down "housewife" and feel very proud of it, and I am quite sure that no woman has any reason for feeling humiliated by the title. It is one of the most skilled professions in the world. When one adds to the business of running a house the care and bringing up of children, there is so much needed preparation for this occupation that I think it could be classed today among the most skilled occupations in the world. To be sure, there are good and bad homes; and there are children who are well brought up and children who are badly brought up. This happens in any business or professional activity. But when one adds up what it means to a nation, one must concede that the well-run home and the well-brought-up children are more important even than a well-run business. More people are affected by the occupation of a housewife and mother than are ever touched by any single business, no matter how large it may be.

Reprinted from "My Day" columns by Eleanor Roosevelt http://www.pbs.org/wgbh/amex/eleanor/sfeature/myday.html.

Excerpts from

The Feminine Mystique (1963)

Instrumental in reviving the American feminist movement in the 1960s, Betty Friedan's best-selling The Feminine Mystique *(1963) called attention to what she believed to be the boredom and alienation suffered by middle-class housewives and mothers in the postwar era. The "housewife syndrome," she wrote, is not a problem of individual adjustment but one of societal identity and restrictive gender role. In this influential work, as well as in her reform efforts over the years, Friedan, a "founding mother" of the women's liberation movement, called for sweeping changes in the structure of society and the role of women.*

The problem lay buried, unspoken, for many years in the minds of American women. It was a strange stirring, a sense of dissatisfaction, a yearning that women suffered in the middle of the twentieth century in the United States. Each suburban wife struggled with it alone. As she made the beds, shopped for groceries, matched slipcover material, ate peanut butter sandwiches with her children, chauffeured Cub Scouts and Brownies, lay beside her husband at night—she was afraid to ask even of herself the silent question—"Is this all?"

For over fifteen years there was no word of this yearning in the millions of words written about women, for women, in all the columns, books and articles by experts telling women their role was to seek fulfillment as wives and mothers. Over and over women heard in voices of tradition and of Freudian sophistication that they could desire no greater destiny than to glory in their own femininity. Experts told them how to catch a man and keep him, how to breastfeed children and handle their toilet training, how to cope with sibling rivalry and adolescent rebellion; how to buy a dishwasher, bake bread, cook gourmet snails, and build a swimming pool with their own hands; how to dress, look, and act more feminine and make marriage more exciting; how to keep their husbands from dying young and their sons from growing into delinquents. They were taught to pity the neurotic, unfeminine, unhappy women who

Fifteen years refers roughly to the period since the end of World War II.

Freudian refers to the psychoanalytic theories of Sigmund Freud (1856–1939) concerning the unconscious mind, sexuality, and their cultural influences.

wanted to be poets or physicists or presidents. They learned that truly feminine women do not want careers, higher education, political rights—the independence and the opportunities that the old-fashioned feminists fought for. Some women, in their forties and fifties, still remembered painfully giving up those dreams, but most of the younger women no longer even thought about them. A thousand expert voices applauded their femininity, their adjustment, their new maturity. All they had to do was devote their lives from earliest girlhood to finding a husband and bearing children. . . .

The suburban housewife—she was the dream image of the young American women and the envy, it was said, of women all over the world. The American housewife—freed by science and labor-saving appliances from the drudgery, the dangers of childbirth and the illnesses of her grandmother. She was healthy, beautiful, educated, concerned only about her husband, her children, her home. She had found true feminine fulfillment. As a housewife and mother, she was respected as a full and equal partner to man in his world. She was free to choose automobiles, clothes, appliances, supermarkets; she had everything that women ever dreamed of.

In the fifteen years after World War II, this mystique of feminine fulfillment became the cherished and self-perpetuating core of contemporary American culture. Millions of women lived their lives in the image of those pretty pictures of the American suburban housewife, kissing their husbands goodbye in front of the picture window, depositing their stationwagonsful of children at school, and smiling as they ran the new electric waxer over the spotless kitchen floor. . . . Their only dream was to be perfect wives and mothers; their highest ambition to have five children and a beautiful house, their only fight to get and keep their husbands. They had no thought for the unfeminine problems of the world outside the home; they wanted the men to make the major decisions. They gloried in their role as women, and wrote proudly on the census blank: "Occupation: housewife." . . .

Census blank refers to the demographic questionnaire distributed in the national census-taking every ten years.

Gradually I came to realize that the problem that has no name was shared by countless women in America. . . . I heard echoes of the problem in college dormitories and semiprivate maternity wards, at PTA meetings and luncheons of the League of Women Voters, at suburban cocktail parties, in station wagons waiting for trains, and in snatches of conversation overheard at Schrafft's. The groping words I heard from other women, on quiet afternoons when children were at school or on quiet evenings when husbands worked late, I think I understood first as a woman long before I understood their larger social and psychological implications.

Schrafft's was a chain of family restaurants.

Just what was this problem that has no name? What were the words women used when they tried to express it? Sometimes a woman would say "I feel empty somehow . . . incomplete." Or she would say, "I feel as if I don't exist." Sometimes she blotted out the feeling with a tranquilizer. Sometimes she thought the problem was with her husband or her children, or that what she really needed was to redecorate her house, or move to a better neighborhood, or have an affair, or another baby. Sometimes, she went to a doctor with symptoms she could hardly describe. . . .

Can the problem that has no name be somehow related to the domestic routine of the housewife? When a woman tries to put the problem into words, she often merely describes the daily life she leads. What is there in this recital of comfortable domestic detail that could possibly cause such a feeling of desperation? Is she trapped simply by the enormous demands of her role as modern housewife: wife, mistress, mother, nurse, consumer, cook, chauffeur, expert on interior decoration, child care, appliance repair, furniture refinishing, nutrition, and education? Her day is fragmented as she rushes from dishwasher to washing machine to telephone to dryer to station wagon to supermarket, and delivers Johnny to the Little League field, takes Janey to dancing class, gets the lawnmower fixed and meets the 6:45. She can never spend more than 15 minutes on any one thing; she has no time to read books, only magazines; even if she had time, she has lost the power to concentrate. At the end of the day, she is so terribly tired that sometimes her husband has to take over and put the children to bed. . . .

It is easy to see the concrete details that trap the suburban housewife, the continual demands on her time. But the chains that bind her in her trap are chains in her own mind and spirit. They are chains made up of mistaken ideas and misinterpreted facts, of incomplete truths and unreal choices. They are not easily seen and not easily shaken off. . . .

I think the experts in a great many fields have been holding pieces of that truth under their microscopes for a long time without realizing it. . . . I became aware of a growing body of evidence, much of which has not been reported publicly because it does not fit current modes of thought about women—evidence which throws into question the standards of feminine normality, feminine adjustment, feminine fulfillment and feminine maturity by which most women are still trying to live.

I began to see in a strange new light the American return to early marriage and the large families that are causing the population explosion; the recent movement to natural childbirth and breastfeeding; suburban conformity, and the new neuroses, character pathologies and sexual problems being reported by the doctors. I began to see new dimensions to old problems that have long been taken for granted among women: menstrual difficulties, sexual frigidity, promiscuity, pregnancy fears, childbirth depression, the high incidence of emotional breakdown and suicide among women in their twenties and thirties, the menopause crises, the so-called passivity and immaturity of American men, the discrepancy between women's tested intellectual abilities in childhood and their adult achievement, the changing incidence of adult sexual orgasm in American women, and persistent problems in psychotherapy and in women's education.

If I am right, the problem that has no name stirring in the minds of so many American women today is not a matter of loss of femininity or too much education, or the demands of domesticity. It is far more important than anyone recognizes. It is the key to these other new and old problems which have been torturing women and their husbands and children, and puzzling their doctors and educators for years. It may well be the key to our future as a nation and a culture. We can no longer ignore that voice within women that says: "I want something more than my husband and my children and my home."

Friedan, Betty. *The Feminine Mystique.* New York: Norton, 1963.

Text of

The Equal Rights Amendment (1923, 1972)

The proposed Equal Rights Amendment (ERA) to the U.S. Constitution was drafted by suffragist Alice Paul in 1921 and introduced in every session of Congress since 1923. A revised version was finally passed by Congress in 1972 and sent to the states for ratification. At the end of the ten-year limit, the amendment had been ratified by 35 states—still three short of the 38 (three-quarters of all the states) needed for adoption. Following are the original text as drafted by Paul and the text passed by Congress in 1972. Following these are lists of the ratifying and nonratifying states.

Original ERA text, introduced in Congress in 1923

- Men and women shall have equal rights throughout the United States and every place subject to its jurisdiction.
- Congress shall have power to enforce this article by appropriate legislation.

ERA text passed by Congress in 1972 and sent to the states for ratification

Section 1. Equality of rights under the law shall not be denied or abridged by the United States or by any state on account of sex.

Section 2. The Congress shall have the power to enforce, by appropriate legislation, the provisions of this article.

Section 3. This amendment shall take effect two years after the date of ratification.

Ratifying States (35)	*Nonratifying States (15)*
Alaska	Alabama
California	Arizona
Colorado	Arkansas
Connecticut	Florida
Delaware	Georgia

Ratifying States (35)	*Nonratifying States (15)*
Hawaii	Illinois
Idaho	Louisiana
Indiana	Mississippi
Iowa	Missouri
Kansas	Nevada
Kentucky	North Carolina
Maine	Oklahoma
Maryland	South Carolina
Massachusetts	Utah
Michigan	Virginia
Minnesota	
Montana	
Nebraska	
New Hampshire	
New Jersey	
New Mexico	
New York	
North Dakota	
Ohio	
Oregon	
Pennsylvania	
Rhode Island	
South Dakota	
Tennessee	
Texas	
Vermont	
Washington	
West Virginia	
Wisconsin	
Wyoming	

Excerpt from

Our Bodies, Ourselves (1970)

From its initial publication in 1970, the groundbreaking Our Bodies, Ourselves: A Book by and for Women *has provided a definitive resource on women's health and sexuality. Researched and written by the Boston Women's Health Book Collective, a nonprofit organization dedicated to women's health education and advocacy, the book offers guidance, information, and additional resources on topics ranging from body image and healthy living to childbearing, birth control, aging, and the health-care system. Published in 19 languages, the work has been updated and reissued as* The New Our Bodies, Ourselves *(1984) and* Our Bodies, Ourselves for the New Century *(1998). The following excerpt on body image is from Chapter 1 of the 1998 edition.*

Take a moment to close your eyes and visualize your body. How do you feel about what you see?

Are your breasts too big or too small? Your butt too big or too flat? What about your stomach or thighs—too fat? Is your nose too broad? Do you wish you were taller or more petite? Is your body too hairy or your skin too dark?

If you're like most women, you answered yes to some of these questions. Almost every woman judges some part of her body—sometimes all of it—as not quite right.

Think about the tremendous diversity of female bodies: we are tall, short, thin, fat, large-boned and hefty, tiny and frail; our eyes vary in color and shape; our skin color ranges from blue-black or ebony to deep browns to copper to olive to pink; our hair is many-colored and has an almost infinite range of textures. Yet, we are all measured against unrealistic standards promoted by the advertising and beauty industries and grounded in fantasies about how a woman should look and behave. A woman who recently quit her job, after a manager told her to change her braided hairstyle or leave, reflects:

Everybody talks about diversity, but if everybody has to fit a certain mold, well, that's not wanting diversity. It's asking people to change who they really are.

What are the forces that lead us to believe we're not okay the way we are? What do we think would change in our lives if we could change our bodies and our looks? What would being more "attractive" give us? More friends? More self-confidence? A better job? How can we learn to feel better about our bodies and more loving toward ourselves and other women despite the onslaught of messages about how we "should" look? Just imagine what would happen if we were to take all the energy we expend trying to conform to society's standards of beauty and direct it elsewhere. What else could we be doing with our time? Our money? Our energy? . . .

How we feel about our looks and how at home we feel in our bodies is complex and develops in response to the many and often contradictory messages we get from society at large and in response to our actual experiences living in our bodies. Some of the pressure to be different from the way we are comes from outside ourselves, from the media images that constantly bombard us, and from the reactions we get from others; some of the pressure comes from deep inside ourselves, from how we internalize our experiences as females in this culture.

Too often our experiences living in our bodies make it difficult for us to accept ourselves. Many of us have experienced violence and abuse that make us feel unsafe in our bodies. One in four women will be raped in her lifetime; one in three girls is sexually abused by age 18. Virtually all of us have experienced unwanted attention from men, whether in the form of compliments, derisive comments, or unsolicited touching. Every woman of color will experience racism. If our culture has different ideals of female beauty from those of the dominant Euro-American culture, the messages we receive from parents and relatives may contradict those of our peers and the media and may cause us additional pain and confusion.

As a result of these violations, many of us have come to feel that our bodies—as they are—are not safe places to be. We may respond by wanting to look like the woman on the cover of a glossy beauty magazine, thinking that if we had the perfect body, we would be shielded from insults to our sense of self and from discrimination. Or we may respond by rejecting our female bodies, feeding our hunger for acceptance with bags of junk food or starving ourselves so that our bodies take on the shapes of preadolescent girls.

We are wounded when a physical characteristic or set of characteristics is loaded with negative expectations. If we have black skin and African features, or olive skin and Asian features, or dark curly hair and a prominent nose as do many Jews and Arabs, or if we have a visible disability, or if we are perceived as "overweight," our experiences from an early age may be marked by other people's negative reactions to our physical selves. We may have come to dislike, mistrust, or even hate our bodies as a result, feeling that they, rather than the society we live in, have betrayed us. . . .

Every society throughout history has had standards of beauty, but at no other time has there been such an intense media blitz telling us what we should look like. Magazine covers, films, TV shows, and billboards surround us with images that constantly reinforce the idea that "beauty" is everything. But what is "beauty" and what does it mean to strive to be "beautiful"? The current ideal woman portrayed in the dominant American culture is white, thin, able-bodied, shapely, muscular, tall, blond, smooth-skinned, and young. The list of what a woman must do to achieve the perfect look is endless, yet paradoxically, it is absolutely essential that in the end she look totally natural! . . .

Never before have there been so many businesses dedicated to selling "beauty" and so many women willing to buy their products. We are sold an infinite array of products and programs to alter our appearance. Almost everywhere we look we receive similar messages: without these jeans (and the skinny body in them), you'll never find a man; without straight, bright, white teeth you'll never find success. The pressure to conform is promoted by a market whose success depends on convincing us that we don't look good enough and is reinforced by employers and others who have control over where we work, where we live, and our opportunities to enjoy good health.

Many of us spend precious time, money, and emotional energy trying to make our bodies conform to standards that have little to do with who we are or what our bodies actually look like. The cost, both economical and psychological, is enormous. We may expose ourselves to serious health hazards: dangerous chemicals in cosmetics, hair products, depilatories, and vaginal deodorants; malnourishment caused by low-calorie diets; skin disorders caused by skin lighteners and suntanning. We may wear clothes and shoes that severely hamper our freedom of movement, making it difficult

Depilatories are hair-removal agents.

for us to defend ourselves if threatened; have tattoos or piercings done in nonsterile environments, putting ourselves at risk of contracting hepatitis or HIV; or undergo highly risky cosmetic surgery to radically change the shape of our eyes, our noses, our faces, our breasts, or our thighs.

HIV stands for "human immunodeficiency virus," the cause of AIDS (acquired immunodeficiency syndrome).

We all participate in maintaining the popular myths and fantasies of how we should look. Not only do most of us try in one way or another to conform, but we have learned to judge others by the same standards we use to judge ourselves. We look at each other in school, on the street, at work, at the gym and compare: we want to know how well we are doing in the competition for female perfection. Sometimes we reject the dominant fantasies about how we should look only to create an alternative ideal, wanting ourselves and our friends to fit other, equally oppressive stereotypes like the Amazon or Earth Mother. . . .

Most of us will, at times in our lives, make some concessions to the dominant ideals for reasons of economic and social survival. If we can recognize, however, when we are reshaping our bodies to fit someone else's demands, we can begin to develop a different relationship to ourselves. As we become conscious of the model body image and the forces that push us to emulate that image, we can learn to know the differences between our authentic selves and the compromises we make with the outside world. We can start feeling freer to make our own choices.

There are many ways to begin this journey. We can explore ways to feel attractive and appreciated that nurture us and respect our integrity as persons. We can find ways of ornamenting our bodies that do not expose us to health risks. We can take the time to learn to appreciate the sheer pleasures of being in our bodies. We can explore ways to enjoy the sensuality of our bodies, through being outdoors, walking, swimming, dancing, taking a hot bath, or getting a massage. We can focus more of our energy on developing other aspects of ourselves through involvement in our communities and through learning and sharing what we know with those around us. We can talk with other women about body image and begin to name the deadly assumptions underlying the standards of female beauty. We can recognize how we've accepted these ideals and how our buying into them reinforces their power.

Thankfully, growing numbers of women question our need to change our bodies to fit the ideals. Many of us are finding power in defining our own standards of beauty. As more of us learn to love and value ourselves and each other just as we are, and as we begin dismantling the stereotypes that equate physical characteristics with our value as persons, media images and social messages will have a lesser impact on our sense of self. Finding new and positive ways of thinking about our bodies allows us to extend the same accepting attitudes to other women and also affects how others perceive us. No matter what our size, shape, color, or physical ability, if we love ourselves and believe in our own beauty, we are more likely to find that others see that beauty, too. And if they don't, believing in ourselves gives others less power over us.

Excerpts from

Testimony of Anita Hill before Senate Judiciary Committee (1991)

In the fall of 1991, the Judiciary Committee of the U.S. Senate opened confirmation hearings on the nomination of federal judge Clarence Thomas to the U.S. Supreme Court. During the course of the hearings, law professor Anita Hill—an African-American woman who had worked as Thomas's assistant—testified that Thomas, also an African American, had repeatedly pressured her for dates and made lurid comments to her. Hill's three days of testimony, heard live on national television, raised a storm of controversy. Thomas vigorously denied the charges, calling the proceedings a "high-tech lynching." Many women in Congress, in executive offices, in factories, and in kitchens said of the all-male panel questioning Hill's veracity, "They just don't get it." The committee eventually confirmed Thomas's nomination; Hill went on the lecture circuit and returned to teaching law. In the aftermath of the hearings, sexual harassment became a widely debated issue throughout the country. In 1992 the Equal Employment Opportunity Commission (EEOC) reported a 50 percent increase in formal complaints of sexual harassment. Professor Hill delivered the following prepared statement to the Judiciary Committee on October 11, 1991.

Mr. Chairman, Senator Thurmond, Members of the Committee, my name is Anita P. Hill, and I am a Professor of Law at the University of Oklahoma. I was born on a farm in Okmulge, Oklahoma in 1956, the 13th child, and had my early education there. My father is Albert Hill, a farmer of that area. My mother's name is Erma Hill, she is also a farmer and housewife. My childhood was the childhood of both work and poverty; but it was one of solid family affection as represented by my parents' religious atmosphere in the Baptist faith and I have been a member of the Antioch Baptist Church in Tulsa since 1983. It remains a warm part of my life at the present time.

For my undergraduate work I went to Oklahoma State University and graduated in 1977. I am attaching to this statement my résumé with further details of my education. I graduated from the university with academic honors and proceeded to the Yale Law School where I received my J.D. degree in 1980.

Upon graduation from law school I became a practicing lawyer with the Washington, D.C. firm of Wald, Harkrader & Ross. In 1981, I was introduced to now Judge Thomas by a mutual friend. Judge Thomas told me that he anticipated a political appointment shortly and asked if I might be interested in working in that office. He was in fact appointed as Assistant Secretary of Education, in which capacity he was the Director of the Office for Civil Rights. After he was in that post, he asked if I would become his assistant and I did then accept that position. In my early period, there I had two major projects. The first was an article I wrote for Judge Thomas' signature on Education of Minority Students. The second was the organization of a seminar on high-risk students, which was abandoned because Judge Thomas transferred to the EEOC before that project was completed.

During this period at the Department of Education, my working relationship with Judge Thomas was positive. I had a good deal of responsibility as well as independence. I thought that he respected my work and that he trusted my judgment. After approximately three months of working together, he asked me to go out with him socially. I declined and explained to him that I thought that it would only jeopardize what, at the time, I considered to be a very good working relationship. I had a normal social life with other men outside of the office and, I believed then, as now, that having a social relationship with a person who was supervising my work would be ill-advised. I was very uncomfortable with the idea and told him so.

I thought that by saying "no" and explaining my reasons, my employer would abandon his social suggestions. However, to my regret, in the following few weeks he continued to ask me out on several occasions. He pressed me to justify my reasons for saying "no" to him. These incidents took place in his office or mine. They were in the form of private conversations which would not have been overheard by anyone else.

My working relationship became even more strained when Judge Thomas began to use work situations to discuss sex. On these occasions he would call me into his office for reports on education issues and projects or he might suggest that because of time pressures we go to lunch at a government cafeteria. After a brief discussion of work he would turn the conversation to discussion of sexual matters. His conversations were very vivid. . . .

Because I was extremely uncomfortable talking about sex with him at all and particularly in such a graphic way, I told him that I did not want to talk about those subjects. I would also try to change the subject to education matters or to nonsexual personal matters such as his background or beliefs. My efforts to change the subject were rarely successful.

Throughout the period of these conversations, he also from time-to-time asked me for social engagements. My reaction to these conversations was to avoid having them by eliminating opportunities for us to engage in extended conversations. This was difficult because I was his only assistant at the Office for Civil Rights. During the latter part of my time at the Department of Education, the social pressures and any conversations of this offensive kind ended. I began both to believe and hope that our working relationship could be on a proper, cordial and professional base.

When Judge Thomas was made Chairman of the EEOC, I needed to face the question of whether to go with him. I was asked to do so. I did. The work itself was interesting and at that time it appeared that the sexual overtures which had so troubled me had ended. I also faced the realistic fact that I had no alternative job. While I might have gone back to private practice, perhaps in my old firm or at another, I was dedicated to civil rights work and my first choice was to be in that field. Moreover, the Department of Education itself was a dubious venture; President Reagan was seeking to abolish the entire Department at that time.

For my first months at the EEOC, where I continued as an assistant to Judge Thomas, there were no sexual conversations or overtures. However, during the Fall and Winter of 1982, these began again. The comments were random and ranged from pressing me about why I didn't go out with him to remarks about my personal appearance. I remember his saying that someday I would have to give him the real reason that I wouldn't go out with him. He began to show real displeasure in his tone of voice, his demeanor and his continued pressure for an explanation. He commented on what I was wearing in terms of whether it made me more or less sexually attractive. The incidents occurred in his inner office at the EEOC. . . .

At this point, late 1982, 1 began to feel severe stress on the job. I began to be concerned that Clarence Thomas might take it out on me by downgrading me or not giving me important assignments. I also thought that he might find an excuse for dismissing me.

In January of 1983, I began looking for another job. I was handicapped because I feared that if he found out, he might make it difficult for me to find other employment and I might be dismissed from the job I had. Another factor that made my search more difficult was that this was a period of a government hiring freeze. In February, 1983, I was hospitalized for five days on an emergency basis for an acute stomach pain which I attributed to stress on the job. Once out of the hospital, I became more committed to find other employment and sought further to minimize my contact with Thomas. This became easier when Allyson Duncan became office director because most of my work was handled with her and I had contact with Clarence Thomas mostly in staff meetings.

In the Spring of 1983, an opportunity to teach law at Oral Roberts University opened up. I agreed to take the job in large part because of my desire to escape the pressures I felt at the EEOC due to Thomas. When I informed him that I was leaving in July, I recall that his response was that now I "would no longer have an excuse for not going out with" him. I told him that I still preferred not to do so.

At some time after that meeting, he asked if he could take me to dinner at the end of my term. When I declined, he assured me that the dinner was a professional courtesy only and not a social invitation. I reluctantly agreed to accept that invitation but only if it was at the very end of a workday. On, as I recall, the last day of my employment at the EEOC in the summer of 1983, I did have dinner with Clarence Thomas. We went directly from work to a restaurant near the office. We talked about the work I had done both at

Education and at EEOC. He told me that he was pleased with all of it except for an article and speech that I done for him when we were at the Office for Civil Rights. Finally, he made a comment which I vividly remember. He said that if I ever told anyone about his behavior toward me it could ruin his career. This was not an apology nor was there any explanation. That was his last remark about the possibility of our going out or reference to his behavior.

In July 1983, I left the Washington, D.C. area and have had minimal contact with Judge Clarence Thomas since. . . .

It is only after a great deal of agonizing consideration that I am able to talk of these unpleasant matters to anyone, except my closest friends. Telling the world is the most difficult experience of my life. I was aware that he could affect my future career but did not wish to burn all my bridges. I may have used poor judgment; perhaps I should have taken angry or even militant steps, both when I was in the agency or after I had left it, but I must confess to the world that the course I took seemed the better, as well as the easier approach. I declined any comment to newspapers, but later, when Senate staff asked me about these matters, I felt that I had a duty to report. I have no personal vendetta against Clarence Thomas. I seek only to provide the Committee with information which it may regard as relevant. It would have been more comfortable to remain silent. I took no initiative to inform anyone. But when I was asked by a representative of this committee to report my experience, I felt that I had to tell the truth.

Reprinted from the University of Maryland Women's Studies Database, www.inform.umd.edu/EdRes/Topic/WomenStudies.

Excerpts from

Violence Against Women Act (1994)

Among the notable legislative successes of the feminist movement in the 1990s was the Violence Against Women Act (VAWA) of 1994. A comprehensive federal law enacted as part of the Violent Crime Control and Law Enforcement Act, VAWA provided a variety of safeguards for victims of sexual assault and domestic violence. Among the provisions were a doubling of prison terms authorized by state statute for repeat offenders; protection of victim confidentiality; grant appropriations for counseling, education, prevention, shelters, information programs and criminal databases, and other measures. At the heart of the legislation was the classification of gender-related crimes as a civil rights violation. Thus, perpetrators would be liable to claims for damages in civil court as well as to criminal prosecution.

Subtitle C (Sec. 40302) Civil Rights

(a) PURPOSE—Pursuant to the affirmative power of Congress to enact this subtitle under section 5 of the Fourteenth Amendment to the Constitution, as well as under section 8 of Article I of the Constitution, it is the purpose of this subtitle to protect the civil rights of victims of gender motivated violence and to promote public safety, health, and activities affecting interstate commerce by establishing a Federal civil rights cause of action for victims of crimes of violence motivated by gender.

(b) RIGHT TO BE FREE FROM CRIMES OF VIOLENCE—All persons within the United States shall have the right to be free from crimes of violence motivated by gender (as defined in subsection (d)).

(c) CAUSE OF ACTION—A person (including a person who acts under color of any statute, ordinance, regulation, custom, or usage of any State) who commits a crime of violence motivated by gender and thus deprives another of the right declared in subsection (b) shall be liable to the party injured, in an action for the recovery of compensatory and punitive damages, injunctive and declaratory relief, and such other relief as a court may deem appropriate.

(d) DEFINITIONS—For purposes of this section—

(1) the term 'crime of violence motivated by gender' means a crime of violence committed because of gender or on the basis of gender, and due, at least in part, to an animus based on the victim's gender; and

(2) the term 'crime of violence' means—

(A) an act or series of acts that would constitute a felony against the person or that would constitute a felony against property if the conduct presents a serious risk of physical injury to another, and that would come within the meaning of State or Federal offenses described in section 16 of title 18, United States Code, whether or not those acts have actually resulted in criminal charges, prosecution, or conviction and whether or not those acts were committed in the special maritime, territorial, or prison jurisdiction of the United States; and

(B) includes an act or series of acts that would constitute a felony described in subparagraph (A) but for the relationship between the person who takes such action and the individual against whom such action is taken.

A *cause of action* is the legal grounds for a civil suit or criminal prosecution.

Under color of here means in legal reliance on, or under the supposed authority of.

Animus is an underlying spirit or motivation.

Section 16 of Title 18, United States Code: The U.S. Code is the complete compilation of federal statutes. Title 18 includes all laws on crime and criminal procedures. Section 16 defines crimes of violence.

SELECTED BIBLIOGRAPHY

Amott, Teresa, and Julie Matthaei. *Race, Gender, and Work: A Multicultural Economic History of Women in the United States,* rev. ed. Boston: South End Press, 1996.

Anderson, Karen. *Wartime Women: Sex Roles, Family Relations, and the Status of Women During World War II.* Westport: Greenwood, 1981.

Anthony, Carl S. *America's First Families: An Inside View of 200 Years of Private Life in the White House.* New York: Touchstone, 2000.

Bailey, Beth, and David Farber. *The First Strange Place: Race and Sex in World War II Hawaii.* Baltimore: Johns Hopkins University Press, 1992.

Boris, Eileen, and Cynthia R. Daniels, eds. *Homework: Historical and Contemporary Perspectives on Paid Labor at Home.* Urbana: University of Illinois Press, 1989.

Boston Women's Health Book Collective. *Our Bodies, Ourselves for the New Century: A Book by and for Women.* New York: Simon & Schuster, 1998.

Brady, Kathleen. *Ida Tarbell: Portrait of a Muckraker.* Pittsburgh: University of Pittsburgh Press, 1989.

Brumberg, Joan Jacobs. *The Body Project: An Intimate History of American Girls.* New York: Random House, 1997

Caffrey, Margaret. *Ruth Benedict: Stranger in This Land.* Austin: University of Texas Press, 1989.

Camhi, Jane J. *Women against Women: American Anti-suffragism, 1880–1920.* Brooklyn, NY: Carlson, 1994.

Caroli, Betty B. *First Ladies.* New York: Oxford University Press, 1995.

Clark-Lewis, Elizabeth. *Living In, Living Out: African American Domestics in Washington, DC, 1910–1940.* Washington, DC: Smithsonian Institute Press, 1994.

Cobble, Dorothy Sue. *Dishing It Out: Waitresses and Their Unions in the Twentieth Century.* Urbana: University of Illinois Press, 1991.

Cohen, Miriam. *Workshop to Office: Two Generations of Italian Women in New York City, 1900–1950.* Ithaca, NY: Cornell University Press, 1992.

Coontz, Stephanie. *The Way We Really Are: Coming to Terms with America's Changing Families.* New York: Basic Books, 1997.

Cott, Nancy. *The Grounding of Modern Feminism.* New Haven: Yale University Press, 1987.

Davis, Allen. *Spearheads for Reform: The Social Settlements and the Progressive Movement, 1890–1914.* New York: Oxford University Press, 1967.

D'Emilio, John, and Estelle Freedman. *Intimate Matters: A History of Sexuality in America.* New York: Harper and Row, 1988.

DuBois, Ellen Carol, and Vicki L. Ruiz, eds. *Unequal Sisters : A Multicultural Reader in U.S. Women's History.* New York: Routledge, 1990.

Edwards, Rebecca. *Angels in the Machinery: Gender in American Party Politics from the Civil War to the Progressive Era.* New York: Oxford University Press, 1997.

Enstad, Nan. *Ladies of Labor, Girls of Adventure: Working Women, Popular Culture, and Labor Politics at the Turn of the Century.* New York: Columbia University Press, 1999.

Ewen, Elizabeth. *Immigrant Women in the Land of Dollars: Life and Culture on the Lower East Side, 1890–1925.* New York: Monthly Review, 1985.

Faue, Elizabeth. *Community of Suffering & Struggle: Women, Men, and the Labor Movement in Minneapolis, 1915–1945.* Chapel Hill: University of North Carolina, 1991.

Filler, Louis. *The Muckrakers.* Stanford, CA: Stanford University Press, 1993.

Finnegan, Margaret. *Selling Suffrage: Consumer Culture & Votes for Women.* New York: Columbia University Press, 1999.

Friedan, Betty. *The Feminine Mystique.* New York: Norton, 1963.

Gamber, Wendy. *The Female Economy: The Millinery and Dressmaking Trades, 1860–1930.* Urbana: University of Illinois, 1997.

Glenn, Susan A. *Daughters of the Shtetl: Life and Labor in the Immigrant Generations.* Ithaca: Cornell University Press, 1990.

Glickman, Lawrence. *Consumer Society in American History: A Reader.* Ithaca: Cornell University Press, 1999.

Gluck, Sherna B. *Rosie the Riveter Revisited: Women, the War, and Social Change.* Boston: Twayne, 1987.

Golden, Claudia. *Understanding the Gender Gap: An Economic History of American Women.* New York: Oxford University Press, 1990.

Goodwin, Joanne L. *Gender and the Politics of Welfare Reform: Mothers' Pensions in Chicago, 1911–1929.* Chicago: University of Chicago Press, 1996.

Gordon, Linda. *Heroes of Their Own Lives: The Politics and History of Family Violence, Boston, 1880–1960.* New York: Viking, 1988.

Hadley-Garcia, George. *Hispanic Hollywood: The Latins in Motion Pictures.* New York: Carol Publishing, 1990.

Hapke, Laura. *Daughters of the Great Depression: Women, Work, and Fiction in American 1930's.* Athens: University of Georgia, 1995.

Hareven, Tamara. *Family Time and Industrial Time.* New York: Cambridge University Press, 1982.

Harrison, Cynthia. *On Account of Sex: The Politics of Women's Issues, 1945–1968.* Berkeley: University of California Press, 1988.

Hartmann, Susan M. *The Home Front and Beyond: American Women in the 1940's.* Boston: Twayne Publishers, 1982.

Hine, Darlene C., and Kathleen Thompson, eds. *A Shining Thread of Hope: The History of Black Women in America.* New York: Broadway Books, 1998.

Hochschild, Arlie R. *The Managed Heart: Commercialization of Human Feeling.* Berkeley: University of California Press, 1983.

Howard, Jane. *Margaret Mead, a Life.* New York: Fawcett Columbine, 1990.

Jacobs, Margaret. *Engendered Encounters: Feminism and Pueblo Cultures 1879–1934.* Lincoln: University of Nebraska Press, 1999.

Jackson, Carlton. *Hattie: The Life of Hattie McDaniel.* Lanham, MD: Madison Books, 1990.

James, Edward T., Janet W. James, and Paul S. Boyer, eds. *Notable American Women, Vol. III.* Cambridge Harvard University Press, 1971.

Jameson, Elizabeth, and Susan Armitage, eds. *Writing the Range: Race, Class, and Culture in the Women's West.* Norman: University of Oklahoma Press, 1997.

Jones, Jacqueline. *Labor of Love, Labor of Sorrow: Black Women, Work, and the Family from Slavery to the Present.* New York: Basic Books, 1985.

Kessler-Harris, Alice. *Out to Work: A History of Wage-Earning Women in the United States.* New York: Oxford University Press, 1982.

Kochersberger, Robert C., ed. *More Than a Muckraker: Ida Tarbell's Lifetime in Journalism.* Knoxville: University of Tennessee Press, 1994.

Kwolek-Folland, Angel. *Incorporating Women: A History of Women and Business in the United States.* New York: Twayne, 1998.

Ladd-Taylor, Molly. *Raising a Baby the Government Way: Mothers' Letters to the Children's Bureau 1915–1932.* New Brunswick, NJ: Rutgers University Press, 1986.

———, and Lauri Umansky, eds. *'Bad' Mothers: The Politics of Blame in Twentieth-Century America.* New York: New York University Press, 1997.

Lehrer, Susan. *Origins of Protective Labor Legislation for Women, 1905–1925.* Albany: State University of New York, 1987.

Lerner, Gerda. *The Majority Finds Its Past.* New York: Oxford University Press, 1979.

Mankiller, Wilma, et al., eds. *The Reader's Companion to U.S. Women's History.* New York: Houghton Mifflin, 1998.

Matsumoto, Valerie J. *Farming the Homeplace: A Japanese-American Community in California, 1919–1982.* Ithaca: Cornell University Press, 1993.

May, Elaine Tyler. *Homeward Bound: American Families in the Cold War Era.* New York: Basic Books, 1988.

Mead, Margaret. *Ruth Benedict.* New York: Columbia University Press, 1974.

Melosh, Barbara. *Engendering Culture: Manhood and Womanhood in New Deal Public Art and Theater.* Washington: Smithsonian Institution Press, 1991.

Meyerowitz, Joanne, ed. *Not June Cleaver: Women and Gender in Postwar America, 1945–1960.* Philadelphia: Temple University Press, 1944.

Meyers, Karen. *Lives and Works.* New York: Grolier, 1999.

Milkman, Ruth. *Gender at Work: The Dynamics of Job Segregation by Sex During World War II.* Urbana: University of Illinois, 1987.

Mintz, Steven, and Susan Kellogg. *Domestic Revolutions: A Social History of American Family Life.* New York: The Free Press, 1988.

Morantz-Sanchez, Regina M. *Sympathy and Science: Women Physicians in American Medicine.* New York: Oxford University Press, 1985.

Morris, Sarah P. *Black Women in America: A Historical Encyclopedia.* New York: Carlson Publishing Inc., 1993.

Moynihan, Ruth Barnes, Cynthia Russett, and Laurie Crumpacker, eds. *Second to None: A Documentary History of American Women,* Vol. II. Lincoln: University of Nebraska Press, 1994.

Muncy, Robyn. *Creating a Female Dominion in American Reform, 1890–1935.* New York: Oxford University Press, 1991.

Paradis, Adrian A. *Ida M. Tarbell, Pioneer Woman Journalist and Biographer.* Chicago: Children's Press, 1985.

Peiss, Kathy L. *Hope in a Jar: The Making of America's Beauty Culture.* New York: Henry Holt and Company, 1998.

Peterson del Mar, David. *Violence and Power: An Intimate History of the North Pacific Slope.* Seattle: University of Washington Press, 2002.

Pleck, Elizabeth. *Domestic Tyranny: The Making of American Social Policy against Family Violence from Colonial Times to the Present.* New York: Oxford University Press, 1987.

Rosen, Ruth. *The World Split Open: How the Modern Women's Movement Changed America.* New York: Viking, 2000.

Ruiz, Vicki L. *Cannery Women, Cannery Lives: Mexican Women, Unionization, and the California Food Processing Industry, 1930–1950.* Albuquerque: University of New Mexico Press, 1987.

Satter, Beryl. *Each Mind a Kingdom: American Women, Sexual Purity, and the New Thought Movement, 1875–1920.* Berkeley: University of California Press, 1999.

Scanlon, Jennifer, ed. *The Gender and Consumer Culture Reader.* New York: New York University Press, 2000.

Schechter, Susan. *Women and Male Violence: The Visions and Struggles of the Battered Women's Movement.* Boston: South End Press, 1982.

Scott, Anne Firor. *Natural Allies: Women's Associations in American History.* Urbana: University of Illinois Press, 1997.

Sicherman, Barbara, and Carol H. Green, eds. *Notable American Women: The Modern Period.* Cambridge: Harvard University Press, 1980.

Sidel, Ruth. *Keeping Women and Children Last: America's War on the Poor.* New York: Penguin, 1996.

Smith, Jessie C., ed. *Notable Black American Women.* Detroit: Gale, 1992.

Ware, Susan. *Beyond Suffrage: Women in the New Deal.* Cambridge: Harvard University Press, 1981.

Weiner, Lynn. *From Working Girl to Working Mother: The Female Labor Force in the United States, 1820–1980.* Chapel Hill: University of North Carolina Press, 1985.

Yung, Judy. *Chinese Women of America: A Pictorial History.* Seattle: University of Washington Press, 1986.

BIOGRAPHICAL INDEX

This index references the biographical main entries and features in this volume. The labels (WF) *and* (TB) *refer to Women's Firsts and Trailblazers features. For organizations, concepts, and additional references to people, see the General Index at the back of this volume.*

GENERAL INDEX

Numbers in bold indicate volume numbers and main entries; *i* indicates illustration.

C

D

E

H

I

J

N

T

U

V

W